# RESEARCH IN ANALYTICAL PSYCHOLOGY

*Research in Analytical Psychology: Empirical Research* provides an original overview of empirical research in Analytical Psychology, focusing on quantitative and qualitative methods. This unique collection of chapters from an international range of contributors covers all the major concepts of Analytical Psychology and provides a strong empirical foundation.

The book covers a wide range of concepts and fields, and is presented in five parts. Part I, Epistemological Foundations, looks at psychological empiricism and naturalism. Part II, Fundamental Concepts of Analytical Psychology, presents chapters on complexes, archetypes, dream interpretation, and image. Part III, Trauma, addresses neuroscience, dreams, and infant observation research. Part IV, Psychotherapy and Psychotherapeutic Methods, examines sandplay, picture interpretation, quality management and training. Finally, Part V, Synchronicity, contains chapters concerning the experience of psychophysical correlations and synchronistic experiences in psychotherapy. Each chapter provides an overview of research in the field and closes with general conclusions, and the book as a whole will enable practitioners to evaluate the empirical status of their concepts and methods and, where necessary, update them. It also presents the necessary material for a re-evaluation of the status of Analytical Psychology within the broader academic field, supporting a move back into the heart of current debates in psychology and psychotherapy.

This book will be essential reading for analytical psychologists in practice and in training, academics and students of Analytical Psychology and post-Jungian ideas, and academics and students of other disciplines seeking to integrate methods from Analytical Psychology into their research. It is complemented by its companion volume, *Research in Analytical Psychology: Applications from Scientific, Historical, and Cross-Cultural Research*.

**Christian Roesler, Ph.D., Dipl.-Psych.,** is a Professor of Clinical Psychology at the Catholic University of Applied Sciences in Freiburg, Germany, and Lecturer of Analytical Psychology at the University of Basel, Switzerland. He is also a Jungian psychoanalyst in private practice in Freiburg and a member of the faculty of the C.G. Jung Institutes in Stuttgart and Zurich.

# RESEARCH IN ANALYTICAL PSYCHOLOGY

## Empirical Research

*Edited by Christian Roesler*

Routledge
Taylor & Francis Group

LONDON AND NEW YORK

First published 2018
by Routledge
2 Park Square, Milton Park, Abingdon, Oxon OX14 4RN

and by Routledge
711 Third Avenue, New York, NY 10017

*Routledge is an imprint of the Taylor & Francis Group, an informa business*

*British Library Cataloguing-in-Publication Data*
A catalogue record for this book is available from the British Library

*Library of Congress Cataloging-in-Publication Data*
Names: Roesler, Christian, 1967– editor.
Title: Research in analytical psychology : empirical research / [edited by] Christian Roesler.
Description: Abingdon, Oxon ; New York, NY : Routledge, 2018.
Identifiers: LCCN 2017059730 (print) | LCCN 2017061386 (ebook) | ISBN 9781315527178 (Master e-book) | ISBN 9781138694903 (hardback) | ISBN 9781138694910 (pbk.)
Subjects: LCSH: Psychology—Research. | Jungian psychology.
Classification: LCC BF76.5 (ebook) | LCC BF76.5 .R46195 2018 (print) | DDC 150.19/54072—dc23
LC record available at https://lccn.loc.gov/2017059730

ISBN: 978-1-138-69490-3 (hbk)
ISBN: 978-1-138-69491-0 (pbk)
ISBN: 978-1-315-52717-8 (ebk)

Typeset in Bembo
by Apex CoVantage, LLC

# CONTENTS

Contributors                                                                    viii

Introduction: empirical research in Analytical Psychology          1
*Christian Roesler*

**PART I**
**Epistemological foundations**                                            **9**

1  Psychological empiricism and naturalism                        11
   *Philip Kime*

**PART II**
**Fundamental concepts of Analytical Psychology**          **27**

2  Complexes and the unconscious: from the association
   experiment to recent fMRI studies                                    29
   *Christian Roesler and Tina van Uffelen*

3  Experimental approaches to the study of the archetype     41
   *Milena Sotirova-Kohli*

4  The relevance of the Jungian concept of "image" to
   contemporary process research through linguistic analysis:
   a bridge between analytical and cognitive psychology        55
   *Alessandra De Coro*

5 Jungian dream interpretation and empirical dream research 69
*Christian Roesler*


**PART III**
**Trauma** **87**

6 Dreaming under fire: the psyche in times of continuous stress 89
*Tamar Kron*

7 Neuroscientific studies of trauma applied to Jungian psychology 102
*Joseph Cambray*

8 The cultural skin in China: the impact of culture upon
development and clinical practice 121
*Brian Feldman*


**PART IV**
**Psychotherapy and psychotherapeutic methods** **135**

9 Sandplay: a method for research with trauma 137
*Denise Gimenez Ramos and Reinalda Melo da Matta*

10 Pictures of transformation and the symbolic attitude: a
research perspective on picture interpretation and the
therapeutic *mundus imaginalis* 154
*Manfred Krapp*

11 Research on the effectiveness of Jungian psychotherapy:
state of the art 173
*Christian Roesler*

12 Quality management and empirical research activities in
Jungian psychotherapy in Germany 187
*Wolfram Keller*

13 Research on training: findings from the evaluation of the
IAAP's International Router training program 203
*John Merchant*

**PART V**
# Synchronicity                                                    225

14  Synchronicity and the experience of psychophysical
    correlations                                                   227
    *Harald Atmanspacher*

15  Synchronistic experiences in psychotherapy: empirical
    studies                                                        244
    *Christian Roesler*


*Index*                                                           *255*

# CONTRIBUTORS

**Harald Atmanspacher**, Ph.D. Physics, Zurich, Switzerland

Senior Scientist and Staff Member at Collegium Helveticum (ETH and University Zurich). President, Society for Mind-Matter Research, Zurich. Faculty Member, C.G. Jung Institute, Zurich. Editor-in-Chief of the interdisciplinary international journal *Mind and Matter*. Research and publications on dual-aspect monism (Pauli–Jung conjecture, mind–matter correlations, exceptional experiences, mental and physical time), contextual emergence (symbolic dynamics, neural correlates of consciousness, mental causation, relative onticity), non-commutative operations in psychology (bistable perception, order effects, learning on networks), and acategorical mental states (representational approaches, unstable cognition, non-conceptual content, exceptional experiences).

**Joseph Cambray**, Ph.D., Santa Barbara, CA, USA

MS, NCPsyA

2015 Visiting Professor, Kyoto University, Graduate School of Education

President, Pacifica Graduate Institute

1997–2010: Faculty member, Harvard Medical School, Center for Psychoanalytic Studies, at the Massachusetts General Hospital, Psychiatry Department.

International Association of Analytical Psychology (IAAP) – Honorary Secretary, 2001–2004; Vice President 2004–2007; President-Elect 2007–2010, President 2010–2013.

*The Journal of Analytical Psychology* – Editorial Advisory Board 2010-present; Consulting US Editor, 2005–2010; US Editor (1997–2005).

**Alessandra De Coro**, Rome, Italy

Psychologist Ph.D., Jungian teaching psychoanalyst (AIPA, Rome, Italy)

Full Professor of Dynamic Psychology at University "Sapienza" of Rome (now retired)

Research on the different theoretical models of psychoanalysis from historical and conceptual perspectives; on clinical implications of attachment theory and of psychotherapy research: application of the Adult Attachment Interview to non-clinical and clinical adolescents (in cooperation with the group of Mary Main, University of California, Berkeley; introduction of the German OPD system (*Operationalized Psychodynamic Diagnosis*) in Italy in collaboration with Rainer Dahlbender (Ulm University) and Manfred Cierpka (Heidelberg University); evaluation of the Referential Activity for the study of the therapeutic process (in collaboration with Wilma Bucci at Adelphi University of New York and Bernard Maskit of Stony Brook University).

**Brian Feldman**, Ph.D. Clinical Psychology, Palo Alto, CA, USA

Jungian analyst, Training Analyst, Inter-regional Society of Jungian Analysts; Faculty, Jung Institute of San Francisco

Visiting Professor, Moscow State University of Humanitarian Sciences; City University of Macau; and Department of Psychiatry, University of Dakar School of Medicine, Senegal, infant observation program. Former chief of clinical psychology, Stanford Medical Center, Department of Child Psychiatry.

Training Member, International Association of Infant Observation (AIDOBB)

Organizational Consultant (ISPSO)

Private practice of clinical psychology and child, adolescent and adult Jungian psychoanalysis

Dr. med. **Wolfram Keller**, Berlin, Germany

Internist/Cardiology, specialized in Psychosomatic Medicine

Training Analyst/Supervisor and Board of managing directors at Institute for Psychotherapy Berlin

Assistant Professor at International Psychoanalytic University Berlin (IPU).

Head of the Inpatient Department of Psychosomatic Medicine and Psychotherapy and Internistic Medicine (Kliniken im Theodor-Wenzel-Werk Berlin), retired March 2011.

Certified Trainer in OPD

**Philip Kime**, Ph.D., Zurich, Switzerland

Dipl. C.G. Jung Institute Zurich, Ph.D. Cognitive Science, M.A. Artificial Intelligence, B.A. Philosophy.

Dr. med. **Manfred Krapp**, Berlin, Germany.

Doctoral dissertation on art therapy and psychotherapy of psychosis (Prof. Benedetti). Specialist in psychosomatic medicine and psychiatry. Analytical training at the C.G. Jung Institute of Zurich. Private practice in Berlin. Tutor at the C.G. Jung Institute in Zurich, at the Academy for Psychosomatic Medicine in Berlin, and the C.G. Jung Institute in Brasília.

**Tamar Kron**, Ph.D., Jerusalem, Israel

Clinical psychologist and Jungian analyst.

Professor Emeritus of Hebrew University and head of the clinical psychology graduate program at the Academic College of Tel-Aviv-Yafo.

Research and publications on the metapsychology of Erich Neumann and its connection to the dialogue philosophy of Martin Buber; dreams of therapists about their patients, and dreams of people living in continuous stress conditions; the relevance of myth to life in modern Western culture, and of the modern couple relationship.

**John Merchant**, Ph.D., Sydney, Australia

Training analyst with the Australian & New Zealand Society of Jungian Analysts and accredited supervisor with the Psychology Board of Australia. Adult education courses in Analytical Psychology at the University of Sydney; workshops and seminars in Australia, New Zealand, the UK, Europe, and the US.

In private practice in Sydney, Australia. See www.johnmerchant.com.au for further details.

Research and publications on: archetype theory and neuroscience, fetal trauma, the use of Skype in analysis and training.

Recent book: *Shamans and Analysts: New Insights on the Wounded Healer* (Routledge).

**Reinalda Melo da Matta**, Ph.D., São Paulo, Brazil

Clinical Psychologist. Area of Research: Psychological Trauma.

Teaching Member of International Society of Sandplay Therapy.

**Denise Gimenez Ramos**, Ph.D., São Paulo, Brazil

Professor and Chair of the Center for Jungian Studies/Post Graduate Program of Clinical Psychology at Catholic University of São Paulo. Member of Brazilian Society for Analytical Psychology (IAAP). Training Therapist, Chair of Research Committee and Vice President for Americas of the International Society of Sandplay Therapy (ISST).

Selected publications: *The Psyche of the Body* (London: Routledge), translated to French, Portuguese and Russian.

Area of Research: Psychosomatics, Cultural Complex, and Psychological Trauma.

**Christian Roesler**, Ph.D., Dipl. Psych, Freiburg, Germany

Professor of Clinical Psychology at the Catholic University Freiburg and of Analytical Psychology at the University of Basel/Switzerland. Visiting professor (research fellow) to Kyoto University, Graduate School of Education, Japan, in 2017.

Jungian psychoanalyst in private practice in Freiburg and member of the faculty of the C.G. Jung Institutes in Stuttgart and Zurich. Training Analyst for the Psychoanalytic Training Institute at the University Hospital Freiburg (Aus- und Weiterbildungsinstitut für Psychoanalytische und Tiefenpsychologisch fundierte Psychotherapie am Universitätsklinikum Freiburg, DGPT).

Research and publications on Analytical Psychology and contemporary sciences, couple and family therapy, postmodern identity construction, narrative research, media psychology.

**Milena Sotirova-Kohli**, Ph.D., Bern, Switzerland

M. Sc. in Clinical Psychology from Texas A&M University, USA, Ph.D. in Psychology from the University of Basel, Switzerland. Currently in training at the C.G. Jung Institute – Zurich Psychotherapist for delegated therapy in Bern, Switzerland, and Mythodrama therapist at the Kantonale Erziehungsberatung (Educational Counseling) in Bern.

Research and publications on creativity, healing and experimental approaches to the study archetypes.

**Tina van Uffelen**, Ph.D., Tübingen, Germany

M.A. Pedagogics, Ph.D. Viadrina University Frankfurt/Oder, Germany, and training candidate at Jung Institute Stuttgart.

# INTRODUCTION

## Empirical research in Analytical Psychology

*Christian Roesler*

It is not a secret that the relationship between Analytical Psychology and academic psychology has been almost nonexistent in the last decade or last few decades. From the side of academic psychology, Jungian psychology has often been accused of not giving any empirical proof for its concepts and the effectiveness of its therapeutic approach. It cannot be denied that Jungian psychology since the days of Jung has developed in most parts far from empirical research and the development of theories and concepts in other disciplines, not only psychology, but also psychiatry, biology, and the neurosciences, to name just a few. This is somewhat surprising given the fact that Jung started his career as an empirical researcher and gained international reputation not with his psychoanalytical work but with his association studies, which gave empirical proof for the existence of unconscious factors and dynamics impacting the functioning of consciousness (Jung, 1992, CW 2). This was the main reason why Freud became interested in Jung's work, because here could be found empirical support for the ideas of early psychoanalysis and the existence of a psychodynamic unconscious. In a letter to Jung, Freud wrote: "*Damit fängt ein neuer Zweig der empirischen Psychologie an*" ("This is the beginning of a new branch of empirical psychology"; translation C.R.) (Freud & Jung, 1974, p. 538).

Over the past several decades, as Analytical Psychology has expanded beyond the first generation of practitioners' clinical focus on theory and practice, there has been an accumulation of research efforts. The movement of Analytical Psychology into academic environments has been a major impetus to this new direction. This reflects Jung's own stated desire to have institutions bearing his name be centers of research and not solely professional training programs (Schlegel, 1999).

Almost unknown, even to many Jungians, is the major influence Jung's concepts had on many fields in psychology, e.g., his invention of the personality dimension extraversion versus introversion, which has now become one of the so-called Big Five personality dimensions in personality psychology and is included in each of the major personality inventories (Roesler, 2010). It is interesting that this concept was found by Jung in his empirical research on application of the association experiment. On the other hand, some of Jung's concepts happen to be "reinvented" by contemporary scholars without acknowledging Jung's original contribution, as is the case for example with the concept of schema in schema therapy, which is nothing more than a reformulation of Jung's concept of the complex (see Roesler & Van Uffelen in this volume).

After his personal conflict and break with Freud, Jung also broke with empirical research and never took it up again. It seems that this tradition of distance to research and academia has somehow continued in the Jungian community up to the present day, even though there are a few places in the world where Jungians have succeeded in establishing Analytical Psychology in university and research contexts – some of whom are contributors to this volume. This break in his biography is difficult to explain, as Jung conducted his empirical research in the psychiatric university hospital in Zurich with great enthusiasm and he earned a tremendous academic reputation, to the extent that between 1906 and 1910 he was one of the most renowned psychologists worldwide. After 1912, however, he conducted only what could be called interpretive or cultural research, as for example his studies in alchemy and religion. It can be said that here he established a highly differentiated research tradition which illuminated the psychological backgrounds and universal patterns of different cultural traditions and belief systems. Some of these studies and the resulting applied research throughout the years can be found in the companion volume, *Research in Analytical Psychology: Applications From Scientific, Historical, and Cross-Cultural Research*. Cambray (in this volume) discusses a possible background for this splitting behavior of Jung's referring to trauma theory.

This volume aims to cover most areas generally considered a part of empirical research in Analytical Psychology, with the exception of research on psychological types, which has its own extensive literature (for an overview and systematic archive, see the website of the Center for the Application of Psychological Type, www.capt. org). Attention is paid to the connections between Analytical Psychology and other related disciplines, e.g., applicable neuroscientific findings, psychotherapy research, developmental research, Freudian psychoanalysis, cultural studies, and so forth. In particular, the essays in this collection seek to highlight the empirical status of Jungian concepts and will be foundational for anyone wishing to conduct future research in Analytical Psychology as it provides the baseline for the current state of the field.

## Epistemological foundations and controversies

In his famous dialogue with the physicist Pauli, and in developing their joint concept of synchronicity, Jung also tried to expand the epistemological frame of psychology as a science by including the perspective of quantum physics (see also Atmanspacher in this volume). Approaches like this and his general interest in parapsychological phenomena seem to have damaged his reputation in academic psychology, where in many circles he is seen as a mystic and the Jungian community as nothing more than a sect. On the other hand, this condemnation of Jung is only possible from the perspective of a psychology which attempts to define itself as a natural science. This approach in psychology has led to such a reduction that it has become almost impossible to investigate inner world phenomena, which should be the main subject of psychology as a science. Kime (in this volume) expands this discussion on what the appropriate epistemological viewpoint for psychology as a science should be.

It cannot be denied, though, that Jung uses the term empirical in his works in a problematic way. He often states that many of his concepts, e.g., the anima, have to be seen as empirical facts. This use of the term is not appropriate, neither today nor in the days of Jung (Shamdasani, 2003). He did not reflect on or even care about the epistemological debates of his time, e.g., the discussion between Karl Popper and the logical empiricists of the Vienna Circle. Here a tendency in Jung – and some of his successors – becomes visible, to isolate themselves from contemporary academic debates or scientific insights, as if they were not relevant at all for Jungian psychology (Roesler, 2012). Even the statement can be found that Jungian psychology is not accessible at all for empirical research – which was also firmly criticized by Jungian scholars (Bash, 1988; Seifert, 1975). From my point of view, this attitude has done great harm to the scientific reputation of Analytical Psychology. Other Jungian scholars have pointed this out much earlier:

> We run the risk of working with increasingly outdated and inaccurate models of the human mind if we avoid subjecting them to the rigour of scientific scepticism, for fear that the numinous or spiritual will be destroyed by the scientific advances in understanding the way the mind actually works, the ways in which it processes information.
>
> *(Knox, 2001, p. 616)*

We Jungians have to acknowledge that we do not live on an epistemological island, and if we continuously neglect the development of theories and empirical findings in psychology and other disciplines, we run the risk of falling out of the scientific world in total. A basic attitude, to which Knox refers, which forms the foundation for investigating how things are by systematic research, is to be skeptical about theories and assumptions – something is not true just because Carl Gustav Jung said it. This is a problem we seem to share with Freudian psychoanalysis (Solms, 2006) – it seems that in the psychoanalytic schools there is a strong tendency for dogmatism, which comes out of an exaggerated adoration of the original founding fathers (Kirsch, 2007).

On the other hand, it has to be acknowledged that Jung struggled over his lifetime to somehow combine the view of a scientist with hermeneutics and with the view of someone who experienced his own soul (Jones, 2003; see also Cambray in this volume), to keep psychology open for insights gained from inner experience (see Shamdasani, 2003, for an extended discussion).

## An overview of Analytical Psychology research

In the last decades, however, the situation of Analytical Psychology has considerably changed. As noted earlier, many of Analytical Psychology's concepts are quite well empirically supported today. Research in Analytical Psychology has grown to a remarkable body of findings and insights which have not yet been carefully mapped and articulated; this volume will strive to bring the field into focus. The aim of this publication is to give an overview, something like the state of the art for a number of major Jungian concepts and their empirical foundation. It also gives an overview of research activities conducted by Jungians or investigating Jungian concepts. This overview makes clear that, first, Jungian concepts can well be empirically investigated; and second, that empirical research in Analytical Psychology can offer tools and perspectives that may be useful for other disciplines. Many of Analytical Psychology's concepts have received strong empirical support, not so much from research efforts in Analytical Psychology itself but often from other disciplines, as can well be demonstrated for the findings of empirical dream research and the support it gives to Jung's theory of dreaming (see Roesler in this volume) as well as for the connection between the neurosciences and Analytical Psychology (see Cambray in this volume).

A first question which has to be addressed is what would be an appropriate methodological approach for research in Analytical Psychology. It is quite clear that the overly positivistic approach in academic psychology, with its exclusive orientation on quantitative measurement and experimental designs, would be too reductive. Philip Kime presents an extended discussion of the problems connected with positivistic reductionism in psychology and describes possible methodological alternatives.

Following this initial discussion of the epistemological foundations of research in psychology in general and Analytical Psychology in particular, a number of authors present research and research findings regarding some of the major concepts of Analytical Psychology: complexes and the unconscious, archetypes and the collective unconscious, images and symbol formation, and dreaming and dream interpretation.

Christian Roesler and Tina van Uffelen give an overview of research with the association experiment and the concept of complexes from Jung's time to recent studies. Also there is a summary of initial findings from a recent study applying the association experiment for diagnostic use in clinical practice and the additional value the experiment gives to the assessment of psychological disorders.

Milena Sotirova-Kohli gives an overview of experimental approaches to the investigation of the concept of archetypes, which has produced some empirical evidence for the existence of archetypal structures in the sense of a collective archetypal memory.

Alessandra De Coro discusses the relationship between Jung's concept of "image," which is a core construct in the Jungian interpretation of psychological processes, and the modern cognitive notion of mental images as constituting a central step in information processing (referring to Wilma Bucci). Cognitive studies, as well as some neuroscience hypotheses about the brain's different modes of processing sensorial and emotional information, seem to confirm the Jungian hypothesis that images are the main content of our thoughts and that thinking itself has its roots in imaging.

Christian Roesler points out that Jung had a major influence on theories of dreaming and dream interpretation in psychotherapy. This chapter provides an overview on findings from empirical dream research that refer to Jung's theory. The research method Structural Dream Analysis (SDA) is described, which allows for systematic and objective analysis of the meaning of dreams produced by patients in Jungian psychotherapies. This ongoing research project aims at building a corpus of cases and forming an empirically grounded theory of the function of dreams for the psychotherapeutic process.

A number of authors have dealt with the impact of trauma on psychological processes and concepts for understanding the development and influence of trauma from the viewpoint of Analytical Psychology. Tamar Kron has investigated dreams of people living under traumatic stress conditions; she can demonstrate how the dreams reflect traumatic experiences which supports the depth psychological understanding of dreaming. From a more general point of view, Joseph Cambray discusses the general field of trauma along with specific insights for Jungian psychology referring to research and findings from the neurosciences. He also presents the results of a Jungian research project conducted by Ruth Lanius and her students at the University of Western Ontario involving fMRI studies on trauma survivors. Brian Feldman presents his research using the infant observation method, focusing on transmission of attachment patterns and intergenerational trauma between infants and their caretakers and the impact of culture in China.

The following section focuses on psychotherapy and its methods in Analytical Psychology. Working with symbols in the form of pictures or sandplay has always been a central method in the psychotherapeutic work in Analytical Psychology. Denise Ramos and Reinalda da Matta present their research method for investigating sandplay pictures. The method was applied to investigate the effect of sandplay therapy (ST) on treating children with trauma caused by abuse, neglect, and abandonment. Results of this intervention showed that children in the intervention group significantly improved regarding internalizing, externalizing factors, and total problems.

Manfred Krapp has developed a research method for investigating pictures and demonstrates its usefulness in a study investigating therapeutic changes in the pictures of psychotic patients in art therapy groups.

Jungian psychotherapy has long been blamed for not giving any empirical proof of its effectiveness. Since the 1990s several research projects and empirical studies on Jungian psychotherapy, its outcome, and process have been conducted mainly in Germany and Switzerland. Christian Roesler gives a critical overview of the studies and results. All the studies show significant improvements not only on the level of symptoms and interpersonal problems, but also on the level of personality structure and in everyday life conduct. These improvements remain stable also after completion of therapy over a period of up to six years. Several studies show further improvements after the end of therapy. Health insurance data show that after Jungian therapy, patients reduce visits to doctors and hospitals to a level even below the average of the total population. Results over several studies show that Jungian treatment moves patients from a level of severe symptoms to a level even below the cutoff where one can speak of psychological health. These significant changes are reached by Jungian therapy with an average of 90 sessions, which makes Jungian psychotherapy an effective and cost-effective method. Nevertheless it has to be noted that several of these Jungian studies had severe problems in finding enough analysts who participated in the study. Also there is still a lack of a randomized controlled trial which would give proof of efficacy of Jungian psychotherapy.

In Germany and Switzerland, Jungian psychotherapy is a well-established part of the health care system which provides good conditions for conducting effectiveness studies. On the other hand, being part of this health care system also makes it necessary to establish systems for ongoing quality management. Wolfram Keller describes a number of studies and approaches in Germany, completed as well as ongoing, which attempt to establish systematic quality management in Jungian psychotherapy.

A not well-investigated field is the training of psychotherapists and how it impacts personality and professional competence. John Merchant gives an overview of the existing research, in psychoanalysis in general as well as in Jungian psychology, and summarizes findings from the International Association for Analytical Psychology's evaluation of their international Router training program.

This volume concludes with two chapters dealing with what may be Jung's most controversial concept: synchronicity. Harald Atmanspacher summarizes the so-called Pauli–Jung dialogue and points out that their epistemological viewpoint can today best be understood as a dual-aspect monism. He discusses the implications for a further development of the concept of synchronicity and its usefulness to better understand mind–matter relations. Christian Roesler gives an overview of empirical studies in the field of synchronicity in psychotherapy and describes a research frame for investigating the appearance of such synchronistic events in the field.

## References

Bash, K. W. (1988). *Die analytische Psychologie im Umfeld der Wissenschaften.* Bern: Huber.

Freud, S., & Jung, C. G. (1974). *Briefwechsel. Hg. v. McGuire & W. Sauerländer.* Frankfurt am Main: Fischer.

Jones, R. (2003). Mixed metaphors and narrative shifts. *Theory and Psychology, 13,* 651–672.

Jung, C.G. (1992). *Experimental researches.* Collected Works, Vol. 2. London: Routledge.

Kirsch, T.B. (2007): *The Jungians: A comparative and historical perspective.* London: Routledge.

Knox, J. (2001). Memories, fantasies, archetypes: An exploration of some connections between cognitive science and analytical psychology. *Journal of Analytical Psychology, 46*(4), 613–635.

Roesler, C. (2010). *Analytische Psychologie heute: Der aktuelle Forschungsstand zur Psychologie C. G. Jungs*. Basel, Freiburg: Karger.

Roesler, C. (2012). A revision of Jung's theory of archetypes in the light of contemporary research: neurosciences, genetics and cultural theory – a reformulation. In P. Bennett (Ed.), *Facing multiplicity: Psyche, nature, culture: Proceedings of the XVIIIth congress of the international association for analytical psychology, Montreal 2010*. Einsiedeln: Daimon.

Schlegel, M. (1999). Forschungskolloquium am C.G. Jung-Institut Zürich: Anschluss an die neue Wissenschaftsentwicklung und Rückbesinnung auf die empirischen Wurzeln der Analytischen Psychologie. *Analytische Psychologie, 30*, 72–79.

Seifert, T. (1975). Von der Notwendigkeit und Möglichkeit wissenschaftlicher Methoden in der Analytischen Psychologie. *Analytische Psychologie, 6*, 26–44.

Shamdasani, S. (2003). *Jung and the making of modern psychology: The dream of a science*. Cambridge: Cambridge University Press.

Solms, M. (2006). Sigmund Freud heute: Eine neurowissenschaftliche Perspektive auf die Psychoanalyse. *Psyche, 60*, 829–859.

# PART I

# Epistemological foundations

# 1

# PSYCHOLOGICAL EMPIRICISM AND NATURALISM

*Philip Kime*

> In so far as [psycho-analysis] is associated with the ultimate reality of the personality, O, it is baseless. This does not mean that the psycho-analytic method is unscientific, but that the term "science," as it has been commonly used hitherto to describe an attitude to objects of sense, is not adequate to represent an approach to those realities with which "psycho-analytical science" has to deal.
>
> (Bion, 1970/2004, p. 88)

## Introduction

When one considers the idea of research, outside of the mainstream cognitive behavioral models of psychology, one is fundamentally involved with philosophical and specifically epistemological questions which complicate things considerably. The notion of research has a very particular bias in that the primary meaning is one of "research into," that is, of a target, a realm of investigation separate from the researcher and separate from the decision or desire to perform research. We often pay lip service to other aspects of the idea when we say that, of course, there is research into concepts and ideas, but this is often with a reservation that this is not quite the same thing, which of course it is not since we have no natural disposition – or at least a much more complicated and ambiguous one – to believe that ideas are ontologically separate in the same way as we pre-theoretically conceive of empirical reality to be separate. Dictionary definitions of research tend to emphasize the *systematic* aspect of investigation, and a systematic approach implies a belief in the systematic organization of the target of the research; this, a subtle, complex vestige of a sympathetic magic whereby one controls and understands by somehow mirroring or copying that which is not yet understood. Sympathetic mirroring of a thing in the structure of the investigation into the thing is part of what it is to believe in a "thing" at all: a sympathy is the first flush of an ontology since it necessitates an alteration in the sympathizer, and the presence of anything which alters us is a primitive and inevitable first ontology. So, the implied subject matter of research and the systematic approach gives us from the very beginning fundamental epistemological and ontological biases. The question is, are these structures adequate for the type of psychology which is called, broadly, "Analytical Psychology"? When we consider psychology as a discipline defined by its subject matter, however one conceives of this, there is little problem in building up a program of empirical research since empiricism indeed is essentially defined by a particular relation to a subject matter to be explored. If, however, as I think we rather should define psychology with respect to its form and the *manner* in which it engages with its purported subject matter, the subject matter it ostensibly investigates drops out of the definition of the field and we are left with a real problem of how to conceive of the notion of "data." I will argue that if we commit to the (metaphysical) structure required by empiricism, we will miss out the essential feature of psychology proper: its particular and unique form. This omission will ensure that what passes for psychology will really only be other fields of a more prosaic structure, albeit obscured by psychological vocabulary which in fact contributes nothing essentially psychological. The great seduction of empiricism obscures and damages the subtle structure of psychology proper which cannot rest satisfied with a metaphysical notion of external "data," no matter how complex the data is said to be.

It is of no help, when considering addressing oneself to a putative empirical Analytical Psychology, to begin with a naïve empiricism since this is questionable even in the most favorable of the physical sciences; any basic text on the philosophy of science will attest to this. Rather one might begin straight away with a more sophisticated model of empiricist ontology such as that developed by Quine since this has been a point of reference in recent relevant work (Atmanspacher, 2014; Atmanspacher & Kronz, 1999). It is necessary to note that there is a significant philosophical lineage from Heidegger through Husserl to Dreyfus's well-known critique of artificial intelligence, which dismisses the significance of a foundational question to which an "empirical psychology" is part of the answer:

> Since that time, many have come to regard it as absurd and wholly obsolete to ask how the subject arrives at knowledge of the so-called "external world." Heidegger has called the persistence of this question the real "scandal" of philosophy.
>
> *(Gadamer, 1962, p. 119)*

Scandal or not, in a modern context where a claim to scientific respectability is heavily biased toward the demonstration of a research paradigm and empirical relevance, arguments starting from a point of incommensurability are too easy to dismiss. It is for this reason that it is worthwhile to begin with a model which is simultaneously able to take seriously the idea of empirical research but is also sophisticated enough to allow for something like psychology.

## Naturalized epistemology

There is no epistemological sophistication seemingly more relevant to psychology than that presented by Quine, if only for the famous sentence about the practice of traditional epistemology:

> But why all this creative reconstruction, all this make-believe? The stimulation of his sensory receptors is all the evidence anybody has had to go on, ultimately, in arriving at his picture of the world. Why not just see how this construction really proceeds? Why not settle for psychology?
>
> *(Quine, 1968a, p. 75)*

At first blush, this seems to be something which the depth psychologist might embrace due to its implied suspicion of arbitrary theorizing, or perhaps intellectualism, but in particular due to the explicit mention of psychology. It seems to advocate praxis, clinical details, and empirical sensibility. The point of a naturalized epistemology is a fundamental suspicion of the normative reconstructions of traditional epistemology leading to a concentration on the processes which actually lead to what we call knowledge. Surely psychology and such a naturalized epistemology have a natural relation, a natural interest in carefully detailing the constructed subtleties and idiosyncrasies in what we claim to know. Indeed this was one of the early (and late) claims of psychoanalysis: it laid bare the strange connective tissue of what we claimed to know and in some way either completed the puzzle or provided the very foundation of the epistemological picture in an ostensibly naturalized manner based on clinical observations. The well-aired suspicions regarding the naturalized credentials of Freud's initial theories notwithstanding, we can be certain that the initial impulse of depth psychology can be characterized as one of descriptive rather than normative epistemics; Freud was used to defend his views by unapologetically affirming that his theory was simply supported by what actually was the case in the consulting room. More sophisticated later theorists such as Bion even went so far as to suggest that the primary phenomenon being worked upon in psychoanalysis was epistemic, the so-called K (Knowledge) link (Bion, 1963).

Thus far we seem to be in a position to advocate naturalized epistemology as a suitable framework in which we can situate Analytical Psychology research. However, this is untenable since the "naturalized" in "naturalized epistemology" derives from the "natural" in "natural science." This is explicit in Quine but often forgotten. Natural science for Quine means empirical science, and psychology for Quine is a part of natural science. A naturalized epistemology is an epistemology characterized by a thoroughgoing empiricism where the essential *explanandum* is "The relation between the meager input and the torrential output" (Quine, 1968a, p. 83) – that is, how we come to build such tremendous models of knowledge given only the "meager" input of the senses. It is clear from this glimpse of the underbelly of a naturalized epistemology that there are fundamental and serious problems with adopting such an epistemological model in Analytical Psychology. This is due in large part to the concept of "archetype" since, ignoring the inappropriate reifications which gather around this idea, it indicates a structuring principle which shapes the sense input far beyond any measure which could reasonably qualify as "meager." We are really in no position, since Kant, to so easily divide the world into "raw" sense data and its post-perceived manipulations, at least in epistemology. Of course Quine has a very famous opinion about this in terms of his attack on the analytic/synthetic distinction which critically sophisticated his empiricism (Quine, 1951). However, the sophistication is to do with the flexibility of scope Quine sees in applying the refutations of experimentation rather than any attack on the empiricist foundations themselves.

The relevant sophistication in Quine's empiricism comes via Duhem (1906/1954) – the well-known thesis of epistemic holism:

> Holism in this moderate sense is an obvious but vital correction of the naive conception of scientific sentences as endowed each with its own separable empirical content.
>
> *(Quine, 1990, p. 16)*

That is, empiricism would not require that every noun in our psychological vocabulary – "self," "archetype," "complex," and so forth – should somehow be connected to a part of the world, giving such terms their reference and thereby meaningful content. Indeed, not even statements expressed as sentences which contain such terms have isolatable empirical content, and this rules out simplistic physical reduction to brain states, for example. Rather, the empirical content of a discipline and thereby the very purpose of research in the discipline is a function of the points at which the theory as a whole touches upon the empirical world. It is this holism which makes Quine's model so useful as a starting point for discussing the empirical content of psychology since it models at the level of meta-theory the justified suspicion of crude versions of materialism which would map every term to a physical state and thereby offer an effectively syntactic method of eliminating psychology altogether.

There are difficulties however, in that points of contact with empirical reality are not so easy to identify in psychology:

> In softer science, from psychology and economics through sociology to history (I use "science" broadly), checkpoints are sparser and sparser, to the point where their absence becomes rather the rule than the exception.
>
> *(Quine, 1995, p. 49)*

Here the "checkpoints" are the "observation categoricals," the points where the theory states something that could possibly conflict with empirical reality, and it is these which provide the touchstones of empiricism for Quine. However sparse or rare these checkpoints might be, they are the foundation of knowledge, and when completely absent relegate a subject to the realms of fiction or groundless metaphysics. This is very important, as it is an insight more colloquially and ubiquitously embraced by many in Analytical Psychology that despite the seeming abstract nature of the concepts involved, there is a hope that these "checkpoints" do exist and provide an empirical touchstone which allows meaningful research and a place in the pantheon of scientific endeavor. I shall argue in this chapter that the nature of psychology proper is that the character of such checkpoints is unique in psychology, and that their empirical nature, when extant, is fundamentally contingent and therefore provides no basis for an empirical attitude.

## Research and ontology

Research requires an object, and this induces a pre-theoretical ontology since what you are researching is to some extent what you think there *is*. Quine formalized this in his maxims regarding quantification and ontology, that ontology is given by the values of the variables one is prepared to quantify over. When researching into $X$, one is generally apt to quantify over variables whose value is $X$. For example, "complexes have a core which can be described using emotionally toned adjectives," or "there is a finite classification of core dream symbols," or even "the Self is a self-organising system of reflexive relations" are all statements of potential research areas in Analytical Psychology that quantify respectively over variables taking as values "complex," "dream symbol," and "Self." There is much to be said for the idea that therefore, such things *are* ontological commitments, regardless of whether one tries to defuse the issue by simply stating that they are not. We must at least thank Quine for teaching us that basing the ontology of a research paradigm on mere statements of ontological commitment is far too naïve.[1]

An empirical basis for any subject requires two things. First, we need an accepted ontology, no matter whether it is finite or infinite or whether it consists of entities concrete (e.g., particles) or abstract (e.g., numbers or complexes). Second, we need some method of converting all unempirical talk into empirical talk in terms of our accepted ontology. The most well-known conversion takes the form of a *reduction* into our accepted ontology; we might wish to eliminate all ontological commitment from a theory which is not commitment to members of the accepted ontology. To take a crude example from the philosophy of mind, we might wish to reduce all talk of beliefs or ideas to talk of neurons firing in particular patterns at particular times, and this would be an ontological reduction from something which we feel uneasy talking about to something about which we feel confident.

There has, of course, been enormous controversy in the philosophy of mind about what might be an acceptable ontology and how one might go about construing mentalistic discourse in terms of such an ontology. Without becoming embroiled in the particulars of the debate, let us keep an eye on the general requirements in respect of theoretical ontological commitment. Quine helpfully codified the abstract structure of the ontological element in all such debates into his notion of a "proxy function," which is a mapping of elements of the ontology of one theory into elements of a theory having a different ontology (Quine, 1968b, pp. 55–62;

Quine, 1966, pp. 214–220; Quine, 1990, pp. 31–33; Quine, 1995, pp. 72–73). Such a proxy function need not be one-to-one and can indeed be many-to-one, and in this case it counts as ontologically reductive. Proxy functions tell us something important about the nature of what is essential in a theory; they tell us that "what justifies the reduction of one system of objects to another is preservation of relevant structure" (Quine, 1966, p. 214). This is very important, as it means that when we recast a theory and its ontological commitments into another theoretical model by way of proxy functions, what we aim to preserve is *structure*.[2] The famous Quinean notion of "ontological relativity" depends on proxy functions because given particular and often typically essential assumptions about the composition of a theory, it is possible to prove that one can always define such a proxy function, and therefore that the ontological commitment of a theory is not fixed and uniquely implicated but rather relative to a complex and pragmatically invisible theoretical background which determines the particular shape of the proxy function. Since the proxy function changes exactly that which determines ontological commitment (for Quine, quantification over free variables), ontology itself is ineradicably relative.

We employ this notion of a "proxy function" in Analytical Psychology when we treat a patient through a medium such as dreams, active imagination, or myths. These variations are seen as a proxy for the psychology of the patient and allow a latitude unavailable to a "direct" approach – this is indeed a central tenet of this form of psychology. We take these "proxy" phenomena as types of maps or structures which somehow "fit" the psychology of a patient and provide a language perhaps more appropriate, coherent, or effective in treatment. I believe Quine to be essentially correct when he emphasizes structure as the essential feature of theory. It is the *shape* of the theory, that is, the geometry of the relations between things in the theory, that *is* the theory; the particular things related are not the point, neither are they stable when one re-maps the theory to the world using a proxy function which preserves the structure. Now, there is a little subterfuge here in this excursion into Quine's philosophy of science due to the presence of an underlying assumption which pervades his work, as it does every empiricist, no matter how sophisticated. The assumption is that the notion of "empirical content" is non-empty, meaning that a restriction on proxy functions is that *all* theories are ontologically committed to at least some things that are real referents of their variables. The assumption, put another way, is that a proxy function cannot map from a theory with empirical content to one without empirical content. This is in fact what *defines* the physical sciences, that their structure is limited to *some* empirical touchstone even though this touchstone might change, indeed sometimes drastically so.

It is this assumption that I reject of psychology. What defines psychology proper is that it *is* structure and that its study is the study of structure only. There need be no empirical touchstones whatsoever, and proxy functions for psychological theory can map to adequate structures which have *no empirical content*. This means that empirical content is inessential for psychology. In fact, it is misleading, as it tempts us into more or less embarrassing scientist diversions. Naturally, such a possibility is not discussed by Quine, the notion of empirical content for quantificational variables being so basic for his philosophical outlook that it is tacitly regarded as a given.

## Fiction and its adequacy

I take folk tales as canonical examples of a proxy function theoretical output in Analytical Psychology. Folk tales are used as a mapping of psychological structure into narratives which help to make clear particular patterns and shapes which are presumably more difficult to see outside of such a narrative. It is their often stark imagery and pervasive historical presence which makes them well suited to their role as useful depictions of psychological geometry.

It is important to point out here that above I said that folk tales are "used" as mappings of psychological structures. It is a completely separate and irrelevant issue as to whether in their genesis they were ever conceived in such a way; as a matter of fact, it is precisely as such mappings that the field conceives of and uses them. The *genesis* of folk tales is not relevant at all for psychology in the same way as the genesis of a theory in the empirical physical sciences is not relevant to its status. This point is indeed one of Popper's (1963) significant contributions to the philosophy of science; following Popper a little further, we can say that it is the *testability* of a theory that matters, not its genesis, and it is here that empirical science and psychology must part company. For folk tales as adequate psychological material are not testable as theory and are not empirical at all. Being both fictional and structurally adequate enough to find enormously broad use across the entire spectrum of modern analytical psychological thought, folk tales are no support for a species of ontological relativity but rather for an outright ontological independence. It is the structural *adequacy* of folk tales which partly defines Analytical Psychology. However, not only are folk tales empirically empty, but this aspect is indeed emphasized in their use when it is pointed out that what matters about the relevance of a folk tale is not the referents of specific imagery, but rather how a folk tale matches the structure of a psychological situation or concept.

I think that it is indeed a hallmark of psychology proper that it is possible to understand it, *without loss*, by a study of fictions. This is not the case in empirical physical science, where every demonstration by way of a toy domain or fictional analogy is accompanied with warnings about lack of adequacy of the demonstration – that it is "only for illustrative purposes" and so forth. Psychology proper is unique in that fictional domains are adequate, and this is because psychology proper *is* structure. This eliminates the necessity of the empirical points of contact which are minimally necessary for empirical research in even sophisticated versions of empiricism. This conclusion is unpalatable to many in the field, and we are tempted time and time again to, for example, identify patients with characters in folk tales and dreams or reduce complexes and transference to brain states.

In my view, it is a misguided tendency which tries to keep psychological theory with one foot in a real, empirical world. The most overt example is cognitive psychology, with its posits of "mental constructs" which survive on a tacit and remote promise of being reduced one day to neuroscience. The antipathy which many depth psychologists demonstrate for mainstream psychology is a little premature, however, because it has similar problems itself once one focuses on the structure of the theory as opposed to the particulars it posits. A popular alternative is a vaguely holistic or New Age psychology which posits a general connectedness, often unfortunately drawing on tremendously difficult and problematic concepts, such as Jung's synchronicity or perhaps upon a superficial misreading of modern physics. Such ideas are structurally no different from the mainstream since they assume a fundamental, empirical disconnectedness which must be overcome by some type of general, pervasive connection. In a thoroughgoing holism, there is no multiplicity and no work for such empirical connections to do (Atmanspacher & Kronz, 1999, p. 280).

A more sophisticated and seemingly relevant example is the impetus taken by the imaginal and Archetypal Psychology schools from Jung's exhortation to "stick to the image" (Jung, 1954, p. 320). In such approaches, the "image" is an epistemic foundation which we treat as *sui generis* and out of which we build our psychology. Structurally, this is not different from standard empiricism since it posits separate images which interrelate in what amounts to a mythological calculus. It is the heterogeneous nature of the images which necessitates some account of connections between them, and this is no different from the heterogeneity of empirical objects and the necessity therefore of some account of *their* interrelations. It should not be thought, then, that a fictional domain is adequate to psychology *because* it is fictional. As Giegerich has argued, the fictional as folk tale and myth are indeed not adequate to psychology proper because of their simplistic pictorial and image-based language (Giegerich, 2013, p. 8). Even though psychology does not require the empirical touchstones of physical science, it does indeed require a structure more subtle than one of separate objects and their relatively simple interrelations. The case of imaginal psychology is instructive because it is sometimes supposed to be an antidote to vulgar empiricism in depth psychology through an insistence on a thoroughly psychological foundation. I rather think that this very idea of "foundation" is where psychology parts company with science – the particularities of the foundation are not relevant. The problem of an "empirical" psychology is not the supposedly "empirical" basis of such an enterprise but rather the *relations* connecting to the putatively empirical foundation. A metaphor helps here. An imaginal psychology is in the position of trying to build a ladder to the moon. Concentrating on the next rung, the construction of the rung, its specific material, joint, strength, and so forth is supposed to be a psychological "staying with the image" and provides a foundation by being "here and now," not abstract and merely theoretical. This is supported by the intuitive idea that when one has added a few rungs to such a ladder, one is indeed closer to the moon. However, it is *this* sense of "closer" that is in fact completely abstract. The next rung of a ladder is only closer to the moon in a sense which has no relation to the realities which in fact determine the relations of ladders with moons – gravity, structural stress, tidal forces, radiation, and so forth. It is undeniable that a ladder 20 meters long is closer to the moon than one 10 meters long, but in concrete reality it is irrelevant how long the ladder is, since it is completely impossible to build a ladder to the moon. It is because the *concrete* facts about such a project render it impossible that once again shows how fundamentally abstract such a desire is.[3] One has to know about the concrete, structural issues in order to have a supportable opinion about the possibility of such a project. The concentration on the "here and now" (of the internal images, for example) instead of the larger structural rules is abstract in the real sense of the word. This definition of "abstract" is the opposite of what is usually meant; structural rules are often criticized for being abstract when it is these that actually provide the concrete, practical import which makes a task possible or impossible. Having one's face against the ladder, concentrating on the next step, pretending that this is concrete, soulful, immediate is merely a pretense which fails to thereby see that the entire enterprise is completely abstract and merely an exercise in playing "let's pretend." This sort of structure mirrors the materialist attempt to build up from foundational physical states to psychology, which is an abstract procedure for the same structural reasons.

A relatively sophisticated way of trying to escape this conclusion is to change the definition of "ladder" to match a solution which could take account of the concrete reality. One redefines "ladder" to mean some sort of sophisticated, expensively engineered machine which, in some very technical sense, does provide some sort of earth–moon connection and which you then call a "ladder." This happens often in psychology: we simply define psychology to be whatever we can do with our method (and which therefore is by definition concrete) and then *post facto* claim that our method is adequate to psychology. All we have done is to redefine "psychology" to fit our methods and thereby established a purely definitional (that is, abstract) idea of psychology. We perhaps define psychology as "the imaginal" and then propose to make a methodology of concentrating on images central to, defining of, psychology. The specific images appear to be concrete and specific when taken alone, but the entire relation between these images and the notion of psychology toward which they tend (and from which they proceed) is completely abstract, since it does not take into account any of the structural, formal characteristics which prevent any accretion of images being adequate to psychology. A ladder nearly a quarter of a million miles long would collapse under its own weight, no matter how authentically, soulfully constructed each individual rung might be. We know this before we start to build the first rung, and so any attempt is essentially willfully abstract, ignoring critical, defining structural problems in order to maintain an innocent, unrealistic, and therefore abstract idea. Of course, from within the definition of psychology as having a foundation in images, an imaginal approach is of course not abstract, which is why it sometimes fools us.

A mere compressed progression, or as Bion would say, "agglomeration" of things is not structural enough to support psychology (Bion, 1957); a succession of images does not have subtlety enough to be adequate to the most subtle of human phenomena. Abstraction is not a matter of whether something feels "dry" or "unsoulful" – this is just an irrelevant personal association – it rather means that the relation one has to an idea is fundamentally unsound, not yet really "in the world," as it ignores ineluctable facts about the structure of the world in order to protect its nascent form. The example of imaginal psychology is instructive, as it demonstrates that the problem with empiricism in psychology has nothing to do with a problem with the empirical itself (since this is manifestly adequate for many things), but rather with the structural relations empiricism establishes for that which is built upon its assumptions.

## Building psychology up from the ground

The desire for a psychological empirical foundationalism, given the philosophical histories of such undertakings, is remarkable mostly for the failure it engenders. From Carnap's *Aufbau* to the attempts of artificial intelligence to build psychology from modular units of empirical certainty, the failure has been thorough and well documented. This failure has been, it must be said, partly obscured by advances in computing and engineering which have turned out impressive robots and behaviors, all of which depend upon rapidly increasing computing power and parallelism designed solely to provide the impressive results, leaving behind any explanatory pretensions.

The simplicity of much of depth psychological flirtations with empiricism, from dream dictionaries to neurological theories of transference or complexes, is surprising since such simplicity has long been questioned by empirically minded philosophers of science, and presumably there are few depth psychologists who would cede the place of their subject for being less complex and deserving of sophisticated treatment. The "bottom-up" nature of theoretical assumptions, despite important caveats in and flat-out contradictions to this sort of model in empirical science, is prevalent in public discourse. The idea that science proceeds by constructing larger things from smaller truths, in the manner of the popular model of progression through, for example, physics, chemistry, biology, and psychology to sociology, is widespread. It is apparent from modern physics that this model will not do for science and it would not do either for modern philosophers who realized that in the realm of epistemology, such a bottom-up model is inadequate for even the basics of semantics. The founders of modern semantics were explicit:

> The concept of truth (as well as other semantical concepts) when applied to colloquial language in conjunction with the normal laws of logic leads inevitably to confusions and contradictions.
>
> *(Tarski, 1933, p. 267)*

Language is not governed by logical laws in such a way that mere adherence to grammar would guarantee the formal correctness of thought processes (Frege, 1882, pp. 84–85).

What then are the chances for a bottom-up empirical reconstruction of the innermost subtleties of human psychology? Tarski and Frege were clear that the bottom-up formalism which so impresses the naïve empiricist is *normative*; it has nothing (explanatory) to do with human beings and how they are in fact constructed. Later, Quine gave up the idea that language is built out of its smallest seemingly foundational units and argued for a starting point strangely later than we would, in our naïve empirical mode, suppose: "We begin with the monolithic sentence, not the term" (Quine, 1990, p. 36). It is, I believe, at this point, with the giving up of the simple-minded empirical notion of bottom-up structure that we begin to approach anything reasonably called psychology, but it involves giving up distinctions which allow us to comfortably remain in the realm of the scientific. If such a model is inadequate for empirical science, it is certainly inadequate for psychology, which trades in far more problematic and subtle concepts.

Ironically, it is to Jung's interaction with modern physics that we owe an important challenge to bottom-up empiricism. It has been argued convincingly (Atmanspacher, 2014) that an account of Jung's psychology as it manifests in his conversations with Pauli requires a top-down and metaphysically subtle theory (dual-aspect monism) to account for it. This theory has no place for a structure, empirical or otherwise, which begs a simple foundation from which to build a complex edifice.[4] The origins of psychology are essentially complex and from the complex manifest epistemic simples, notably the mind/matter distinction which then fools us into attempting the reverse speculation of constructing mind from matter.

We may tease out this point to useful end via an example of the dialectic internals of a well-regarded example of empirical psychology. Nisbett and Ross's generally excellent *Human Inference* (1980) is rightly regarded as a central text touching upon many areas of cognitive functioning within the framework of mainstream cognitive psychology. A merit of this work lies in its periodic realization that the inner structure of the subject matter is too much for the empirical assumptions to bear, and although such moments are rare, they are crucial. Nisbett and Ross reveal the relation of their method to the empirical foundation in many places but none more revealing than when discussing the fundamental empirical matter of "data coding," that is, mapping empirical observables to phenomena of a putatively psychological nature in order to forge a link supporting quantification and analysis. Their example is of detecting eye contact by measuring degree of visual angle and then extrapolating from this to a discussion about distinguishing various psychological predicates (Nisbett & Ross, 1980, p. 67). The possibility of "data coding" is essential to empiricism in order to forge the link to an empirical base of observables, constituting as it does, in modern parlance, the fundamental insights of the British empiricist tradition from Locke and Hume. Nisbett and Ross mention that, despite small changes in visual angle being important in regulating social conduct, "no one seems immune to serious coding errors in attempting to distinguish shyness from aloofness, feigned enjoyment from genuine pleasure or political conviction from political rhetoric" (Nisbett & Ross, 1980, p. 67). Here we see an implicit shift from the uncontroversial discussion of "coding errors" of assigning angles to eye contact to a highly problematic comparison of discussing the "coding error" of assigning, for example, shyness to eye contact and by transitivity, to visual angles – the "real" empirical base.

This is a failure to understand the nature of psychological predicates. In the case of eye contact, there is a good proxy in the form of visual angles of incidence, and the task is to "code" eye contact in terms of the proxy of visual angle. However, in the case of shyness, the establishment of a measurable, empirical proxy would constitute a solution to Wittgenstein's language game problem that there is no one common thing which all "games" (here, events of shyness) have in common. In the case of what we might call "psychological predicates," there is no data to code because "coding" whether something is shyness is really to *define* whether something is shyness, since there is no shyness proxy with which we can compare our decision to see if it is correct. Deciding whether an X is a Y without any fixed standard of Y is in fact an act of *defining* X. This is the essential form of psychology, that there is a necessary component of defining what one seems to be "coding," and therefore the idea of "data," of empirical evidence, is simply not available in the simple form in which it exists in the physical sciences. Of course, it always seems like it is possible to "code" an empirical proxy for psychological phenomena since the act of defining something is guaranteed to succeed.

Sophisticated mainstream psychologists like Nisbett and Ross do seem to intuit this but account for it in an inadequate way by trying to reconstruct the definitional aspect of psychological concepts by suggesting that "coding" errors are not so obviously errors if there are good pre-evidential reasons to warrant such errors (Nisbett & Ross, 1980, pp. 68–69). Uneasy about a simple empirical proxy, they then advocate coding "shyness" based on a pre-existing theory about what other things normally accompany shyness, which of course means that the whole idea of an empirical proxy has been undermined by the language game of defining "shyness" once more. An empirical proxy which can be error-prone due to philosophical matters of definition and semantics, rather than inadequate equipment, experimental error, and so forth, is not a purely empirical basis at all, which is simply to repeat Quine's famous "Two Dogmas" conclusion.

It should be clear that "data coding" is just another name for Quine's proxy functions since a proxy function is a way of turning a theoretical language into another language, usually with the aim of arriving at a tractable or empirically connected vocabulary more amenable to some sort of work (the practice of science, for example). We can now classify three forms of proxy functions:

1   The form where the source language is *defined* by the target language. For example, we define "shyness" as a measure of eye contact, in turn proxied by angle of visual incidence. The definitional aspect of this is often implicit, disguising its form.
2   The normal empirical scientific form, where the target language touches by necessity upon empirical reality in places, providing empirical content to the theory as a whole.
3   The form of pure structure, where the target language has no empirical points of contact but is structurally isomorphic to the source language. There is no necessary empirical content.

Form 1 is often encountered in cognitive psychology, where the entire psychologi-cal aspect is effectively bypassed by implicitly redefining terms. This does indeed give an empirical base, but the implicit redefinition of terms it involves typically means that the same empirical base equally well supports fields such as anthropol-ogy, neurology, biology, or sociology, removing the need for anything essentially psychological. Form 2 is the normal situation in the empirical sciences as described by Duhem and Quine, where empirical content is a distributed value derived from points of observational contact. The problem with mainstream psychology is that the definition involved in form 1 is implicit which causes a confusion of 1 with 2, thus leading to an inappropriate empiricism because it seems as though a connec-tion has been *found* between psychology and empirical data, whereas it has actually been stipulated. Psychology, conceived of as a subject in its own right, rather than merely as a vocabulary variant of another subject, takes form 3 above. The lack of necessity of empirical content in formally adequate target languages is defining of psychology and has one particular consequence, in that the difference between "normative" and "descriptive" disappears and means nothing in psychology since the subject is itself essentially concerned with the collapse of this distinction. This is a restatement of the idea that fiction is adequate to psychology and is a modern restatement of Hegel's critique of the ontological argument as described in the context of psychology by Giegerich (2013, p. 171).

The idea of empirical content, even when sophisticated to the limits of the notion by a model such as Quine's, is not adequate to psychology. Psychology requires more subtle geometry than any foundational epistemology can provide, and this must inevitably inform our notion of research.

## Conceptual research

When empirical content is inessential, research is not essentially empirical. Research in psychology is essentially conceptual: it is the analysis and refinement of the structure of the very idea of psychology. Despite the somewhat crude empirical narratives with which both Freud and Jung tried to justify their work, the service rendered to the history of ideas by their work was conceptual: sophisticating and fundamentally defining and refining concepts such as "unconscious" and "psyche." An inessential empirical aspect remains relevant, however, in that the framing of dis-cussions, their scaffolding and vocabulary are often (and often necessarily) given in empirical language. Indeed, just as with language where the contingent vocabulary is inessential and may be varied while conveying the same content, our empirical investigations in psychology must be seen as tools serving to clarify conceptual distinctions. These clarifications are not toothless abstractions because as Jung was wont to say, psychology always only speaks of itself and therefore it is not a failure when it fails to speak of something other than itself.

Psychological research which seeks to *use* terms such as "unconscious" or "arche-type" in discussing or even explaining putatively empirical phenomena is in fact contributing solely to a *definition* of the terms. This reflects the essential irrelevance of the normative/descriptive distinction in psychology mentioned previously. Such definitional activity is of great value since the defining and refining of terms is the simultaneous traversing and creation of the psychic landscape. Notice how this is also a description of the practice of analysis itself with the consequence that analysis proper *is* research and not something one does with tools which research provides.

A good example of this idea of "research" is Giegerich's Hegelian program, which is a sophisticated attempt to properly define and refine notions such as "unconscious" in that it, for example, urges a conceptual change from treating such terms as nouns and discusses them rather as adjectives. This is a significant conceptual change in the very ontology of Analytical Psychology which has vast structural ramifications in how we think, discuss, and practice. Another example of the "research" aspect of Giegerich's work is the use of Hegel to avoid the hypostatization of structurally simple, given (and therefore pseudo-empirical) "opposites" as the source of psychic tension. A dialectical model is given which demonstrates how inessential pre-existing oppositional poles are in accounting for the dynamics of psychological movement.[5] This work removes the need for an untenable, crude empirical base and does justice to the peculiar geometry of the psychological, generating itself from itself without the need for a reductive empirical substrate. This is real psychological research, changing the very substance of psychology which is not the empirical substance of any material thing. If we reject this conceptual approach, we are simply accepting that there is nothing to psychology other than a convenient vocabulary which merely summarizes empirical regularities which are really the province of the natural sciences. Much mainstream psychology either explicitly or implicitly does precisely this. However, it is a terrible error, made as it is on the basis of an untenable and inadequate philosophical knowledge, ignorant of the subtleties of the concepts necessary for the task of describing a phenomenon as complex and subtle as human psychology.

## Notes

1 Compare Giegerich's related comment about the futility of denials of ontological commitment (Giegerich, 2013, p. 265).
2 Technically, this means that when we change the referents of terms, we also change the predicates which are true or false of those terms, so that all propositions true in the old theory are true in the new theory.
3 Compare Giegerich (2013, p. 162).
4 Compare Giegerich's similar stress on the necessity of ongoing incarnation of theory in psychology (Giegerich, 2013, pp. 349–353).
5 See in particular Giegerich (2014, ch. 7).

## References

Atmanspacher, H. (2014). Notes on psychophysical phenomena. In H. Atmanspacher & C.A. Fuchs (Eds.), *The Pauli-Jung conjecture and its impact today* (pp. 181–199). Exeter, UK: Imprint Academic.

Atmanspacher, H., & Kronz, F. (1999). Relative onticity. In H. Atmanspacher, A. Amann, & U. Müller-Herold (Eds.), *Quantum, mind and matter: Hans primas in context* (pp. 273–294). Dordrecht: Kluwer.

Bion, W.R. (1957). Differentiation of the psychotic from the non-psychotic personalities. *International Journal of Psychoanalysis, 38*(3–4).

Bion, W.R. (1963). *Elements of psycho-analysis.* London: Heinemann.

Bion, W.R. (2004). *Attention and interpretation.* Lanham, MA: Rowman and Littlefield (Original work published 1970).

Duhem, P. (1954). *The aim and structure of physical theory* (P.W. Wiener, Trans.). Princeton, NJ: Princeton University Press (Original work published 1906).

Frege, G. (1882). Über die wissenschaftliche Berechtigung einer Begriffsschrift [On the scientific justification of a logical notation]. In T.W. Bynum (Ed.), *Conceptual notation and related articles* (Vol. 81, pp. 48–56). Oxford: Oxford University Press.

Gadamer, H-G. (1962). The philosophical foundations of the twentieth century. In D.E. Linge (Ed.), *Philosophical hermeneutics* (pp. 107–129). Berkeley: University of California Press.

Giegerich, W. (2013). *Neurosis: The logic of a metaphysical illness.* New Orleans, LA: Spring Journal Books.

Giegerich, W. (2014). *Collected english papers: Vol. 6. Dreaming the myth onwards: C.G. Jung on Christianity and on Hegel* (Vols. 6). Part 2 of The Flight into the Unconscious. New Orleans, LA: Spring Journal Books.

Jung, C.G. (1954). *The collected works: Vol. 16. The practice of psychotherapy* (2nd ed.). (H. Read, M. Fordham, G. Adler, W. McGuire, Eds.; R.F.C. Hull, Trans.). Princeton, NJ: Princeton University Press.

Nisbett, R., Ross, L. (1980). *Human inference: Strategies and shortcomings of social judgement.* Century Psychology Series. Englewood Cliffs, NJ: Prentice-Hall.

Popper, K.R. (1963). *Conjectures and refutations: The growth of scientific knowledge.* London: Routledge.

Quine, W.V. (1951). Two dogmas of empiricism. In *From a logical point of view* (pp. 20–46). Cambridge, MA: Harvard University Press.

Quine, W.V. (1966). *The ways of paradox and other essays.* Cambridge, MA: Harvard University Press.

Quine, W.V. (1968a). Epistemology naturalized. In *Ontological relativity and other essays* (pp. 69–90). New York: Columbia University Press.

Quine, W.V. (1968b). Ontological relativity. In *Ontological relativity and other essays* (pp. 26–68). New York: Columbia University Press.

Quine, W.V. (1990). *The pursuit of truth.* Cambridge, MA: Harvard University Press.

Quine, W.V. (1995). *From stimulus to science.* Cambridge, MA: Harvard University Press.

Tarski, A. (1933). Pojęcie prawdy w językach nauk dedukcyjnych [The concept of truth in formalized languages] (J.H. Woodger, Trans.). In J. Corcoran (Ed.). *Logic, semantics and metamathematics: Papers from 1923 to 1938* (2nd ed., pp. 152–278). Indianapolis, IN: Hackett.

## PART II

# Fundamental concepts of Analytical Psychology

# 2

# COMPLEXES AND THE UNCONSCIOUS

## From the association experiment to recent fMRI studies

*Christian Roesler and Tina van Uffelen*

Analytical Psychology and Jung's career started with his research using the association experiment (AE). This research led Jung to conceive of the concept of the unconscious complex. This chapter presents an overview of research with the AE and the concept of complexes from Jung's time to today. Also discussed is a summary of the initial findings from a recent study applying the AE for diagnostic use in clinical practice and the additional value the AE gives to the assessment of psychological disorders.

## The association experiment

From 1904–1911, when working together with Eugen Bleuler at the psychiatric hospital "Burghölzli" of Zurich University, Jung conducted research with the association experiment (AE; Jung, 1992, CW II). Jung took over this experiment from the so-called father of experimental psychology, Wilhelm Wundt, who developed it to test associative processes in his psychological laboratory at Leipzig University. The origins of the AE can be traced back to the founding fathers of psychology as a science, Francis Galton and Stuart Mill. In this experiment, a list of 100 words is presented to subjects who have the task to react as quickly as possible with the first association coming to their mind for each word; additionally, a psychogalvanometer was used to record physiologic responses to the word. It was found that some of the words stimulated emotional reactions in the subject, but this remained unconscious to the person. The emotional reaction leads to "failures," i.e., prolonged reaction time, inability to reproduce the association in the second round, laughing, commentaries, or other forms of emotional expression. The words from the list connected with such failures were investigated more deeply by asking the subjects for more associations to these words, the so-called context. Up to this point the AE was a pure experiment under controlled conditions without the introduction of any kind of subjective interpretation. Taken together, these words form a network of meaning for which Jung coined the term *complex*.

## The concept of a complex

A complex is an unconscious organized set of memories, associations, fantasies, expectations, and behavior patterns or tendencies around a core element which is accompanied by strong emotions. It is derived from early developmental experiences which have a problematic or even traumatic character circling around unresolved needs and topics. The complex can be triggered in later life by structurally similar cues, e.g., situations or relationships. In this case, the complex takes hold of the person or, better to say, of the ego; this is accompanied by strong emotions and typical behavior patterns influenced by the complex. Complexes can also be described as personality parts which, as an organized entity, have a certain autonomy from the ego as the center of the personality. When a complex is at work, it has a strong impact on the state of mind and the person, under its control, feels and behaves differently, e.g., strongly irrational, compared to his or her normal and conscious way of acting. Complexes are not necessarily maladaptive; they can act as organized behavior sets in the sense of social roles, e.g., in the professional field. In the case of maladaptive, unintegrated complexes, these tend to be suppressed or split off, and psychodynamic theories consider them to be at the core of neurotic disorders.

It is interesting that Jung's career started with empirical research and the use of an experimental setting which is at the core of what is called "normal science." Jung's association studies (Jung, 1992) gave empirical proof of the existence of unconscious, emotionally laden factors which impact behavior. That was the reason why Freud became interested in this research and took over the term complex for his theory of psychoanalysis, e.g., the Oedipus complex. Even Freudian psychoanalysts who have conducted empirical research on unconscious processes have valued highly Jung's contribution to the empirical investigation of the unconscious in his early studies with the AE and have called him psychoanalysis' first experimental researcher (Leuschner, Hau, & Fischmann, 1998). They even criticize Freud for his rejection of any kind of experimental research in psychoanalysis which, as they argue, was motivated by the personal conflict with Jung, whereas in the beginning of their relationship he was fascinated by Jung's empirical orientation and its contribution to early psychoanalysis.

Other early psychoanalysts also made use of the concept of the complex, e.g., Alfred Adler developed his theory of the inferiority complex. In early psychoanalysis, a complex was considered to be at the core of neurosis and was then conceptualized as an inner conflict between an unconscious drive impulse, e.g., an aggressive impulse, coming from the id, and an opposing suppressive force coming from the superego. In later conceptualizations, namely from the British school of object relations theory (M. Klein, W. Fairbairn, D. Winnicott), the complex was considered to be an unconscious representation of conflictual or frustrating experiences with a primary caregiver; the complex then consists of an inner scenario of self in an interaction with an other accompanied by a specific affect. For example, a boy grows up with the repetitive experience of being devaluated, belittled, and disparaged by his own father. This experience is accompanied by feelings of frustration, shame, low self-esteem, and so forth. Over time in the psyche of the boy, an authority complex is formed. This complex in adult life is triggered by having a demanding boss at work, where just facing this person provokes the same old feelings of shame, low self-esteem, and so forth. This is also an illustration of the fact that complexes tend to be projected on persons or situations in current life; they also form the basis for transference phenomena.

In developmental research it could be demonstrated how such patterns develop out of experiences with primary caregivers. Attachment theory and research identifies different attachment patterns or types (secure, insecure avoidant, etc.) in empirical studies which depend on the sensitivity of the caregiver. These attachment patterns, also called internal working models, are formed in the first 2 years of life with long-lasting effects into adulthood, e.g., these patterns influence the way the adult person takes up intimate relationships. In infant observation research (Stern, 1985) it could be empirically demonstrated how infants build stable patterns of expectations depending on their experiences with their caregivers which are called representations-of-Interactions-Generalized (RIGs). Attachment patterns as well as RIGs can be seen as early forms of complexes; the insights from infant observation were adapted to Analytical Psychology by Mario Jacoby (1998). Prominent authors who have adapted concepts from attachment theory to Analytical Psychology are Anthony Stevens (2003) and Jean Knox (2003): "Jung's concept of the complex is very close to that of the 'internal working model' of attachment theory" (Knox, 2003, S. 627).

## The psychodynamic unconscious and recent conceptions from cognitive psychology and the neurosciences

Whereas for the greater part of the 20th century there was controversy between psychodynamic positions and academic psychology and psychiatry regarding the existence and the relevance of unconscious processes, today it can be summarized that also the cognitive sciences take the existence of an unconscious for granted. An important part in this development took the research on subliminal perception, where it could be demonstrated that images presented to subjects below the level of conscious perception can have massive effects on psychological processes and behavior (Libet, Wright, Feistein, & Pearl, 1979; Crick & Koch, 1995). Even cognitive psychologists do not deny that there is a cognition without awareness; some even argue that there is evidence for the fact that more than 95% of all mental activity remains totally unconscious (Kihlstrom, 1984). The German psychoanalyst Wolfgang Mertens (2005) points out that the human brain processes 10–100 million bits of information per second, of which only 10–40 bits will become conscious. This is interesting, because it would support Jung's position that consciousness is just an island in a sea of unconscious, and that the unconscious is able to create meaningful structures and owns a certain kind of wisdom.

Research in the neurosciences has produced the distinction between explicit and implicit memory, and implicit (i.e., unconscious) schemas are considered to be the content of this implicit memory (Kandel, 2008). The neuroscientists Mark Solms and Oliver Turnbull (2005) argue that the implicit or procedural memory can be seen as identical with the psychodynamic unconscious; this can explain why clients in psychoanalysis cannot speak about the crucial experiences in their development because they are stored in the procedural memory, which cannot be put into words but only acted out in, mainly, interpersonal behavior. Other findings from the neurosciences support many other positions of the psychodynamic view on the unconscious: also unconscious perceptions can be emotionally valued, and especially those stimuli which are connected with conflictual experiences tend to have stronger emotional responses; there are neurobiological processes which lead to an unconscious suppression of emotionally negative memory content – this means that there are unconscious processes which interpret perception and select emotionally negative or disturbing content for suppression, and this can also be applied to very complex information such as narratives. Earlier experiences lead to the formation of cognitive schemas (complexes) which influence the perception of recent information input, which is called top-down information processing in the cognitive sciences (Anderson, 1983). The influence of these cognitive schemas can be so strong that it overrides the actual information input, which is a nice proof for the existence of what is called projection in psychoanalysis – human beings are able to "perceive" information which is actually not there just because they expect it to be there. This is exactly what Jung meant with his concept of the complex, of which he says that new information is adapted to the pre-existing complex structure.

## Partial personalities and dissociation

Complexes are not necessarily pathological. Representations of experiences with parent figures and other caregivers form the basic structures of the psyche. Whether such complexes become pathological depends on their accessibility for conscious reflection and on the degree of their integration into the whole of personality. In Analytical Psychology also, the ego is considered to be a complex which is in large part under conscious control. If a child can build a secure attachment pattern with caregivers, this complex will most likely lead to stable and satisfying relationships. Only if a complex builds around a conflictual or unresolved experience and, because of the painful emotions connected to it, is suppressed into the unconscious does it become pathological. In its most extreme form, such a pathological complex is totally split off from the rest of the personality. This can lead to dissociative disorders, e.g., multiple personality disorder, where a split-off part of the personality can suddenly take over control.

Jung himself was very much influenced by the French school of psychiatry of the late 19th century (Charcot, Janet), in which dissociation played a major role in the explanation of psychological disorders. Therefore it was quite natural for him to see the psyche as a structure which can be subject to dissociation. Outside of psychodynamic psychology the term dissociation was not used in academic psychology until the 1980s, when there was a new focus on dissociative disorders, e.g., multiple personality disorder (Kluft, 1987). The Jungian analyst Noll (1989) brought these studies together with the use of the concept of the complex and points out: "it is demonstrated that essential characteristics of Jung's 'autonomous complexes' are congruent with the phenomenology of the 'alternate personalities' or 'personality states' of this disorder" (p. 368). Since then the idea of more or less autonomous parts of personalities and the need for their integration into the whole of personality has influenced different schools of psychotherapy, e.g., ego state therapy and inner family systems therapy. Contemporary cognitive psychology has developed similar concepts, as for example implicit schemas, which are also applied in contemporary approaches of cognitive therapy like schema therapy (Young, Klosko, & Weishaar, 2003).

## Research with the association experiment

Even though research with the AE marked the beginning of the formation of Jung's concepts, it has almost disappeared from contemporary Analytical Psychology. With his leaving the university in 1911, Jung also left empirical research behind and never took it up again. Later Carl A. Meier, the first president of the Zurich Jung Institute, systematically collected Jung's unfinished research studies and results and published them in a coherent volume called *Die Empirie des Unbewußten*" ("Empiry of the Unconscious"; Meier, 1968/1994). In his summary of Jung's research with the AE, he concluded that the results give proof that the associative process is an unconscious process which allows for forming a psychological typology of the person, especially whether he or she is an extraverted or introverted type; that failures point to unconscious (pathological) complexes which have emotion as a dynamic component; and that the results support Freud's assumption that free association leads to the uncovering of suppressed content.

Also in Jung's lifetime there were a few empirical studies that made use of the AE (Pohl, 1939; Schaffner, 1951). After Jung's death, for decades no research was conducted using the AE. Beginning again in 1979 a systematic investigation was conducted to develop norm(ative?) data for the AE word list (Schlegel, 1979) and a detailed manual for the application and interpretation of the AE in the context of psychotherapy (Kast, 1988). Schlegel (1979) in his investigation focused on the correlations between the findings in the AE and psychophysiological measures. Jung in his investigations had made use of the measurement of the skin resistance, and an early form of what later became the polygraph (for details, see Jung's "Experimental Researches"/CW 2 and Meier's [1968] summary). Schlegel's measurements included skin resistance, heart rate, breath, muscle activity, laughter, and movement, and demonstrated clear correlations between somatic reactions and activated complexes.

Recently there has been a certain renaissance of the use of the AE in research designs. A group of Jungian analysts from Korea (Shin, Lee, Han, & Rhi, 2005) investigated the effects of complexes on learning processes using serial reaction time tests (SRT), a very common research design used in cognitive psychology. In SRTs, a series of visual stimuli is presented to subjects who have to identify the images correctly as quickly as possible. The presentation follows a hidden pattern, and it can be demonstrated that subjects can identify the pattern without being conscious of that, but their reaction time is reduced significantly. Before the SRT an association experiment was conducted with the subjects using the Korean version of Jung's 100-word list (Rhi, 2000). From the results of the AE, a list of complex words was formed to which most of the subjects had reacted with failures. As a control, a neutral, non-complex word list was formed. With these two lists, an experiment was conducted with the experimental group receiving the complex word list and the control group the neutral list. It was expected that the experimental group, because of the complex words and the emotional reaction stimulated in the subjects, would have more problems in learning the material. The results were contradictory: in the experimental group, learning processes were accelerated. The authors explained these results by assuming that the activation of unconscious complexes had heightened the awareness of the subjects during the test because it was connected with a general arousal, which facilitated subliminal learning processes. Even if one is not willing to accept this explanation, the experiment could demonstrate that complex stimuli create a significant difference in the results, which gives proof of the fact that unconscious emotional factors have effects on learning processes (Shin, Lee, Han, & Rhi, 2005).

## Complexes in neuro-imaging studies

Recent neuro-imaging studies have even found neuronal correlates of complexes (Kehyayan et al., 2013; Petchkovsky et al., 2011). A study of participants involved in taking the Word Association Test has demonstrated the neuronal activation pattern that underlies an activated complex (Bechtel, 2013), thereby providing evidence for the neural correlates of the processes at work that cause a disturbance of consciousness when a complex is triggered and supporting Jung's assertions. The research group around Leon Petchkovsky (Petchkovsky et al., 2011, 2013) conducted the AE with 12 normal subjects (i.e., without psychological disorders). Parallel to the AE an fMRI study was conducted which made those areas of the brain visible that were activated during complex reactions to the word stimuli. The researchers were able to demonstrate that the reaction to complex laden words followed a typical pattern of brain activation (corrected $z$-values between 4.90 and 5.69). Also they could demonstrate that there is an exchange between the brain hemispheres during association processes and that the left hemisphere, responsible for logical thinking, can within a few seconds deactivate the right hemisphere, responsible for emotion processing, intuition, and creativity. On the other hand, at the moment when a complex is activated, the dominance of the left hemisphere is broken, which the authors see as a "window of opportunity," a sensitive state of brain functioning in which new things can more easily be learned.

> We found that when a complex is activated, brain circuits involved in how we sense ourselves, but also other people, get activated. However, as there is no external person, the "other" circuits really refer to internalized programs about how an "other" person might respond. When a hot button gets pressed, "internal self" and "internal other" get into an argument.
>
> *(Petchkovsky in Wiley, 2013)*

Future studies should focus on the differences in complex reactions and parallel imaging between normal subjects and subjects with specified psychological disorders, e.g., schizophrenia, posttraumatic stress disorder, and so forth.

In Germany, the research group around the neuroscientist Nikolai Axmacher (Kehyayan, Best, Schmeing, Axmacher, & Kessler, 2013) from the University of Bonn has become quite famous recently because of their studies applying the AE, in which they could find empirical evidence for the process of suppression. In these studies subjects had to associate to conflict-related sentences. After a 1-hour break, the subjects were asked to repeat the sentences. It could be demonstrated that conflict-related words were "forgotten." Through neuroimaging, the researchers were able to demonstrate that through those words that were later forgotten; areas in the brain were activated which are connected with conflict processing. Apparently this activation resulted in such a disturbance of retrieval processes that the subjects were not able to remember the words correctly – and the whole process was totally unconscious to the subjects. This was interpreted as a proof for Freud's assumption of the defense mechanism of suppression.

It can be concluded that even though the concept of complexes is more than 100 years old, it has found its way into different fields of contemporary psychology, it has been empirically validated, and it has proved to be an effective tool in different approaches of psychotherapy.

## *Comparing the association experiment with standardized diagnostic measures*

In this section we will describe our own study which followed an earlier pilot single case study conducted by Vezzoli et al. (2007). In this study the AE in its original version (Jung's 100-word list) was applied to a single case, first at the beginning of a psychotherapy and again after completion of the therapy. In the pre–post comparison it could be demonstrated that the complex structure of the person had changed in the course of the therapy in a positive direction, that is the ego complex became more differentiated from the father and mother complexes. The most interesting part of this pilot for our study was the combining of the AE with standardized clinical measures: Structured Clinical Interview for DSM (SCID), the Symptom Checklist-90-R (SCL-90-R), and the Minnesota Multiphasic Personality Inventory (MMPI). Unfortunately the authors did not give any details about the correlations between these measures and the AE. In the following publication, they extended the presentation of the results to include a detailed description of the transference processes (Vezzoli et al., 2008).

In our own study we replicated the design in the sense that we investigated the results of the AE in comparison to a set of standard measures:

- Symptom Checklist-90-R (SCL-90-R): this instrument evaluates psychological distress and psychiatric disorders in individuals. The test is a 90-item self-report scale that uses a 5-point Likert scale. The SCL has good internal and test–retest reliability (for Global Severity Index [GSI], Cronbach's $\alpha$ = .97–.98) and is the most widely used clinical measure for psychological distress with reference data from non-clinical samples available (Franke, 2002).
- Freiburg Personality Inventory, revised version (FPI-R): instead of the MMPI, we used a comparable German personality inventory, which is the most widely used personality inventory in the German-speaking countries. As a personality inventory it investigates stable personality dimensions, e.g., extraversion versus introversion, neuroticism, openness, and other central personality dimensions which are part of the so-called Big Five. The test has very good reliability and validity values, and reference data from clinical as well as nonclinical samples (Fahrenberg, Hampel, & Selg, 2010).
- The AE with the 50-word list from Schlegel (1979).
- A depth psychological clinical and biographical interview ("Anamnese") focusing on the biographical development of the person, problems, and resources (Schneider & Jansen, 2009).

The aim of the study was to compare the results of the AE with the findings from the other measures regarding parallels and differences. All of the measures were applied to a sample of 18 clients (17 to 69 years; $M$ = 43 years) who requested therapy in a community counseling center.

Since the study combines qualitative and quantitative data for the interpretation of the results, we used a mixed-method design (Teddlie & Tashakkori, 2003). For the standardized measures (SCL-90-R and FPI-R), T-values were computed which put the individual in relation to the reference group. For the interpretation of the biographical interview as well as for the results of the AE, a discursive interpretation group consisting of experts from the field was used. The group had the task to evaluate the findings from the two qualitative measures and transform them into individual values on a scale from 1 to 5 (1 = no symptoms, 2 = light symptoms,

3 = clear symptoms, 4 = severe symptoms, 5 = very severe symptoms) for a defined set of categories:

1 Self-esteem
2 Norm orientation
3 Aggression inhibition
4 Aggression
5 Depression/inferiority complex
6 Anxiety
7 Psychosomatic problems
8 Obsessive-compulsive tendencies
9 Unresolved grief
10 Trauma
11 Performance orientation
12 Shame and blame complex.

These 12 categories were formed as a synthesis of the dimensions that are covered by the standardized measures as well as by the AE and the clinical interview.

## Results

Our study demonstrated that all the symptoms and problem areas which could be identified in the standardized measures could also be identified in the AE.

For 8 out of 18 subjects, the results from the standardized measures were identical to the findings in the clinical interview, and in the AE as well, as to the subject's own description of their symptomatology. This applies especially to the dimensions: depression/inferiority complex, aggression/aggression inhibition, anxiety, and obsessive-compulsive tendencies. The category of psychosomatic problems produced identical findings over all the applied measures for the total sample of 18 subjects.

For another group of 10 out of 18 subjects, symptoms and problem areas were identified, whereas these were not found in the standardized measures; here the subjects had nonsignificant or nonclinical values on the relevant dimensions (T-values not > 64, PST value in SCL-90-R not ≥ 60, stanine values in FPI-R in not more than two categories > 6 or < 4). In these cases the results from the AE could be verified by the clinical interview and the subject's own description of their symptoms and problems. An interesting finding in this group is that especially those subjects belong to this group who have significantly higher values in the sense of a strong adaptation to social norms and social orientation (stanine ≥ 7) and very low values in openness (stanine ≤ 4). These subjects suffered significantly more from shame and guilt complexes and a low self-esteem as compared to the first group – which could be identified in the AE as well as in the clinical interview – and it seems that because of these problems the subjects were "faking good" in the standardized measures. We assume that the subjects attempted to hide the severity of their psychological problems in the self-rated measures and tried to present themselves in the sense of social desirability. This can be interpreted as speaking for the fact that standardized measures, as applied in this study, have a weakness in identifying psychological symptoms if subjects are not willing to communicate their problems openly, whereas the AE has the advantage of identifying the symptoms even if the subject is not willing to communicate them or they are unconscious to the person.

Another advantage of the AE is its ability to identify the problem areas of inferiority/low self-esteem, unresolved grief, aggression inhibition, and traumatization, which the standardized measures do not measure systematically because these areas are mostly unconscious. Apart from identifying symptoms, problems, and conflicts, the AE is able – via the assessment of the context, associations to the stimulus words – to link the symptoms and problem areas with biographical information in the sense of a better understanding of how the personality developed over the life course. In this sense, the application of the AE does not only identify symptoms and conflicts but also creates information for a psychodynamic understanding of how the problems developed and how the person deals with the conflict areas in the sense of defense mechanisms and coping strategies. Additionally, the AE is able to give at least some hints on resources in the person in terms of what in Analytical Psychology is called the finalistic aspect, the kind of development which is necessary to overcome the problems.

## Conclusion

Our findings support the insight that the AE, even though it is more than 100 years old and has rarely been applied in clinical psychology, is capable of identifying symptoms and problem areas for diagnostic purposes to the same extent as standardized clinical measures. Additionally, the AE is capable of identifying unconscious tendencies and problem areas which subjects in clinical interviews have difficulties communicating, as for example low self-esteem and feelings of guilt and shame. The AE is also capable of putting these problems into context in the sense of collecting biographical information which can be formed into a psychodynamic understanding of how symptoms, defense mechanisms, and coping strategies form a coherent whole in the person. These findings encourage us to recommend the use of the AE as a standard instrument at the beginning of analytical psychotherapies. To our knowledge, even in Jungian training institutes there is often no training for candidates in the application of the AE. In the German-speaking countries, until now only the Jung Institute Zurich had a compulsory seminar for candidates to train in the application of the AE. As a result of this study a number of training institutes in Germany, namely Stuttgart and Berlin, have started to offer seminars for training in the application of the AE. Our findings support the viewpoint that the AE in the form in which it was applied by Jung is one of the jewels of Analytical Psychology and should be promoted much more strongly in the Jungian community. Our findings demonstrate that, even though the application of the AE takes considerable time and effort, this is worthwhile since it supports the therapist in systematically collecting information for a coherent psychodynamic hypothesis for the case as well as for the therapy plan.

In future Analytical Psychology research, the AE should play a prominent role. First, we hope that there will be studies replicating our design to strengthen the finding that the AE is capable of identifying symptoms and problems systematically and with high clinical validity. Apart from that, the AE should be part of systematic psychotherapy outcome studies in Analytical Psychology, applied in a pre–post comparison design, as the AE is able to identify not only symptoms and problems but also changes in the personality structure over the course of therapy (see Vezzoli et al., 2007). This should not only be tested in single case studies but also in studies with larger samples.

## References

Anderson, J.R. (1983). *The architecture of cognition*. Cambridge, MA: Harvard University Press.

Bechtel, P. (2013). *The effect of complex stimulus words determined by means of the Word Association Test on Functional Magnetic Resonance Imaging* (Unpublished thesis). Zürich: C.G. Jung Institute.

Crick, F., & Koch, C. (1995). Are we aware of neural activity in primary visual cortex? *Nature*, *11*, 121–123.

Fahrenberg, J., Hampel, R., & Selg, H. (2010). *Freiburger Persönlichkeitsinventar*. Manual 8, erweitere Auflage. Göttingen: Hogrefe.

Franke, G. H. (2002). *SCL-90-R – Die Symptom-Checkliste von L. R. Derogatis (2. vollständig überarbeitete und neu normierte Auflage)*. Göttingen: Beltz Test.

Jacoby, M. (1998). *Grundformen seelischer Austauschprozesse: Jungsche Therapie und neuere Kleinkindforschung*. Zürich: Walter.

Jung, C.G. (1992). *Experimental researches. Collected Works, Vol. 2*. London: Routledge.

Kandel, E.R. (2008). *Principles of Neural Science* (5th ed.). New York: McGraw Hill.

Kast, V. (1988). *Das Assoziationsexperiment in der therapeutischen Praxis*. Fellbach: Bonz.

Kehyayan, A., Best, K., Schmeing, J.B., Axmacher, N., & Kessler, H. (2013). Neural activity during free association to conflict – related sentences. *Frontiers in Human Neuroscience*, 7, 705–713. https://doi.org/10.3389/fnhum.2013.00705

Kihlstrom, J.F. (1984). Conscious, subconscious, unconscious: A cognitive perspective. In K. Bowers & D. Meichenbaum (Eds.), *The unconscious reconsidered*. New York: Wiley-Blackwell.

Kluft, R.P. (1987). An update on multiple personality disorder. *Hospital and Community Psychiatry*, *38*, 363–373.

Knox, J. (2003). *Archetype, attachment, analysis: Jungian psychology and the emergent mind*. Hove: Brunner-Routledge.

Leuschner, W., Hau, S., & Fischmann, T. (1998). Couch im labor: Experimentelle Erforschung unbewusster Prozesse. *Psyche*, *52*, 824–849.

Libet, B., Wright, E.W., Feistein, B., & Pearl, D.K. (1979). Subjective referral of the timing for a conscious sensory experience. *Brain*, *102*, 193–224.

Meier, C.A. (1994). *Die Empirie des Unbewussten: Mit besonderer Berücksichtigung des Assoziationsexperiments von C.G. Jung*. Band 1 (2. Aufl.). Einsiedeln: Daimon.

Mertens, W. (2005). Das Unbewußte in der Kognitionspsychologie. In M. Buchholz (Hg.), *Das Unbewusste in aktuellen Diskursen* (pp. 282–309). Gießen: Psychosozial-Verlag.

Noll, R. (1989). Multiple personality, dissociation, and C.G. Jung's complex theory. *Journal of Analytical Psychology, 34*, 353–370.

Petchkovsky, L., Petchkovsky, M., Morris, P., Dickson, P., Montgomery, D., Dwyer, J., & Burnett, P. (2013). fMRI responses to Jung's Word Association Test: Implications for theory, treatment and research. *Journal of Analytical Psychology, 58*(3), 409.

Petchkovsky, L., Petchkovsky, M., Morris, P., Dickson, P., Montgomery, D., Dwyer, J., Burnett, P., & Strudwick, M. (2011). The fMRI correlates of psychological "complexes": Exploring the neurobiology of internal conflict. *Journal of US-China Medical Science, 8*(11), 647–660.

Pohl, W. (1939). *Ein Assoziationsexperiment mit Störungsreiz* (Dissertation). Bonn: University of Bonn.

Rhi, B.Y. (2000). *Analytical psychology*. Seoul: Iljogak.

Schaffner, J. (1951). *Die "Versager" im Formdeutversuch von Rorschach und im Assoziationsexperiment von Jung* (Dissertation). Zürich: University of Zürich.

Schlegel, M. (1979). *Psychologische und psychophysiologische Aspekte des Assoziationsexperiments* (Dissertation). Zürich: University of Zürich.

Schneider, W., & Jansen, P. (2009). Biographische Anamnese. In P. Jansen, P. Joraschky, & W. Tress (Hrsg.), *Leitfaden Psychosomatische Medizin und Psychotherapie*. Köln: Deutscher Ärzte-Verlag.

Shin, Y.W., Lee, J.S., Han, O.S., & Rhi, B.Y. (2005). The influence of complexes on implicit learning. *Journal of Analytical Psychology, 50*, 175–190.

Solms, M., & Turnbull, O. (2005). *The brain and the inner world*. New York: Other Press.

Stern, D. (1985). *The interpersonal world of the infant: A view from psychoanalysis and development*. New York: Basic books.

Stevens, A. (2003). *Archetype Revisited: An updated natural history of the Self*. Toronto: Inner City Books.

Teddlie, C., & Tashakkori, A. (2003). Major issues and controversies in the use of mixes-methods in the social and behavioral sciences. In A. Tashakkori & C. Teddlie (Hrsg.), *Handbook of mixed methods in social and behavioral research* (pp. 3–50). Thousand Oaks, CA: Sage.

Vezzoli, C., Bressi, C., Tricario, G., Boato, P., Cattaneo, C., Visentin, U., & Invernizzi, G. (2007). Methodological evolution and clinical application of C.G. Jung's word association experiment: a follow-up study. *Journal of Analytical Psychology, 52*, 89–108.

Vezzoli, C., Boato, B., Jandoli, I., Manoussakis, C., Sgobba, C., Tricarico, G., Zucca, P., Bressi, C. (2008). *Research update on Jung's Word Association Test: Empirical observation on the influence of transference on the complexes – Psychotherapy in public health services*. Orta di St Giuglio: JAP-Conference (Speech).

Wiley. (2013). A rather complex complex: Brain scans reveal internal conflict during Jung's word association test. *ScienceDaily*. Retrieved February 15, 2015 from www.sciencedaily.com/releases/2013/06/130610133131.htm

Young, J.E., Klosko, J.S., & Weishaar, M.E. (2003). *Schema therapy: A practitioner's guide*. New York: Guilford Press.

# 3

# EXPERIMENTAL APPROACHES TO THE STUDY OF THE ARCHETYPE

*Milena Sotirova-Kohli*

## Jung's definition of archetypes

Unlike Freud, Jung believed that the unconscious was not just the seat of sexual and aggressive instincts and repressed wishes. Through his work with the association experiment, the study of myths and fairy tales, and the study of the fantasies produced by psychotic patients, Jung reached the conclusion that there was a layer of the unconscious which contained universal images, patterns of behavior, and modes of perception which were accessible to the whole of the human race and to the animal world as well. These specific patterns of perception and behavior which crystallize in consciousness in the form of symbols he named archetypes (after Plato) and suggested that these were "empty and purely formal . . . a possibility of representation given *a priori*" (Jung, 1954, para. 155, p. 79). Further on, Jung stressed that "the representations themselves are not inherited only the forms" (Jung, 1954, para. 155, p. 79). In this sense, Jung believed that the archetype-as-such is unknowable and "irrepresentable" (Jung, 1947, para. 415, p. 215). We come to know the effect of archetypes through the impact they have on consciousness due to their "ability to organize images and ideas" (Jung, 1947, para. 440, p. 231).

The archetype in Jung's view "can be named and has an invariable nucleus of meaning – but always only in principle" (Jung, 1954, para. 155, p. 80). Anything we say about the archetype remains a visualization which is made possible by the current state of consciousness in a respective moment. Archetypes are numinous and are associated with strong affective responses. Furthermore, Jung believed that the archetype had a "psychoid nature" (Jung, 1947, CW 8, para. 419, p. 215). He clarified this as follows: "the archetype describes a field which exhibits none of the peculiarities of the physiological and yet, in the last analysis, can no longer be regarded as psychic, although it manifests itself psychically" (Jung, 1947, para. 420, p. 215). Jung considered archetypes to represent a spectrum ranging from the physical to the psychic and even to the transcendent. So, archetypes-as-such, while being universal, are also unknowable; although archetypes have a profound impact on consciousness and the life of the individual, they do not belong just to the psychic sphere and seem to be given *a priori* as a possibility or a form without content (similar to Plato's view that psyche and soma are integrated in one whole).

## Modern approaches to archetypes

These qualities of the archetype have contributed a lot to the controversies that surround it, as contemporary Jungian scholars try to reformulate the theory of the archetype in terms of modern science. Among one of the most well-formulated approaches is the model which theorizes that what Jung might have meant with the archetype is similar to what contemporary cognitive semantics calls image schemas (Knox, 2003, 2004, 2009; Merchant, 2006, 2009; Sotirova-Kohli, Rosen, Smith, Henderson, & Taki-Reece, 2011). In this approach, the archetype is looked at as an early achievement of development resulting from the qualities of the brain as a dynamic system and the interactions between the individual (biological and psychological) and the environment (social, cultural, and physical). This understanding of the archetype uses a dynamic systems approach to cognition and action. This approach relates to the process of formation of pre-verbal image schematic representations in the infants' brain which are largely determined by the history of the brain as a system, i.e., based on the experience the system has in the physical world and the ability of the brain as a dynamic system to self-organize (Thelen & Smith, 1994). Later on, these pre-verbal neuronal activation patterns serve as a foundation for the development of conceptual thought – categories and concepts. In themselves these neuronal activation patterns constitute attractor states for the dynamic system of the brain.

Varela, Thompson, and Rosch (1991) propose a slightly different approach to cognition and action, namely, an enacted cognition approach to the study of mental processes and representations. This concept suggests that cognition is "enaction: a history of structural coupling that brings forth a world" (Varela et al., 1991, p. 27), which seems in unison with most of the aforementioned basic ideas. These authors go even a step further to suggest that "the cognitive system projects its own world, and the apparent reality of this world is merely a reflection of internal laws of the system" (Varela et al., 1991, p. 172) Among Jungian scholars, George Hogenson (2009) looked into the connection between archetypes and the mirror neurons and proposed understanding the archetype as an "elementary action pattern" (p. 325), which sounds close to some of the ideas of the enacted cognition approach of Varela, Thompson, and Rosch.

Other Jungian scholars stress the non-linear dynamics which underlie both the functioning of the brain as a system and some aspects of the archetype in their reinterpretation of the nature of the archetype. For example, synchronicity, enantiodromia, or the therapeutic relationship looked at as a dynamic open system.

George Hogenson proposed that the archetype could be understood as an "iterative moment in the self-organization of the symbolic world" (Hogenson, 2004, p. 279). Saunders and Skar have suggested that the archetype was an emergent structure which derived from the self-organizing properties of the brain (basically not contradicting the theory of the image schema; Saunders & Skar, 2001). McDowell stressed that the archetype was a pre-existing principle of organization of the personality (McDowell, 2001), while Van Eewynk looked at archetypes as strange attractors of the dynamic system of the psyche (Van Eewynk, 1991, 1997) whose non-linear dynamics underlie individuation and the therapeutic relationship.

Maybe the aspect of the archetype theory that raises the strongest discussions at present is innateness. How do we understand innateness and what Jung actually meant when he stated that the archetypes are *a priori* given to us? Furthermore, how do we understand the innateness of archetypes in an age in which we know that no symbolic information can be transmitted genetically?

There are Jungian scholars who find arguments in defense of the innateness of the archetype from contemporary research. Among these are such phenomena as the doctor–patient relationship (Rosen, 1992), the deep structure of language (Haule, 2010), attachment patterns (Stevens, 2003), and basic emotions, language acquisition mechanisms, and the face recognition program (Roesler, 2010, 2012). We can also add the basic affective systems as proposed by Panksepp (e.g., 2011). Roesler (2012) pointed out Seligman's concept of "preparedness" – the readiness to learn – as a further example of innateness that could be applied to archetypal theory. Erik Goodwyn (2010, 2012) used findings from evolutionary psychology and neuroanatomy in defense of innateness. However, even scholars like Anthony Stevens, known for his work in defense of genetically transmitted innateness, look at the archetype-as-such as "innate neuropsychic centers" (Stevens, 2003, p. 86), thus getting very close to the position of the earlier described understanding of the archetype-as-such in terms of embodiment and enacted cognition.

While there are still proponents of the idea that archetypes are transmitted genetically, many believe that the discussion of nature versus nurture is obsolete and stress the interactionist nature of human development (Knox, 2004; Hogenson, 2009; Merchant, 2009; Rosen et al., 2010; Roesler, 2010, 2012), or point out the psychological factors in evolution in the argument against a purely genetically transmitted innateness (Hogenson, 2001). The innate aspect of the archetype can also be looked at as a predisposition to a genetic condition which needs certain environmental cues to find expression (Roesler, 2010, 2012). Jungian scholar Pietikäinen (1998) suggested a radical departure from the discussion about innateness and proposed that with the help of a Cassirerian approach archetypes could be understood as "culturally determined functionary forms organizing and structuring certain aspects of man's cultural activity" (Pietikäinen, 1998, p. 325).

Regarding inborn behavior and archetypes, we need to mention the work of Jungian scholars who give examples of innateness which have found empirical support in experimental psychology. Among these are such phenomena as the doctor–patient relationship (Rosen, 1992), the deep structure of language (Haule, 2010), attachment patterns (Stevens, 2003), basic emotions, language acquisition mechanisms, and face recognition programs (Roesler, 2010, 2012). Roesler (2012) points out Seligman's concept of "preparedness" as a further example of innateness that can be applied to archetypal theory. Erik Goodwyn (2010, 2012) uses in defense of innateness findings from evolutionary psychology and neuroanatomy.

We can also say that the controversies concerning innateness and the archetype reflect the controversies in psychology at large. While the dynamic systems approach to cognition and action, cognitive semantics, embodiment, and enacted cognition as approaches in the study of cognitive processes enjoy widespread popularity, there are also many scholars who conduct experimental work in connection with innate mechanisms. The experimental work of developmental psychologists such as Spelke provides data which supports the hypothesis of multiple innate mechanisms with which infants are equipped at birth. Spelke suggests that "perception, thought, value and action depend on domain-specific cognitive systems" and "each system has its own innate foundations and evolutionary history" (Spelke, 2010, p. 204). Interestingly, in a recent study Izard, Sann, Spelke, and Streri (2009) report research data which supports the assertions that infants at birth are equipped with abstract, numerical representations. It thus seems that cognitive science at large has not answered the question concerning innateness as a basic ideological factor.

The debate around the nature of the archetype is further enriched by Archetypal Psychology which sees the place of the archetype in imagination and stresses the transcendental nature of the archetype (Roesler, 2010, 2012). Although this approach to the archetype might not resonate with many mainstream psychologists, there are tendencies in contemporary studies of consciousness which sound in agreement with the ideas of Archetypal Psychology. The Hameroff and Penrose quantum theory of consciousness (Hameroff & Penrose, 2003) and the hypothesis that the brain does not produce consciousness but serves the purpose of receiving and transmitting information which exists from beyond it (Beauregard, 2011) can be seen to resonate with some of the basic ideas of the Archetypal Psychology concerning the archetype. Furthermore, the notion of synchronicity – meaningful coincidences based on an acausal connection principle – which Jung developed in exchange with Wolfgang Pauli and Albert Einstein, and which can be seen as an expression of a constellated archetypal field at work (Jung, 1952; Cambray, 2002), finds support in recent days through the discoveries in complexity theory and the dynamics of complex adaptive systems (Cambray, 2009).

Given all these ideas, how do we understand the archetype? Are archetypes transmitted biologically, or are they transmitted by culture as Roesler (2012) asks? Can we understand the collective unconscious in terms of subliminal transmission and inter-individual neuronal format as Roesler (2012) proposed, or is the collective unconscious a form of archetypal (collective unconscious) memory as Rosen et al. (1991) suggested? Or is the basis of the archetype and the collective unconscious both innate and environmental?

## Archetypes as image schemas

Among one of the most well-formulated modern approaches to the archetype is the proposed reformulation of the archetype theory in terms of image schemas (Knox, 2003, 2004, 2009; Merchant, 2006, 2009; Sotirova-Kohli et al., 2011). Jean Knox first proposed the connection between the image schema and the archetype-as-such. In the tradition of Talmy (1983), Johnson (1987), and Lakoff (1987), the image schema can be defined as a "dynamic, recurring pattern of organism-environment interactions" (Johnson, 2007, p. 136). They are "structures of sensorimotor experience that can be recruited for abstract conceptualization and reasoning" (Johnson, 2007, p. 141). They are "preverbal and mostly nonconscious" (Johnson, 2007, p. 144). In this sense, image schemas are suggested to be a neural activation pattern which resulted from repeated interactions between the individual and the environment (see Sotirova-Kohli et al., 2011). In this sense the archetype is looked at as an early achievement of development resulting from the qualities of the brain as a dynamic system to self-organize and the interactions between the individual and the environment (social, cultural, and physical). This understanding of the archetype uses a dynamic systems approach to the development of cognition and action. This approach to cognition and action relates to the process of formation of pre-verbal image schematic representations in the infants' brains, which are largely determined by the history of the brain as a system, i.e., based on the experience the system has in the physical world and the ability of the brain as a dynamic system to self-organize (Thelen and Smith, 1994). Later on, these pre-verbal neuronal activation patterns serve as a foundation for the development of conceptual thought – categories and concepts. In themselves these neuronal activation patterns constitute attractor states for the dynamic system of the brain. Furthermore, the ideas of Talmy, Johnson, and Lakoff concerning image schema find support in the contemporary research on embodiment, where embodiment is defined as the meaning of symbols to an agent and the reasoning about meaning and sentence understanding which "depends on activity in systems also used for perception, action and emotion" (de Vega, Glenberg, & Graesser, 2008, p. 4). Neuroimaging studies support the idea that sensory and motor systems are involved in concept understanding and retrieval (Binder & Desai, 2011). Thus, image schemas can be understood as the neuronal activation patterns which encode embodied experience in the world. They function automatically, i.e., unconsciously, and underlie concepts, narrative, and ritual (Hampe, 2005), all qualities which can be attributed also to the archetypes. It is important to note that in Johnson's (2007) theory of image schema and embodiment, feeling and emotion are attributed to an important role in the assessment and evaluation of the environment and in meaning-making.

Relevant to the idea of the archetype as an image schema is also the contemporary understanding of the inner world as a simulated interaction with the environment, at the core of which is the understanding that the phenomenal experience of an inner world is a result of the ability to activate motor and sensory structures suppressing the urge to act (e.g., Heslow, 2011). The inner world of the human being is given central place in Jung's work. Fantasy as a form of simulation is also central in Jungian analytic work and related to the archetypal dynamics at work which promote healing and integration of the personality. This specific form of fantasy work of imagination Jung called active imagination and defined it as "his method of psychotherapy" (Chodorow, 1997, p. 17).

## Empirical studies on archetypes

Contemporary empirical investigation of the hypothesis of the archetypes is sparse. There are two experimental paradigms which aim to test the hypothesis of the archetype, namely, the Rosen and Smith (1991) paradigm, which will be described in this section, and the Maloney (1999) paradigm. Maloney studied the preference ratings of images presenting archetypal themes such as the theme of the hero and the mother in a large community sample and found that archetypal themes determined affective responses of adults as hypothesized by Jung's theory of the archetypes.

The Rosen and Smith paradigm was built on the basis of studying the associations between a set of 40 archetypal symbols and their associated meanings – the Archetypal Symbol Inventory (ASI). C.G. Jung conducted psychological evaluations of patients using the Word Association Test as mentioned previously, and this was one of his approaches for studying the archetype (Roesler, 2010). Interestingly, as Rosen et al. (1991) pointed out, Jung never used symbols in his association experiments. To provide an instrument with which archetypal memory can be studied by means of symbols, the aforementioned authors developed the Archetypal Symbol Inventory (ASI), which consists of 40 archetypal symbols and 40 associated words indicating the archetypal meanings of these symbols (Rosen et al., 1991). Furthermore, Rosen and Smith designed a series of three experiments to test the hypothesis of collective unconscious memory. The two preliminary experiments – a free association task and a forced association task using the 40 symbols from the ASI – tested to what degree the participants had spontaneous conscious knowledge of the archetypal meanings of the symbols and provided empirical evidence that there is practically no conscious knowledge of these meanings (Rosen et al., 1991).

In their main study, Rosen et al. (1991) investigated the learning effect and recall rate of the 40 archetypal symbols and their related meanings from the ASI. The experimental design of Rosen et al. (1991) utilized a cognitive psychological approach to testing the hypothesis of the collective unconscious (memory). Rosen and coworkers hypothesized that pre-existing collective unconscious memory would have qualities similar to "semantic memory" (Tulving, 1972). The authors further adopted a list-learning procedure to test for pre-existing knowledge of archetypal symbols. This procedure presupposes that participants are presented with lists of stimuli (often pairs of words) to be learned, and later their memory of the learned stimuli was tested by showing only one of the words from the learned pair (the cue). There is empirical evidence which suggests that words are learned better if they are cued by semantically related words (e.g., Thompson & Tulving, 1970;

Koriat & Bjork, 2005). The experimental design of Rosen and team utilized the list-learning procedure where the stimuli pairs consisted of a symbol and a word, and later a cued-recall (archetypal symbols used as cues) task was used to test the memory of the items from the learning procedure. Thus, the 40 archetypal symbols from the ASI were presented to the participants; half of them were paired with their associated meanings and the other half with random incorrect meanings. The participants were later shown the symbol and were asked to recall the word they saw previously paired with the symbol. As hypothesized, the study found that the archetypal meanings were recalled better when in the learning phase they were presented matched with the symbols they were associated with, i.e., when correctly matched in the learning phase. This allowed the authors to conclude that the archetypal symbols and their associated meanings were strongly associated. Since in their preliminary studies the authors found that there was no spontaneous conscious knowledge of the meaning of the symbols, they concluded that the effect they observed in the main study of the paradigm demonstrated pre-existing knowledge of the symbols, which was triggered through an effect of priming when the symbols were presented to the participants paired with their correct archetypal meanings. This first study of Rosen et al. (1991), as well as subsequent studies of Huston (1992) and Huston, Rosen, and Smith (1998), provided empirical support for the existence of what these authors called archetypal, collective unconscious memory.

Subsequently, Huston et al. (1998) proposed a possible mechanism for evolutionary collective unconscious (archetypal) memory. They explained the effect of better recall of meanings when they were matched correctly with a symbol as being a result "of interhemispherical connection, mediated by the corpus callosum, which allows for the recall of the accurate meaning of the archetypal symbol triggered by the affective response" (Huston et al., 1998, pp. 145–146). According to these authors, the right hemisphere was the seat of archetypal patterns, symbols, and their affectively charged visual images, while the left hemisphere was the seat of verbal knowledge. It was proposed that when an archetypal symbol was presented, matched with its correct meaning, there was an affective response which constellated an archetypal image in the right hemisphere. This was explained as the effect of priming the evolutionary unconscious archetypal memory. The authors further suggested that it was this affective response which facilitated retrieval of the correct meaning (word) of the symbol when the symbols were presented by themselves later in the cued recall task (Huston et al., 1998).

The Rosen et al. study stimulated discussions among Jungian scholars. Jill Gordon (1991) raised the question as to whether the images used by the team could at all be considered to be archetypal before conducting cross-cultural research. Gordon stressed the importance of conducting multiple cross-cultural studies to determine whether the images used really had the qualities of archetypal images, namely, whether these were "forms that provoke more or less similar or even identical associations from a majority of people" (Gordon, 1991, p. 229). Raya Jones argued in a similar fashion that the results observed by Rosen et al. could be explained with "cultural convention or as artifacts of the statistical procedure" (Jones, 2003, p. 707).

## Kanji as archetypal image

Chinese characters (*kanji*) originated as a semiotic system independent from the spoken language and were adopted as a writing system in the Chinese language and later in the Japanese language where they are presently used as a component of a mixed system of writing together with two syllabaries (*hiragana* and *katakana*), sets of characters which write the smallest segment of language in Japanese – the *mora*. However, Japanese *kanji* function non-phonetically in the system of language and contribute to a slightly different structure of the linguistic sign as a graphic image. There is right-hemispheric advantage for *kanji* and left-hemispheric advantage for *kana* (*hiragana* and *katakana*) processing in the case of Japanese speakers. This fact suggests that *kanji* are linked to visual schemas or archetypal images. *Kanji* reading is said to more heavily involve visual orthographic retrieval and lexical-semantic system via the ventral route, while *kana* transcriptions of *kanji* words require phonological recoding to gain semantic access through the dorsal route. Considering the circumstances of the origination of Chinese characters, as well as the peculiarity of their mode of cognitive processing as part of the system of Japanese language, Sotirova-Kohli et al. (2011) theorized that Chinese characters might represent symbolic archetypal images, and we sought to test this premise empirically.

Our study was built on the previously described Rosen and Smith (1991) paradigm for studying archetypal (collective unconscious) memory. We conducted a series of three experiments to test the hypothesis that *kanji* are archetypal images. Experiments 1 and 2 were studies based on the original research of Rosen et al. (1991) to test if there is any conscious/cultural knowledge of the correct meaning of the 40 Chinese characters which would facilitate learning and recall of the characters. Experiment 3 (the main study) was designed to test whether showing characters matched with the correct meaning would have an effect on learning and recall. In all three experiments we used the same set of 40 characters written in *Tensho* style.

Experiment 1 was a free association task. Twenty-nine randomly assigned undergraduate students of psychology were shown the 40 characters for 20 seconds, and in this time were asked to come up with a word that best represented the image. Only 3 characters were recognized correctly out of 1,080 (40 × 27) possible correct answers. The results revealed little if any conscious knowledge of the characters.

Experiment 2 was a forced association task. Twenty-nine different, randomly assigned undergraduate students in psychology were given the 40 characters and a list of 80 words – 40 correct meanings of the characters and 40 incorrect meanings, and were asked to choose from the list the word that in their opinion best represented the meaning of the respective image. Twenty-six characters were recognized correctly out of 1,160 (40 × 29) possible correct answers. Analysis demonstrated that participants were poorer than expected by chance at matching characters with their correct meaning (Sotirova-Kohli et al., 2011). The results confirmed that the participants have no conscious knowledge of the meaning of the characters.

Experiment 3 was a paired-associate learning task. We hypothesized that if kanji characters, like archetypal images (Rosen et al., 1991), were matched with their correct meanings, these correctly matched pairs would have a higher rate of learning and recollection than characters paired with incorrect meanings. Two different groups of randomly assigned introductory psychology students at Texas A&M University (a total of 192) took part in the study. The set of 40 Chinese characters was divided into two sets, each consisting of 20 characters. Each of the two groups of students was presented with both sets of characters; however, in each group a different set was matched correctly with the meaning-word. The students were shown first the character-word pairs for 5 seconds and, after a rest of 1 minute, they were shown only the characters for 8 seconds each and asked to write down the word they saw previously paired with the character.

The results were scored strictly. Only words which were the same as the presented stimuli words were counted in the process of scoring (i.e., synonyms were not accepted as correct answers). A repeated-measures factorial ANOVA with one within-subjects variable (matching-matched vs. mismatched) and one between-subjects variable (counterbalancing) was conducted to analyze the data. The main effect of matching was significant, $F(1, 168) = 12.986, p < .001$; i.e., significantly more meanings were recalled for matched pairs than for mismatched pairs. Matching Chinese characters with their correct meanings at the time of study benefited learning and subsequent recall. This result mirrors the results of Rosen et al. (1991) and supports the idea that kanji characters are associated with their correct meanings; such pre-existing knowledge makes paired associates easier to learn and recall, as compared to paired associates that are not meaningfully paired. Given the results of experiments 1 and 2, it appears that this pre-existing knowledge of kanjis' meanings is unconscious.

The results from experiment 1 and experiment 2 demonstrated that there was little or no spontaneous conscious knowledge of the meaning of the Chinese characters. The results from the main study (experiment 3) lend weight to the hypothesis that there is unconscious knowledge of the Chinese characters and their meanings that is triggered as a result of priming when subjects are shown correctly matched pairs of characters and their meanings. The results from our study are similar to the previous studies of collective unconscious (archetypal) memory of Rosen et al. (1991), Huston (1992), and Huston et al. (1998). We can say that kanji, in a certain sense, behave on a cognitive level in a similar fashion to archetypal symbols. These findings are encouraging in that they reaffirm the possibility of empirical study, the existence of collective unconscious (archetypal) memory, and reinforce the proposed connection between the archetype and its cognitive semantic nature as image schema (Knox, 2003). Although our experiments were not designed to test whether Chinese characters are metaphoric extensions of image schemas, embodied cognition seems to be another possible explanation of the observed results. As we pointed out earlier, kanji as visual images were developed following certain systematic rules which were supposed to enable these images to encode the signified of the linguistic sign independent of, but in a fashion similar to the phonetic image/signifier, i.e., they encode the same content but independent from the phonetic signifiers/sound images of the words and do not function phonetically. One of the key assertions of cognitive semantics is that image schemas underlie thought and language. As pointed out earlier, they are considered to be neuronal activation maps, "experiential gestalts which momentarily emerge from ongoing brain, body and world interactions" (Gibbs, 2005, p. 115), and can be "turned on" by either performing an action or having an actual experience, observing this experience or action, or thinking, speaking, reading, or writing about it. Thus, image-schematic thought and linguistic processes involve embodied simulation of experience using one's body (Gibbs, 2005, p. 115). Research demonstrated that activation of certain image schematic spatial or temporal relations affects linguistic comprehension, human actions, and memory (Hampe, 2005). Therefore, we can hypothesize that one possibility to explain the results from our study is that both kanji or visual stimuli and their archetypal meanings – verbal stimuli – recruit similar image schematic internal maps which facilitates learning and recall of the symbols matched with their correct (archetypal) meaning. However, future research is needed to empirically demonstrate the validity of these theoretical speculations, as well as the assertions that archetypes are what cognitive semantics call image schemas.

## Cross-cultural evidence of collective unconscious memory

Intrigued by the question of whether the results observed by Rosen and team described previously are replicable in a different language and in a different cultural context, we decided to conduct the same experiment in the German-speaking part of Switzerland. We presumed that if the significant effect of matching on learning and recall of the associated meanings of archetypal symbols from the Archetypal Symbol Inventory (ASI) observed by Rosen and team (1991) was related to the archetypal nature of the symbols used in the experiments, then these results should be replicable in cross-cultural studies conducted in a different language and a different cultural context. Thus we hypothesized that correctly paired archetypal symbols and their German associated meanings would also lead to significantly better learning and recalling the associated words than in the case of mismatched pairs.

As a first step for testing the hypothesis, our team translated the original English ASI into German. For this purpose the team of Sotirova-Kohli, Roesler, and Opwis translated individually the 40 items from English to German, and through a process of inter-rater agreement (where all three agreed on the translation) they determined the German translations of the 40 symbols. An external expert from the Baumann Foundation (Basel) was asked to proofread the translations as well. The question as to the adequateness of the procedure of attaching a "correct meaning" to the symbols was discussed. However, the main idea of the present study was to test the hypothesis of replicability of the results from the initial Rosen et al. (1991) study in a different cultural and linguistic context; it was agreed, therefore, to apply the exactly same procedure for the experiment.

The participants in this experiment were 398 first- and second-year medical students from the University of Bern and 14 psychology students from the University of Basel. Students were assigned randomly to the two counterbalancing conditions.

Ten protocols were excluded from the analysis due to systematic mistakes or for not filling out the protocols properly.

We utilized the same experimental procedure as Rosen et al. (1991) in their original main study. The 40 symbols were divided in two sets of 20 symbols, and each set was presented to both of the counterbalancing conditions. However, in one condition they were matched correctly with the associated meanings and in the other one they were mismatched. The pairs were presented first for 5 seconds each, and after a rest of 1 minute the symbols were presented in the same order for 8 seconds each, in which time the participants were asked to remember and write down the word they saw originally paired with the symbol.

The protocols were coded strictly. A repeated-measures factorial ANOVA was conducted with one within-subjects variable (matching) and one between-subjects variable (counterbalancing). The main effect of matching was significant, $F(1, 401) = 125.83$, $p < .0001$, $MSE = 3.047$, $\omega^2 = 0.22$; statistically significantly more meanings were recalled for matched pairs than for mismatched pairs. Matching the symbols with their correct meanings benefited the learning and the subsequent recall. These results replicated the findings of Rosen and team (1991) done in a sample of English-speaking students. Being able to replicate the findings that matching symbols correctly with their meanings facilitates learning and subsequent recall in a German-speaking sample provides further evidence that archetypal symbols are truly associated with their meanings. Furthermore, this cross-cultural evidence of the associations between archetypal symbols and their meanings demonstrates that it is less likely that the observed effect is related to a cultural context or is a linguistic artifact. In this sense, it can be said that our results provide further evidence that the collective unconscious and archetypes as hypothesized by C.G. Jung have a universal nature.

However, although the cross-cultural replication of the original study with the ASI replicated the findings, there still are many issues that deserve further research. Although there is obviously a strong association between the archetypal symbols and their meanings independent of linguistic and cultural context, it still is not exactly clear how this can be explained. Are the observed results due to the effect of embodiness on cognition in terms of the dynamic system's approach to cognition and action and the theory of image schema? Or do these results support the debated innateness of the archetype? In a recent study (Rosen et al., 2010) with medical students it was demonstrated, for example, that environmental factors such as hope and spiritual meaning serve as protective factors against depression in medical students genetically predisposed to depressive disorder. Further investigations are necessary to be able to answer any of these questions convincingly.

Although we could demonstrate that participants from two different language and cultural backgrounds could easier learn and recall correctly matched symbol-meaning pairs, the question still remains whether these results could be observed in different age samples, since archetypes are hypothesized to be universal and should be present not only in representatives of different cultures but also in people from different age groups. In this sense it would be important to see if the results are replicate among elderly and/or children. Furthermore, it would be of particular interest to conduct the experiment with patients who have amnestic syndrome, as already pointed by Huston et al. (1998). Results from such a study would be revealing as to the type of memory involved in the mechanisms which underlie the observed effects.

Given the answers of the participants to the questions in the subjective report, it seems also worthwhile to investigate the subjective experience of the participants when they are presented the symbol-word pairs, and in this sense to systematically use symbols in the study of personal associations in a manner similar to the studies conducted using the Word Association Test.

This study demonstrated that the effect of matching exerts a statistically significant effect on learning and recall independent of language and culture which supports the hypothesis of the universality of the archetype. However, there is need of further experimental work to be able to answer many of the questions concerning the nature of the archetype and the collective unconscious.

## References

Beauregard, M. (2011). Neuroscience and spirituality – Findings and consequences. In H. Walach, S. Schmidt, & W.B. Jonas (Eds.), *Neuroscience, Consciousness and Spirituality*. New York: Springer.

Binder, J.R., & Desai, R.H. (2011). The neurobiology of semantic memory. *Trends in Cognitive Science, 15*(11), 527–536.

Cambray, J. (2002). Synchronicity and emergence. *American Imago, 59*(4), 409–434.

Cambray, J. (2009). *Synchronicity: Nature and Psyche in an interconnected universe*. College Station: Texas A&M University Press.

Chodorow, J. (Ed.) (1997). *Jung on active imagination*. Princeton, NJ: Princeton University Press.

De Vega, M., Glenberg, A.M., & Graesser, A.G. (Eds.) (2008). *Symbols and embodiment: Debates on meaning and cognition*. Oxford: Oxford University Press.

Gibbs, R.W., Jr. (2005). The psychological status of image schemas. In B. Hampe (Ed.), *From perception to meaning: Image schemas in cognitive linguistics*. New York: Mouton de Gruyter.

Goodwyn, E. (2010). Approaching archetypes: Reconsidering innateness. *Journal of Analytical Psychology, 55*(4), 502–521.

Goodwyn, E. (2012). *The neurobiology of gods: How brain physiology shapes the recurrent imagery of myth and dreams*. New York: Routledge.

Gordon, J. (1991). Comment on paper by David H. Rosen et al. *Journal of Analytical Psychology, 36*, 229.

Hameroff, S., & Penrose, R. (2003). Conscious events as orchestrated space-time selections. *NeuroQuantology, I*, 10–35.

Hampe, B. (2005). *From perception to meaning: Image schemas in cognitive linguistics*. New York: Mouton de Gruyter.

Haule, J.R. (2010). *Jung in the 21st Century: Evolution and Archetype*, vol. I. New York: Routledge.

Heslow, G. (2011). The inner world as simulated interaction with the environment. *Toward a science of consciousness, Stockholm 2011*, plenary presentation.

Hogenson, G.B. (2001). The Baldwin effect: A neglected influence on C.G. Jung's evolutionary thinking. *Journal of Analytical Psychology, 46*, 591–611.

Hogenson, G.B. (2004). Archetypes: Emergence and the psyche's deep structure. In J. Cambray & L. Carter (Ed.), *Analytical psychology: Contemporary perspectives in Jungian analysis.* New York: Brunner-Routledge.

Hogenson, G.B. (2009). Archetypes as action patterns. *Journal of Analytical Psychology, 54*(3), 325–337.

Huston, H. (1992). *Direct and indirect tests of archetypal memory* (Unpublished Master's thesis in psychology). Texas: A&M University.

Huston, H.L., Rosen, D.H., & Smith, S.M. (1998). Evolutionary memory. In D.H. Rosen & D.C. Luebbert (Eds.), *Evolution of the psyche.* Westport: Praeger.

Izard, V., Sann, C, Spelke, E.S., & Streri, A. (2009). Newborn infants perceive abstract numbers. *PNAS, 6*(25), 10382–10385.

Johnson, M. (1987). *The body in the mind.* Chicago: University of Chicago Press.

Johnson, M. (2007). *The meaning of the body.* Chicago: University of Chicago Press.

Jones, R. (2003). On innateness: A response to Hogenson. *Journal of Analytical Psychology, 48*, 705–718.

Jung, C.G. (1947). *On the nature of the psyche* (CW 8). Princeton, NJ: Princeton University Press.

Jung, C.G. (1952). *Synchronicity: An acausal connecting principle* (CW 8). Princeton, NJ: Princeton University Press.

Jung, C.G. (1954). *Archetypes of the collective unconscious* (CW 9-I). Princeton, NJ: Princeton University Press.

Knox, J. (2003). *Archetype, attachment, analysis: Jungian psychology and the emergent mind.* New York: Brunner-Routledge.

Knox, J. (2004). From archetypes to reflective function. *Journal of Analytical Psychology, 49*(1), 1–19.

Knox, J. (2009). Mirror neurons and embodied simulation in the development of archetypes and self-agency. *Journal of Analytical Psychology, 54*(3), 307–323.

Koriat, A., & Bjork, R.A. (2005). Illusions of competence in monitoring one's knowledge during study. *Journal of Experimental Psychology: Learning, Memory, and Cognition, 31*, 187–194.

Lakoff, G. (1987). *Women, fire and dangerous things: What categories reveal about the mind.* Chicago-London: The University of Chicago Press.

Maloney, A. (1999). Preference rating of images representing archetypal themes. *Journal of Analytical Psychology, 44*, 101–116.

McDowell, M.J. (2001). Principle of organization: A dynamic-systems view of the archetype-as-such. *Journal of Analytical Psychology, 46*(4), 637–654.

Merchant, J. (2006). The developmental/emergent model of archetype, its implications and its application to shamanism. *Journal of Analytical Psychology, 51*(1), 125–144.

Merchant, J. (2009). A reappraisal of classical archetype theory and its implications for theory and practice. *Journal of Anaytical Psychology, 54*(3), 339–358.

Pietikainen, P. (1998). Archetypes as symbolic forms. *Journal of Analytical Psychology, 43*, 325–343.

Roesler, C. (2010). *Analytische Psychologie heute: Der aktuelle Stand der Forschung zur Psychologie C. G. Jungs.* Basel: Karger Verlag.

Roesler, C. (2012). Are archetypes transmitted more by culture than biology? Questions arising from conceptualizations of the archetype. *Journal of Analytical Psychoogy, 57*(2), 223–246.

Rosen, D.H. (1992). Inborn basis for the healing doctor-patient relationship. *The Pharos, 55*, 17–21.

Rosen, D.H., Mascaro, N., Arnau, R., Escamilla, M., Tai-Seale, M., Ficht, A., Sanders, C., . . . Stevenson, K. (2010). Depression in medical students: Gene-environment interactions. *Annals of Behavioural Science and Medical Education, 16*(2), 8–14.

Rosen, D.H., Smith, S.M., H.L., & Gonzalez, G. (1991). Empirical study of associations between symbols and their meanings: Evidence of collective unconscious (Archetypal) memory. *Journal of Analytical Psychology*, 211–228.

Saunders, P., & Skar, P. (2001). Archetypes, complexes and self-organization. *Journal of Analytical Psychology*, *46*(2), 305–323.

Sotirova-Kohli, M., Rosen, D.H., Smith, S.M., Henderson, P., & Taki-Reece, S. (2011). Empirical study of kanji as archetypal images: understanding the collective unconscious as part of the Japanese language. *Journal of Analytical Psychology*, *56*, 109–132.

Spelke, E. (2010). Innateness, choice and language. In J. Frank and J. Bricmont (Eds.), *Chomsky notebook*. New York: Columbia University Press.

Stevens, A. (2003). *Archetype revisited: An updated natural history of the Self.* Toronto: Inner City Books.

Talmy, L. (1983). How language structures space. In H.L. Pick, Jr. & L.P. Acredolo (Eds.), *Spatial orientation: Theory, research and application*. New York: Plenum Press.

Thelen, E., & Smith, L.B. (1994). *A dynamic systems approach to the development of cognition and action*. Cambridge, UK: MIT Press.

Thomson, D.M., & Tulving, E. (1970). Associative encoding and retrieval: weak and strong cues. *Journal of Experimental Psychology*, *86*(2), 255–262.

Tulving, E. (1972). Episodic and semantic memory. In E. Tulving & W. Donaldson (Eds.), *Organization of memory*. New York: Academic Press.

Van Eewynk, J.R. (1991). Archetypes: The strange attractors of the psyche. *Journal of Analytical Psychology*, *36*(1), 1–25.

Van Eewynk, J.R. (1997). *Archetypes and strange Attractors: The chaotic world of symbols.* Toronto: Inner City Books.

Varela, F.J., Thompson, E., & Rosch, E. (1991). *The embodied mind: Cognitive science and human experience*. Cambridge, MA: MIT Press.

# 4

# THE RELEVANCE OF THE JUNGIAN CONCEPT OF "IMAGE" TO CONTEMPORARY PROCESS RESEARCH THROUGH LINGUISTIC ANALYSIS

## A bridge between analytical and cognitive psychology

*Alessandra De Coro*

The concept of "image" is a basic premise of Jungian psychology: conceptualizing the role of the image within an individual's mental processes and as part of the therapeutic dialogue is one of C.G. Jung's seminal contributions. This chapter will examine the notion of "image" and its clinical applications: first, the development of Jung's theoretical framework about images will be synthetically explored, as well as the role of images in the analytical work; second, an empirical system that is applicable to the process research in dynamic psychotherapy will be described, illustrating the role of the images in the therapeutic change process. Some empirical studies will be briefly presented and potential directions for future research will be indicated.

## The origins and meaning of the concept of "image" in Carl Gustav Jung's psychological model

Jung's interest in imagination (in German *Einbildungskraft*: literally "energy to form images") is in my opinion at the core of his original disagreement with Freudian psychoanalysis. In *Symbols of Transformation* (1912/1952), the Swiss psychiatrist proposes his vision of the unconscious way of thinking as an imaginative thinking, abandoning Freud's original interpretation of a "dynamic" unconscious, grounded on the intervention of repressive forces. According to Jung the causal explanation – however revolutionary at the beginning of psychoanalysis – was still reductive if it could not include the "spontaneous activity" of the unconscious psyche rooted in ancestral memories. In his earliest essays on psychopathology, Jung repeatedly affirmed that "visual images" are "autonomous transformations of elementary stimuli," namely the result of spontaneous psychical processes which elaborate sensorial configurations deriving from external or internal stimulations (Jung, 1902, para. 99). And significantly, from a clinical point of view, these images, appearing in delusions and in the neologisms of psychotic patients, as well as in ordinary fantasies, transform the unconscious contents associated with painful emotions into metaphors, allowing them to emerge into consciousness (Jung, 1907, para. 300). Jung's approach to mental phenomena was in line with the ideas of the American empiricist psychologist William James, who affirmed that both consciousness and unconsciousness couldn't be defined as entities. James defined consciousness as a continuous "stream of thought" (1890, chap. 9), distinguishing however between two kinds of human thinking: "reasoning on the one hand, and narrative, descriptive, contemplative thinking on the other." The latter kind of thinking "consists of a procession through the mind of groups of images of concrete things, persons, places, and events, together with the feelings which they awaken" (James, 1898, p. 911). These images can follow an order "derived from our actual experience of the order of things in the real world," or else "our thoughts merely bud one out of the other according to the caprice of our revery" and "there may occur very abrupt transitions between one set of images and the next" (James, 1898, p. 911).

Jung discovered the relevance of mental images in psychopathology both through his clinical work with psychiatric patients in Burghölzli and by means of his empirical studies of verbal associations. These studies led to the recognition of the nuclear theoretical bond between the unconscious individual meanings and the deep layers of human collective unconscious, opening a new pathway to the understanding of the complexity of the psyche. Since 1911, working on the fantasies of Miss Miller, Jung developed a strong interest in the different mythologies existing all over the world in different cultures, and began to collect evidences that all these mythological figures were in fact referring to some universal symbols. The biological roots of the embodied mind in human species could reasonably justify the commonality of these few general categories, like those *patterns of behavior* discovered by ethologists in different animal species. At the same time, however, the specific ability of the human mind to symbolize could produce as many different images as there are cultural forms alive in different times and different geographical areas. Building on James's definition of narrative thinking, Jung proposes that images are the most direct expression of the "not directed thinking" which "leads away from reality into fantasies of the past or future" (1912/1952, para. 18).

By virtue of their similarity with mythologems, images acquire a therapeutic value because they allow new connections between the unconscious and consciousness, thus obtaining the goal of reducing dissociation. The function of imagination helps the individual mind to reconnect the personal consciousness with both the personal and collective unconscious, because, as Jung frequently states, unconscious images, as "psychic attitudes," are "the deposits of all our ancestral experiences" (1928, para. 300). The hypothesis of a naturally dissociated psyche is the basis of Jung's notion of a complex architecture of the human mind: "the psyche is not an indivisible unity but a divisible and more or less divided whole. [. . .] I have called these psychic fragments 'autonomous complexes,' and I base my theory of complexes on their existence" (Jung, 1920/1948, para. 582). Therefore, the multiplicity of images in the individual mind alludes to the multiplicity of the unconscious complexes which constellate the psyche and which constitute a continuous source of creative energy oriented toward development. Jung describes this multiplicity as the "multiple luminosities of the unconscious": "complexes possess a kind of consciousness, a luminosity of their own," symbolically represented by powerful alchemical images like the multiple eyes of fishes in the sea or the starry heaven (Jung, 1955/1956, para. 270). Jung attributes the possibility of the integration of such a plural and dissociated psyche to a "transcendent function" which drives the different complexes to the unity of the self, as experience of internal integrity and of communion with the external world (Young-Eisendrath, 2000). The self is defined as a goal of the individual's development, but at the same time as the developmental process itself, bringing to "a new equilibrium, a new centering of the total personality, a virtual centre which, on account of its focal position between conscious and unconscious, ensures for the personality a new and more solid foundation" (Jung, 1928, para. 365). Such a process, in life as in psychotherapy, is activated by the "transcendent function," and is also the basis for a dialogue with the external "other" in human community. Images are central in such a dialogue, even if they present some difficulties in interpretation:

> it is undoubtedly more complicated [. . .] where only visual products are available, speaking a language which is eloquent enough for one who understands it, but which seems like deaf-and-dumb language to one who does not. Faced with such products, the ego must seize the initiative and ask: "How am I affected by this sign?"
>
> *(Jung, 1957/1958, para. 188)*

In summary, Jung's notion of image is considered to be strictly built upon his hypothesis that the human psyche is founded on innate energetic potentials, analogous to the species-specific innate releasing mechanisms defined by ethologists, but including ancient imprinting of the cultural history of the human species (archetypes: see Jung, 1935/1954). The most accredited interpretation of Jungian archetypes today is that they are innate dispositions to form "coherent affectively charged images (archetypal images) that are expressed unconsciously in dreams, mythologies, folklore, art, religion, rituals, and literature in similar forms the world over" (Young-Eisendrath, 2000, p. 428). This view of a "core arousal state, connected with affective images, is now supported by Edelman's and Le Doux's work on emotional memory" (Young-Eisendrath, 2000, p. 428). In this sense Jung's images can be compared to some contemporary definitions of "mental images" in cognitive science, where images are intended as the "material" from which emotional meanings are constituted at a first level of the symbolization process. Moreover, they are the way through which symbols can be formed in our minds. Antonio Damasio, reflecting on the theoretical implications of modern neuroscience for the notion of consciousness, maintains that human consciousness has its basis in the "feeling of what happens," which is translated by images in our brain. The first step in the process of becoming aware is the formation of images which indicate the relationship between the organism and the object (internal, like emotions, as well as external, like perceptions). Damasio's notion is that images are the "basic currency" of our mind: he even affirms that movies are the most reliable external representation of such processes happening in our mind (Damasio, 1999, 2010), providing – via this unusual thesis – a sort of conceptual bridge between individual images and collective ones.

## Mental images: a fruitful construct in contemporary research studies on cognitive processes

In the last quarter of the 20th century, Allan Paivio (1971) and other cognitive psychologists (e.g., Stephen Kosslyn, 1983) were defined as "psychologists of images" because they tried to put images at the center of the mental processes aimed at knowing the world. They starkly affirmed that images are completely different from propositional representations. Cognitive processes underlying images are similar to those underlying perception. Images represent objects by analogy of structural relationships between their parts; images represent an object or a scene from a specific point of view; and an image can be transformed continuously in the mind through changes of perspective. Paivio (1986) formulated the "dual code" theory of cognition, giving the same weight to images and to verbal propositions in the constitution of our thoughts. According to this theory, the human mind uses two different codes in order to reach new knowledge and to recall past memories. Some studies on the development of thought and language in infants have also considered that conceptual patterns originate by "image schemes": infants, moving from global perceptive and sensory-motor procedures, learn to recognize objects and relations between them through image schemes. These schemes are formed by spatial structures and include non-verbal characteristics, namely images, which can be available to be described in a propositional format when the baby begins to use verbal language (Mandler, 1992).

In the 1990s Wilma Bucci, a New York psychoanalyst who had previously collaborated with Paivio, was interested in the evidence that some people are more capable than others at associating words to pictures. Specifically, she asked herself how the "cure by words" could be effective also with patients who are not really able to use words to describe their emotions and indeed can use words to "deviate" the analytical conversation from the therapeutic goal (Bucci, 1997). Like many psychoanalysts involved in proving analytic psychotherapy's effectiveness, Bucci was looking for an explanation of the patients' changes during psychoanalysis that could be empirically assessed. With this aim, she looked at the possibility of assessing "psychological capacities" that could be "consensually accepted as reflecting underlying structural change": the definition of such capacities should offer a common language for the clinical approach to possible empirical studies, even if their results might "be formulated differently by adherents of different theoretical positions in psychoanalysis" (Wallerstein, 1995, p. 309).

The structural change is defined in classical psychoanalysis as a result of the integration between primary and secondary processes in mental functioning. Following Paivio's different codes of information processing, Wilma Bucci elaborates a "multiple code theory" of emotional information processing. Just like cognitive information processing, Bucci postulated that sensations and emotions (originally perceived at the body level) are integrated into verbal thoughts by means of three different processing codes, which contribute to the production of what analysts call "emotional meaning." The first is the subsymbolic code: sensory, motor, visceral, and emotional information is immediately processed by the brain in an analogic and continuous way, and is stored in parallel, so that it can be recalled later only at an implicit, bodily level. The following code is characterized by the appearance of images that chunk subsymbolic information into meaningful discontinuous units, specific for different sensorial aspects (visual images are different from auditory or tactile ones); the images are sequentially stored so that they can be recalled, implicitly as well as explicitly, by associative processes or in dreams. This is the non-verbal symbolic code, which represents the bridge between the bodily emotional experience and the reflection activity about the meaning of such experience: images are the beginning and the core of the symbolization processes. The third code is the verbal symbolic one: images are processed through the linguistic organization, originating verbal propositions that can be further combined, generating further new meanings that can be recalled both at an implicit and an explicit level, and can be communicated to others in explicit form (Bucci, 1997; Bucci & Maskit, 2007).

## The referential activity system and the study of the psychoanalytic process

The mental function connecting these three different codes of emotional elaboration is called referential activity (RA) (Bucci, 1997). It operates going up and down through the three levels of the organization of emotional meanings. As a measure of trait, RA indicates how much a person is capable of linking emotions with bodily sensations, images, and verbal thought. As a measure of variability, RA can be used to understand which changes (in the connecting ability of the same person) are observable in the course of a time period, depending on the person's physiological and emotional conditions as well as on the interpersonal context. RA, in fact, operates also as a function of interpersonal communication: its variations can denote the person's oscillations in communicating real and present emotions through her/his discourse, but also in listening to the emotional communication by the interlocutor. This is why Bucci suggests investigating the effectiveness of the analytic process through the measure of RA, as it varies in the verbal exchanges between patient and analyst in a single session, as well as in a series of sessions. The variations of RA can tell us how much each of the two participants is separately using emotionally charged words and how much the flow of emotional communication is connecting patient and analyst together (Bucci, Maskit, & Hoffman, 2012). More specifically, the appearance of images in the analytic dialogue (for instance, through the use of metaphors or sensorial words, or through the narration of very clear and detailed episodes or dreams) seems to be a reliable indicator of the activation of this connecting process in the client's and/or in the analyst's mind. So the use of imagistic language by the patient can be interpreted by the analyst as a cue that sensorial and emotional contents, formerly dissociated and not accessible to symbolization, are beginning to be connected to symbolic meanings, and possibly will be integrated with the verbal thought, opening the way to reflection.

The question of the formation of symbolic meaning is relevant, according to a majority of contemporary analysts from different schools, in order to define the therapeutic change. Even if the concept of "symbol formation" presents different nuances in post-Jungian and post-Freudian literature, many analysts today, discussing clinical material, would agree on the following indicators of positive changes in their patients minds:

1 The ability to give names to their authentic and spontaneous emotions;
2 The increased ability to communicate their emotional experience to the analyst through their discourse in the sessions;
3 The increased association capacity, linking different episodes of their past and present life to specific emotional experiences;
4 The ability to find new and "surprising" meanings in the narration of their personal history;
5 The amplification of their affective meanings through comparisons and analogies with other people's emotions (recognized either in real life or in literature, arts, movies, etc.).

For instance, James Fosshage (1997), a Jungian-trained psychoanalyst with a focus on self-psychology, emphasized the function of dreams in the spontaneous development of a healthy mind, and has more recently tried to define the therapeutic change as follows:

> REM, dream, infant, and cognitive research evidence suggests that imagistic symbolic capacity exists at birth. Learning and remembering using imagistic symbolic processing could suggest a more easily translatable connection with later developed verbal symbolic processing and a closer, although varied, interconnection between implicit and explicit (symbolic) memory systems. [. . .] Implicit mental models, it is proposed, are variably modifiable through two different change processes: (1) accommodation or transformation of expectancies through new implicit procedural experience (not requiring explicit focus) and (2) diminished activation and increased capacity to deactivate implicit mental models through explicit/declarative processing and the establishment of contrasting implicit models through new implicit procedural experience.
>
> *(Fosshage, 2005, pp. 516–517)*

Likewise, the Jungian analyst Polly Young-Eisendrath (2000) points to changes from the domain of non-representational memories to the domain of the representational ones: "in non-representational memories, we react to immediate stimuli because they have elicited a primitive emotion – usually fear – sometimes without conscious perception of them"; this is the case of memories "that are triggered in the amygdala" and activate rigid kinds of responses. Instead, representational memories "are complex, affective images that I would call metaphors [. . .] because they map cues from earlier domains of experience to later ones" (Young-Eisendrath, 2000, p. 428). Non-symbolic, implicit bodily experience inevitably reactivates old patterns of action and response; the passage from this experience to a symbolic imagistic or metaphorical kind of emotional communication makes it possible to create new variations of the old patterns, which is a necessary clinical step in the therapeutic process.

According to Bucci (1997), the patient's higher or lower ability to communicate to the analyst her/his emotions and vivid sensory experience through images and concrete, detailed, and clear linguistic formulations in a given moment shows the degree of activation of referential activity in her/his mind at this very moment. This means that, when a patient is using a clear, sensory and detailed language which evokes vivid images also in the listener, then her/his "real" and "present" emotional, sensory, and visceral experience is substantiating her/his words. The "cure of words," in fact, can be effective only when, at least from time to time during a session, the patient is able to evoke emotions in the actual relationship with the analyst through her/his flow of words, so that afterwards both can reflect together on such experiences and elaborate them, giving new shared meanings to the patient's old affective experiences. Therefore an analytic process, which aims to an activation of what analysts call the *symbolization process*, may be described in this frame as an emotional reciprocal interaction that puts into motion the referential activity, both in the patient's and in the analyst's mind. Due to the power of the emotionally charged verbal exchanges in the analytic relationship, the patient may experience old and new emotional situations that become significant only when images help her/him to build a bridge between body and mind, between sensations, feelings, visceral movements, and verbal thinking.

## Clinical research using RA: understanding clinical interactions

### Research design

According to Bucci's theory, measuring the variations of RA both in the patient's and in the therapist's discourse along a series of sessions can evidence the increasing (or the decreasing) of the patient's ability to express and reflect on her/his emotions, as well as the critical interactions between therapist and patient for such changes. Micro-changes in the ability to connect words and emotions can be discovered applying the measure to a single session.

The first instrument developed to measure RA was based on the four scales of Concreteness, Clarity, Specificity and Imagery, created by Bucci and her research group at Adelphi University on the basis of features seen as central for vivid and evocative writing (Bucci & Kabasakalian, 1992). Precisely, Imagery refers to a quality of the spoken language, which evokes images in the listener's mind. These scales are applied to audio-recorded psychotherapy sessions, previously divided into segments corresponding to "idea units" by judges, who have obtained a sufficient reliability following the instructions given in the manual (Bucci et al., 1992). The manual has been translated into German, French, Spanish, and Italian (De Coro & Caviglia, 2000). The RA score for each segment of the session corresponds to the mean value of the scores assigned for the four scales, from 0 to 10.

On the basis of the results of her first studies applying the RA manual scales to clinical material, Bucci (1997) proposed a model of the RA variations in the "ideal" analytical process, a pattern which can cover the space of a session or, more frequently, can be repeated more than once in the same session. This model, called the referential process, can be described by a "normal" curve designed by the variations of the RA values and is articulated in three phases:

1   *Arousal*: at the beginning of a session, a problematic emotion schema is activated in the patient's mind, accompanied by painful feelings and implicit ideas associated to it; the affective core of the schema is expressed through bodily and sensory experience, that is at a subsymbolic level. Verbal communication is not fluent, sometimes flat, or even silent: RA values are very low.

2   *Narrative/Symbolizing*: at a certain point, sometimes after an intervention from the analyst, some aspects of the problematic schema appear in the form of a vivid narrative; maybe the patient tells a recent episode, or a memory, or a dream, activating in the analyst's mind attention and possibly images. This is, according to Bucci, the essential phase of the symbolizing process, because the speaker, emotionally engaged in her/his still unrecognized schema, is however connecting the subsymbolic flow of experience to language, through images coming from recalling a memory or a dream. This phase is characterized by high values of RA.

3   *Reorganizing*: once the emotion schema has been experienced and reported in a narrative form, usually the analyst steps into the dialogue by some interventions aimed to interpret, explore, and reflect upon the issues that are being expressed. In this third phase, RA is decreasing again, because the discourse of both participants moves to a more rational level, following the rules of the linguistic organization but still elaborating on the previous emotion schema. According to Bucci, the potential for new connections and changes in the patient's emotional organization lies in this type of mutual exchanges between patient and analyst. In fact the sessions, which are evaluated by expert psychoanalysts as "good hours," present a regular alternation of these three phases (Bucci, 2002; Bucci & Maskit, 2007).

These first studies, however, showed two difficulties: (1) in the application to a relevant number of sessions, the method resulted to be time-consuming and required at least two or three judges to be completely reliable; (2) in the evaluation of results, the simple assessment of the RA variable could not allow to explain the differences between the first and the third phase of the referential process, neither from a linguistic point of view nor from the clinical one.

## Building on the measurement of RA: the WRAD dictionaries, studies, and overall results

With the help of mathematician Bernhard Maskit of Stony Brook University, the RA system underwent a radical transformation, increasing the complexity of the assessment of clinical exchanges. First of all, the variations of RA became measurable through a computerized procedure, enabling future comparison studies among institutions. Second, more computerized dictionaries were created, adding further measures for linguistic variables, in order to obtain a more articulated picture of the referential process.

The first goal of this computerization was to graph the text files of an analytic session showing the variability of RA during the session. This is possible by virtue of a special program (Discourse Attributes Analysis Program, or DAAP) based on a weighted dictionary that attributes a RA value to each word in the text. Initially, the weights have been determined using the RA values attributed by expert judges on the RA scales to transcribed texts of audio-recorded clinical material; the DAAP, however, is able to model the initial weights, considering the linguistic context in which the single words appear (i.e., counting the weights of the preceding and following words). The English Weighted Referential Activity Dictionary (WRAD) includes 697 frequently used linguistic items which cover from 83% to 87% of the spoken language used in the data set originally employed to build it.

Studying the variations of the RA measures obtained over different treatments (i.e., successful and unsuccessful psychotherapies) and expanding upon the study of the three phases of the referential process in a single session, or in many consecutive sessions of the same patient, Bucci and Maskit arrived at the conclusion that more dictionaries were required in order to model the different functions which correspond to the referential process' different phases. At present the DAAP operates on the basis of the relationships among four different measures: referential activity (WRAD), affect (AFF), reflection (REF), and disfluency (DF). The three new dictionaries were developed using standard computerized content analysis procedures (Bucci & Maskit, 2007). The affect dictionary includes words that are referring to emotional experience and can accompany the increasing RA in the second phase. The reflection dictionary contains words referring to processes of thought, which are most used in the third phase, where RA tends to decrease. The disfluency dictionary contains few words or vocal utterances that indicate that the speaker is struggling to communicate ("like," "well," "uh," "ehm," etc.), and are more likely to be used in the arousal phase. More precisely, the operation of the referential process appears to be associated with a negative WRAD/REF covariation, indicating sequential rather than concurrent occurrences of these two processes. The patient's covariation between WRAD and REF (WRAD/REF) has been shown to be related to clinical judgments of effectiveness in more than one study where the same sessions were assessed through the DAAP dictionaries and by expert analysts: the analysts were asked to give a qualitative evaluation of the "good hours" versus the ineffective ones, and to look also inside each single session for the good exchanges between patient and analyst (Bucci & Maskit, 2007; Bucci, Maskit, & Hoffman, 2012).

Other measures which have been found relevant for the evaluation of the clinical process are the mean WRAD for both patient and therapist in each session; the high WRAD proportion, which indicates how much of the time the patient is in the narrative/symbolizing style (that is, using words with RA values above .5); and the mean high WRAD, which is designed as a measure of the intensity of the patient's emotional engagement, indicating the average amount by which the WRAD function lies above its neutral value (Mariani, Maskit, Bucci, & De Coro, 2013).

## *An Italian research study*

In Rome, at the University "La Sapienza," after having applied the manual RA scales in some clinical studies (Solano et al., 2001; De Coro, Tagini, Andreassi, & Pazzagli, 2002; Mariani, Iberni, & De Coro, 2007), we have built an Italian computerized multidimensional dictionary (I-WRAD) with the contribution by the Roman research group under my supervision and by some psychotherapists and researchers from Milan (Mariani, 2009; Rivolta, Mariani, & Tagini, 2009; Mariani et al., 2013). The I-WRAD is much larger than the English dictionary, containing 9,596 words, which cover 97% of the spoken language used in the data set originally employed to build it (132 participants). In a second set of texts (32 participants) that have served to test its reliability, the I-WRAD has covered nearly 94% of the language and has shown a good concurrent reliability with the RA manual scales (see Mariani et al., 2013).

In order to test the clinical validity of the Italian computerized measures, the four Italian dictionaries (IWRAD, IREF, IAFF, and IDF) have been applied to a number of transcribed sessions extracted from the dynamic psychotherapies of three single cases (Mariani et al., 2013): three young women treated by three different female therapists at the Department of Dynamic and Clinical Psychology of "La Sapienza" University, with weekly sessions during a period from 25 up to 28 months. The Shedler-Westen Assessment Procedure, a psychodynamic instrument (SWAP-200; Westen & Shedler, 1999; Shedler, 2009) was used to assess their respective personalities at the beginning of each psychotherapy, and to measure the changes observed at the end of the therapies. The application of this procedure on the first four sessions of each patient assessed the presence of clinically significant features of one or more personality disorders (PD), but no diagnosis for PD;[1] moreover, all three had psychological health indices below the "high functioning" threshold.

Ms. A, a 23-year-old, was studied through the computerized analysis of 10 sessions after the first four ones (two non-consecutive sessions every 6 months); for

Ms. B (aged 18), the investigated sessions were 23; and for Ms. C (aged 24) they were 33, randomly selected every 2 weeks. At the end of each treatment, the T-scores for personality disorders had decreased in the three cases, and the psychological health indices were clearly above the "high functioning" threshold, showing that the three patients had reached non-clinical levels of psychological functioning. The SWAP was applied in blind by three students who had been trained in this procedure.

As for the linguistic measures, we found that in all three therapies the clinical improvements were accompanied by increasing values of mean IWRAD and of high IWRAD proportion both in patient and therapist. While for Ms. A and Ms. B these two measures were higher in the patient than in the therapist, as expected, along the entire treatment, in Ms. C's speech the two measures were constantly lower than in her therapist's speech. Ms. C was also the only one who still showed significant features in two personality disorders at the end of her treatment. For all three cases the patient was higher in disfluency than the therapist and lower in reflection and affect. The negative co-variation of IWRAD and IREF in the patient's speech was increasing over time in all three therapies, even if the case of Ms. C showed more frequent oscillations. Since this measure implies the operation of the referential process, characterized by the activation of imagery and narratives followed by reflection, this result appears to be coherent with the clinical improvement of the three patients (Mariani et al., 2013, p. 14).

## Conclusion

The findings from research studies based on the multiple code theory of Wilma Bucci point to the relevance of the construct of referential activity for a dynamic interpretation of the verbal exchanges in psychotherapy and of their possible effectiveness in bringing about a structural change in the client's mind. This theory attributes to imagery such as it appears in words through some peculiar characteristics of the language, a central role in the activation of the connecting function called referential activity. In fact, according to Bucci's studies, the appearance of images in the patient's speech has a double relevant effect on the analytical process. The recall of specific autobiographic events, as well as the narration of a dream through detailed visual representations, appear both to indicate the activation of a new connection inside the client's mind between emotion schemas and verbal thought, and to activate in the interpersonal dialogue analogous images in the listener's mind so that patient and analyst can share precious moments of mutual emotional regulation.

Half a century before, Jung claimed that to perceive and to give form to images (even by concrete means, like pencils or brushes or clay) is useful to the therapeutic process only when the patient can overcome an "aesthetic attitude" and recognizes that she/he is "participating to the action": in this case a real "confrontation with the unconscious" occurs, bringing the patient to the "*unio mentalis*" (Jung, 1955/1956, para. 752). A few years later, James Hillman (1960), reviewing a large scientific and philosophic literature about emotion, proposed that emotional development is the aim of psychotherapy "beyond the cure of symptoms and the problems of social adjustment": such a therapy requires "an active confrontation of analyst and analysand [. . .] and openness to the elaboration of symbolic images." Emotion itself brings about transformation, if there occurs an integration between conscious and unconscious perspectives: "*emotion is always to be valued more highly than the conscious system alone*" (pp. 284–285). He writes: "The symbol is the efficient cause of emotion: it is its stimulus. Where there is emotion there is a symbol. Or, as the cause is an aspect of the event itself, *the symbol is thus the emotion itself in the aspect of an exciting image*" (p. 258). The emotional contact occurring in the transference phenomena "has such a primary role in psychotherapy" because "emotion is wholeness and affective contact is the first level of healing, of making whole" (pp. 274–275).

Further theoretical and empirical investigation would allow for expansion of the possible implications of this parallelism for further developments of Jungian theory and of the analytic clinical work. My limited aim here was to put into evidence that, even in different languages, referring to different theoretical frames, modern studies on the analytic process seem to offer an empirical confirmation of Jungian intuition about the value of images in the therapeutic dialogue – images as an intrapsychic bridge between different layers of consciousness and different cognitive modalities, but also images as a preferential way to an interpersonal communication, based on the possibility of sharing the individual's authentic emotional life.

## Note

1 In the SWAP quantitative personality profiles, the T-scores between .50 and .60 in one or more PD categories indicate that the person's functioning shows significant features of that or those personality disorders, without attaining the threshold for a proper diagnosis of PD. T-scores above .60, instead, suggest the presence of a structured PD (Shedler, 2009).

## References

Bucci, W. (1997). *Psychoanalysis and cognitive science*. New York: Guilford Press.

Bucci, W. (2002). Multiple code theory and the referential process: Applications to process research. In P. Fonagy et al. (Eds.), *An open door review of outcome studies in psychoanalysis* (2nd ed., pp. 192–195). London: International Psychoanalytical Association.

Bucci, W., & Kabasakalian, R. (1992). The Referential Activity Research Group. In *Scoring referential activity: Instructions for use with transcripts of spoken narrative texts*. Ulm: Ulmer Textbank.

Bucci, W., & Maskit, B. (2007). Beneath the surface of the therapeutic interaction: The psychoanalytic method in modern dress. *Journal of the American Psychoanalytic Association, 55*, 1355–1397.

Bucci, W., Maskit, B., & Hoffman, L. (2012). Objective measures of subjective experience: The use of therapist notes in process–outcome research. *Psychodynamic Psychiatry, 40*(2), 303–340.

Damasio, A. (1999). *The feeling of what happens: Body and emotion in the making of consciousness*. Orlando, FL: Harcourt Inc.

Damasio, A. (2010). *Self comes to Mind: Constructing the conscious brain*. New York: Random House.

De Coro, A., & Caviglia, G. (Eds.) (2000). *Wilma Bucci: La valutazione dell'attività referenziale.* Roma: Edizioni Kappa.

De Coro, A., Tagini, A., Andreassi, S., & Pazzagli, C. (2002). Il 'processo primario' e la ricerca empirica. Una nota sul modello di Wilma Bucci per lo studio della psicoterapia psicoanalitica. *Rassegna di Psicologia, 2,* 73–90.

Fosshage, J.L. (1997). The organizing functions of dream mentation. *Contemporary Psychoanalysis, 33,* 429–458.

Fosshage, J.L. (2005). The explicit and implicit domains in psychoanalytic change. *Psychoanalytic Inquiry, 25,* 516–539.

Hillman, J. (1960). *Emotion: A comprehensive phenomenology of theories and their meanings for therapy.* Evanston, IL: Northwestern University Press.

James, W. (1890). *The principles of psychology.* Vol. 1. New York: Dover Publications, 1950.

James, W. (1898). Brute and human intellect. In *Writings 1878–1899.* New York: The Library of America, 1992.

Jung, C.G. (1902). *On the psychology and pathology of so-called occult phenomena.* CW 1. London: Routledge & Kegan Paul, 1970.

Jung, C.G. (1907). *The psychology of dementia praecox.* CW 3. London: Routledge & Kegan Paul, 1960.

Jung, C.G. (1912/1952). *Symbols of transformation.* CW 5. London: Routledge & Kegan Paul, 1956.

Jung, C.G. (1920/1948). *The psychological foundations of belief in spirits.* CW 8. London: Routledge & Kegan Paul, 1969.

Jung, C.G. (1928). *The Relations between the ego and the unconscious.* CW 7. London: Routledge & Kegan Paul, 1966.

Jung, C.G. (1935/1954). *Archetypes of the collective unconscious.* CW 9/1. London: Routledge & Kegan Paul, 1959.

Jung, C.G. (1955/1956). *Mysterium coniunctionis.* CW 14. London: Routledge & Kegan Paul, 1970.

Jung, C.G. (1957/1958). *The transcendent function.* CW 8. London: Routledge & Kegan Paul, 1969.

Kosslyn, S.M. (1983). *Ghosts in the mind's machine: Creating and using images in the brain.* New York: Norton Press.

Mandler, J. (1992). How to build a baby. II. Conceptual primitives. *Psychological Review, 99,* 587–604.

Mariani, R. (2009). *Per uno studio del Processo Referenziale in psicoterapia: Il dizionario delle parole riflessive (I-REF), un indicatore linguistico in relazione all'I-WRAD* (Ph.D Thesis, supervised by A. De Coro, unpublished). Roma: Università "La Sapienza."

Mariani, R., Iberni, E., & De Coro, A. (2007, March). The therapeutic relationship as co-construction and development of Referential Activity. *Book of Abstracts: SPR European Chapter Annual Meeting.* Funchal (Madeira, PT).

Mariani, R., Maskit, B., Bucci, W., & De Coro, A. (2013). Linguistic measures of the referential process in psychodynamic treatment. *Psychotherapy Research,* 1–19. https://doi.org/10.1080/10503307.2013.794399

Paivio, A. (1971). *Imagery and verbal processes.* New York: Holt, Reinehart & Winston.

Paivio, A. (1986). *Mental representations: A Dual Coding approach.* New York: Oxford University Press.

Rivolta, L., Mariani, R., & Tagini, A. (2009, October). The Italian Reflection (I-REF) and Affect (I-AFF) dictionaries as measures of mental functioning. *Book of Abstracts: SPR European Chapter Annual Meeting.* Bolzano (IT).

Shedler, J. (2009). *Guide to SWAP interpretation.* Retrieved from www.SWAPassessment.org

Solano, L., Zoppi, L., Barnaba, L., Fabrizi, S., Zani, R., Murgia, F., & Seagal, J. (2001). Health consequences of differences in emotional processing and reactivity following the 1997 earthquake in Central Italy. *Psychology, Health & Medicine, 6*(3), 267–275.

Wallerstein, R.S. (1995). The effectiveness of psychotherapy and psychoanalysis: Conceptual issues and empirical work. In T. Shapiro & R.N. Emde (Eds.), *Research in psychoanalysis: Process, development, outcome* (pp. 299–312). Madison, CO: International Universities Press.

Westen, D., & Shedler, J. (1999). Revising and assessing Axis II. Part I: Developing a clinically and empirically valid assessing method. Part II: Toward an empirically based and clinically useful classification of personality disorders. *American Journal of Psychiatry, 155,* 258–285.

Young-Eisendrath, P. (2000). Self and transcendence: A postmodern approach to analytical psychology. *Psychoanalytic Dialogues, 10,* 427–441.

# 5

# JUNGIAN DREAM INTERPRETATION AND EMPIRICAL DREAM RESEARCH

*Christian Roesler*

From its very beginning, psychoanalysis has seen the dream as the royal road to the unconscious. Nevertheless, in the different psychoanalytic schools quite different approaches to the interpretation of dreams in psychotherapy have developed. Also in the last decades different authors have offered a series of reconceptualizations of Freud's original theory of dreaming. This has led to a convergence of contemporary Freudian theories of the dream toward Jung's understanding of the dream. This development was at least partly initiated by results from empirical dream research. Following the discovery of rapid eye movement (REM), which accompanies dreaming during sleep, a large corpus of empirical research has developed on dreaming, its functions, and its connection to waking life.

Referring to Barrett (2001), the results of empirical dream research can be summarized in the following theory of dreaming: in the dream the brain is in a mode where it does not have to process new input but can use larger capacities for working on problems and finding creative solutions. The dream focuses especially on experiences in waking life that have emotional meaning for the dreamer. The dreaming mind can find solutions for problems more easily because it is able to connect very different areas and functions of the brain. It becomes obvious here that empirical dream research, though not having any intention of testing Jungian theory, has become quite supportive of Jung's theory of the dream. The findings of empirical dream research have led to some modifications in the Freudian theory of dreaming (e.g., no difference between manifest and latent meaning, the dream is not "the keeper of the sleep," etc.; see overview in Fiss, 1995). As a result of this process, contemporary Freudian dream theories have incorporated a number of aspects of Jungian dream theory (Werner & Langenmayr, 2005; Fisher & Greenberg, 1977, 1996). An example of this convergence can be found in the dream theory of James Fosshage (1987, 1997), which focuses on the functions of the dream as a regulator of emotions and integrating factor of psychological organization; the author explicitly refers to the strong analogies with Jung's theory.

## Jungian dream theory

Generally speaking, there are two different theories of the dream to be found in Jung's works. The first sees the dream as a spontaneously produced picture of the current situation of the psyche in the form of symbols (Jung, 1925/1971, § 505); the second emphasizes the compensation of conscious attitudes (Jung, 1984). The two theories can easily be merged into one general theory of the dream. Via dreams, the unconscious brings new information to consciousness. This process is more compensating the stronger the tension is between conscious orientation and the unconscious process of individuation. In this sense the unconscious contains a broader and more holistic knowledge about the development of personality. This is supportive of the hypothesis that the psyche is a self-regulating system. As the information brought to consciousness from the unconscious takes the form of symbols and images, it needs translation to be understood by the conscious ego.

## Research on dreaming and its psychological function

In his overview of experimental dream research, Schredl (2007) points to the strong connections between experiences, especially emotional and stressful ones, in waking life and the dream. There is extensive evidence that dreams have an influence on emotion regulation in waking life, e.g., nightmares have a positive effect on coping (Picchioni & Hicks, 2009). In recovering from trauma, dreams can even have a therapeutic effect (Hartmann, 1998).

> In sum, evidence from a variety of types of studies supports the notion of an emotion regulation function of dreaming and the more specific suggestion that dream characters and their emotion-laden interactions with the dream self may mediate this regulatory effect.
>
> *(Nielsen & Lara-Carrasco, 2007, p. 274)*

Dreams also seem to have a strong influence on creativity just in the way Jung postulated. There is a systematic collection by the dream researcher Barrett (2001) of a large number of artists and scientists stimulated by their dreams. The influence of dreams on creativity was also investigated in experimental studies (Schredl, 2007). Dreaming plays a central role in the consolidation of memory content (Hallschmid & Born, 2006) and promotes insight, learning processes, and problem-solving (Wagner, Gais, Haider, Verleger, & Born, 2004; Fiss, 1979). Therefore contemporary theories of dreaming based on empirical research see the dream as an information processing activity which is task oriented, adaptive, and has a regulating function for emotion, stress, and memory (Moffitt, Kramer, & Hoffmann, 1993; Kramer et al.,

1976; Hartmann, 1996). These findings support the view that dreaming is part of the self-regulating function of the psyche.

Even more interesting is the research on the content of dreams initiated by Hall and Van de Castle (1966), who could show that it is possible to draw a personality profile based only on the dreams of the person. In a study on dreams of people with multiple personality disorder, Barrett (1996) could show that the split-off parts of the personality appeared personified in the dreams, which would support Jung's approach in dream interpretation. In this research tradition it also became obvious that there is a high continuity of the themes in the dreams of a person over a long period of time (Levin, 1990). Cartwright (1977) found that the themes in dreams change when a person goes through psychotherapy. These findings support the view that the unconscious tries to communicate with ego consciousness via dreams to initiate changes in the attitude of the ego.

There is also systematic research on the use of dreams in psychotherapy and their effects. In part, this research was conducted by psychoanalysts. Greenberg and Pearlman (1978) compared the content of dreams of patients currently in psychoanalysis with the protocols of therapy sessions from the time of the dream and found a strong connection between the themes in the dreams and in psychotherapy, especially those connected with strong emotions. An interesting point here is that these authors point out that there is no latent meaning in the dream to be deciphered, but the dream can be read directly as a report about the current conflictual themes in the waking life of the dreamer. In a similar way, Palombo (1982) could show that analysands reprocess contents from the last analytical session in the following dreams. Popp, Luborsky, and Crits-Christoph (1990) investigated dreams and narratives from therapy sessions with the methodology of the core conflictual relationship theme; they found that both narratives and dreams were structured by the same unconscious relationship patterns.

Even more interesting is the research conducted by the group around Clara Hill (1996), who investigated the effects of the use of dream work in psychotherapy. They developed a model of psychotherapeutic work with dreams that is very close to the Jungian approach in many aspects. In the overview of her research, Hill and Spangler (2007) gives the following summary of her findings: clients in psychotherapy regard working with dreams as more helpful than sessions without dream work, and they receive fundamental insights through this work; insight is focused on specific problems from the life of the clients, and effects from the dream work focusing on a specific problem can be found even after just one session of dream work; this insight is not just on the cognitive level but leads to significant changes in the everyday life of the clients, e.g., better coping with the problem worked on; dream work leads directly to a reduction of depressive symptoms and improves subjective well-being. In one study, the research group (Bradlow & Bender, 1997) even found that the initial dream from an analytical psychotherapy contains information on the central topics of the client which had to be dealt with in the course of psychotherapy.

There is only a small number of empirical studies from Analytical Psychology focusing on the use of dreams in psychotherapy, and these findings have to be interpreted with care due to strong limitations of the research design (Faber, 1983; Kluger, 1955). In the Jungian approach there is also a certain tradition of studies investigating the unconscious influence of the orientation of the therapist on the dreams of the patient. Both Kron and Avny (2003) and Fischer (1978) found evidence for a strong unconscious communication or reciprocal influence between therapist and patient which shows up in the contents of the dream.

So there is some evidence for psychodynamic theories of dreaming and its role in psychotherapy. Nevertheless, there is a strong need for more systematic studies on the relationship between the content of the dreams of a person, namely the development of recurrent themes and figures in a series of dreams; and the course of psychotherapy, namely the development of core conflictual themes of the patient and the overall development of the personality. In Germany there is a certain tradition in psychoanalysis for developing elaborate coding systems for dream content and their use in studies investigating processes in psychotherapy (e.g., Moser & von Zeppelin, 1996). To understand the meaning conveyed by the dream, it has to be interpreted. In the psychodynamic schools of psychotherapy, this interpretation of dreams takes place in an interaction between therapist and client. For a systematic research on the meaning of dreams, it would be necessary to have a method of interpretation which produces more objective and reliable results, and the method of "structural dream analysis" presented here is an attempt in this direction.

## Structural dream analysis (SDA)

In psychotherapeutic processes, dreams point to the core problems/conflicts, but they also contain elements to solve these problems. During the course of a psychotherapy, the analyst assumes that the series of dreams follows an inner structure of meaning. SDA aims at identifying this inner structure of meaning from the series of dreams alone without referring to additional information about the dreamer, the psychodynamics, or the course of psychotherapy. The meaning conveyed by the dream is analyzed in a systematic series of interpretive steps which makes use of analytic tools developed in narratology (Gülich & Quasthoff, 1985); especially two earlier methods of narrative analysis were incorporated into the SDA study:

1    Russian researcher Vladimir Propp (1975) developed a method called structural analysis/functional analysis and applied it to fairy tales. Each fairy tale is divided into its functional parts (e.g., "The King is ill and needs healing"; "The hero fights the Dragon") and each functional part receives an abstract symbol, e.g., a letter or number. As a result, each fairy tale can be written as an abstract formula of symbols, and then different fairy tales can be compared regarding their structure.

2    Brigitte Boothe (1994) of the University of Zurich developed the narrative method, JAKOB, for the analysis of patient narratives from analytical

psychotherapies and their development over the course of psychotherapy. An important element in this method is to analyze the role that the narrator takes in the narrative in terms of activity versus passivity and his/her relation to other protagonists in the narrative.

SDA also makes use of amplification, which was systematized in the form of a manual.

The interpreters, who are blinded regarding all other information about the case, receive a series of 10 to 20 dreams covering the whole course of a psychotherapy, ideally marking core points and topics. The dreams are provided by practicing analysts who also write a case report about the psychopathology and psychodynamics of the patient involved as well as about the development of core conflicts and themes in the course of the therapy.

## Overview of the research methodology

1   Segmentation of the narrative
2   Episodic models
3   Fate of the protagonist: the dream narratives are analyzed regarding the position of the ego (ego is actively involved, a passive observer, is marginalized, etc.)
4   Functional analysis (following Propp)
5   Integrating the preceding steps into a structural framework describing the whole dream series
6   Amplification of core symbols: symbols that appear in several dreams or have a central position to the dream series are analyzed using symbol dictionaries and translated into a hypothesis of their psychological meaning
7   Amplifications are included into the framework of the dream series
8   Overall interpretation of the meaning of the whole dream series in psychological language.

Further details about the nature of the research steps are provided in the following sections.

### *Exemplary dream series*

To illustrate the application of this method, the preceding steps are taken to analyze the following dream series (originally written down by the dreamer in German and handed over to the therapist; the translation follows the original style of the client):

1   I walked down the street in the darkness, on both sides small houses behind fences. Lots of barking dogs jumped against the fences. I was frightened but then I became brave. I barked like a dog myself aggressively and the dogs immediately fell silent.

2 I am on my way with my bicycle up a hill. It is demanding. Around me are large trees, it's like in the mountains. Arriving on top there is a little white poodle, it barks, it is on a leash. I'm driving home downhill in sharp curves. Doberman dogs are behind me, I cannot get rid of them because of the curves. They run at my side and bark at me. Then it is light and sunny, arriving on the pass it's beautiful. There is a restaurant, like in Italy, beautiful houses. On top of the pass the black dogs are coming.

3 There is a stillwater, a river? There is a little bridge, somebody on the other side. He falls into the water, he somehow slipped as if under a log. I pull him out, but first I hesitate. He is like dead. But that guy has a sharp knife and he cuts the other helper's throat. I flee.

4 In black and white: at a nearby train station. A girl and another person, who seems to be masochistic, and a very energetic black dog. The dog pulls the other person into the little pond, then pulls the person out of the water and up the hill. The person gives himself a blow job, then to the dog. Then I am at the foot of a tall building. I say: the dog must be put on a leash. The masochistic person says: you have to stroke the dog. I say: no, it must be put on a leash and then removed. The masochistic person is angry and goes into the tall building. The other person says: you have to follow him, he is sad. The dog smells, I put him on a leash but it is disgusting.

5 An elderly, badly smelling dog is with me and my girlfriend in Paris. It just found us. We get on the bus, the badly smelling dog could not go with us, we left it outside. We are already outside of the city limits, but will return to the city on the highway. The dog would not have been able to come along behind us.

6 I was the manager of a café in the house. I was promoted like Joseph in the house of Potifar. Everybody says goodbye to a father with his little son, he's in the backyard. There is an elderly man with a Pitbull. He says: I can show you how evil the dog is. But I just had to go. I walked into a vineyard. The dog runs from its leash and goes behind me, but I jump over fences and walls. The path goes uphill through the yard and back down on the other side.

7 In a country restaurant. Two Romanians come in and start begging. I remember: the last time the two of them were masked and committed a robbery. I drive away with the motorcycle. I want to report to the police, because now I know their faces.

8 A little baby is in danger. I cover it with newspaper and carry it with me through a sewerage system. Then I forget about it and leave it somewhere. But then I realize that the baby is missing and go back and find it again. I carry it with me and feed it. I think: the baby is so small, it should get mother's milk, but I can just feed him solid food.

9 I'm sitting on the couch in the garden. A man with two bottles of beer is by my side and offers one to me, maybe my father? I get the feeling of being unfair to the other person. We are having a beer together.

10 My father dies at the age of 49 years. I'm not moved at all. It was strange that he died so young. We don't have such a long life as my grandma with her 102 years of age.

11 I saw a giant toe and found it is my toe. The skin on the nail was grown very wide. I thought: this has to be removed. It could be moved back easily. There was another level of skin below, this one could be taken off easily, too. I was surprised that it did not hurt. Below the skin were very small black worms, everything was rotten, but you could remove it without difficulty. Below that everything was new.

## Step 1: segmentation

Each dream is separated into its narrative segments before further steps of analysis are applied (Lucius-Hoene & Deppermann, 2004).

## Step 2: episodic models

As described earlier, a narrative consists of a starting point, a development, and a conclusion; this basic structure can be differentiated into different dynamic models. In SDA, 10 different episodic models (Boothe, 1994) are used to describe the dynamic of the development in the dream narrative.

1 Continuity: a static image, no destabilizing momentum
2 Climax: a process of growth and optimization
3 Anticlimax: a process of decline
4 *Restitutio ad integrum* (after deintegration): after deintegration, a return to normal conditions
5 *Restitutio ad integrum* (after climax): after climax, a return to normal conditions
6 Approbation: validation after denigration, by successfully passing an examination or test
7 Frustration: after a short gradation there is strong degradation
8 Chance: positive development; the protagonist adapts to conditions and stabilizes
9 Anti-chance: negative development; the protagonist adapts to negative conditions and stabilizes
10 Unexplainable changes: the normal course of the narrative is disrupted; something unexpected happens.

## Step 3: fate of the protagonist

Analysis of the position the ego takes in the narrative:

1 Only ego initiative: in all phases of the narrative the ego has the initiative; the ego is always in the subject position.

2 Only other's initiative: only other agents have the initiative throughout the narrative; the ego is never in the subject position.
3 Loss of initiative: initially the ego has the initiative, also parallel to other figures, but at the end is in a passive position.
4 Regain the initiative: the ego is at the beginning and at the end in the initiating position; during the course of the narrative the ego loses the initiative to other actors.
5 Embedded in others' initiative: the ego is from time to time in the course of the development in the initiative position, but not at the beginning and not at the end.

Applying these systematic steps to the preceding dream series leads to the following structure (Table 5.1).

**TABLE 5.1** Episodic models and fate of the protagonist for total dream series

| | Episodic model | Fate of the protagonist |
|---|---|---|
| **Dream 1** | Restitutio ad integrum (after deintegration) | Regain the initiative |
| **Dream 2** | Anticlimax | Loss of initiative |
| **Dream 3** | Anticlimax | Regain initiative |
| **Dream 4** | Not definable | Embedded in others' initiative |
| **Dream 5** | Continuity | Embedded in others' initiative |
| **Dream 6** | Frustration | Regain initiative |
| **Dream 7** | Approbation | Regain initiative |
| **Dream 8** | Chance | Only ego initiative |
| **Dream 9** | Antichance | Loss of initiative |
| **Dream 10** | Continuity | Not definable |
| **Dream 11** | Approbation | Only ego initiative |

After this step of analysis, a first summarizing interpretation of the development over the course of the dream series is possible. On both levels of analysis, there is a certain development from patterns of decline in the first half of therapy to patterns of approbation or chance which could be called more optimistic. Regarding ego initiative, there is a development from patterns of loss of initiative or the ego being subjected to others' initiative to patterns dominated by ego initiative. Psychologically speaking, there is a certain development from a situation in which the ego is more of a victim of conditions or others' initiative to a situation where ego consciousness is more capable of taking over initiative and controlling the situation.

## Step 4: functional analysis (following Propp)

In this step, each dream is segmented into its functional parts and each part receives an abstract symbol. Here, the interpreter has to decide how far the abstraction of the narrative segment should go. The aim here is to reduce the dream narrative down to its structural elements so that they become comparable. In the current state of the development of SDA, the definition of structural elements has to be developed for each new series of dreams; in the long run, the aim is to build up a corpus of analyzed cases which will allow for a generalization of structural elements across cases.

Table 5.2 shows the functional analysis for all the dreams of the preceding dream series. Recurrent structural elements are marked.

## *Step 5: identification of repetitive structural elements*

Repetitive structures that were marked are now extracted:

**Dream 1:** threat, constructive strategy
**Dream 2:** threat, pursue, flight, threat
**Dream 3:** help/support, threat, flight
**Dream 4:** disgust
**Dream 5:** pursue, disgust, pursue
**Dream 6:** threat, pursue, flight, end pursue
**Dream 7:** pledge for help/support, threat, constructive strategy
**Dream 8:** pledge for help/support, help/support, inadequate measures
**Dream 11:** wish for modification, modification, renewal/regeneration.

## *Step 6: amplification of major symbols*

To combine the preceding structural elements of the dreams with content in the next step, the meaning of central symbols of the dreams will be analyzed by using Jung's original method of amplification. To arrive at a scientific approach to the interpretation of symbols via amplification in the application of SDA, this step is clearly defined. Amplification of symbols is restricted to the use of a set of symbol dictionaries (e.g., Cooper, 1978) which give information about the cultural background of symbols in the sense of their use and understanding in religious traditions, mythology, cultural beliefs, and so forth. This is to certify that interpretation of the symbols is done in a way that is as objective as possible.

This step of interpretation is applied only to a very restricted number of symbols, ideally those which appear repeatedly in the dreams or seem to be especially important to the series of dreams (see Table 5.3).

## *Step 7: integration of the previous steps*

The preceding findings just give information about the field or context of meaning of the symbols. In the next step, this has to be integrated in the structure of the dream series. This is clearly the more psychological step in the interpretation, which makes use of psychological/psychodynamic concepts. Still, this step of interpretation attempts to stay as objective as possible, therefore the aim here is not to formulate definite interpretations of the dreams but to translate the preceding structures

**TABLE 5.2** Functional analysis for total dream series

| | Function I | Function II | Function III | Function IV | Function V | Function VI | Function VII | Function VIII |
|---|---|---|---|---|---|---|---|---|
| **Dream 1** | 0 Initial situation | BD Threat | S Constructive strategy | | | | | |
| **Dream 2** | 0 Initial situation Situation | ↑ Way up | BD Threat | ↓ Way down | V Pursue | F Flight | ↑ Way up | BD Threat |
| **Dream 3** | 0 Initial situation | W Water | WT Death/damage | H Help/support | BD Threat | F Flight | | |
| **Dream 4** | 0 Initial situation | VSCH deference | & sexual act | KS conflict | KL Conflict solution | EK Disgust | | |
| **Dream 5** | 0 Initial situation | V Pursue | EK Disgust | O Change of place | V End Pursue | | | |
| **Dream 6** | 0 Initial situation | ‖ Gradation | VE goodbye | BD Threat | V Pursue | F Flight | V End Pursue | |
| **Dream 7** | 0 Initial situation | BH Pledge for help/ support | BD Threat | S Constructive strategy | | | | |
| **Dream 8** | BH Pledge for help/support | H Help/support | VG Neglect | HW Taking up action | IH Inadequate measures | | | |
| **Dream 9** | 0 Initial situation | UH Unjust act | | | | | | |
| **Dream 10** | WT Death/damage | | | | | | | |
| **Dream 11** | GM Wish for modification | M Modification | RE Renewal/regeneration | | | | | |

**TABLE 5.3** Amplification of symbols

| Symbol | Dreams | Amplification |
|--------|--------|---------------|
| Dog | 1, 2, 4, 5, 6 | In a number of cultures the dog is related to death. In old Egypt and Greece, the dog guards the underworld and is a mediator between the worlds of the living and the dead. Those gods either living in the dark or being ambiguous figures often appear in the form of dogs. The dog clearly has ambiguous meaning: on the one hand, it is connected with wisdom, grace, and religion, especially the white dog; on the other hand, the dog is connected with primitive affects, impurity, vice, and envy, especially dark dogs. Also the dog is related to sexuality, because dogs in the streets are promiscuous. In some cultures the dog appears as ancestor and creator of man and of civilization because of the wisdom and the sexual power that is related to it. |
| Child | 8 | The child is a symbol for impeccably clean purity and innocence because it is so close to birth. It also represents the original and therefore is related to an abundance of possibilities. |
| Foot/toe | 11 | The foot/toe is that part of the body which is closest to the earth. Therefore symbolically as an organ of movement it is in a strong relation to the will. In the context of psychoanalysis, the foot is also seen as phallic. Related to this aspect of the symbol, naked feet can have a decisive role in rituals of initiation and generativity. |
| Worm | 11 | The worm is a being that lives below the earth and in the dirt. Therefore in several cultures this animal is connected with the snake and the devil. Also the worm is related to darkness and death and the rebirth of life from death. |

into a psychological language. As was mentioned earlier, dreams do not represent a linear structure of development but usually take up symbols and patterns repeatedly which undergo a process of transformation. In this step of interpretation it should be attempted to reconstruct this repetitive use of symbols and patterns in the dreams and the transformative process, if there is any. The focus here is on more general topics appearing repetitively in the dreams. This is illustrated in Table 5.4, where the structural elements are combined with a psychological interpretation of symbols and their meanings and included in an overall description of the dream series.

## Step 8: summarizing interpretation of the dream series

The last step is to integrate all the findings from the preceding steps into a general description or summary of the series of dreams from a psychological point of view:

In the first half of the process the ego is confronted with threatening aspects; by (?) analyzing the symbol of the dog these aspects can be characterized as having

**TABLE 5.4** Integration of amplification into dream structure

| *Threat* | *Constructive strategy* |
|---|---|
| *The ego is threatened by shadow aspects.* | *The ego takes over forms of expression of shadow aspects and by doing that, succeeds in making these aspects give up their threatening position.* |

1   The ego is threatened by shadow aspects in the form of dogs. By taking over the act of barking from the shadow aspects, the ego succeeds in making the shadow aspects stop their threatening behavior.

2   Threat *The ego is threatened by shadow aspects*    Pursue *and pursued by them*    Flight *and flees from them*    Threat *but the threat persists.*

2   In reaction to the confrontation and pursue by shadow aspects in the form of dogs, the ego flees. But the ego does not succeed and gets caught by the shadow aspects.

| 3 | Help/support | Threat | Flight |
|---|---|---|---|
| | *The ego starts actions to give help/support to other aspects of the psyche.* | *The ego is threatened by shadow aspects.* | *The ego flees from threatening shadow aspects.* |

3   The ego tries to take a supportive stance toward a helpless aspect of the psyche. But this part of the psyche comes out to be threatening and destructive. In reaction to the threat, the ego flees into an area in which it is no longer threatened by shadow aspects.

4   Disgust
   *The ego feels disgust toward shadow aspects.*

4   The ego is confronted with shadow aspects in the form of dogs. The ego denies and pushes away these aspects out of disgust.

| 5 | Pursue | Disgust | End Pursuit |
|---|---|---|---|
| | *The ego is pursued by shadow aspects.* | *The ego feels disgusted by shadow aspects.* | *The pursuit is successfully brought to an end.* |

5   The ego tries to flee from the confrontation with shadow aspects in the form of dogs. This is the fact because the ego feels strong denial and disgust toward the shadow aspects. The ego succeeds in getting away from the confrontation.

| 6 | Threat | Pursue | Flight | Interrupted Pursuit |
|---|---|---|---|---|
| | *The ego is threatened by shadow aspects.* | *The ego is pursued by shadow aspects.* | *The ego flees from threatening shadow aspects.* | *A pursuit through shadow aspects is interrupted.* |

6    In reaction to being threatened by shadow aspects in the form of dogs, the ego flees. The ego succeeds in getting away from the shadow aspects.

| 7 | Pledge for help/support | Threat | Constructive strategy |
|---|---|---|---|
| | *The ego becomes aware of aspects of the psyche that need help/support.* | *The ego is threatened by shadow aspects.* | *The ego is able to recognize in time a danger that comes from shadow aspects. It starts out to activate forces of order and security.* |

7    The ego tries to give support to a part of the psyche that needs help. But this part of the psyche comes out to be threatening and destructive. The ego is able to recognize the approaching danger in time and activates components of the psyche that are able to reestablish order and security.

| 8 | Pledge for help/support | Help/support | Inadequate forms of help |
|---|---|---|---|
| | *The ego recognizes aspects of the psyche that need help/support.* | *The ego goes into action to give help/ support to other parts of the psyche.* | *The ego is missing adequate forms to give help to other parts of the psyche.* |

8    The ego recognizes a part of the psyche in form of an infant which needs help and support. The ego already has an idea how to give support. But still it is missing the adequate measures to realize this support.

| 11 | Wish for modification | Modification | Renewal/regeneration |
|---|---|---|---|
| | *The ego realizes the necessity to modify a part of the psyche.* | *The ego begins to modify a part of the psyche.* | *Through activity of the ego, a process of regeneration and renewal becomes visible on a part of the psyche.* |

11    The ego realizes the necessity to modify a part of the psyche. This is a part connected with willpower and movement. Through activity of the ego, a process of renewal and regeneration on this part of the psyche comes about.

an aggressive and destructive, even murderous character, also they seem to be connected with sexuality. Finally they carry a certain ambiguity, changing between aggressiveness and helpless neediness. In the beginning the ego is threatened and experiences strong fear, it is not capable of coping with these aspects but flees from them. In the beginning even flight is not always successful but the ego gets caught and overwhelmed by these destructive aspects.

In the further course of the dream series, the shadow aspects begin to lose their threatening character. The ego now experiences disgust regarding these parts of the psyche and rejects them. Now a new thematic field is introduced. It is centered around situations where the ego is asked to act in a helpful and supportive way and to be active. Some pledges for help appear to be dangerous, because these parts of the psyche that ask for help are also destructive powers. The ego therefore is in danger of supporting destructive energies and being destroyed itself in the process. It can be assumed that in this change the original ambiguity of the shadow aspects is contained and they move toward the helpless and needy side.

In the image of the infant needing help, these parts have finally lost their destructive aspects, and the ego meets a pure, positive part of the psyche which points to a new beginning. These parts of the psyche need support, but the ego has some difficulty in overcoming disgust and rejection and finding a supportive attitude toward these parts. Then the ego realizes more and more how these parts have to be cared for, even though some of the necessary means and strategies are still missing. Toward the end of the dream series, the ego actively takes part in a process where some parts of the psyche experience a process of death and renewal. These aspects of the psyche can be associated with willpower and intention.

## Case description (delivered by the analyst)

The client is a young man (30 years old). Before starting psychotherapy, the client was imprisoned, having committed physical violence in more than 100 cases. Being not openly violent any more after imprisonment, he suffered from feelings of strong tension, unrest, and emptiness that were almost unbearable, against the background of a severe depression. The only means to deal with these depressive states was a strong compulsion to consume pornographic media, especially those containing physical violence toward women.

The client came from a broken home. The father suffered from severe alcoholism and tended to be violent against his wife and children. On several occasions the client experienced fear of death and was almost killed by his father. The father also seems to have been suffering from a sexual obsession: he collected pornographic videos in large numbers and stored them in his bedroom. This aspect of the father's life was always fascinating for the client. The mother grew up in the former Yugoslavia and was never able to speak German properly; it might be that the mother was slightly mentally disabled. The client stated that "she was too dumb to understand what I needed." In adolescence, the client was taken out of his family by the welfare authorities because of the difficult situation and was given into custody.

Later he joined a group of hooligans and committed a large number of violent crimes. While in prison the client experienced a religious conversion and became member of a fundamentalist Christian sect. He came into psychotherapy with the explicit intention of overcoming his aggressive impulses. His intimate relationships often followed a sadomasochistic pattern. *Psychodynamics*: the client seems to have experienced severe abandonment, helplessness, and anxiety in childhood. The frustration of his basic needs has led the client to compensatory aggression. From the psychodynamic viewpoint, the client suffers from severe depression based on a narcissistic disorder connected with a strong sexual drivenness toward violent contact with women. There is a deep contempt in the client toward women, originating on the one hand from the frustration experienced with the mother, but also influenced by the father's sexual obsession. The denigration of women also seems to have the function of defense against depression. The religious conversion has equipped the client with a strong superego which helps him to control himself in social life, nevertheless this does not solve the inner conflicts. There is a very strong and violent destructive complex in the psyche which formerly was dealt with by directing it outwards to other people; now it goes up against the ego.

*Course of therapy*: in the first years of therapy, the focus was on helping the client to formulate his needs and feelings and communicate them in social relationships, which helped to decrease the pressure of frustration aggression. In the transference, the therapist came into the position of the threatening father. The experience of security in the therapeutic relationship which also included a certain control over the analyst helped to integrate these experiences and strengthen ego functions. In the course of therapy, the relationships with women changed and the client became capable of building a marriage and family. When his first son was born, the client experienced such panic that he felt aggressive impulses toward the infant. By working through these impulses and their connection to early experiences in life, the inner pressure of frustration and aggression slowly receded. At the end of therapy, the client was living in a very solid social, family, and job situation. From time to time the client still needs to use violent pornographic videos to control his inner states of emptiness and frustration. In social life the client is now fully adapted. The low-frequency therapy took 6 years with two minor interruptions and 206 hours.

## Comparison between the results of structural dream analysis and the course of therapy

The parallels between the structure of the dream series and the psychodynamics and course of therapy are apparent. The negative complex leading to aggression and sexual compulsiveness can easily be identified in the symbol of the threatening dogs, also because the dog symbolically is connected with sexuality; on the other hand, the image of the pursuing dogs is a very direct expression of the experience of the violent father. In the course of therapy, the dreamer becomes more and more conscious of the neediness and helplessness behind the destructive complex, which culminates in the image of the helpless infant. To the extent that the client can accept these needs and take care of them, the ego gains control over the complex and the destructive aspects become integrated. In the end, with the symbol of renewal, a new state of ego strength and willful control over the personality is established.

SDA is currently applied by research teams in Switzerland, Germany, Japan, and the United States. The aim of the joint international project is to build up a corpus of at least 30 cases which will allow for identifying structures across cases. The following questions will be investigated: Are generalized structures to be found in the development of dreams in successful psychotherapies compared to failed ones? Are there connections between type of psychopathology, e.g., depression, and the symbols and structures in the dreams?

An interesting preliminary result is that in successfully completed therapies a general structure can be found:

> Initially the dream ego is threatened by a dream figure representing a complex – the ego applies inadequate measures (flight, paralysis) and the threat persists. This pattern changes over the course of therapy to a pattern where the dream ego can manage the threatening figure with a constructive strategy and the threat vanishes or is incorporated. Threatening animal figures become human (like in the exemplary case above). In all cases strong parallels between the symbolism of the dreams and the themes in therapy were found. The overall aim is to formulate an empirically grounded theory of the meaning of dreams and their development in the course of psychotherapies.

## References

Barrett, D. (1996). Dreams in multiple personality. In D. Barrett (Ed.), *Trauma and dreams*. Cambridge, MA: Harvard University Press.

Barrett, D. (2001). *The committee of sleep: How artists, scientists, and athletes use dreams for creative problem-solving*. New York: Crown.

Boothe, B. (1994). *Der Patient als Erzähler in der Psychotherapie*. Göttingen: Vandenhoek & Ruprecht.

Bradlow, P.A., & Bender, E.P. (1997). First dreams in psychoanalysis: A case study. *Journal of Clinical Psychoanalysis, 12*, 387–396.

Cartwright, R.D. (1977). *Night life*. Englewood Cliffs, NJ: Prentice-Hall.

Cooper, J.C. (1978). *Dictionary of traditional symbols*. London: Thames and Hudson.

Faber, P.A. (1983). Induced waking phantasy: Its effects upon the archetypal content of nocturnal dreams. In P.A. Faber (Ed.), *Analytical psychology*. London: Academic Press.

Fischer, C. (1978). *Der Traum in der Psychotherapie: Ein Vergleich Freud'scher u. Jung'scher Patiententräume*. München: Minerva.

Fisher, S., & Greenberg, R.P. (1977). *The scientific credibility of Freud's theories and therapy*. Hassocks, Sussex: Harvester Press.

Fisher, S., & Greenberg, R.P. (1996). *Freud scientifically reappraised: Testing the theories and therapy*. New York: Wiley-Blackwell.

Fiss, H. (1979). Current dream research. A psychobiological perspective. In B. Wolman (Ed.), *A handbook of dreams*. New York: Van Nostrand.

Fiss, H. (1995). The post-Freudian dream: A reconsideration of dream theory based on recent sleep laboratory findings. In H. Bareuther, K. Brde, M. Evert-Saleh, & N. Spangenberg (Hg.), *Traum und Gedächtnis: Materialien aus dem Sigmund-Freud-Institut* (Bd. 15; pp. 11–35). Münster: Lit.

Fosshage, J.L. (1987). New vistas on dream interpretation. In M. Glucksman (Ed.), *Dreams in new perspective: The royal road revisited*. New York: Uman Sciences Press.

Fosshage, J.L. (1997). The organizing functions of dreaming mentation. *Contemporary Psychoanalysis, 33*, 429–458.

Greenberg, R., & Pearlman, C. (1978). If Freud only knew. A reconsideration of psychoanalytic dream theory. *International Review of Psychoanalysis, 5*, 71–75.

Gülich, E., & Quasthoff, U. (1985). Narrative analysis. In T.A. van Dijk (Ed.), *Handbook of discourse analysis, Vol. II: Dimensions of discourse* (pp. 169–197). London: Academic Press.

Hall, C.S., & Van De Castle, R.L. (1966). *The content analysis of dreams*. New York: Appleton-Century-Crofts.

Hallschmid, M., & Born, J. (2006). Der Schlaf der Vernunft gebiert Wissen. In M.H. Wiegand, von F. Spreti, & H. Förstl (Hg.), *Schlaf und Traum: Neurobiologie, Psychologie, Therapie* (pp. 75–106). Stuttgart: Schattauer.

Hartmann, E. (1996). Outline for a theory on the nature and functions of dreaming. *Dreaming, 6*, 147–170.

Hartmann, E. (1998). *Dreams and nightmares: The new theory on the origin and meaning of dreams*. New York: Plenum Trade.

Hill, C.E. (1996). *Working with dreams in psychotherapy*. New York: Guildford Press.

Hill, C.E., & Spangler, P. (2007). Dreams and psychotherapy. In D. Barrett & P. McNamara (Eds.), *The new science of dreaming. Vol. 2: Content, recall and personality correlates* (pp. 159–186). Westport: Praeger.

Jung, C.G. (1971). *Allgemeine Gesichtspunkte zur Psychologie des Traumes*. GW Bd. 8. Olten: Walter.

Jung, C.G. (1984). *Die praktische Verwendbarkeit der Traumanalyse* (GW Bd. 16). Olten: Walter.

Kluger, Y. (1955). Archetypal dreams and "everyday" dreams. *Israel's Annals of Psychiatry and Related Disciplines, 13*, 6–47.

Kramer, M., Hlasny, R., Jocaobs, G., & Roth, T. (1976). Do dreams have meaning? An empirical inquiry. *American Journal of Psychiatry, 133*, 778–781.

Kron, T., & Avny, N. (2003). Psychotherapists' dreams about their patients. *Journal of Analytical Psychology, 48*, 317–339.

Levin, R. (1990). Psychoanalytic theories on the function of dreaming: A review of the empirical dream research. In J.M. Masling (Ed.), *Empirical studies of psychoanalytic theories*. Hillsdale, NJ: Erlbaum.

Lucius-Hoene, G., & Deppermann, A. (2004). *Rekonstruktion narrativer Identität: ein Arbeitsbuch zur Analyse narrativer Interviews*. Wiesbaden: VS Verlag für Sozialwiss.

Moffitt, A., Kramer, M., & Hoffmann, R. (Eds.) (1993). *The functions of dreaming*. Albany, NY: State University of New York Press.

Moser, U., & von Zeppelin, I. (1996). *Der geträumte Traum: Wie Träume entstehen und sich verändern*. Stuttgart: Kohlhammer.

Nielsen, T., Lara& -Carrasco, J. (2007). Nightmares, dreaming, and emotion regulation: A review. In D. Barrett & P. McNamara (Eds.), *The new science of dreaming. Vol. 2: Content, recall and personality correlates* (pp. 253–284). Westport: Praeger.

Palombo, S.R. (1982). How the dream works: The role of dreaming in the psychotherapeutic process. In S. Slipp (Ed.), *Curative factors in dynamic psychotherapy* (pp. 223–242). New York: McGraw Hill.

Picchioni, D., & Hicks, R.A. (2009). Differences in the relationship between nightmares and coping with stress for Asians and Caucasians. A brief report. *Dreaming, 19*, 108–112.

Popp, C., Luborsky, L., & Crits-Christoph, P. (1990). The parallel of the CCRT from therapy narratives with the CCRT from dreams. In L. Luborsky & P. Crits-Christoph (Eds.), *Understanding transference: The CCRT method* (pp. 158–172). New York: Basic Books.

Propp, V. (1975). *Morphologie des Märchens*. Frankfurt am Main: Surkamp.

Roesler, C. (2010). *Analytische Psychologie heute: Der aktuelle Stand der Forschung zur Psychologie C. G. Jungs*. Freiburg-Basel: Karger.

Schredl, M. (2007). *Träume: Die Wissenschaft enträtselt unser nächtliches Kopfkino*. Berlin: Ullstein.

Wagner, U., Gais, S., Haider, H., Verleger, R., & Born, J. (2004). Sleep inspires insight. *Nature, 427*, 352–355.

Werner, C., & Langenmayr, A. (2005). *Der Traum und die Fehlleistungen: Psychoanalyse und Empirie* (Bd. 2). Göttingen: Vandenhoeck und Ruprecht.

# PART III
# Trauma

# 6

# DREAMING UNDER FIRE

## The psyche in times of continuous stress

*Tamar Kron*

Since September 2000, the town of Sderot and the kibbutzim and villages on the border of the Gaza Strip have been under the terror of rocket attacks and wars. Studies done in Sderot and the surrounding villages and kibbutzim show that a significant proportion of the population suffers from at least one posttraumatic stress disorder (PTSD) symptom. Even residents of the area who did not report a specific symptom did report suffering from emotional distress (Gelkopf, Berger, Bleich, & Silver, 2012).

Sadly, Sderot and the surrounding area can be considered a "natural laboratory" for a field study of the psychological state of people living for a long time under continuous stress. Continuous stress and trauma are manifested in dreams. The study of dreams can expand our knowledge concerning the unconscious reactions to trauma and the efforts of coping with continuous traumatic situations.

In this chapter I will present my research on dreams of Israeli residents of the area bordering with the Gaza Strip. The first discussion is an overview of history of research on traumatic dreams. Then I review the characteristics of traumatic dreams and their possible healing function. The second part of the chapter is a presentation of my studies in the field and their results, followed by conclusions.

## A brief history of research on traumatic dreams

Research on traumatic dreams had not been the center of theoretical and research attention until the end of the Vietnam War (1955–1975). An estimated quarter of all soldiers sent to Vietnam from 1964 to 1973 required some form of psychological help. The post-Vietnam syndrome, increasingly diagnosed in veterans in the seventies, ultimately led to the adoption of PTSD as a diagnostic category in 1980 in *DSM-III* (Crocq & Crocq, 2000). Traumatic dreams and nightmares have been recognized as one of the main symptoms of PTSD. With the awareness and acknowledgment of the prevalence of chronic and delayed PTSD in combat soldiers populations, traumatic reactions of civilians living under conditions of continuing stress came to the attention of the helping professions.

Despite this development, not much has been written on traumatic dreams in the psychoanalytic and analytic psychology literature about dreaming. In his book *The Interpretation of Dreams* (1900), Freud did not even mention traumatic dreams. Only after World War I, when material on "war neurosis" dreams was brought to his attention, did Freud refer to traumatic dreams. In 1920, aware of the inconsistency of traumatic dreams with his wish-fulfilling theory, Freud explained the nature of trauma in war and trauma neurosis:

> Such external excitations as are strong enough to break through the barrier against stimuli we call traumatic. . . . The flooding of the psychic apparatus with large masses of stimuli can no longer be prevented: on the contrary, another task presents itself – to bring the stimulus under control, to "bind" in the psyche the stimulus mass that has broken its way in, so as to bring about a discharge of it.
>
> *(Freud, 1920, p. 34)*

In a seminar that Jung delivered in 1938 exploring the dreams of individuals suffering from "shell shock," he explains how recurring dreams after war trauma indicate an absolute shift in the psychic system. They are

> completely identical repetitions of reality. That is proof of the traumatic effect . . . The attempt to transform a shock into a psychical situation that may gradually be mastered can also succeed toward the end of a treatment, however, as I have observed myself in a series of dreams of an English officer. In this man's dreams, the explosion of the grenade changed into lions and other dangers that he was then able to tackle. The shock was, so to speak, absorbed. In this way, the dreamer was able to master the effect of the shock as a psychical experience.
>
> *(Jung, 2010, pp. 21–22)*

## Characteristics of traumatic dreams

Even though traumatic dreams were not the focus of interest for Freud and Jung, their short comments cited earlier correspond to some of the main findings of current research. Both refer to typical traumatic dreams being concrete and not symbolical, a characteristic which, as we shall see in what follows, has been found in all research on traumatic dreams. The need mentioned by Freud, "to 'bind' in the psyche the stimulus mass that has broken its way in" (1920, p. 34), is described by Ernest Hartmann, a prominent researcher of traumatic dreams, as one of the healing functions of the dream (see below). The gradual change of traumatic dreams from concrete to symbolic, as an outcome of therapy, is described by

Jung in the preceding citation, and was found in research on psychotherapy for PTSD patients.

In the wake of the recognition of PTSD as a separate diagnostic criteria and the rising number of patients suffering from PTSD during the 1980s, research on traumatic dreams expanded. In 1982, at the 135th annual meeting of the American Psychiatric Association, Van der Kolk et al. presented their research on nightmares and trauma. They found that chronic traumatic nightmares of men who had been in combat differ from the lifelong nightmares of veterans with no combat experience, in that they tended to occur earlier in the sleep cycle, were more likely to be replicas of actual events, and were more commonly accompanied by gross body movements (Van der Kolk et al., 1984).

Harry A. Wilmer, a Jungian analyst and psychiatrist who worked with Vietnam veterans reports, in a paper published in 1982, that in the records of the Vietnam veterans he had seen in his ward, there has been no documentation of the contents, frequency, and nature of their dreams and nightmares. Being a Jungian analyst, he himself was interested in the patients' dreams, and conducted group meetings where the patients related their dreams and discussed them (Wilmer, 1982). In a later article, Wilmer reports his study of 359 dreams of Vietnam veterans he collected, in which he found that more than 50% of the dreams were classified as actual – the dream describing the actual traumatic scene (Wilmer, 2001).

As noted earlier, Ernest Hartmann, psychiatrist and psychoanalyst, devoted himself to the study of sleep and dreams, and is considered a prominent researcher of dreams. On the basis of the results of his numerous research studies (Hartmann, 1995; Hartmann et al., 1998, 2000, 2001; Hartmann & Basile, 2003; Hartmann & Brezler, 2006, to mention a few), Hartmann constructed a theory of dreaming, the basic premise of which is that traumatic dreams have a healing function (Hartmann, 2008). The main points of his theory are the following:

- Dreaming is hyperconnective.
- The connections are not made randomly. They are guided by the emotions of the dreamer.
- The dream has a central image, which can be detected, and expresses the dreamer's emotion.
- The central image is a measure of the power of the emotion.

The making of connections guided by emotion has an adaptive function, which is conceptualized as "weaving in" new material – in other words taking new experiences, especially if they are traumatic, stressful, emotional, and gradually connecting them, multiply connecting them, into existing memory. This weaving in is the basic function of dreaming. The dream interconnects the traumatic experience to existing network of connections, making it easier for the next traumatic experiences to be woven in.

Hartmann suggests that dreaming has a quasi-therapeutic function (Hartmann, 1995, 2000) which can be seen most clearly after trauma. Dreaming, like therapy, can be considered the making of connections in a safe place. In therapy, the safe place allows the patient to tell the traumatic narrative and try to integrate the trauma. Dreaming makes connections in a safe place and allows for gradual integration of the traumatic event and the emotions stirred by it.

In the last 20 years, the research of traumatic dreams has extended to civilian populations under stressful conditions: war, terror, and refugee situations. Recent studies regarding the dreams of people who live in situations of continuous stress show that the content and characteristics of traumatic dreams are determined by a number of variables, each related to the trauma itself and to the participative experience. In general, the dreams of people who have experienced stress and trauma are more concrete than symbolic, and include more fragmentary narratives than dreams of those who have not experienced trauma (Nadar, 1996; Varvin et al., 2012). Dreams of children under continuous stress because of war and terror were found to be characterized by negative emotions, anxiety, horror, and the absence of solutions to problems (Punamäki et al., 2005; Valli et al., 2005; Valli et al., 2006; Helminen & Punamaki, 2008).

## Dreaming under fire: dreams under continuous threat of rocket attacks and in times of war

Immediately after the Gaza War (2008–2009), also known as Operation Cast Lead, a group of clinical psychology graduate students[1] under my supervision started to collect dreams and interview residents of Sderot and villages near the Gaza border as part of their master's thesis research. The methodology used, the population, and the results of that research follow.

### Participants and methodology

Participants included 44 women and 18 men, all residents of the Sderot area. There are two reasons for the greater number of women participants in the study: first, more women than men agreed to take part in the research; second, results of research into gender differences in dream recall indicate that women have more frequent dream recall than men (Schredl & Reinhard, 2008).

The participants were recruited by the chain-referral or "snowball" sampling process.

The youngest participant was 14 years old and the oldest was 65 years old. Three age groups of the women participants will be described in more detail in the results section.

All the participants agreed to be interviewed and signed an informed consent form. In the case of participants under the age of 18, their parents signed a form consenting to their participation in the study.

The researchers met twice with each participant. The first meeting consisted of an open interview of 30 to 40 minutes, where questions were asked relating to background, residence in the area and its consequences, feelings, and their manner of coping. Participants were also asked about their sleep and dreaming patterns. At the end of the first meeting, each participant received a dream diary and a notebook prepared by the researchers, which included an instruction page. Each page began with the same sentence: "Last night I dreamed that . . ." Participants were instructed to write down their dreams and all associations to the dream for 4 weeks. During the 4 weeks, the researchers maintained telephone contact with the participants to follow up on the performance of the task and to answer questions and respond to problems they raised. After the 4 weeks, the researchers met with the subjects once again. The participants handed in their dream diaries and were asked to tell about their experiences during the past month. They were also asked to fill in two questionnaires: one on coping and the other on self-control.

In this manner, a total of 661 dreams were collected: 525 dreams of women and 136 of men.

## Content analysis

In analyzing the dreams, we looked for recurrent "central themes" which could be related to the continuous stressful situation. Three judges assessed the dreams separately and indicated (0 for "No" and 1 for "Yes") the presence of each theme per dream. Initially starting with a long list of themes, those finally selected appeared in at least 10% (53) of the total cohort of dreams.

Table 6.1 summarizes the list of themes, each theme's definition, and the percentages of dreams in which the theme appears.

The main findings of the content analysis of the total cohort of dreams are as follows: there were almost no differences between the two calculations of percentages of theme occurrences described above. The most prevalent dream themes were togetherness and active ego. These themes might be related to waking life strategies for coping with stress situations, and will be discussed in detail later. Other themes

**TABLE 6.1** List of themes and the percentage of dreams in which they appeared for total sample

| Theme | Young (14–19) | Middle (20–40) | Old (41+) |
| --- | --- | --- | --- |
| **Stress situation related** | 37% | 25% | 23% |
| **Fear and anxiety** | 35% | 30% | 29% |
| **Helplessness and loss of control** | 33% | 33% | 33% |
| **No escape** | 10% | 18% | 14% |
| **Active ego** | 60% | 64% | 63% |
| **Coping with the situation** | 26% | 23% | 20% |
| **Together** | 78% | 60% | 66% |
| **Symbolic** | 22% | 40% | 36% |
| **Masochism** | 50% | 54% | 44% |
| **Shadow** | 24% | 35% | 28% |
| **PI** | 29% | 45% | 51% |

that seem to be related to the situation (stress situation related, fear and anxiety, helplessness, and loss of control) appear in about one-third of the dreams, while half of the dreams are masochistic dreams. These findings are an unconscious manifestation of the reality of concrete danger and distress as a result of living under continuous threat of rocket attacks.

Generally, the frequency of symbolic dreams is quite low, corresponding with findings in other studies of dreams in traumatic situations. The frequency of shadow images is also generally low, contradicting the expectation that the shadow of "the enemy" would appear in high frequency in this population. Is the absence of shadow images related to the fact that rockets have no face and the danger comes "from above"?

## Helpless Heroes: the dreams of men in the shadow of continuous, life-threatening rocket attacks

### (Kron, T. & Hareven, O., 2011, 2012)

For historical reasons, the ideal of the muscular and masculine Jew has occupied a central place in the Israeli culture, mainly as a reaction to the figure of the weak and persecuted Jew in the Diaspora and also as a survival necessity.

The men living under conditions of continuous threat of rocket attacks have to cope with pressures which derive from the social expectations of men in general, and pressures deriving from unconscious persona and/or repressed male archetypes, which are not fulfilled in the face of the constant threat.

"Helpless Heroes" are the men whose dreams we studied – civilians who have to survive continuous rocket attacks by taking shelter. In addition to the basic content analysis described above, we analyzed their unconscious conceptions of themselves by looking at male archetypes and the Hero's Journey in their dreams. The mirror image of the men's unconscious conception of themselves, as reflected in their dreams, is the women's unconscious conception of the figure of the man (the Animus) as reflected in their dreams. The comparison between the men's and women's dreams reflected the unconscious expectations of both women and men, and the gaps between them.

Eighteen men participated in the study. The youngest was 16 years old and the oldest was 54 years old. A total of 136 dreams were collected from the men. For the purposes of this study, we analyzed only those dreams of women in which a man figure played a central role. Twenty-three of the women participants reported dreams in which a male figure appeared. The youngest of these was 15 years old, and the oldest was 62 years old. A total of 69 dreams were collected from them.

The main findings of the content analysis were as follows: 42% of the men's dreams were concrete and 58% were symbolic. Thirty-one percent of them indicated fear and anxiety, while in 20% the theme of helplessness was conspicuous. Thirty-seven percent were defined as masochistic dreams according to the Beck scale.

Jungian analysis yielded interesting results. A striking finding is that an Anima figure appeared only in one dream! The archetype that appears more than any other male archetype in the men's dreams is that of the hero's journey (20% of the dreams). The need for symbols of the hero arises when the ego needs strengthening. But the picture of the hero's journey that emerges in the men's dreams is one of a truncated journey, in which there is a departure, characterized by the effort to distance oneself and flee from the difficulties of daily life, and an attempt to enlist various helpers. The beginning and end of the journey are almost completely removed from the men's dreams, and none of them is a dream in which the full process is reflected.

The following is a dream of a "Helpless Hero" – a 35-year-old man living in a kibbutz near the Gaza border:

> On the way to the town, we lost our car, lie on the sand. Soldiers say something about a skirmish with terrorists. The soldiers move about, shoot in all directions, explosions are heard from afar, and get closer. The soldiers throw hand grenades, also backwards in our direction, we have to move forward, mortars explode, somebody moves backwards and then falls down. A hand grenade falls near him but he doesn't move, I move away and shout to him to move, but it doesn't help. I start to move in the direction of the crossroads, has to take care that the enemy will not catch sight of me.

In contrast to their conscious position, expressed in interviews, of denial or making light of the experience of fear and anxiety, the traumatic elements appearing in their dreams fill in the partial picture.

The women's Animus dreams show almost the opposite of the dreams of men. 40% of the women's Animus dreams indicate fear and anxiety, and the Animus might be "invited" into these dreams because of a need for it. In 26% (!) of the women's dreams the Animus is presented as a savior, protector, or guide. An additional and similar compensatory process in this context is hidden beneath the following fact: figures of an admired Animus appear in the women's dreams – a famous actor or another well-known male figure, usually strong, talented, and masculine. The need for the figure of the Ideal Man can perhaps be understood seeing the lack of such figures in the women's life experience.

Difficulty in making allowances for the weakness of the men also appears as a motif in the search for help in the dreams. While the men turn for some kind of help in 24% of their dreams, the Animus in the women's dreams turn for help in only 6% of the dreams. It appears that the men need help far more than the women are willing to accept or able to understand.

Whereas in many cases the men feel week and incompetent in the situation, the women continue to expect that they should be strong, rescue them, and fulfill their masculine vocation as fathers and spouses. It appears that helplessness, confusion, and the need for help are inconsistent with the unconscious model that the woman have for men, and therefore they receive less consideration from the women. These gaps give a clear sense of the system of expectations with which the men must cope, which exert great internal and external pressure upon them.

## Dream Dome: do dreams shield the psyche in times of continuous stress?

### (Kron, T. Hareven, O. & Goldzweig, G. (2015))

The title of this study – "Dream Dome" – alludes to the rocket defense system named "Iron Dome," employed by the Israel Defense Forces in defending Sderot and its surrounding areas against attacks.

As mentioned in the "participants and methodology" section (see p. 92–93), more women than men agreed to take part in the research. It seemed important to study the women group separately. This group included 44 women, all residents of the Sderot area. The youngest participant was 14 years old and the oldest was 65 years old. A total of 531 dreams collected from the women's group were analyzed.

We divided the research population into three age groups – *Young* 14–19 (19 participants; 204 dreams); *Intermediate* 20–44 (17 participants; 222 dreams); *Old* 45–65 (eight participants; 105 dreams) – and looked for differences in the appearance of themes in their dreams. The percentage of occurrences of each theme in the total number of dreams was calculated for each age group separately.

Looking at the differences in frequency of themes across the three age groups, we found that there are no differences for some themes. Helplessness and loss of control seem to be a common experience for all participants and appear in the dreams of the three age groups with almost the same frequency. The Active ego appears in more than 60% of the dreams, with no differences between the age groups. The Masochism theme appears in 50% of the dreams, again with no differences between the age groups, and can be understood in connection to the reality of the life-threatening stress situation. Altogether, *the differences between age groups indicate that the young age group is the most vulnerable of all.* Indeed, the younger age group has significantly higher frequencies of situation-related stress themes. The frequency of Symbolic dreams is significantly low within the younger age group in comparison to the two other groups. This finding may reflect the traumatic response and the vulnerability of this group as well as corresponding to other findings in dream research regarding people who have experienced stress and trauma (Nadar, 1996; Varvin et al., 2012).

In the following dream of a 17-year-old girl, the present trauma of rocket attacks is associated with the Holocaust:

> It's the holocaust. I am in the sport room with my class mates when suddenly men come in and want to take us. I run away with two friends, somebody captures my friends and I escape into the club, but there someone with long hair and slanted eyes tries to capture me. I hide, and he looks around for me, calling "Jewess, Jewess." I run to the toilettes and hide there, the man comes after me, he has some sort of hammer in his hand and he says he will use it if needed. He doesn't see me but stand right facing me, I breath hard and am afraid that he will hear my breathings and discover me. Suddenly my father

and brother arrive and we succeed in throwing him into a cart, and taking his gun. I hold the gun and shoot at him, the bullets hit his forehead, but he doesn't die, it looks like a computer game. Then my father gives me a pistol and I shoot at him from close range, but he doesn't get hit, so father takes the pistol and hold it close to his head and shoot. He died, his face didn't change and only a little blood came out.

The younger age group has the highest frequency of the theme Togetherness (78%), significantly more than the other two groups. This finding may be understood as seeking social support on an unconscious level as a means of coping with chronic stress. It can safely be hypothesized that the theme Togetherness is compensatory to the traumatic reactions to the harsh reality.

A different portrayal of reactions to the chronic stress situation on the unconscious level surfaces in the dreams of the old age group, where the frequency of the theme "PI" is the highest (51%). Although this finding was not statistically significant, it is compatible with Erich Neumann's principle of "centroversion," which derives from Jung's theoretical premise of individuation (Neumann, 1954). Centroversion is the movement of the psyche toward integration, a process which involves the ego's shifting from preoccupation with the outside reality to the inner world. According to Jung and Neumann, this shift usually occurs about midlife.

The intermediate group records the highest level (18%) of the No-escape theme (dreams which describe futile attempts to run away from the dangerous area), which is significantly more and nearly double that of the younger age group. This finding surprised us at first, as we predicted that this group, including a majority of mothers with young children, would be the most preoccupied with active coping also on the unconscious level. At the same time, this finding can explain the high level of the Active ego theme in this group (64.4%). It can be safely assumed that the ambivalence on the mothers' part in regard to remaining in or leaving the area is more profound. In order to cope with the stress situation these women also need deeper inner work which is conveyed through the relatively high frequency of Symbolic dreams (40.09%, the highest of all the groups and significantly higher when compared to the younger age group). This finding echoes the outcome in a study by Kron and Brosh (2003) on the relationship between dreams during pregnancy and postpartum depression. They found that women whose dreams during pregnancy reflected inner work as preparation for the upcoming birth did not suffer from postpartum depression, while women whose dreams were shallow and "nice" during their pregnancies did suffer from postpartum depression.

The following is a dream of a woman from the intermediate group:

> I was near the kibbutz dining room with my younger son and met my two daughters with another boy. I asked them: "Where will you run to if you hear the warning siren?" They pointed to the house of one of the grandmothers

which has a security room. I said "OK," and started to walk with them in the direction of the house. Suddenly, a huge helicopter came out of this house and flew very low in the direction of the dining room. I looked at it admiringly and said to one of the kids: "Look, it's a show," believing that these were our soldiers, but suddenly the helicopter opened up and out came figures from *Star Trek* and started shooting. One figure shouted: "Run for your life," and I started to run in the direction of our home with my son.

All elements of trying to cope with the danger are in this dream. The dreamer prepares herself and her children for the coming attack, and as kind of compensation the enemy is not real but phantasy figures. But reality is stronger than phantasy, and the dreamer runs for shelter, defending her son.

## Psyche under stress: dreams of Israelis and Palestinians in a time of war

### *(Kron and Halfon (2015, 2016))*

The last research presented here is a study of the recent war (2014–2015) between Israel and Hamas (called in Israel Operation Protective Edge) as reflected in the dreams of two groups, the inhabitants of southern Israel and Palestinians on the West Bank.

Participants included 38 Palestinian women and 25 Palestinian men, as well as children, living in villages and towns in the West Bank and 18 Israeli women and 10 Israeli men, residents of the Sderot area near the Gaza border. The disproportionately low number of Israeli subjects may have been due to the difficulty of their participation in the midst of the rocket attacks.

A total of 141 dreams were collected, 109 from Palestinians and 32 from Israelis. Table 6.2 summarizes the list of themes and their frequencies in the Palestinians and the Israelis groups.

Although we did not find statistically significant differences between the two groups in the frequencies of trauma indicators, we did find differences in the themes. The most statistically significant difference we found among the groups is a preponderance of symbolic dreams in the Palestinian group as opposed to a preponderance of concrete traumatic dreams in the Israeli group. As we understand it, the significant difference between the two groups is due to the proximity of the Israeli subjects to the war zone in Gaza where they were under constant bombardment and threat of terrorism, while the effects of the war on the West Bank where the Palestinian dreamers live were experienced indirectly.

There is a higher percentage of themes related to symbols, imagination, religion, and magic in the dreams of the Palestinian group. Animals and imaginary creatures are a common theme in Palestinian dreams, one that never appeared in the dreams of the Israeli group. Most of the animals and creatures were described as dangerous and threatening, bearing death and destruction to the dreamer and causing the dreamer to flee or slay them.

**TABLE 6.2** Themes' frequencies in both research groups

| Israelis | Palestinians | Themes |
|---|---|---|
| (75%) 24 | (12.04%) 13 | Concrete traumatic dream |
| (15.63%) 5 | (31.48%) 34 | Symbolic traumatic dream |
| (90.63%) 29 | (43.52%) 47 | Total number of traumatic dreams |
| (71.88%) 23 | (2.78%) 3 | Concrete enemy |
| (6.25%) 2 | (21.3%) 23 | Symbolic enemy |
| (78.13%) 25 | (24.08) 26 | Total number of enemy |
| (3.13%) 1 | (2.78%) 3 | Non-threatening animals |
| (0%) 0 | (6.48%) 7 | Imaginary animals and creatures |
| (3.13%) 1 | (11.11%) 12 | Dangerous animals |
| (6.25%) 2 | (16.67%) 18 | Total number of animals with imaginary animals and creatures |
| (34.38%) 11 | (1.85%) 2 | Soldiers |
| (15.63%) 5 | (0.93%) 1 | Rockets |
| (15.63%) 5 | (0%) 0 | Tunnels |
| (56.25%) 18 | (2.78%) 3 | Total number of soldiers, rockets and tunnels |
| (3.13%) 1 | (18.52%) 20 | Positive elements |
| (3.13%) 1 | (20.37%) 22 | Religion and magic |
| (68.75%) 22 | (18.52%) 20 | Violence |
| (28.13%) 9 | (10.19%) 11 | Threats to the home |

The following dream of a 27-year-old Palestinian man is an example:

> I dreamed I was driving away from town out near the desert. And suddenly there was thunder and lightning and rain fell. The roads filled with water. I noticed that the wheels were on fire and made a lot of noise. I stopped the car and got out and a big bird swooped down from the sky and snatched up the car and I stood there feeling sad.

In many of the traumatic concrete dreams within the Israeli group, men see themselves as either fighting or helpless and in flight – in similar fashion to the dreams of men in the study "Helpless Heroes." Women dreamers express concern for others.

In both groups, however, archetypal symbols of evil like snakes and terrorists emerge from underground, in keeping with the Jungian approach to the collective unconscious. Another parallel is the appearance of archetypal evil swooping down from the sky in the form of predatory birds and rockets. The enemy in both groups is dehumanized and without individual identity, a projection of the shadow which threatens to destroy the collective.

## In conclusion

Dreams can help us identify people who suffer from emotional distress, even if they do not report specific symptoms of PTSD, and seem "OK." Early detection and treatment can help prevent later severity of delayed PTSD. Working with dreams can enhance coping with continuous stress situations and recovering from emotional distress. Many of our subjects reported that writing the dreams in the dream diary was for them, as formulated by a woman from Sderot, "self therapy." Last, but not least, dreams, like emotions and feelings, are part of our human nature. I believe in the power of dream telling and hearing to open a way to the possibility of dialogue with the "Other," even when that Other is perceived as the enemy.

## Note

1 Many thanks to my dedicated and creative students: Adina Dick, Tamar Halfon, Or Hareven, Noam Knoler, Inbal Klein, Tal Lotem, Iris Maneri, and Irit Vaadya.

## References

Crocq, M.A., & Crocq, L. (2000). From shell shock and war neurosis to posttraumatic stress disorder. A history of psychotraumatology. *Dialogues Clin Neurosci, 2*(1), 47–55.

Freud, S. (1920). *Beyond the pleasure principle: Standard Edition 18* (pp. 3–36). London: The Hogarth Press.

Gelkopf, M., Berger, R., Bleich, A., & Silver, R.C. (2012). Protective factors and predictors of vulnerability to chronic stress: A comparative study of four communities after seven years of continuous rocket fire. *Social Science and Medicine, 74*, 757–766.

Hartmann, E. (1995). Making connections in a safe place: Is dreaming psychotherapy? *Dreaming, 5*, 213–228.

Hartmann, E. (2000). The waking-to-dreaming continuum, and the effects of emotion. *Behavioral and Brain Sciences, 23*, 947–950.

Hartmann, E. (2008). The nature and functions of dreaming. In D. Barrett & P. McNamara (Eds.), *The new science of dreaming* (Vol. 3; pp. 171–192). Westport: Praeger.

Hartmann, E., Rosen, R., & Grace, N. (1998). Contextualizing images in dreams: More frequent and more intense after trauma. *Sleep, 21S*, 284.

Hartmann, E., & Stickgold, R. (2000). Contextualizing images in content obtained from different sleep and waking states. *Sleep, 23S*, A172.

Hartmann, E., Zborowski, M., Rosen, R., & Grace, N. (2001). Contextualizing images in dreams: more intense after abuse and trauma. *Dreaming, 11*, 115–126.

Hartmann, E., & Basile, R. (2003). Dream imagery becomes more intense after 9/11/01. *Dreaming, 13*, 61–66.

Hartmann, E., & Brezler, T. (2006). A systematic change in dreams after 9/11/01. *Sleep, 29-S*, A-48.

Helminen, E., & Punamaki, R-L. (2008). Contextualized emotional images in children's dreams: Psychological adjustment in conditions of military trauma. *International Journal of Behavioral Development, 32*(3), 177–187.

Jung, C.G. (2010 Paperback edition). *Children dreams: Notes from the seminar given in 1936–1940.* (Ed. Meyer-Grass M. & Jung L). Princeton, NJ: Princeton University Press.

Kron, T., & Brosh, A. (2003). Can dreams during pregnancy predict postpartum depression? *Dreaming, 13*(2), 67–81.

Kron, T., & Halfon, T. (2015). The Psyche under stress: Dreams of Israelis and Palestinians in a time of war. *3rd European Conference on Analytical Psychology, Trieste, Italy – Analysis at the Cultural Crossroads.*

Kron, T., Halfon, T. (2016). Dreaming under fire: Dreams of Israelis and Palestinians in a time of war. *Prague conference on Civilians at War. Losses, Recovery and the Experience of the Helpers.*

Kron, T., & Hareven, O. (2011). Helpless heroes: The dreams of men and women in the shadow of continuous life-threatening missile attacks. *28 Annual Conference of the International Association for the Study of Dreams.* Kerkrade: The Netherlands.

Kron, T., Hareven, O. (2012). Dreams in the nights of terror: Continuous stress and coping. In *Montreal 2010 facing multiplicity: Psyche, nature, culture. Proceedings of the XVIIIth congress of the international association for analytical psychology.* Zurich: Daimon Pub.

Kron, T., Hareven, O., & Goldzweig, G. (2015). Dream dome: Do dreams shield the psyche in times of continuous stress? *Dreaming, 25*(2), 160–172.

Nadar, K. (1996). Children's traumatic dreams. In D. Barrett (Ed.), *Trauma and Dreams* (pp. 11–24). London: Harvard University Press.

Neumann, E. (1954). *The origins and history of consciousness.* Translated from the German by R.F.C. Hull. Bollingen Series XLII. Princeton, NJ: Princeton University Press.

Punamäki, R-La., Ali, K.J., Ismahil, K.H., & Nuutinen, J. (2005). Trauma, dreaming, and psychological distress among Kurdish children. *Dreaming, 15*(3), 178–194.

Schredl, M., & Reinhard, I. (2008). Gender differences in dream recall: A meta-analysis. *Journal of Sleep Research, 17*, 125–131.

Valli, K., Revonsuo, A., Pälkäs, O., Ismahil, K.H., Ali, K.J., & Punamäki, R-L. (2005). The threat simulation theory of the evolutionary function of dreaming: Evidence from dreams of traumatized children. *Consciousness and Cognition, 14*, 188–218.

Valli, K., Revonsuo, A., Pälkäs, O., & Punamäki, R-L. (2006). The effect of Trauma on dream content: A field study of Palestinian children. *Dreaming, 16*(2), 63–87.

Van der Kolk, B.A., Blitz, R., Burr, W., Sherry, S., & Hartmann, E. (1984). Nightmares and trauma: A comparison of nightmares after combat with lifelong nightmares in veterans. *American Journal of Psychiatry, 141*(2), 187–190.

Varvin, S., Fischmann, T., Jovic, V., Rosenbaum, B., & Hau, S. (2012). Traumatic dreams. Symbolization gone astray. In P. Fonagy et al. (Eds.), *The significance of dreams.* London: Karnac.

Wilmer, H.A. (1982). Vietnam and madness: Dreams of schizophrenic veterans. *Journal of Academic Psychoanalysis, 10*(1), 46–65.

Wilmer, H.A. (2001). The healing nightmare: War dreams of Vietnam veterans. In D. Barrett (Ed.), *Trauma and dreams* (pp. 85–99). Cambridge, MA: Harvard University Press.

# 7

# NEUROSCIENTIFIC STUDIES OF TRAUMA APPLIED TO JUNGIAN PSYCHOLOGY

*Joseph Cambray*

## Introduction

Beginning with the hypothesis that Jungian analysis is a trauma-based psychology stemming from Jung's own history, this chapter will proceed to examine some of the neurobiological correlates of mind, especially those associated with traumatic injuries. This takes us to the psychosomatic pole of archetypal dynamics and into the realm of the psychoid. The unique contribution Jungian psychology can offer in these areas will be brought forward.

In *Memories, Dreams and Reflections*, Jung notes a key transformative moment when as a young man he was reading a textbook by Krafft-Ebbing. A flash of illumination came with the resolution to what had been a major vocational dilemma; his two interests, natural science and spirituality, could be legitimately combined by going into psychiatry. It offered "an empirical field common to biological and spiritual facts . . . the place where the collision of nature and spirit became a reality" (Jung, 1961a, pp. 108–109). This transformative experience was predicated on Krafft-Ebbing's description

> of the "subjective character" of psychiatric textbooks. So I thought, the textbook is in part the subjective confession of the author. With his specific prejudice, with the totality of his being, he stands behind the objectivity of his experiences and responds to the "disease of the personality" with the whole of his own personality. Never had I heard anything of this sort from my teacher at the clinic. . . . these few hints cast such a transfiguring light on psychiatry that I was irretrievably drawn under its spell.
>
> *(Jung, 1961a, p. 109)*

This guiding insight remained with Jung throughout his life.

In a 1929 article contrasting himself with Freud, Jung wrote about the "truth" of psychology in similar language:

> true expression consists in giving form to what is observed.
>
> The modern psychologist, however ambitious, can hardly claim to have achieved more than this. Our psychology is the more or less successfully formulated confession of a few individuals, and so far as each of them conforms more or less to a type, his confession can be accepted as a fairly valid description of a large number of people.
>
> *(Jung, 1961b, paras. 771–772)*

And again, in 1935 in a discussion after his fourth Tavistock lecture, he commented:

> I consider my contribution to psychology to be my subjective confession. It is my personal psychology, my prejudice that I see psychological facts as I do. I admit that I see things in such and such a way. But I expect Freud and Adler to do the same and confess that their ideas are their subjective point of view. So far as we admit our personal prejudice, we are really contributing towards an objective psychology. We cannot help being prejudice by our ancestors, who want to look at things in a certain way, and so we instinctively have certain points of view.
>
> *(Jung, 1976, para. 275)*

Taking Jung at his word, then, requires us to view his theories at least in part through the lens of his subjective experiences in conjunction with his personality. In doing so, I wish to briefly draw upon his early developmental history to suggest Jung had significant multiple traumas in childhood, which inflluenced his construction of psychological theories.

For the sake of space I will only mention a few of the known facts about potentially traumatizing events in Jung's life. First was the condition of his mother even prior to his conception. She had had two stillborn daughters and a son who only lived for 5 days; Carl Gustav was her first surviving child. She became lethargic and depressed, even after a move to Laufen 6 months later (Bair, 2003, pp. 18–20). Apparently she had postpartum depression and marital tension grew; Carl was cared for by a maid and often slept with his father. Eventually his mother was hospitalized for her depression on several occasions, with long stays away from home, and he was taken to live for a time with an older aunt. A series of distressing events ensued: at his father's vicarage the bodies of those who drowned in the falls nearby, often suicides, were brought to an outbuilding – young Carl, fascinated, sought to observe. This was repeated when the family moved to Kleinhüningen. After a dam broke and the ensuing flood killed a number of local people, Carl, then about five years old, searched for and found a body (Bair, 2003, p. 26). After the birth of his younger sister when he was 9, his mother appeared to him to have an uncanny side, especially at night – in part a manifestation of attachment difficulties.

At school Carl began to have conflicts with peers and was ferocious in his defense of self. He developed school phobia for a time, which he heroically pushed through, but clearly had become psychologically complexed. Later in his correspondence with Freud, he revealed that as an adolescent he had been a "victim of a sexual assault" by a highly admired figure, likely a priest to whom his father was close. Given his size and strength at the time, it seems unlikely that he was physically overpowered (Bair, 2003, p. 71); that he linked it with his disgust at having a "religious crush" on Freud points to the ambivalence in his feelings about these events.

After medical school, study of mental illness and trauma became Jung's daily work in his first professional position, as medical staff at the Burhölzli psychiatric asylum in Zurich. As a part of his psychiatric training, after a couple of years on staff, he was sent to Paris to work with Pierre Janét at the Salpetriere Hospital. Janét's work with hysterics had led him to develop a dissociative model of the psyche. This has come to be recognized as a key early theory of trauma psychology. Jung adopted much of it in his own theories (for discussion, see Haule, 1984, 1986).

Jung's subsequent research at the Burghölzli, which included making psychophysical measurement during word association experiments, led him to formulate one of his signature concepts, the feeling-toned complex. This research correlated various types of disruptions to normal associative processing of language with simultaneous physiological measures of anxiety, such as changes in galvanic skin response, breathing rhythms and intensity, blood volume in a finger, pulse rates, and so on. This work was not only the first experimental validation of Freud's conception of a dynamic unconscious, but also supported the notion of the natural dissociability of the psyche for Jung, bringing him in line with the French dissociationists, as well as having forensic applications (effectively, the first "lie detector" device). These experiments could be seen as early forms of cognitive neuroscientific research, highlighting the impact of affect on cognitive processing. This places Jung and his theories in a precursor role to some contemporary explorations in the neuroscience of trauma. Thus both Jung's personal history and his early professional work reflect an orientation to trauma studies.

However, the most significant and meaningful processing of a traumatic experience began about a decade later for Jung. In the wake of his break with Freud, amid much soul-searching as to his direction in life, Jung underwent a tremendous psychic upheaval starting in late 1913. During the initial period, he felt he was "menaced with a psychosis" (Jung, 1961a, p. 176). Though he emerged within six months from the most intense aspects of this encounter with the unconscious, it took more than 15 years for him to fully digest these experiences. The results of this processing of psychological trauma are recorded in his *Red Book*, recently published, but they are also reflected in many of his major theoretical conceptualizations and clinical practices, which came from this period and afterwards – for example, the initial personal development and subsequent clinical use of "active imagination" (Cambray, 2015, pp. 83–84). Key ideas such as the archetypes, the collective unconscious, the self (as a holistic, supraordinate archetype), individuation, psychological types, and synchronicity all arose out of his metabolizing of these experiences

(Shamdasani Intro to RB; the SF RB conf. papers, etc.). This transformative period made him into the figure most contemporary people think of, when he is brought up. It is what made Jung *Jung*.

Contextualizing Jung's transformative period, we can readily see it is occuring against a backdrop of massive, collective trauma: the First World War and the consequent reconfiguration of nation states. The subsequent rise of facism and the horrors of the Second World War immersed Jung in further, prolonged cultural trauma, even as he became more skillful at handling his and his patients' individual responses to these traumas.

In the face of these massive cultural traumas, Jung continued to pursue the fundamental impulse that led him into psychiatry, a marriage of nature and spirit. One aspect of this was his growing interest in the traditions of alchemy, with its imaginings of riches obtained through transformations of the unwanted, taken by Jung as meaningful psychological metaphors for the individuation of the personality. Another aspect of this desire for union was the dialogue with modern physics, especially through his engagement with Wolfgang Pauli. Together the two, physicist and psychologist,[1] forged a radically new vision of the relationship between matter and psyche, the psychoid archetype, and articulated in depth the idea of synchronicity as a psycho-physical reality, based on descriptions of acausal but meaningful coincidences.

## Jungian and post-Jungian uses of neuroscience and complexity theory

While microscopic studies of individual neuron had begun in the late 19th century, Jung did not actively incorporate much of this material into his theories. However, after World War II, the wealth of new technologies available along with the advent of molecular biology generated discoveries that began to interest Jung's followers. By 1953, Nathaniel Kleitman and Eugene Aserinsky observed rapid eye movement (REM)sleep; this was soon associated with dreaming. Several Jungians including Tom Kirsch published articles on this in the psychiatric literature of that era; see Kirsch's "The Relationship of the REM State to Analytical Psychology" (1968). During the 1950s, Paul McClean proposed the triune brain (reptilian brain stem and cerebellum; limbic; and neo-cortical systems), and imaginings about where archetypes might reside in these brain systems entered into Jungian discussions.

By 1957, Roger Sperry and colleagues were beginning research that lead to the study of patients who had had their corpus callosums severed to prevent the spread of grand mal epileptic seizures. Sperry's ongoing research on the quality of consciousness associate with each hemisphere and lateralization of functions earned him a Nobel Prize. The models of the mind derived from these works were recognized as having affinities with Jung's ideas, and some Jungian authors incorporated these ideas (e.g., Rossi, 1977). Jenny Yates, a Jungian analyst, became a visiting associate in Sperry's lab in 1984 after completing her analytic training in Zurich. She eventually published her finding in *Psyche and the Split-Brain*. While interesting speculations emerged from Sperry's work, the assignment of specific Jungian concepts to the results of this early brain research were overly optimistic and premature, although stimulating and well intentioned.

More recently, surveying the past 20 years, an important new direction began with David Tresan's 1996 paper "Jungian Metapsychology and Neurobiological Theory." Tresan brought the challenge of integrating contemporary brain research into Jungian theory building and highlighted the utility of studies in complexity theory for deepening our understanding of the mind–body relationship. It should be noted that most of the information in the neurobiological literature up to this time was from patients who either had brain injuries, lesions, or significant psychological traumas. As with the entire analytic enterprise, the study of the psyche arose from exploration of traumatic, unconscious, or pathological states.

Following Tresan's work, a number of authors suggested ways to employ studies from complexity research, especially those focusing on self-organizing systems with emergent properties. These ideas were applied to the Jungian notions of complexes and archetypes, and therefore by extension to trauma psychology (Saunders & Skar, 2001; Knox, 2003; Hogenson, 2001, 2004; McDowell, 2001). In 2002, Cambray first applied this approach to synchronicity and that has generated more literature on the topic from multiple authors. Clinical applications of complexity have also been made, e.g., François Martin Vallas has produced a series of articles in the last decade employing an emergentist perspective in studies of the transference/countertransference field (see for example 2006 and 2008); and at the 2010 International Association for Analytical Psychology (IAAP) Congress, Cambray presented clinical material based on "moments of complexity" in work with a patient with a multiple, complex trauma history (Cambray, 2011).

Around the same time, a related topic which gained interest in Jungian circles was the role and importance of mirror neurons first observed by the research group around Giacomo Rizolatti at the University of Parma. These neurons fire both in the performance of an action and in the observation through various sensory channels of the same action. They therefore are thought to form a fundamental link between the perceptual and interior worlds, though they are certainly not the only components. Many psychologists and neuroscientists see these neurons as holding one key to the experience of empathy, though again this is far more complex than can be accounted for by this neuronal category. Nevertheless, research on this class of neurons has brought about a revival of interest in empathy, as these neurons seem to be at the core of our ability to know the minds of others, what is known as "theory of mind," and have an important role in our abilities for aesthetic appreciation. Therapeutically they may be deeply involved in forming interactive fields and are something we are born with; but it would seem there also might be some plasticity with these neurons, e.g., psychotherapeutic and analytic trainings may partial involve enhancement of neural pathways with such neurons, or even more speculatively may stimulate some neurogenesis of these neurons. Deficits in these neurons and/or the networks they participate in are thought to be important in autism and psychopathy. Failures in empathy and difficulties sorting out inner and outer experiences are also typical in cases of traumatized individuals. However, the relevant neurobiology of those who suffer from trauma has been focused on brain networks, as will be discussed below. The interrelationship between the mirror neuronal systems and various brain networks has yet to be ascertained and is one area in which future developments are sought.

In the last several years a growing number of publications by analytical psychologists attempting to integrate the impact of these neurons into theory and practice have been made. A reassessment of the relevance of imitation in analytic learning has been considered (Cambray, 2007), as well as arguments both supporting an emergentist view of archetypes (Knox, 2009), and challenging this notion and that of a psychodynamic unconscious (Hogenson, 2009). As the embryology, post-natal development, and full distribution of this class of neurons remains unknown at present, it is hoped that more research will be conducted to give a fuller picture that will assist in developing a more complete picture of the overlaps and differences between brain, mind, and psyche (likely a series of highly complex, nested, emergent relations susceptible to disruptions by trauma).

There are also other groups of neurons that display fascinating properties and likewise deserve attention, for example, spindle or von Economo neurons. In brief, these are large nerve cells with quite long axons, and are thought to be involved in rapid transmission of neural signals, getting information quickly to disparate parts of the brain for processing. They appear to occur only in social animals; besides being found in humans, they have been discovered in the great apes, whales, and dolphins. These neurons are primarily located in the anterior cingulate cortex (ACC) and frontal insula (FI), which are linked with social emotions and self-awareness – they are also regions which are involved in the brain networks to be discussed below. These neurons seem poised to transmit neural data about the social environment to many other regions in the brain. For large brained creatures this facilitates rapid assessment and response to social information, indicating it is of great importance to survival. When these cells are lost or destroyed, through illness such as frontotemporal dementia, the afflicted exhibit losses in self-awareness and empathic capacities, traumatic for themselves and their loved ones. Jungian analyst Dyane Sherwood discussed these neurons and their implications in a chapter titled "The Embodied Psyche: Movement, Sensation, Affect" (Sherwood, 2010).

## Memory and the future

The field of memory studies has undergone an explosive resurgence in the past several decades, especially as technological innovations have allowed remarkable levels of monitoring of brain activities correlated with action associated with memory. According to a number of current researchers (e.g., Moscovitch, 2007, pp. 17–18), "memory does not exist until it is recovered . . . until it is revealed in behavior or thought". For these researchers memory is multi-staged, occurring through distributed processes (operating in a variety of brain regions) of encoding of representations, consolidation, storage, and retrieval, often with re-consolidation to follow as a recalled event is stored anew.

Modern conceptions of the forms of memory encompass a great variety of phenomena. For example, we now have many categories of memory with some overlapping functions: references can readily be found to explicit, implicit, procedural, emotional, semantic, working, declarative, and non-declarative, as well as the more commonly held notion of episodic or autobiographical memory. However, even the act of remembering events from our personal past, using episodic memory, is now recognized as a (re)constructive activity in its own right, involving multiple brain centers and having a creative-synthetic dimension rather than being a simple reproduction of statically stored contents (see Addis, Wong, & Schacter, 2007, p. 15, and Schacter, 2007) – this bears resemblance to some contemporary understandings of Freud's notion of *Nachträglichkeit* as a retranscription of memory.

In a series of papers, Daniel Schacter of Harvard University and colleagues have been using fMRI studies to investigate the relationship of the regions of the brain which appear activated when subjects remember past events as compared with their imagining future events. The data has led the researchers to conclude that "all regions active during the construction and elaboration of past events were also active during future event construction and elaboration" (Addis, Wong, & Schacter, 2007, p. 15). Further, they note "future events recruited a number of additional regions thought to be involved in prospective thinking and generation" (p. 16), though with differing intensities. For example, only the future imaginings activate the right hippocampus.

Based on their results, this group has made a radical but reasonable suggestion that the episodic system may actually have as its primary role "not reminiscence but rather future thinking" (Addis, Wong, & Schacter, 2007, p. 15), and that this would also help to explain "the pattern of episodic deficits in amnesic patients, who exhibit significant impairments in not only past, but also future episodic thinking" (p. 15). In presenting a "constructive episodic simulation" hypothesis, in which "episodic memory supports the construction of future events by extracting and recombining stored information into a simulation of a novel event" (Schacter & Addis, 2007), they are indeed creating a mental marriage of memory and the future. This has parallels with prospective function of the psyche in Jungian theory, individuation as maturation of the personality into its fullest potentials.

Schacter et al. have extended their model to memory problems generally:

> some of the vulnerabilities of episodic memory, such as memory distortions and illusions, may be attributable to the role of the episodic system in allowing us to mentally simulate our personal futures by flexibly drawing on elements of the past.
>
> *(Addis, Wong, & Schacter, 2007, p. 15)*

Thus in working with patient's memories, therapists do well to attend to their prospective and metaphoric or symbolic significance, while recognizing the impact of the context in which they are occurring, i.e., at this particular moment, with this therapist – what could be termed the *kairos* of recall. The suggestion is that memory is not only an emergent process arising from interactions among elements of a distributed neurological base, but also that the act of recollection in therapy is a reflection of the state of the dyad including the field they are in; the action of memory in therapy can therefore be considered indicative of a moment of complexity.

In the recent past, consideration of ways to interrupt the reconsolidation of traumatic memories as a means to reduce PTSD symptoms have become a focus of research interest. For example in "Xenon Impairs Reconsolidation of Fear Memories in a Rat Model of Post-traumatic Stress Disorder (PTSD)," Meloni, Gillis, Manoukian, and Kaufman (2014) model the way xenon gas might be applied to erase traumatic fears and anxieties. However, tampering with memory risks meddling with what makes us who we are and raises ethical concerns about manipulations of our construction of reality.

## Three brain networks

By the mid-1970s, biological psychiatry researchers were exploring regional patterns of activity in the brain. However, this was still primarily formulated into a kind of contemporary phrenology, with neurobiological brain "modules" serving as loci of mental functioning. Then around 2001, as scientific advances allowed enhanced resolution in a number of brain imaging technologies, some curious, unanticipated phenomena emerged. As with so much of discoveries made in science, serendipity played a significant role, which hints at a synchronistic core in the discovery process, linked to the cultural moment when it appears. The surprising finding came when measurements of metabolic process were made of the whole brain when it was not engaged actively in a task but was in a "passive" state. The anticipation was that such passive states would be "rest states" with decreased brain activity. However, the evidence was completely contrary based on the total amounts of glucose and oxygen being consumed (measured by PET and fMRI scans). The research team lead by Marcus Raichle concluded with verifying "the existence of an organized, baseline default mode of brain function that is suspended during specific goal directed behaviors baseline" (Raichle et al., 2001). This "default mode functioning" in turn generated a search for where the metabolic activity was occurring when no overt mental task was being undertaken. The default mode was quickly recognized as comprising numerous components widely dispersed throughout the cortex (Mazoyer et al., 2001).

Cortical networks for working memory and executive functions sustain the conscious resting state in man. The specific loci involved and the mental function implicated in what is now termed the "default mode network" (DMN) were reviewed in detail by Buckner, Andrews-Hanna, and Schacter in 2008.[23] There are actually two closely interacting subsystems here. The hippocampus and adjacent areas in the MTL (medial temporal lobe), which are associated with episodic/autobiographical memory, have been found to be correlated with the other key hubs of the of the default network including the cingulate, pre-frontal and inferior parietal cortices. This second cluster of sites of the DMN have been linked to self-referential mental simulations which include reflecting on the mental activities of others (theory of mind) while drawing upon the memory system, and include imaginative constructions of possible future scenarios. Buckner et al. in their extensive 2008 review suggest the DMN "*is* the core brain system associated with spontaneous cognition, and further that people have a strong tendency to engage the default network during moments when they are not otherwise occupied by external tasks" (2008, p. 15), which they liken to William James's "stream of consciousness." Furthermore, recent studies suggest that the degree of segregation of components of the DMN vary with age and brain condition/mental state, including degree of traumatization; this will be discussed later.

A number of important internal mental processes that require mental simulation evoke activity in brain regions overlapping the DMN as noted in the review, including autobiographical memory, envisioning the future, theory of mind, and moral decision making. Fortunately there has been an implicit normalizing and valuing of the DMN along with the various psychological activities associated with it in the recent neuroscience literature. This may be especially important to the analytic community as Buckner et al. observe: "[t]here [i]s a strong correlation in regional default network activity with the participants' daydreaming activity" (2008, p. 16).

Thus, the evidence suggests that this is *the* neurological system which becomes active when we enter into states of reverie – a topic that has direct bearing on the kind of consciousness essential to the analytic process and possibly part of the neurology engaged when "active imagination" is undertaken. Looking forward, this is an area I anticipate will revitalize broad interest in internal and introspective states of mind and so holds great promise for Analytical Psychology.

Additional evidence demonstrated that there is "competition between sensory processing and spontaneous default network fluctuations . . . [and] that transient lapses in the control of attention may lead to a shift in attention from the external world to internal mentation" (Buckner et al., 2008, p. 17). The opposition between what is termed the central executive network (CEN), consisting of dorsolateral prefrontal and posterior parietal cortices engaged in higher-order cognitive and attentional control, including verbal learning and executive functioning, and DMN systems is seen as a dynamic equilibrium. Initially framed as an "anticorrelation" between the two networks (when one is "on," the other is "off"), related studies revealed that a third network, the salience network (SN), controls the switching between the CEN and the DMN (Seeley et al., 2007; Menon & Uddin, 2010).

In particular, the SN[4] is thought to monitor "the saliency of external inputs and internal brain events" and serve as an integral hub mediating other functional networks (Menon & Uddin, 2010, fig. 2). Thus when the SN is alerted to significant external stimuli it initiates a switch between the DMN and the CEN. According to Menon and Uddin, "in our model, sensory and limbic inputs are processed by the anterior insula (AI), which detects salient events and initiates appropriate control signals to regulate behavior and homeostatic state" (2010, fig. 4). These studies are part of an evolving paradigm for understanding the way the brain processes sensations, emotions, and cognitive tasks via functional networks marked by intrinsic connectivity between the different nodes within the networks, moving toward a synthesis of body, brain, and mind.

High DMN activity would therefore likely be a significant neurological correlate of introversion and suggest further explorations of this link are warranted. The research on DMN as a normal function of our mental life also can potentially be of practical assistance in dealing with the larger culture. Thus, the tendency to pathologize introversion by making it a part of a syndrome of reclusiveness, withdrawal, and affective constriction was successfully countered in discussions of the criteria for inclusion in the DSM-V.

In the past decade, research on the DMN has indicated that dysfunctions associated with it are involved in at least three major psychiatric illnesses/disease: autism, schizophrenia, and Alzheimer's; some researchers would also add depression. One major viewpoint on autism is that

> [d]evelopmental disruption . . . linked to the MPFC [medial pre-frontal cortex] might result in a mind that is environmentally focused and absent a conception of other people's thoughts. . . . the failure to modulate the default network in ASD [autism spectrum disorder] is driven by differential cognitive mentation during rest, specifically a lack of self-referential processing.
>
> *(Buckner et al., 2008, pp. 26–27)*

However, the argument has subtleties, as the authors were careful not to specifically locate the origins of autistic pathology in the DMN but rather view ASD as adversely impacting the DMN:

> disruptions . . . may not be linked to the originating developmental events that cause ASD but rather reflect a developmental endpoint. That is, dysfunction of the default network and associated symptoms may emerge as an indirect consequence of early developmental events that begin outside the network. . . . the default network may be largely intact in ASD but under utilized perhaps because of a dysfunction in control systems that regulate its use.
>
> *(Buckner et al., 2008, pp. 26–27)*

Given there is also a substantial body of research identifying mirror neuron deficits with ASD, an implication of these last remarks is worth making explicit. The dysfunction here could be seen as inhibiting the full emergence of the self and can easily be confused with the impact of trauma.

If this argument has merit, we may be witnessing in this phenomenon a cultural equivalent in the 21st century of the role played by hysterics at the turn of the 20th century. The discovery of the dynamic unconscious within the context of psychoanalysis came from Freud's work with hysterics. Jung was able to deepen this, in part by examining the mental processes of schizophrenic patients, into a rich, archetypal world of symbolism.[5] However, symbolic approaches are not particularly useful as interventions with autistic conditions/sectors, instead creating space for emergent processes to arise seem more helpful (recent publications by Toshio Kawai are pointing in this direction, e.g., Kawai, 2009). My suggestion is that ASD patients may be leading us into a new (revised) view of the how the brain-mind-psyche operates at the far edges of our psychological universe. The other group of patients who have come to capture our collective imagination are the trauma survivors, and we will need to be careful to differentiate the two groups.

## Altered states, trauma, and brain networks

Applying graph theoretic models derived from mathematics, physics, and computer science to understand complex systems with multiple interacting parts has proven quite useful in the exploration of brain networks outlined earlier. Dynamic changes, as over a lifetime, are now being investigated. For example, researchers at the University of Texas–Dallas present "findings indicate that increasing age is associated with decreasing segregation of functional brain systems" and that "individuals with less segregated association system exhibited the poorest memory ability" (Chan et al., 2014, E5002). Healthy aging brains tend to become less segregated and less specialized; the global efficiency (GE) of the brain is thereby enhanced. The potential benefits of the increased GE were not explored by these researcher, but may have relevance to the individuation process. Trauma also impairs connectivity (see below).

In a new study, Robin Carhart-Harris and his colleagues at Imperial College London observed:

> LSD reduces connectivity within brain networks, or the extent to which nerve cells or neurons within a network fire in synchrony. LSD also seems to reduce the extent to which separate brain networks remain distinct in their patterns or synchronization of firing. Overall, LSD interferes with the patterns of activation in the different brain networks that underlie human thought and behavior.
>
> *(American College of Neuropsychopharmacology, 10 December 2015)*

Again segregation was decreased throughout the networks, this time by the use of LSD. While this study focused on the chaotic brain state engendered by LSD, it did not discuss recent, renewed interest in therapeutic uses of psychedelics. One research area would then be to explore any potential value these less segregated states might have for the development of the personality.

Other recent research links brain networks to religious beliefs (Kapogiannis et al., 2014), early detection of neurodegenerative disorders (Pessina, 2015), and to traumatic brain injuries with PTSD symptoms (Spielberg, McGlinchey, Milberg, & Salat, 2015). According to Spielberg et al.:

> weaker connectivity was linked to higher PTSD re-experiencing symptoms, one of which was present only in veterans with comorbid mTBI [mild trauma brain injury]. Re-experiencing was also linked to worse functional segregation (necessary for specialized processing) and diminished influence of key regions on the network, including the hippocampus.
>
> *(2015)*

The hippocampal involvement could be linked with the tendency to overreact to benign stimuli that echo an aspect of a traumatic memory.

Even more generally, adverse impacts of trauma on brain networks of individuals when PTSD does not develop has now been demonstrated (Stark et al., 2015). These authors note: "Results suggest that trauma has a measurable, enduring effect upon the functional dynamics of the brain, even in individuals who experience trauma but do not develop PTSD." This raises important issues for therapists working with individuals who have been robust and/or fortunate enough not to manifest full PTSD symptomatology but nevertheless suffer, often unconsciously, in the aftermath of traumatic experience. As indicated in the introduction, I believe C.G. Jung would be classified in this last group.

In an excellent review of the intrinsic connectivity networks (CEN/DMN/SN) involvement in PTSD and related disorders, Ruth Lanius and colleagues detail how each of these networks are effected by traumatic experiences. They proceed then to offer neural, pharmacological, and psychotherapeutic interventions to counter the adverse effects of the trauma experinces (Lanius et al., 2015). Previously, the team headed by Professor Lanius examined alterations in connectivity of the SN activated by direct gaze for PTSD sufferers; this research was co-sponsored by the IAAP (Thome, Frewen, Daniels, Densmore, & Lanius, 2014).

An initial report of this research was given by Margaret Wilkinson at the IAAP Congress in Copenhagen in 2013. In particular it was noted:

> PTSD symptom severity was positively associated with the integration of the right anterior cingulate cortex (ACC) and left insula within the SN in patients with PTSD. . . . [A]nalyses revealed a higher activation of the SN during direct gaze as compared to avert gaze, which was more pronounced in patients with PTSD as compared to healthy control subjects. . . . [P]articipants with PTSD showed enhanced coupling of the amygdala and the insula within the SN as compared to healthy control subjects.
>
> *(Wilkinson and Woodhead, 2014)*

These results confirm clinical intuitions with neuroscientific evidence, indicating accentuated sensitivity (hypersensitivity) linked to constraints of the SN in individuals exposed to prolonged childhood abuse (the PTSD population used). The more adaptive "top-down" cortical pathways found in controls exposed to direct gaze (allowing social interactions to be assessed and processed by the CEN) are not available to individuals with PTSD. Instead, direct gaze leads to sustained activation of sub-cortical routes for processing eye contact information, i.e., amplification of alarm states. The tighter coupling of the amygdala (which correlates with fear responses) with the insula in those suffering with PTSD appears to inhibit switching to or accessing the CEN, rendering those afflicted refractory to verbal interventions when in states of arousal. This mechanism is also likely responsible in part for the heightened unconscious communications prevalent in therapeutic encounters with this client population.

## Synchronistic phenomena in the treatment of a trauma survivor

In a case I previously discussed of a woman (Ms. A) with a history of severe sexual abuse as a child, a number of enigmatic events occurred (Cambray, 2002). Initially, any disruption of the schedule, with absences of a week or more, required prophylactic hospitalization. After considerable progress in containment was achieved, Ms. A requested to remain out of the hospital during a 10-day hiatus due to my travels. After reflection and consultation I agreed. The time for a call was arranged before I left we spoke at the designated hour.

At first she was agitated, quickly recounting a short dream from the night before that: "you (the analyst) were in the Black Forest and lost to me." She was manifestly terrified (i.e., her amygdala was highly activated presumably enslaving the SN) and asked if I was in Germany. Aware that her difficulty in retaining affective memory of our work together was leaving her exposed to severe abandonment anxieties, I responded in kind, concretely, reassuring her that I was not in Germany but could see that she felt in danger of losing contact with me. We discussed her concerns; she acknowledged the fragmentation occurring and we focused on reestablishing her feeling of connection our work, and through that to mundane reality as she seemed in danger of regressing into a terrifying fairy tale world of archetypal figures, witches, and monsters. Our contact was sufficiently containing that Ms. A's regained stability was sustained and she remained at home, out of the hospital, until I returned.

The following day, I went for a scuba diving lesson. After a morning of pool work, the diving instructor decided on the spot that I should come along on the afternoon's dive, my first in open water. It was therefore with some trepidation that I joined the other seasoned divers as we headed out to sea. It was only as we neared the site that the divemaster told us about the dive. I was profoundly surprised to discover that the site chosen was called "the Black Forest." After the momentary disruption caused by recognition of the pre-cognitive aspect of Ms. A's dream, I found myself aware of the asymmetry in our respective attitudes about the "Black Forest." The realm I was about to enter, though unknown and containing some real risks, was in fact a potential source of enjoyment. Indeed, the name of the site refers to the black coral that is a part of the reef at that spot and the trip underwater to visit this was exquisite to say the least, fortunately not marred by external incident.

There was a transitory somatic countertransference in the shock induced by the meaningful coincidence; it gave a fleeting "taste" of the constricted SN the patient had to endure much of the time. This constriction had to be metabolized before I could psychologically proceed into the waters. A related, larger transferential concern was also expressed in the dream: if the "black forest" is taken as a metaphor for the numerous anomalous experiences that surrounded this woman at this period in the treatment, then there was the danger that the analyst might become absorbed (or fascinated) and lost in these elliptical, synchronistic communications and miss her very real human suffering. Yet to not acknowledge and be receptive to them would only intensify her desperation. Remaining *near* the emergent edge was an implicit requirement if the therapy was to proceed.

Ms. A's traumatic history left her immersed in a world of psychic chaos whenever she perceived danger. However, in the act of providing her a measure of containment, offering a sense of ordered understanding, reciprocally I was left more open to the dissolving effects of the chaotic elements in the field. My more rational orientation toward the dream contents was undermined by a compensatory, unconscious shift toward the chaotic pole. Although I chose not to disclose to the patient what had occurred while I was away, my attitude and attention to the communicative power of her unconscious processes were certainly heightened. The synchronicity of the dream/dive site appears to have had an opposite effect on each of us resulting in both of us, and the analysis itself, moving more toward the edge of chaos and order.

This framing of the interactive field seeks to link the synchronistic occurrences with emergent phenomena. Over the past two decades, I have sought to understand anomalous experiences occurring in analysis from a systemic perspective and have used the study of complex adaptive systems as a useful theoretical formulation. The self-organization characteristic of these systems tends to produce emergent phenomena, and I have suggested many clinical synchronistic phenomena could be fruitfully discussed from this perspective.

The emergent edge in the dyad system of analyst and traumatized patient is also the locus of transformation in therapy. It is not a permanent condition to be attained and then sustained; rather it tends to be a metastable transitional state in which new configurations can appear through self-organization of the interacting parts. Under facilitating conditions the new forms can then proceed to evolve into more complex forms with autonomous existence, which may have temporary or more permanent existence.

Emergent phenomena are inherently value neutral, neither good nor bad, so conscious reflection and choice are essential to the type of outcome achieved. Emergence elicits and requires ethical considerations, often prodromal dilemmas arise marked by ambiguity, such as the decision to allow a phone call during a time when I was out of the office. By staying in the complexity of the dilemma and talking it through, we came to a "now moment" as we moved toward an agreement to speak by phone.

According to Daniel Stern and Boston Process of Change Study Group (BPCSG) colleagues, "when the traditional therapeutic frame risks being, or is, or should be, broken" and passes through "an unknown and unexpected intersubjective space," a charged now moment can lead to a "moment of meeting" (Stern et al., 1998, p. 912). Additionally, a now moment is understood by the group as being "a potential emergent property of a complex dynamic system" (p. 912) which they related to the Greek concept of *kairos* (p. 911), a seizing of the right moment. This indeed happened in Ms. A's case: she was genuinely surprised at my agreeing to her request for a phone call and felt she had achieved a breakthrough in our communications. The edge here had both positive (trust) and negative (manipulative) elements, hence the need for discernment before proceeding. Furthermore, an affective response of surprise is often a hallmark of emergence, especially as an unanticipated new, more complex form of interaction is coming into being.

The further evolution of the moment of meeting into a "moment of complexity" (MoC), as I call productive synchronicities in therapy (Cambray, 2011), began with the actual phone call. With the appearance of the "black forest," the analytic field itself was intensifying; unconscious dynamics were re-organizing our interactions. From complexity science we know that for any increase in complexity in a system, i.e., for emergent phenomena to manifest, there needs to be a break or lowering of symmetry. In this case that break came in the shock of the synchronicity, when I could recognize that Ms. A and I were "in" the same image yet experiencing it from significantly different vertices, generating an MoC.

In the months following my return there were a number of additional MoCs with Ms. A. The dynamic attunement between us was clearly heightened. Despite my never having overtly revealed the synchronistic event, Ms. A. had a series of dreams in which she would find me underwater and I would share my air regulator with her – termed buddy breathing in the diving community, a form of rescue when a diver is out of air. Obviously this dream image is highly overdetermined, though I won't comment on the multiplicities of meanings here beyond noting her capacity to locate me in a shared realm where I could offer assistance when she might otherwise "drown," but note that as with other patients with trauma histories, there is often a psychological porosity to paraverbal communications within the field.

## Conclusions

While not all anomalous experiences occur with PTSD patients, nor do all such experiences happen only with this patient population, the element of surprise is characteristic. Ordinary modes of perception are frequently challenged in these situations. An emergentist perspective offers a useful approach to understanding these phenomena, which are key to a Jungian analytic attitude (Bright, 1997).

From research on individuals with PTSD from childhood abuse, there is likely a neurological predisposition to a range of anomalous experiences. Arousal of the amygdala together with its enslavement of the insula leave a traumatized individual in intense, negatively charged affective states of alarm, with diminished cognitive processing capacities but hypersensitive to perceived or imagined dangers. Often these states lies outside of language; they are unspeakable and often feel unbearable; communication must go through alternative channels. Such states profoundly impact the therapeutic field, especially when the therapist is sensitive to or open to alterations in the field. Hence intensification of countertransferential responses is common around these activations, perhaps through mirror neuronal/empathic resonance pathways.

Beginning with internal acknowledgment of the occurrence of such events, therapists can go on to partially metabolize the associated affect by recognizing asymmetries in shared field experiences. In effect, freeing up one's own anterior insula from an amygdalar hold can re-establish functional switching between the DMN and the CEN needed to process experience (in the model of an induced, syntonic, transient traumatic countertransferential response to an activated field). Thus the preconditions for an elliptical communication through unconscious channels can precipitate self-organizing behavior in the analytic field. Re-engaging one's cognitive processing in the midst of a flood of affective communications submerging consciousness, can be therapeutic provided it is not a dissociative withdrawal from the affect. I believe this was poetically imaged in Ms. A's dreams about our "buddy breathing," which of course intensified other transferential feelings, but exploring those are for another time.

## Notes

1 From the period when he stopped actively working on the *Red Book*, about 1930, Jung began to identify himself increasingly with the psychological aspect of his work. When he returned to the university in 1932, after a hiatus of about 18 years, he no longer wished to teach psychiatry but instead asked, and was granted, to teach psychology (Graf-Nold, 2007).

2 The key regions of the DMN are the ventral medial prefrontal cortex (vMPFC), posterior cingulate/retrosplenial cortex (PCC/Rsp), inferior parietal lobule (IPL), lateral temporal cortex (LTC), dorsal medial prefrontal cortex (dMPFC), and hippocampal formation (HF).

3 While the DMN is relatively symmetrical in normal individuals, in schizophrenics there are distinct hemispheric asymmetries and in certain "oddball" auditory tasks; see Swanson, N., Eichele, T., Pearlson, G., Kiehl, K., Yu, Q., & Calhoun, V.D. (2011), "Lateral differences in the default mode network in healthy controls and patients with schizophrenia," *Human Brain Mapping*, *32*(4), 654–664, https://doi.org/10.1002/hbm.21055.

4 The SN is composed of the dorsal anterior cingulate cortex, bilateral insular cortices, amygdala, and ventral midbrain.

5 Buckner et al. suggest "the complex symptoms of schizophrenia could arise from a disruption in this control system resulting in an overactive (or inappropriately active) default network" (2008, p. 27). If accurate this would suggest that much of Jung's theories could be reconsidered in light of the DMN, in a manner complementary to reviewing them in terms of emergence theory.

## References

Addis, D.R., Wong, A.T., & Schacter, D.L. (2007). Remembering the past and imagining the future: Common and distinct neural substrates during event construction and elaboration. *Neuropsychologia, 45*, 1363–1377.

American College of Neuropsychopharmacology. (2015, December 10). LSD changes consciousness by reorganizing human brain networks. *ScienceDaily*. Retrieved August 30, 2017 from www.sciencedaily.com/releases/2015/12/151210144910.htm

Bair, D. (2003). *Jung: A biography*. Boston-New York-London: Little, Brown and Company.

Bright, G. (1997). Synchronicity as a basis of analytic attitude. *Journal of Analytical Psychology, 42*(4), 613–635.

Buckner, R.L., Andrews-Hanna, J.R., & Schacter, D.L. (2008). The brain's default network: anatomy, function, and relevance to disease. *Annals of the New York Academy of Sciences, 1124*, 1–38. https://doi.org/10.1196/annals.1440.011

Cambray, J. (2002). Synchronicity and emergence. *American Imago, 59*(4), 409–434.

Cambray, J. (2007). Reconsidering imitation. In Ann Casement (Ed.), *Who owns jung?* London: Karnac.

Cambray, J. (2011). Moments of complexity and enigmatic action: A Jungian view of the therapeutic field. *Journal of Analytical Psychology, 56*(2), 296–309.

Cambray, J. (2015). Jung, science, German romanticism: A contemporary perspective. In Mark E. Mattson, Fredrick J. Wertz, Harry Fogarty, Margaret Klenck, & Beverley Zabriskie (Eds.), *Jung in the academy and beyond*. New Orleans: Spring Journal, Inc.

Chan, M.Y., Park, D.C., Savalia, N.K., Petersen, S.E., & Wig, G.S. (2014). Decreased segregation of brain systems across the healthy adult lifespan. *Proceedings of the National Academy of Sciences USA, 111*(46), E4997–E5006.

Graf-Nold, A. (2007). C.G. Jung's position at the "Eidgenössische Technische Hochschule Zürich" (ETH Zürich) – the "Swiss Federal Institute of Technology Zurich." *Jung History, 2*(2), 12–15.

Haule, J. (1984). From somnambulism to the archetypes: The French roots of Jung's split with Freud. *The Psychoanalytic Review, 71*(4), 635–659.

Haule, J. (1986). Pierre Janet and dissociation: The first transference theory and its origins in hypnosis. *American Journal of Clinical Hypnosis, 29*(2), 86–94.

Hogenson, G. (2001). The Baldwin effect: A neglected influence on C.G. Jung's evolutionary thinking. *Journal of Analytical Psychology, 46*(4), 591–611.

Hogenson, G. (2004). Archetypes: Emergence and the psyche's deep structure. In J. Cambray and L. Carter (Eds.), *Analytical psychology: Contemporary perspectives in Jungian psychology*. East Sussex-New York: Brunner-Routledge.

Hogenson, G. (2009). Archetypes as action patterns. *Journal of Analytical Psychology, 54*, 325–357.

Jung, C.G. (1961a). *Memories, dreams, reflections*. New York: Pantheon Books.

Jung, C. G. (1961b). Freud and Jung: Contrasts. In *Freud and psychoanalysis* (CW 4). Princeton, NJ: Princeton University Press.

Jung, C. G. (1976). Tavistock lectures. In *The symbolic life* (CW 18). Princeton, NJ: Princeton University Press.

Kapogiannis, D., Deshpande, G., Krueger, F., Thornburg, M.P., & Grafman, J.H. (2014). Brain networks shaping religious belief. *Brain Connectivity, 4*(1), 70–79. https://doi.org/10.1089/brain.2013.0172

Kawai, T. (2009). Union and separation in the therapy of pervasive developmental disorders and ADHD. *Journal of Analytical Psycholgy, 54*(5), 659–675.

Kirsch, T. (1968). The relationship of the REM State to analytical psychology. *American Journal of Psychiatry, 124*, 1459–1463.

Knox, J. (2003). *Archetype, attachment, analysis: Jungian psychology and the emergent mind*. London: Brunner-Routledge.

Knox, J. (2009). Mirror neurons and embodied simulation in the development of archetypes and self-agency. *Journal of Analytical Psychology, 54*, 307–353.

Lanius, R.A., Frewen, P.A., Tursich, M., Jetly, R., & McKinnon, M.C. (2015). Restoring large-scale brain networks in PTSD and related disorders: a proposal for neuroscientifically-informed treatment interventions. *European Journal of Psychotraumatology, 6*, 27313. http://doi.org/10.3402/ejpt.v6.27313

Martin-Vallas, F. (2006). The transferential chimera: A clinical approach. *Journal of Analytical Psychology, 51*(5), 627–641.

Martin-Vallas, F. (2008). The transferential chimera II: Some theoretical considerations. *Journal of Analytical Psychology, 53*(1), 37–59.

Mazoyer, B., Zago, L., Mellet, E., Bricogne, S., Etard, O., Houde, O., Crivello, F., Joliot, M., . . . Tzourio-Mazoyer N. (2001). Cortical networks for working memory and executive functions sustain the conscious resting state in man. *Brain Research Bulletin, 54*, 287–298.

McDowell, M.J. (2001). Principle of organization: A dynamic-systems view of the archetype-as-such. *Journal of Analytical Psychology, 46*, 637–654.

Meloni, E.G., Gillis, T.E., Manoukian, J., & Kaufman, M.J. (2014, August 27). Xenon impairs reconsolidation of fear memories in a rat model of post-traumatic stress disorder (PTSD). *PLOS One*. https://doi.org/10.1371/journal.pone.0106189

Menon, V., & Uddin, L.Q. (2010). Saliency, switching, attention and control: A network model of insula function. *Brain Structure and Function*, doi 10.1007/s00429-010-0262-0, published on-line 29 May, 2010.

Moscovitch, M. (2007). Memory: Why the engram is elusive. In Henry L. Roediger, Yadin Dudai, & Susan M. Fitzpatrick (Eds.), *Science of memory concepts*. New York: Oxford University Press.

Pessina, L-A. (2015). Observing brain network dynamics to diagnose Alzheimer's disease. *ScienceDaily*. Retrieved December 12, 2015 from www.sciencedaily.com/releases/2015/07/150716091528.htm

Raichle, M.E., MacLeod, A.M., Snyder, A.Z., Powers, W.J., Gusnard, D.A., & Shulman, G.L. (2001). A default mode of brain function. *Proceedings of the National Academy of Sciences of the USA, 98*(2), 676–682.

Rossi, E. (1977). The cerebral hemispheres in analytical psychology. *Journal of Analytical Psychology, 22*(1), 32–51.

Saunders, P., & Skar, P. (2001). Archetypes, complexes and self-organization. *Journal of Analytical Psychology, 46*, 305–323.

Schacter, D.L. (2007). Memory: Delineating the core. In Henry L. Roediger, Yadin Dudai, & Susan M. Fitzpatrick (Eds.), *Science of memory concepts*. New York: Oxford University Press.

Schacter, D.L., & Addis, D.R. (2007). The cognitive neuroscience of constructive memory: Remembering the past and imagining the future. *Philosophical Transactions of the Royal Society B, 362*, 773–786.

Seeley, W.W., Menon, V., Schatzberg, A.F., Keller, J., Glover, G.H., Kenna, H., Reiss, A.L., & Greicius, M.D. (2007). Dissociable intrinsic connectivity networks for salience processing and executive control. *The Journal of Neuroscience, 27*(9), 2349–2356.

Sherwood, D. (2010). The embodied psyche: Movement, sensation, affect. In Raya A. Jones (Ed.), *Body, mind and healing after Jung: A space of questions*. London-New York: Routledge.

Spielberg, J.M., McGlinchey, R.E., Milberg, W.P., & Salat, D.H. (2015, February 18). Brain Network disturbance related to posttraumatic stress and traumatic brain injury in veterans. *Biological Psychiatry, 78*(3), 210–216. https://doi.org/10.1016/j.biopsych.2015.02.013

Stark, E.A., Parsons, C.E., Van Hartevelt, T.J., Charquero-Ballester, M., McManners, H., Ehlers, A., Stein, A., & Kringelbach, M.L. (2015, July 17). Post-traumatic stress influences the brain even in the absence of symptoms: A systematic, quantitative meta-analysis of neuroimaging studies. *Neuroscience & Biobehavioral Reviews, 56,* 207–221. https://doi.org/10.1016/j.neubiorev.2015.07.007

Stern, D.N., Sander, L.W., Nahum, J.P., Harrison, A.M., Lyons-Ruth, K., Morgan, A.C., Bruschweiler-Stern, N., & Tronick, E.Z. (1998). Non-interpretive mechanisms in psychoanalytic therapy: The "something more" than interpretation. The Process of Change Study Group. *The International Journal of Psychoanalysis, 79*(5), 903–921.

Thome, J., Frewen, P., Daniels, J.K., Densmore, M., & Lanius, R.A. (2014). Altered connectivity within the salience network during direct eye gaze in PTSD. *Borderline Personality Disorder and Emotion Dysregulation, 1*(1), 17.

Tresan, D. (1996). Jungian metapsychology and neurobiological theory. *Journal of Analytical Psychology, 41,* 399–436.

Wilkinson, M., & Woodhead, J. (2014). Report and Clinical Reflection on the Research carried out by Professor Ruth Lanius and her team in the Department of Psychiatry at the University of Western Ontario, and Margaret Willkinson and Dr. Judith Woodhead with the support of the IAAP academic, sub-committee and Dr. Joe Cambray, the advisor to the project. In "Copenhagen 2013 100 Years On: Origins, Innovations and Controversies. Proceedings of the 19th Congress of the International Association for Analytical Psychology. Editor, Emilija Kiehl. Einsiedeln, Switzerland: Daimon Verlag.

Yates, J. (1994). *Psyche and the split-brain.* Lanham, MD: University Press of America.

# 8

# THE CULTURAL SKIN IN CHINA

## The impact of culture upon development and clinical practice

*Brian Feldman*

## Introduction

In this chapter I would like to present the idea that culture provides a form of social containment – a cultural skin in which we are able to create shared meanings that provide a scaffolding and structure for both our individual and group life. The cultural skin mediates experiences between the subjective and symbolic realm of images and the inter-subjective dialogues that take place in the social spaces between self and other. I would like to explore the cultural skin as it emerges in infant observations that I have been involved with in China with groups of observers in Mainland China, Macau, and Hong Kong and to link this to our analytical work.

I became interested in the concept of the cultural skin when as a graduate student I attended seminars with the psychoanalyst Erik Erikson. Erikson based his work on the careful observation of infants and children in different cultural contexts. He explained in his seminars that culture is transmitted from one generation to the next primarily through the early sensuous/bodily interactions between (m)other and infant. For Erikson, sensuous bodily contact was the foundation for cultural transmissions and can be seen as one of the origins of what Jungians now identify as the cultural complex. I became intrigued with Erikson's concept of the early transmission of culture through bodily interaction and decided to study this myself. I utilized the infant observation method that I was introduced to by Michael Fordham and through the seminars on infant observation and development that I attended with Mary Ainsworth, who with John Bowlby developed attachment theory. I have found that in practicing analysis and teaching clinical and infant observation seminars in China, North America, Latin America, and Russia that the language and concepts utilized to describe psychological experience can be divergent in different cultures, as each culture develops their unique approach to psychological experience based on generations of cultural experience. Jung has taught us that while the archetypes are universal, their expression differs in each distinct cultural context. The nature of subjectivity, inter-subjectivity, and the forms and patterns of interpersonal relationships that emerge within each distinct cultural framework are unique and need to be empathically and sensitively encountered. Patterns of attachment can also be quite different within distinct cultural frameworks. From a Jungian standpoint, attachment is archetypal and emerges through the ongoing bodily, inter-subjective, and affective exchanges between the archetypal needs of the infant for safety, security, and comfort and the caregiver's sensitivity, awareness, and accurate interpretation of the infant's emotional and physical needs, as well as an appropriate and prompt response to those needs (Ainsworth, 2015).

From a Jungian perspective Neumann perceptively states that

> not only is there a temporal succession of psychic dominants (archetypes) unfolding autonomously (in the infant), but this entire process, whose predisposed course is ingrained in the species, is at the same time dependent on the influence of a specific environment. The human child . . . is by nature not only a psychobiological being, but from the very beginning a social being conditioned by culture.
>
> *(Neumann, 1959)*

A Jungian approach to infant observation involves an appreciation of the aesthetic and spiritual components of the infant's psychological and emotional experience. The aesthetic and spiritual emerge in the domain of implicit relational knowing, that domain of knowledge that is non-verbal, non-symbolized, unnarrated, and non-conscious (Stern, 2010). The rhythm of the caregiver's (father or mother) heartbeat and breath, the melody of their voice, and the gaze of their eyes are all significant aspects of the infant's experience of being held and contained within the emotional and mental experience of an other, and are important components of the evolution of secure attachment. The innate archetypal need for and experience of mutuality and intimacy play a part in aesthetic and spiritual experience and the creative process. Infant observation and infant research have taught us about the importance of the complex interpersonal and inter-subjective relatedness of the infant and the affective interplay that characterizes the parent–infant dyad. The internalization of these rhythms in the infant–(m)other relationship provide the bedrock of the aesthetic and spiritual experience. The infantile origins of the sense of beauty and the experience of spirituality can be seen in the longed-for experience of connection, security, and pleasure found within the early (m)other–infant attachment that has both personal and archetypal components. Early sources of beauty and spirituality lie in the early relational and inter-subjective experiences: the recognition of the (m)other's face, eye-to-eye contact, affective attunement, and the moments of meeting (Stern, 2010) that affirm the infant's spontaneous gesture (Winnicott, 1971) and help give shape and form to the unique subjectivity of each individual infant. The spontaneous gesture when responded to in an affectively attuned manner takes on aesthetic form as it is sculpted through interaction with the (m)other in the transitional space, the area of play which is the matrix of the aesthetic and spiritual experience. The music of the vocalizations between (m)other and infant, the sharing of warmth, the rhythmic interaction of mutual touching, and the attunement of affect in facial interaction are all sources of meaning, imaginative and creative fantasy, and form the bedrock of the aesthetic and the spiritual. The facial mirroring between (m)other and infant is a primary foundation of intimacy throughout life. The modulation and subtlety in facial interactions influence internal representations of time, space, and affect and are a primal source of the affectively charged, formal organization in which space, shape, rhythm, sound, and color all come together in an engrossing and recurring aesthetic and spiritual experience.

## The Chinese cultural skin

In the Chinese cultural context, philosophy, spirituality, and culture provide a skin that functions as a container for psychological experience. Jung was keenly interested in Chinese philosophy and culture and wrote interesting commentaries on the *Tao Teh Ching* and the *I Ching* – two of China's great wisdom books. Jung wrote perceptively about the paradoxes and complexities of Chinese philosophy and spirituality stating that "in Lao-tzu's *Tao Teh Ching* there is no position without its negation. Where there is faith, there is doubt; where there is doubt, there is credulity; where there is morality there is temptation" (Jung, 1958). This play of opposites is an indication of the complexity of Chinese culture, of its many paradoxes, and for a Westerner like myself its mysterious and often inscrutable nature. The *I Ching* has great importance for the understanding of the Chinese cultural skin, as the *I Ching* values the uniqueness and endless diversity of the present moment with all of its unpredictability, synchronicities, and aliveness. The configuration of the sticks that are thrown in the *I Ching* to determine a unique structure or pattern are the result of chance events at the moment of observation and form the basis for the generation of meaning and significations. Jung utilized the *I Ching* to support his concept of synchronicity – a theory based upon meaningful coincidences as opposed to a strict theory of causality. In China the understanding and experience of self is embedded in these emergent and meaningful moments. The *I Ching* provides a cultural skin, a cultural container and envelope in which shared meanings coalesce into a philosophy of life that form a complex cultural mosaic or gestalt. Culture according to anthropologist Clifford Geertz (1973) comprises these shared meanings that make possible the experience of subjectivity as well as interpersonal and inter-subjective communication. Christopher Bollas in his book *China on the Mind* (2013) has also written about the importance of these masterpieces of Chinese culture and utilizes his experience of these works to understand the Chinese psyche. Culture provides a form of social containment, a cultural skin, in which we are able to create shared meanings that provide a scaffolding and structure for both our individual and group life, sense of identity and self. In this chapter I will be exploring how the infant observation method helps us to gain an understanding of Chinese culture from the perspective of the infant–caregiver relationship.

## Notes on the infant observation method

I would like to outline the infant observation method that we have utilized in our study. Infant observation is a tool utilized to train analytical psychotherapists in the understanding of pre-verbal emotional development of the infant, and the impact of infancy upon later psychological development. Infant observation is concerned with teaching the developing analyst to both sharpen and deepen their observational skills in a supportive context. Infant observation as developed by Esther Bick (1964) and utilized within the Jungian tradition by Michael Fordham does not involve the experimental manipulation of variables and behavior between the infant and their caregiver, nor are observations conducted in a laboratory setting. Rather, it involves the observation in the naturalistic setting of the home of infant–parent interaction. Each infant is observed within the context of their primary attachments 1 hour each week from birth through the second year of life. The purpose of this 2-year experience is to provide an opportunity to observe firsthand, from an analytically oriented perspective, the unfolding of the infantile psyche within the context of the early infant–caregiver relationships. The infant observation study group usually consists of four to five participants who meet for 2 hours weekly to discuss the observations and to reflect upon the interactions and make inferences with regard to the developing intrapsychic/emotional states of the infant. Aspects of symbolic development, such as the evolution of a concept of an internal space through the experience of the skin as the first container of inner experience, are at times a focus of the discussions. Overall there is an attempt to understand the totality of the infant's experience and the impact that experience has upon ongoing development. Through these detailed observations and discussions, the participants gain firsthand knowledge of the infant psyche and are able to begin to think about the relevance of this knowledge and experience for the practice of child and adult analysis. Participants in the seminar have found the observations helpful in their clinical work with both children and adults. They report gaining greater insight into and empathy for the infantile and early childhood aspects of their analysand's experiences, as well as in becoming more sensitive to the pre-verbal, unconscious, and intra-subjective aspects of the analytical relationship.

Before becoming a more standard adjunct of Jungian analytic trainings, infant observation had a long history and evolution within the psychoanalytic world. Infant observation began as part of the analytical training course for child psychotherapists at the Tavistock Clinic in 1948, when the training in child psychotherapy began. Melanie Klein's (1975) emphasis on describing early infantile states of mind, combined with John Bowlby's (1982) work on attachment theory, led the originators of the child psychotherapy program at the Tavistock Clinic in London (Esther Bick, 1964) to institute a seminar in infant observation covering the first 2 years of life. Within the field of Analytical Psychology, Michael Fordham introduced infant observation into the child analysis curriculum of the Society of Analytical Psychology in London in the early 1970s. Infant observation was instituted at the Society of Analytical Psychology by Michael Fordham to enable the analytic trainees to conceptualize vividly the infantile experience of their child and adult analysands. Fordham also believed that the training in infant observation would increase the child analyst's understanding of the child's non-verbal behavior and his play, and would help the child analyst when he interviewed the parents and enable him to better understand their account of the child's history. At this time infant observation is taught at a number of Jungian institutes throughout the world such as in the US, UK, Italy, and Germany as well as with Jungian groups in Russia and China.

Infant observation allows the student a unique opportunity to observe the development of an infant starting from birth in the context of his own home and in relation to the caregivers in his life. The observers are able to discover for themselves how these important attachments emerge and develop. They are also able to compare and contrast their observations with those of their fellow students in the weekly infant observation seminars.

The observers do not take notes during the observation sessions. It is felt that note taking could interfere with the capacity of the observer to feel emotionally and empathically involved with the family and especially with the infant–caregiver relationship. It is important that the observer be able to experience the emotional and psychological impact of the infant–caregiver relationship upon themselves and not to offer either advice or criticism to the caregiver, which could undermine the caregiver's emerging sense of getting to know the baby in their own way. Utilizing this structure, the observer is able to develop through empathy an ongoing relationship with the emotional give and take of the earliest period of an infant's life. The seminar format helps the participants explore the projections of the different family members upon the observer. At times the group discussions are very difficult and painful. Especially difficult are the times when the group discusses and reflects on the impact of an attachment figure's depression upon the infant. When depressive mood states are prominent, the caregiver (mother, father, or grandparent in China) often experiences emotional detachment from the baby, and a sense of helplessness in understanding and meeting the baby's need can emerge. At other times, the group can experience with the observer the dynamic thrust of a facilitating parent–infant relationship where the parent is attuned to the baby's needs and desires and is able both to empathize with them and meet them in a synchronous manner. During these times we begin to experience together as a group how the episodes of affect attunement lead to the development of a stable sense of self. We are continually impressed by the capacity of the infant to actively participate in the creation of his own universe and the manner in which the infant attempts to make his wants and desires known to his caregivers. The strong developmental thrust of the infant engenders hopefulness and enables the group to understand that not all lapses in empathy lead to developmental deviations. The participants in the group are thus sensitized to the ups and downs of normal infant development and they are able to observe the impact of the environment upon the developing infant.

Data from infant observation, infant research and attachment theory all point to the hypothesis that a secure attachment relationship between a neurologically healthy baby and a stably present, mindful, and sensitive attachment figure(s) – male and/or female, father and/or mother, or parents of either gender in a homosexual relationship – forms the foundation for symbolization, as well as reflective and imaginative functions upon which the scaffolding of all later psychological development takes place.

Infant observation has an important relevance for the practice of analysis. Utilizing the (m)other–infant metaphor, we can hypothesize that in analysis the development of symbolization processes in the analysand are dependent upon the analyst's capacity to maintain a symbolic attitude that provides a secure internal space in which the meanings of images, reveries, memories, and sensory experiences can unfold and take shape in the potential space of the analytical encounter. Jung's concept of the analyst's symbolic attitude can be linked to Bion's conception of maternal reverie. Utilizing the mother-infant metaphor, Bion postulates that the (m)other in a state of reverie is able to receive, via projective identification, the infant's unmetabolized, unmentalized sensory experiences, and transform them through a striving for understanding into a bearable and manageable emotional/bodily experience for the baby. Through these interactional sequences, the baby feels more adequately held by the (m)other and more contained within her/his mind. The caregiver provides mediation, a form of support and understanding that fosters the infant's growth and development. Given a healthy baby (neurologically and developmentally), this leads to the baby's becoming calmer and more secure (from an attachment standpoint), and fosters the experience of the (m)other as a secure base where he can find safety and comfort, which then becomes internalized and helps the child to separate and individuate. A similar process occurs within the analytic relationship.

## Infant observation in China

During the past 6 years I have been involved in the planning, organization, and supervision of infant observation groups in China. The Chinese observers have gone into the homes of participating families with the task of observing the moment-to-moment interactions between the infant and their caregivers starting at birth through the second year of life. Each participant finds a family to observe in their local community and visits the family each week for an hour during a 2-year period. After the observation, a narrative is written that is based upon what is observed in the baby, what is observed in the interactions between baby and caregiver, and what is observed within themselves; the narrative is distributed to the group for discussion. This is a daunting task for the observers as they are encountering the most primitive states of the human psyche and observing a helpless infant who is completely dependent upon her caregivers. The experience can generate a great deal of anxiety within the observer, and the group meetings that take place 2 hours weekly on Zoom provides a skin or container for the observers to help reflect upon and generate meanings from their experiences. I would like to focus in this chapter upon some of the important issues that have emerged during the course of infant observations in China and some of the beginning hypotheses that these observations have generated.

One of the most significant aspects of infant observation work, like the *I Ching*, is that it is based in the present moment. The observer's task is to remain in the present moment without memory and desire (Bion, 1977), and to utilize their imagination and intuition to observe the cross currents that take place in the observation. We look at both conscious verbal and behavioral communications and the unconscious communications that take place between the infant and her caregivers, as well as between the different family members and the observer. The observer has the task of finding within the family a stable and comfortable space within which the observation can take place without the observer unduly impacting the ongoing everyday life of the family. The understanding of the methodology of infant observation and its usefulness for the practice of infant, child, adolescent, and adult analysis takes a good deal of time, but once it is understood and integrated, the observers have found the experience indispensable toward the development of their analytical and personal identities. Infant observation also provides us with a method to more deeply understand the transmission of culture and trauma, the emergence of attachment styles within the primary relationships of the infant with their caregiver, and the emergence of self and identity.

## The emergence of self in China

The self in the Chinese cultural context emerges through different types and qualities of interactions than in the West. The self is more socially contextualized, as the infant develops within a complex social system that includes a wide circle of caregivers, both parents and grandparents. We have found that the family communicates to the infant from an early age the need for accommodation to family social norms and the acceptance of social prohibitions. The emphasis upon individuation, autonomy, and self-expression is less emphasized than in Western culture. The infant's sense of self and identity are an expression of the culture in which she is embedded. Self and identity are impacted by the interactions that take place at both the interpersonal and inter-subjective levels. From a Jungian viewpoint, Fordham's (1985) concept of actions of the self (self emergence) originates in the mirroring by the caregiver of the infant's spontaneous gestures and vocalizations. The emergence of self in China takes place in a different manner as accommodation to the wishes and needs of others is seen as a primary developmental task for the infant. We have to be careful in our infant observations not to superimpose Western values upon the Chinese families, but rather to observe carefully the impact of interpersonal and inter-subjective interactions upon the infant's development.

From our research in infant observation, we observe the infant's experience of self emergence from the beginning of the baby's life. As self emerges and transforms, we observe the earliest and most primitive states of physical and psychological cohesion that involves being contained within a skin that provides an envelope for sensory, affective, and inter-subjective experiences. At the inter-subjective level (m) other and baby sculpt and shape their mutually co-created experiences through the depth and breadth of their affective and unconscious communications. Stern (2010) calls these shapes vitality forms. Stern's vitality forms provide a temporal envelope for emotional, inter-subjective, and interpersonal experience and lead to the infant's felt experience of aliveness. (M)other and infant form a primal coniunctio that emerges as the attachment archetype is stimulated through interaction with the significant others in the infant's life. This early constellation of the coniunctio provides an important foundation for the emergence of later relational coniunctios.

We need to be cautious how we utilize concepts of the self in China, as the infant's inter-subjective experience with an other is more subtle and nuanced than in the West, and the self often emerges in a space that is more internal, more private. The following episodes illustrate this aspect of the Chinese baby's encounter with prohibitions related to the body and the search for comfort, security, and safety with mother that facilitates the emergence of self.

When I (the observer) go to the home of baby A, mother and grandmother are in the living room of their small apartment. Baby A is 3 months and 3 days old at the time of observation. Mother and grandmother greet me, and I go over to the chair in the living room where I have found a safe and comfortable place from which to observe. The baby has been breast-fed for 2 months but mother feels anxious about the breast-feeding and fears that she will not have enough milk for her baby's nourishment, so she has supplemented the breast-feeding with formula. Grandmother is feeding the baby formula from a bottle, and as she sucks on the bottle baby's eyes are closed; grandmother does not attempt to make either verbal or visual contact with baby, who appears to be struggling with the bottle as she is unable to control the flow of the formula. Realizing that baby is struggling with the bottle, grandmother removes it, and baby then begins to move her hands, arms, and legs as if she wants to express her feelings about the feeding. Baby touches her mouth with her finger and grandmother takes the finger out of her mouth, saying that it is dirty and she should not put her finger in her mouth. After grandmother takes her finger out of her mouth, baby tries to put it back in again; grandmother takes it out saying it is dirty and bad to do that. This interaction continues as baby explores her face and mouth with her finger. Baby appears more and more frustrated with grandmother's prohibition and starts to cry. Mother then comes over to baby, picks her up, and tries to console her. Baby then calms down and falls asleep in mother's arms. Mother here was able to relate to baby's distress and affirm her need for holding and containment, experiences that foster self-emergence.

At 4 months and 15 days, I come to the home and am met by grandmother and baby A. Grandmother complains to me that baby A is being naughty by refusing to drink formula from a bottle. Grandmother attempts to feed baby but she does not want to drink. Mother then comes into the room and gives baby a toy to play with, which baby begins to suck on. Baby then starts to lick the toy, and mother quickly replaces it with the bottle saying that she must now be hungry. Baby spits out the milk and starts to cry. Mother puts the toy back in baby's mouth and then quickly replaces it with the bottle when baby starts to suck on the toy. I begin to feel a sense of frustration and anger as baby struggles with the bottle. After a few minutes, baby becomes sleepy and is put in a basket on the floor, and while in a half-sleep state mother puts the bottle in baby's mouth and she begins to suck on it and drinks most of the formula. I have the feeling that baby needed to accommodate to the caregivers' wishes and cannot not assert her autonomy and independence.

In my analytic work in China, I have been struck by the personal narratives of my analysands who describe the need for respect of the authority of elders, parents, teachers, and the needs of the larger social order. Analysands describe this as the Chinese social contract: the family provides for and takes care of the baby, and as the child grows and develops she needs to keep in mind the needs of the family and the ancestors and to prevent shame or disappointment. What I have found in China is that the actions of the self, while present, need to be contained and controlled within the individual in order to live successfully in the outer world. The Chinese social contract has helped the society to evolve. We need to be careful and cautious about how we apply the concepts of actions of the self and individuation to our clinical understanding as the self is more socially contextualized than in the West. Perhaps this is something that baby A is teaching us.

## Skin and psyche

The concept of the psychic skin is utilized in infant observation research as the skin is the first container of emotional and symbolic experience, and as development proceeds the skin becomes internalized and symbolized as a psychic skin, providing a containing function for the psyche/soma. The transmission of culture takes place through bodily and affective interactions between infant and caregiver often on the surface of the skin and through skin-to-skin interactions. Touch and sensuality are intimately linked to the development of attachment security as the secure infant explores her own body image through the interaction with the body of the other. Interactions between baby and (m)other that involve the surface of the body, the skin, are critical in the evolution of the infant's sense of a bounded internal space that is separated from the external world through a boundary experienced as the skin. When the experience of the skin as a boundary between the internal and external realms has evolved, the individual is able to experience living within their own individual skin, separate but interconnected with significant others. Secure attachment is facilitated through the evolution of a primary skin function (Feldman, 2004) that can serve as a container of psychological and emotional experience. The (m)other's capacity to both tolerate, mediate, soothe, and transform the often terrifying mental states of the baby into more manageable and digestible experiences is another significant factor in the evolution of a secure attachment relationship and in the evolution of a primary skin function.

Through the careful observation of infants, we have been able to see that as development unfolds, the skin becomes an increasingly important container of psychological, emotional, and erotic/sensuous experience for the infant. The transformation of the somatic skin into an internalized psychic skin is facilitated through complex interactional sequences between baby and (m)other: the infant's ongoing bathing in words, the emotional interchanges that provide the baby with the psychological nourishment related to affective attunement, and physical touch which when sensitively experienced provides a foundation for the evolution of the primary skin function (Feldman, 2004). Early interpersonal experiences within the infant–(m)other couple that impede the development of a coherent psychic skin or primary skin function are often a major focus in the analysis of children, adolescents, and adults who suffer from identity disorders, eating disorders, disorders of the skin, sleep disorders, and auto-sensuous addictions that can impede both psychological growth and the development of individuation processes. These disorders can be related to the emergence of a secondary skin function that impedes psychological and emotional development through the excessive use of bodily defenses. When bodily defenses are dominant in the personality, emotional development can be severely impacted and can lead to the development of autistic defenses or defenses of the self.

An example of the importance of skin emerged in the following observation of baby B at 3 months, 14 days.

Baby B seems happy when I arrive at the apartment. Baby is lying in a small cradle in the large room off from the kitchen. As I enter, baby looks at me and I feel welcomed by him into the observational space. When I sit down, mother seems concerned and tells me that baby does not want to eat and that he has developed severe eczema all over his body. He has had eczema before, but now it is appearing more serious and difficult to control. I can see that large red spots cover the baby's skin. In a worried and anxious manner, mother tells me that she and father have taken him to the dermatologist and that the doctor has let her know that she needs to put special lotions on him and that he will need special baths so that he can be more comfortable. I see baby attempt to rub and scratch his skin as he seems uncomfortable. The skin disorder has emerged during the past 2 months of observation, starting when mother went back to work full time and an au pair, who does not speak Chinese, began taking care of him. Mother lets me know that he sleeps with the caregiver and that father is not home very much now as his work and travel schedule have intensified. I wonder about the separation from mother and how this may be impacting baby B. I do not observe baby B being held by mother, and when baby is upset the au pair comes quickly into the room to try to soothe him, which he accepts. Mother continues to look very nervous and approaches baby and touches him, offering some words of comfort and reassurance saying, "Oh, my poor baby, how you are suffering." Mother puts her hand on baby's stomach and continues to try to calm him while he is held in the arms of the caregiver. Mother says that baby has not been sleeping well because of the skin problems that have become more serious, and that both baby and au pair do not sleep through the night. Mother appears very sad and depressed about the skin difficulties. Mother tries to play with baby, but he is not responsive to her and he appears sleepy and lethargic. She then tries to feed baby and he appears uninterested in the bottle that she tries to give him. I feel that baby is rejecting mother and perhaps he is expressing his feelings of rejection and abandonment by her when she went back to work full time. I feel a sense of depression within myself as I leave the observation.

In our group of infants in China, the emergence of skin disorders has been a common phenomenon, appearing in more than half of the infants observed. Skin disorders can be common in infancy and there are immunological issues that are impacted by the interaction of psyche and soma. In the case of baby B, he was developing an anxious/avoidant attachment with his mother, and mother was unable to get in synch with her baby after the prolonged separations for work. The au pair also did not appear to offer him a feeling of security and comfort, and perhaps he was trying to hold himself together through the emergence of eczema. Research on eczema from an analytical perspective indicates that when individuals feel poorly contained and held, they can develop skin disorders, and the rubbing and scratching of the skin helps to achieve momentary feelings of calmness and increased comfort – a primitive form of a self-care function. The eczema has become an expression of a secondary skin function to help hold the infant's fragile psyche/soma. Perhaps baby B's eczema was also a communication to his caregivers about his need for more secure bodily/affective containment and holding.

## Inter-generational transmission of trauma

The inter-generational transmission of trauma related to the historical events of the Mao era, such as the Cultural Revolution and other historical and collective traumas, is an important theme in our observations. During the years of the Cultural Revolution (1962–1976), between 1.5 and 2 million people were killed, lives were often ruined through endless denunciations, false confessions, struggle meetings, and persecution campaigns (Dikotter, 2016). The Cultural Revolution was characterized by loss at many levels of Chinese society. The Chinese cultural skin became torn and tattered as historical temples and shrines were destroyed, and traditional spiritual values such as the ideas of Confucius and Lao-tzu were considered outmoded. Many experienced a loss of social and economic status, and many intellectuals and teachers lost their careers as universities and schools were closed and they were sent to the countryside to work in the fields. Students turned against those teachers and professors who were suspected of being against Mao's ideology. This loss of security and trust, usually provided by the cultural skin, created fear and mistrust that led to tears in the Chinese cultural skin that have been difficult to heal. These tears in the cultural skin can only be healed through processes of open dialogue and cultural atonement, and in China this reparative process has failed to fully occur.

The inter-generational transmission of trauma has emerged in many of our infant observations as well as being a major theme in analytic treatment in China. We have observed that trauma could be communicated both consciously and unconsciously to the infant by the caregiver. Often these are hidden wounds experienced by the individual and the collective that can only be integrated through elaboration at both symbolic and verbal levels of discourse. A safe space is needed to elaborate the impact of individual and collective trauma, as we have learned from our extensive experience with Holocaust survivors and their children and grandchildren. Infant observation and analysis appear to provide a safe space where this process of elaboration and integration can take place.

This emerged in the observation of baby C. Baby C appeared during the first year of observations to have developed a disorganized attachment with his mother. The observer was concerned about the high level of disorganization in the infant as the child's behavior included hitting himself, hitting his mother and grandmother, and not being able to manage separations from mother that were unpredictable and lacking in transitioning behavior. Mother told the observer that she was having difficulty managing her baby and grandmother was not able to provide adequate containment. Mother requested a referral for psychotherapy that she subsequently appreciated and benefited from.

The following vignette at 12 months and 2 weeks describes some of this difficulty.

> When I arrive for the observation, baby C is beginning to stand and walk on his feet with some difficulty. I become concerned because he is teetering on his feet holding onto the table and chairs and could fall at any moment. Mother is present but does not do anything to prevent the fall that is imminent. Baby C starts to cry, but mother does not come over to him; instead she appears to ignore him. I feel pain in empathy with the baby, and after several minutes I go over to him and lift him up. Mother then comes over to hold him and grandmother comes into the room. Baby does not wear diapers and has been taught to urinate into the trash basket that is on the floor. During the observation I notice that he pees on the floor and that there are wet spots on the carpet. Mother comments that he has not yet learned to control his bladder or bowel movements. Mother then asks if she can talk to me and she asks grandmother to come into the room to take care of baby. She takes me aside and starts to tell me how difficult her life is with her husband, and how she was traumatized as a child, which included being chained to a bed when her parents were not at home. I listened and experienced her torment when she told me this. I began to think that the difficulty that she has with the separations from her infant might be linked to the childhood trauma she is telling me about. She then talks about how her parents were mistreated, ostracized, and beaten during the Cultural Revolution as they were suspected of being capitalists. Some relatives were killed during this period and the family went through emotional upheavals, dislocations, and loss. I stayed in an empathic mode of listening to her and she appeared calmed by this. When I left the observation, I realized I spent as much time with mother as I did observing baby, but this seemed significant as mother appeared to be able to

hold baby in mind more effectively after this conversation. She needed to have her own infantile/child self seen and acknowledged, and her rivalry for my attention in the observation seemed to diminish.

## The former one child policy and the infant's relationship with her caregivers

In our group of Chinese babies, most are only children, the products of the one child policy that has currently undergone modifications. Recently families are now allowed to have two children. Parents who previously were allowed only one child often experienced pain about this policy. What we have found in our observations is that a high level of ambivalence is often expressed by both parents and/or the grandparents verbally or else communicated unconsciously, usually to the female child, and was more problematic if the female child was an only child. In the observation of baby D the following interchange occurred at 4 months and 3 weeks.

When the observer came to the home he reported the following sequence:

> Baby D is being held by the grandmother and appears to be happy and in a good mood as baby is smiling and there appears to be an active and engaging interchange of vocalizations and sustained eye contact. Mother is close to the baby and also trying to make contact with her by touching her feet and tickling her tummy. Grandmother and mother start to talk with each other in a playful manner and start to talk about the baby. They say to the baby "one day we may abandon you and then how may you feel?" They laugh with each other and the baby while they say this. I am feeling very confused about this but stay in my observational position and do not ask any questions. Grandmother and mother continue to say these comments about the baby directly to her and while they do this they are smiling and the baby starts to smile as well. Mother had told me on a previous occasion that they had hoped for a baby boy when she conceived. I sensed that she was disappointed both in the baby and with herself and that this was being projected into the baby.

Grandparents play a major role in the lives of most infants in China. The one child policy made it more common for grandparents to have one child and then in turn their child has one child, so there are few grandchildren. The infants in our observations often developed strong attachments to grandparents and early on needed to begin to differentiate mother, father, and grandparents. This can be difficult for the infant and parents, especially the mother, who can experience rivalry, competition, jealousy, and envy toward the grandmother (her mother or often the husband's mother). We have observed intergenerational conflict about infant rearing practices that can be difficult to sort out. Often the mother tries to form a bond with the observer, as she feels that the observer has a more "modern" approach to child rearing, and mother can utilize the observer to triangulate against her mother or mother-in-law. Fathers can have difficulty emotionally supporting mother as their allegiances can be torn between their own mother and their wife. We have found that Chinese fathers have a hard time being included in the life of the baby. They seem not to have role models for the father–infant attachment that is so important in the life of the baby. Many of the fathers have become interested in the observational experience and try to interact with their baby while the observer is present. In this way the observation itself has a therapeutic impact on the infant's development.

## Conclusion

Infant observation in China has taught me about cultural humility, the importance of maintaining an appreciation of differing cultural contexts and psychological frameworks. We enter into the observation focused upon the present moment and utilize our imaginative and intuitive capacities to perceive what is happening both on the surface level of interaction and beneath the surface that include the nuances of inter-subjective and symbolic communication. In this way we are able to reflect upon what is common to us all as meaning making subjects and the richly woven tapestries of our divergent cultural heritages.

## References

Ainsworth, M. (2015). *Patterns of attachment*. London: Routledge.
Bick, E. (1964). Notes on infant observation in psychoanalytic training. *International Journal of Psychoanalysis, 45*, 558–566.
Bion, W. (1977). *Seven servants*. New York: Aronson.
Bollas, C. (2013). *China on the mind*. London: Routledge.
Bowlby, J. (1982). *Attachment and loss*. London: Hogarth Press.
Dikotter, F. (2016). *The cultural revolution*. London: Bloomsbury.
Feldman, B. (2004). Skin for the Imaginal. *Journal of Analytical Psychology, 49*(3), 285–311.
Fordham, M. (1985). *Explorations into the self*. London: Academic Press.
Geertz, C. (1973). *The interpretation of cultures*. New York: Basic Books.
Jung, C.G. (1958). *Psychology and Religion* (CW 11). Princeton, NJ: Princeton University Press.
Klein, M. (1975). *Envy and gratitude*. London: Hogarth Press.
Neumann, M. (1959). The genetic aspect for analytical psychology. *Journal of Analytical Psychology, 4*(2), 125–137.
Stern, D. (2010). *Forms of vitality*. London: Oxford University Press.
Winnicott, D.W. (1971). *Playing and reality*. London: Tavistock Publications.

# PART IV

# Psychotherapy and psychotherapeutic methods

# 9

# SANDPLAY

## A method for research with trauma

*Denise Gimenez Ramos and Reinalda Melo da Matta*

The psychotherapeutic technique of sandplay has been increasingly employed due to the excellent results obtained using this process in the treatment of different pathologies. This technique was developed by the Jungian analyst Dora Kalff (2003) in the 1950s with the objective of encouraging the patient to express his/her conscious and unconscious feelings in a non-verbal way using miniatures and two sand trays, one with wet sand and another with dry sand. The use of a protected and free space (the sand tray) to create scenes with or without figures and objects facilitates patients' expression of deep unconscious content.

Dr. Kalff noted that this expression of unconscious content and thus awareness was experienced on a pre-verbal level (Weinrib, 1993; Kalff, 2003; Pattis, 2011). Friedman and Mitchell (2003) have found that this form of treatment allows for the emergence of unconscious traumatic components, which are normally contained via defense mechanisms, to be symbolically revealed in the sandplay scenes, allowing the expression of aggressive impulses.

Friedman and Mitchell (2003) observed that the role of the therapist is to be present without any judgment or interpretation. This attitude may help the patient to review, reflect, and appropriate his/her own process, making the scenes an act of creation and consciousness. The scene may also facilitate the therapist–patient relationship depending on the quality of the transference process. Furthermore, the fact that sand tray pictures are photographed and archived is unique among the various Jungian techniques. This process of photography and archiving allows for the collection of data that can potentially be utilized for comparative and effectiveness research.

At this time, qualitative analysis is the predominant research approach used by Jungian clinicians. Due to the nature of this type of research, the results of these processes have been restricted to the description and interpretation of sandplay scenes, without an analysis that allows generalization over experiences and comparison of results.

In the Clinical Graduate Program at the Catholic University of Sao Paulo, the authors began to work with a database of sandplay pictures to explore the effectiveness of sandplay therapy for different conditions and among patients. Our first study goal was to construct a method to analyze the results of the therapeutic data from sandplay and to standardize data from the pictures and verbal expressions used by the patients while working with sandplay. Our objective was also to conduct qualitative and quantitative analysis, compare data among several patients, and compute the results obtained by different therapists, within a homogeneous pattern. As an example of our approach, we offer the data from three male patients between 6 and 8 years old, suffering with obsessive compulsive disorder (OCD; Ramos & Matta, 2008).

## The sand tray data

The data analyzed here were from the archives of the authors. We had used the categories established by Grubbs (1995) and Mitchell and Friedmann (1994). It is possible that new categories may emerge, as has happened in this research, according to the dynamics and psychopathologies of the patients.

## Research methodology

Our research methodology focused on three elements: capturing and classifying verbal and non-verbal expressions from the three mentioned cases, verifying and classifying miniatures, and classifying the individual scenes.

*Capturing expressions*: In this work, we consider verbal expressions as well as non-verbal expressions (pictures) produced by the subjects throughout the making of the scenes. These expressions are grouped in categories established and defined by the authors for this study. New categories can surface according to the emerging material in each clinical study. Here we will describe only the categories found in the study mentioned earlier. We start by gathering all verbal expressions through literal transcription of the spontaneous verbal expressions as well as stories that the subject tells during the construction of scenes. These verbal expressions are grouped in categories in relation to the central idea of the scene.

*Survey of miniatures in each scene*: To be able to duplicate the results, it is also necessary to verify the amount and kind of miniatures present in the therapist's office and the grouping of such by theme. We add the number of miniatures presents in each theme, remembering that all the miniatures in the therapeutic room are already classified by theme before the beginning of the treatment. The miniature classification method developed by Grubbs (1995) can be here utilized.

For instance, in Figure 9.1 we have four miniatures within the theme "wild animals." It is important to observe that the same miniature can be used in different contexts. Although they might be kept in the same theme, they still could

**FIGURE 9.1**  Photograph of scene 1 of a patient

be classified in another category following the general dynamic of the scene. For instance, the theme "ball" can be classified in the destruction category when it is used as "bomb" or classified as celebration when used as "Christmas ball." Another example is a lion or a tiger, which belong to the theme "wild animals" but can be classified in the category conflict (if they are in an attack position) or in the category ego identification (when the patient uses one of these animals as an expression of himself/herself).

*Scene classification:* The description and categorization of scene dynamics are made by the observation of each picture. Here, through the notes made by the therapist during the making of the scenes and observation of the photographs taken, a scene is described using the Grubbs (1995), Friedmann and Mitchell (2003) classification system. The description includes the position of the miniatures in the sandbox (for instance, elephant in the lower half), the use of water (dry or wet sand), and the orientation and movement of the sand (excavations or elevations and their position within the box). The analysis of these factors allows us to classify the dynamic of the scenes within one or more categories. The classification was made by the therapists who were also the researchers. For instance, a scene with an excavation with water in the center is classified in the category descendent movement, but if the patient has drowned animals or people in the water, the scene is also classified in the category destruction. In this way, a scene may contain more than one category.

The therapist observes and evaluates both the construction and the final aspect of the scene and attributes it to one or more predominant categories. For instance, when a patient in the construction of the scene throws the miniatures on the sand, the therapist might consider this an aggressive behavior and classify it in the category conflict. This way, the therapist's interpretation is considered and computed in the final statistical analysis.

In Table 9.1 we see an example of the data assessment using one scene of a patient.

As shown in Table 9.1, three categories emerge from our evaluation of the sandplay scene: destruction, defense, and conflict.

Along the psychotherapy process, all the scenes are organized in similar way so that we have a table with all the scenes of the patient classified in categories.

*Assessment of the categories' frequency*: The total time in the treatment process is divided into three periods. For instance, if the patient has been in analysis for 816 days, this total is divided into three phases: initial, intermediate, and final. The patient made a total of 38 scenes during this period. We identified the total number of categories and the number of times that each one appears in each phase. In this case, in the whole process, 14 categories were identified. These categories repeat themselves: in the initial phase we had 11 categories used 40 times; in the intermediate phase 11 categories were used 52 times; and in the final phase 10 categories were used 43 times.

We then add the number of times that each category appears in the different phases. For instance, the category defense appears 5 times out of 40 in the initial phase, 4 times out of 52 in the intermediate phase, and zero times in the final phase. That is 12.5% ($5 \times 100/40$) in the initial phase; 7.7% ($4 \times 100/52$) in the intermediate phase; and 0% in the final phase. These calculations allow us to observe a clear decrease of the defense mechanisms on the scenes.

The category centralization appears a total of 18 times. In the initial phase, it appears 3 times out of 40, or 7.5%; in the intermediate phase 5 times out of 52, or 9.6%; and in the final phase 10 times out of 43, or 23.3%. Through this we notice a gradual increase in the centralization movements. The category automatism appears 2 times out of 40, or 5%; 4 times out of 52, or 7.7%; and zero times in the final phase, demonstrating an increase in the middle of the process followed by a decrease until disappearance. If we consider the total number that each category was used, we have a more precise picture of the all process of a patient. As an example of this methodology the data of three male patients between 6 and 8 years old suffering with OCD were gathered and computed in Table 9.2.

We can observe that the categories most used in the initial phase were automatism and defense, whereas in the final phase the most frequent were centralization and integration.

With this table, we can clearly visualize how some categories evolve throughout the process and make corresponding interpretations. It is expected, based on the patient's pathology, that determined categories indicating conflict decrease and others indicating harmonization increase. A hypothesis can be raised according to the patient's clinical case. For instance, we can raise the hypothesis that the application of the sandplay technique will decrease the neurotic symptoms of a patient, expressed here as OCD.

**TABLE 9.1** Description and categorization of the scene 1

| No. of scene | Date | Patient's verbalization | Verbal expression: category | Miniature's themes | Scenario's dynamics | Clinical observations | Imagery expression: category |
|---|---|---|---|---|---|---|---|
| 1 | 09/04/04 | "The city is separated from the forest" | Defense | 5 Wild animals<br>1 Nature figure<br>1 Monument<br>2 Construction figures<br>1 Ball (bomb-destruction)<br>6 Celebration figures 5 Barrier figures | Threaten figures separated by fences in order to prevent them to invade the superior part of the scenario where there is a Christmas tree with presents. There is a bomb next to the nativity set and the Statue of Liberty. | The picture shows threatening situations. The symbols of celebration are limited by fences and surrounded by objects of destruction. | Destruction Defense Conflict |

**TABLE 9.2** Evolution of categories through three points of measurement (initial, middle, and final) of the sandplay process of three patients (G, L, and A)

| Categories | G | | | L | | | A | | |
|---|---|---|---|---|---|---|---|---|---|
| | Initial | Middle | Final | Initial | Middle | Final | Initial | Middle | Final |
| Automatism | 5.0% | 7.7% | 0.0% | 9.0% | 5.0% | 0.0% | 1.8% | 0.0% | 0.0% |
| Defense | 12.5% | 7.7% | 0.0% | 10.6% | 5.0% | 4.2% | 5.5% | 3.5% | 1.6% |
| Centralization | 7.5% | 9.6% | 23.3% | 4.5% | 7.5% | 5.9% | 9.2% | 15.3% | 17.5% |
| Integration | 0.0% | 5.8% | 20.9% | 4.5% | 1.3% | 7.6% | 1.8% | 3.5% | 15.9% |

Through the analyses of the scenes, we may observe any change in the patient's clinical state. The sandplay data may also be compared to the medical, academic, and family reports.

This method also allows us to compare the evolution and development of different patients. As an example, we use data of three children with OCD (Matta, 2006) to verify similar patterns among them as well as any differences.

## Evaluation questions

- What is the most predominant category between the three patients?
- Can we observe a disease's pattern?
- Is there a predominant category in each phase for the three subjects?
- Do the patients follow a similar pattern of evolution through the process?

Data presented in a single table can show the percentage of the categories by phase for the three patients, giving a general idea of the evolution of the categories for all. Table 9.3 shows the categories' evolution in each of the three patients.

As we can we observe in the table, there has been an increase in the categories integration and transformation and a decrease in the categories automatism, conflict, defenses, and destruction. Other possible comparative figures (Figures 9.2 and 9.3):

As we can see, the use of this method enables objectively following the evolution and development of the patient as well as a comparison to other patients. Here we have a possibility to verify if there are patterns of development in a sandplay, according to the determined pathology or age group. In the other hand, the classification of scenes and the categorization of the patient's verbalization depend on the therapist's ability as well. These categories must be described in the clearest way so that it allows other researchers to use it, creating a database.

The ideal when doing this research is that the classification of the scenes is made by someone other than the therapist himself/herself. Although, of course, the way that the therapist will describe his/her observations will be highly important, for only he or she will be able to set the proper tone to what took place in the sessions. Thus, the transference, countertransference, and resonance questions may be only be answered by the therapist and then included in the categories.

It is clear that the increase or decrease of a determined category throughout the process does not necessarily mean a progress in the patient's clinical case. For instance, the increase in the category conflict can mean an improvement in a patient who is passive and submissive. Although our observations indicate the tendency for classified scenes to translate as positive transformation, the patient's final evaluation depends on his general clinical case, and it cannot be dependent on a literal transcription of the scenes. The data then obtained need to be evaluated in comparison to other clinical and behavioral observation.

**TABLE 9.3** Evolution of all categories throughout the processes of the three patients

| Categories | G | | | A | | | L | | |
|---|---|---|---|---|---|---|---|---|---|
| | *Initial* | *Middle* | *Final* | *Initial* | *Middle* | *Final* | *Initial* | *Middle* | *Final* |
| Automatism | 5.00% | 7.70% | 0.00% | 9.00% | 5.00% | 0.00% | 1.80% | 0.00% | 0.00% |
| Defenses | 12.50% | 7.70% | 0.00% | 10.60% | 5.00% | 4.20% | 5.50% | 3.50% | 1.60% |
| Destruction | 0.00% | 9.60% | 4.70% | 3.00% | 5.00% | 7.60% | 7.30% | 1.80% | 0.00% |
| Conflict | 15.00% | 15.40% | 11.60% | 8.50% | 5.60% | 9.30% | 12.80% | 5.90% | 9.50% |
| Congestion | 5.00% | 5.80% | 9.30% | 6.50% | 0.60% | 2.50% | 3.70% | 0.60% | 0.00% |
| Transference | 12.50% | 0.00% | 2.30% | 3.00% | 3.10% | 6.80% | 2.80% | 1.20% | 0.00% |
| Celebration | 5.00% | 0.00% | 7.00% | 3.50% | 1.30% | 0.00% | 7.30% | 6.50% | 11.10% |
| Egoic Identification | 15.00% | 21.20% | 9.30% | 14.10% | 18.80% | 21.20% | 14.70% | 4.70% | 11.10% |
| Ascending mov. | 7.50% | 1.90% | 0.00% | 9.50% | 9.40% | 10.20% | 5.50% | 14.10% | 1.60% |
| Descending mov. | 10.00% | 7.70% | 0.00% | 11.10% | 18.10% | 14.40% | 22.90% | 30.00% | 19.00% |
| Submersion | 5.00% | 7.70% | 2.30% | 4.00% | 9.40% | 4.20% | 4.60% | 12.90% | 3.20% |
| Transformation | 0.00% | 0.00% | 9.30% | 8.00% | 10.00% | 5.90% | 0.00% | 0.00% | 9.50% |
| Centralization | 7.50% | 9.60% | 23.30% | 4.50% | 7.50% | 5.90% | 9.20% | 15.30% | 17.50% |
| Integration | 0.00% | 5.80% | 20.90% | 4.50% | 1.30% | 7.60% | 1.80% | 3.50% | 15.90% |

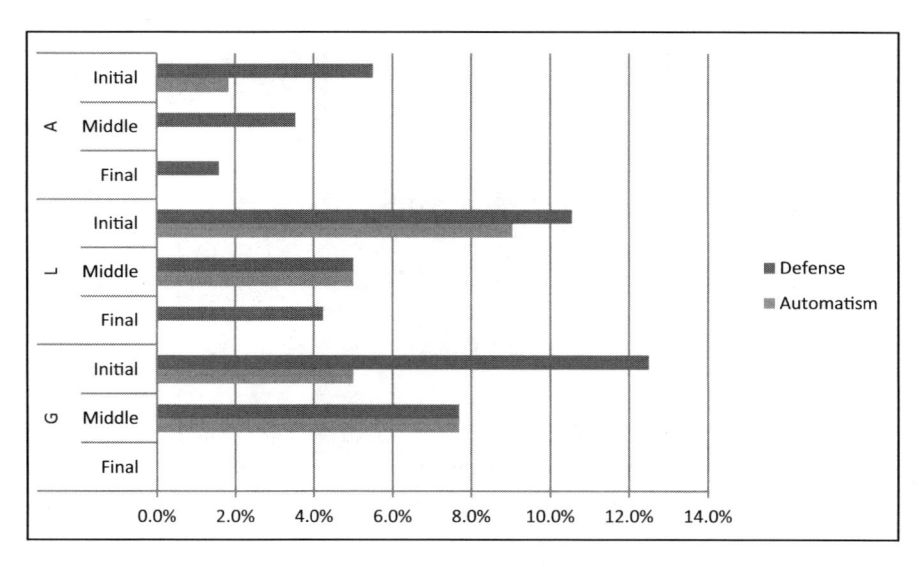

**FIGURE 9.2** Evolution of the categories automatism and defense in three cases

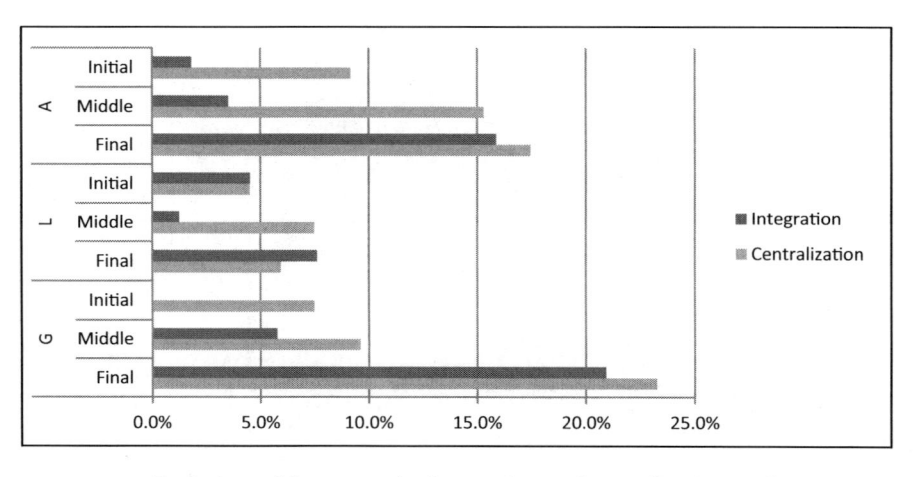

**FIGURE 9.3** Evolution of the categories integration and centralization in three cases

Next, we show the application of the effect of the sandplay therapy method on children with symptoms of trauma linked to abuse, neglect, and abandonment.

## Research with traumatized children

The research literature in the field of trauma indicates that traumatic experiences in childhood can cause irreversible damage to a child's psyche, especially for victims suffering from abusive practices by their caregivers. Several studies confirm the need for effective therapeutic techniques for the treatment of traumatized children prior to a manifestation of chronic patterns of disorganization and destructiveness directed toward themselves and others.

Van der Kolk (2005) considers the major challenge in this field to be the development of effective interventions for traumatized children to acquire the ability to cope with uncomfortable physical sensations and to be able to process their traumatic experiences.

One of the techniques developed to this end is Sensory Integration, created by Howe (2005). This technique aims to help children maintain a state of calm and relaxation, and to recognize, control and distinguish between different sensations. The inclusion of non-verbal therapy techniques such as sandplay therapy may be useful. According to Howe, cognitive behavioral therapy (CBT) should not be used to initiate the treatment of traumatized children, as this technique presupposes sufficient control of the frontal cortex over the emotional limbic system. The author further posits that prematurely initiated cognitive therapies may lead to fight-or-flight and/or freezing responses, and will not result in adequate treatment outcomes in traumatized children. In accordance with this view, a systematic review of the effectiveness of CBT in sexually abused children (MacDonald, Higgins, & Ramchandani, 2011) revealed that while CBT may have a positive impact on the sequelae of abuse, its results are not statistically significant. Similarly, van der Kolk (2005) criticized verbal therapies for increasing the risk of activating those implicit memories and physical or physiological sensations linked to trauma which may lead to the experience of strong negative emotions.

Despite the obvious need for developing effective interventions with trauma victims, there are currently few research studies that address this challenge. If, as previous studies have hypothesized, trauma becomes sedimented in subcortical structures including the hypothalamus and therefore remains unconscious and non-verbalized, non-verbal therapy techniques may represent the most effective treatment strategies (Schore, 2003). In addition, it is well established that play represents the primary means for young children to facilitate the emergence of unconscious content. Thus, the development of interpersonal, cognitive, emotional, and physical techniques that integrate recreation and stimulate non-verbal symbolism are likely to promote mental health without the risk of re-traumatization.

Therefore, non-verbal techniques could facilitate the expression of unconscious processes linked to trauma, as was demonstrated by clinical studies where the transduction of sensations and physiological/emotional symptoms to a more conscious level was facilitated using non-verbal material (Ramos, 2006). We have also observed that clinical cases studies of ST conducted with adult, teenage, and child patients have shown that symbolization of the trauma allowed for psychic content to be integrated and for aggressive and destructive tendencies to be acknowledged – converting the core of defensive structures into creative structures instead and gradually modifying and strengthening the victim's ego (Kalff, 2003; Adams, 2007; Balfour, 2008; Rivière, 2008; Herrmann, 2008, 2011; Hong, 2011; Freddle et al., 2015).

The present study aims to investigate whether traumatized children experience improvement in clinical symptoms related to internalizing factors, externalizing factors, and total problems (as scores on the CBCL/6–18), as well as in perceptual ability, visual spatial analysis, conceptual abstraction ability and subjective evaluation of well-being following psychotherapeutic treatment with sandplay therapy (ST).

## Method

### Participants

Children aged between six and a half and 10 years of age residing in foster care institutions in four cities in the state of São Paulo, Brazil, participated in the study from May 2012 to December 2014.

*Exclusion criteria*: children undergoing psychological treatment.

*Sample selection*: Eighty-six children ages 6–10 years old residing in foster care institutions at the time of testing were evaluated using the Child Behavior Checklist (CBCL/6–18) by two caregivers at the institution where the children lived. All children scored borderline and/or clinical outcomes in the aggregate scores of internalizing factors, externalizing factors, and total problems. These results are consistent with past studies, which have reported significant differences in performance by traumatized children on these scores (Spinazzola et al., 2013). In the course of the study, 26 children dropped out due to being returned to their family or adopted, resulting in a total sample of 34 boys and 26 girls.

*Instruments*: ID Form: age, sex, cause for admission, duration of foster care; Child Behavior Checklist (CBCL/6–18; Rocha, Pereira, Arantes, & Silvares, 2010); Cubes and Vocabulary sub-tests WISC-III (Wechsler, 2011); Autoquestionnaire Qualité de Vie Enfant Imagé/AUQEI (translated and adapted by Assumpção, Kuczinski, Sprovieri, & Aranha, 2000); sandplay therapy material: two sand trays with wet and dry sand (size 72 cm × 50 cm × 7.5 cm); miniatures representing humans, greenery, stones, animals, buildings, vehicles, and mythical figures.

Placebo therapy material: one sand tray with dry sand (size 40 cm × 30 cm × 5 cm) with a 2 cm layer of sand, six white stones, and rake.

### Camera

*Procedure*: The participants were divided into three groups: Experimental (EG), Placebo (PG) and Control (CG) according to the availability of participants in each institution. Participants from the same institution participated in only one of the groups to prevent participants in the PG and CG from feeling excluded from the EG. Thus, sample randomization was not performed for ethical reasons.

*Evaluations were made in three stages:* T0 (baseline evaluation); T1 (second evaluation) after 20 weeks of treatment for all groups; T2 (third evaluation) at a 6-month follow-up after T1 for EG only.

## Treatment procedure

### Experimental group (EG)

ST was performed individually by three psychologists at weekly intervals, with each session lasting an average of 45 minutes. In the first meeting, the therapist gave instructions to the child: "There are several miniatures and two trays of sand: one with dry sand and one with wet sand. You can play with the objects in this room. I would like you to build a scene using the miniatures you want. After you finish your scene and leave the room, I will photograph what you built." The child was also requested to tell a story about the scene following completion.

Each therapist annotated the child's verbal production and acknowledged their feelings and verbalizations. The session ended once the child communicated that he/she had finished and wanted to leave. After the child left the room, the therapist photographed the scene.

### Placebo group (PG)

The PG procedure was performed individually by six research assistants in individual sessions at weekly intervals, with an average duration of 45 minutes. A sand tray was shown to each child with the following instructions: "You can play with these objects: a sand tray, rake and stones." Following instruction, the child was free to verbalize their feelings but not requested to do so. The session ended when the child communicated that he/she had finished and wanted to leave.

### Control group (CG)

The CG procedure consisted of the psychological evaluation that was performed individually by research assistants.

The director of each foster care institution that participated in the study signed a global consent form authorizing the participation of the children under foster care and an individual consent form for each child as their legal guardian.

The study was approved by the Research Ethics Committee at the Pontifical Catholic University of Sao Paulo, with registry number 29730. CAAE: 01873412.8.0000.5482.

The participants in the PG and CG whose clinical symptoms persisted after T1 were referred to a specialist clinic.

An initial analysis was performed on differences in the four scores (CBCL, Cubes sub-test, Vocabulary sub-test, AUQEI) between the three groups at T0. Normality distribution was assessed via the Shapiro-Wilk test, which is suitable for smaller sample sizes. All variables rejected the null hypothesis of normality, thus adhering to a normal distribution.

Due to satisfaction of all relevant statistical assumptions, a parametric method (ANOVA) was employed for data analysis.

## Results

### Population characteristics (T0)

All groups met the criteria for homogeneity for age ($p = 0.276$), sex ($p = 0.28$), cause for admission ($p = 0.766$), and duration of foster care ($p = 0.133$). Results from the CBCL/6–18 revealed no significant differences between the three groups for internalizing factors ($p = 0.237$), externalizing factors ($p = 0.339$), and total problems ($p = 0.183$) before the intervention.

Results from the WISC-III sub-tests (Cubes and Vocabulary) were also equivalent across the three groups, with 76, 7% of the sample (Cubes sub-test; $p = 0.108$) and 80% of the sample (Vocabulary sub-test; $p = 0.362$) scoring below the average for the 6–10 age group. These results confirm research conducted by Van IJzendoorn and Juffer (2006), who found one of the primary characteristics of institutionalization to be a lack of motor, sensory, and cognitive stimulation, with subsequent delays in language development and cognitive function.

All participants across the three groups showed a high subjective sensation of quality of life on the AUQEI test ($p = 0.330$).

### Between-groups comparisons (T1)

#### AUQEI results

Analysis of quality of life (QOL) revealed no significant differences between T0 and T1 (i.e., all participants assessed their quality of life as the same level before and after the intervention): EG ($p = 0.542$), CG ($p = 0.142$), and PG ($p = 0.587$). Foster care appears to have had a protective effect, at least in the case of this sample. Access to education, food, clothing, health care, and security appeared to be important factors for the children in this research sample, regardless of whether they received psychological treatment.

#### WISC-III results

There were no significant differences in the WISC-III results between T0 and T1 for the three groups on both the Vocabulary sub-test, EG ($p = 0.114$), CG ($p = 0.536$), and PG ($p = 0.126$); and the Cubes sub-test, EG ($p = 0.157$), CG ($p = 0.705$), and PG ($p = 0.560$).

#### CBCL/6–18 results

Table 9.4 shows significant differences in all CBCL factors for the EG and a significant improvement in externalizing factors for the CG between T0 and T1.

**TABLE 9.4** Differences among groups after intervention (CBCL/6–18)

| Variables | EG | | | CG | | | PG | | |
|---|---|---|---|---|---|---|---|---|---|
| | T0 | T1 | p-value[1] | T0 | T1 | p-value[1] | T0 | T1 | p-value[1] |
| Internalizing factors | 62.8 | 52.1 | **< 0.001** | 62.3 | 62.0 | 0.637 | 65.1 | 64.3 | 0.486 |
| Externalizing Factors | 70.2 | 59.2 | **< 0.001** | 68.5 | 65.5 | **0.009** | 71.2 | 70.1 | 0.366 |
| Total Problems | 66.7 | 57.9 | **<0.001** | 66.1 | 64.2 | 0.079 | 68.3 | 64.0 | 0.090 |

EG: Experimental Group; CG: Control Group; PG: Placebo Group.

[1] T-Test for paired samples.

**TABLE 9.5** General linear model for repeated measurements (CBCL/6–18)

| Variables | Mean Values[1] | | | Standard Deviation | | | p-value[2] |
|---|---|---|---|---|---|---|---|
| | T0 | T1 | T2 | T0 | T1 | T2 | |
| Internalizing Factors | 59.6 | 53.4 | 54.3 | 6.8 | 4.5 | 3.2 | 0.269 |
| Externalizing Factors | 68.3 | 55.4 | 56.5 | 4.9 | 4.5 | 8.4 | **0.020** |
| Total Problems | 65.5 | 55.5 | 53.3 | 1.1 | 2.6 | 2.9 | **0.032** |

[1] The 12 cases were considered valid in the three measurements.
[2] Significance of Pillai's Trace test.

## Differences among groups after intervention (CBCL/6–18)

### EG results at 6-month follow-up (T2)

A follow-up evaluation 6 months after the intervention could only be conducted with the .EG ($n = 12$), as several children in the three groups were referred for psychological treatment, released, or adopted. Analysis of variance revealed no significant differences in the AUQEI and WISC tests between T1 and T2.

The results from the CBCL/6–18 in Table 9.5 reveal that while there were similar internalizing factor scores in T2, there was an increased improvement in externalizing factors and total problems compared to T1, 6 months after treatment.

### Sandplay scene analysis

Two categories of themes were defined for this investigation (see Table 9.6): (A) themes suggesting suffering and conflict and (B) themes relating to transformation and the possibility of psychological improvement. Each of these categories encompassed seven themes (based on categorization by Friedman & Mitchell, 2003):

> Category A: Threat/conflict; chaos/destruction; rage; wounds, neglect, defenses/schisms, and hidden/secret/mystery. Category B: Celebration, centralization, integration, pathfinding, nurture, protection/care, and transference.

**TABLE 9.6** Test for differences among rates of negative themes (A1 and A2) and positive themes (B1 and B2) in ST

| Variables | Experimental Group | |
|---|---|---|
| | Ratio | p-value[1] |
| A1 – Ratio of scenes with negative themes and total scenes (sessions 1–10) | 46.3% | 0.333 |
| B1 – Ratio of scenes with positive themes and total scenes (sessions 1–10) | 53.7% | |
| A2 – Ratio scenes with negative themes and total scenes (sessions 11–20) | 35.6% | **0.001** |
| B1 – Ratio of scenes with positive themes and total scenes (sessions 11–20) | 64.4% | |
| A1 – Ratio of scenes with negative themes and total scenes (sessions 1–10) | 46.3% | **0.002** |
| A2 – Ratio of scenes with negative themes and total scenes (sessions 11–20) | 35.6% | |
| B1 – Ratio of scenes with positive themes and total scenes (sessions 1–10) | 53.7% | **0.002** |
| B2 – Ratio of scenes with positive themes and total scenes (sessions 11–20) | 64.4% | |

[1] T-test for paired samples.

Each scene contained one or more themes. To better analyze the therapeutic process, we split the data into two phases: phase 1, sessions 1 through 10; and stage 2, sessions 11 through 20:

A1 = sessions 1 to 10, with focused on themes from category A
B1 = sessions 1 to 10, with themes related to category B
A2 = sessions 11 to 20, with themes related to category A
B2 = sessions 11 to 20, with themes associated with category B.

We observed no significant differences between negative themes (A1) and positive themes (B1) at the beginning of the process. Therefore, the participants revealed a similar frequency of positive and negative scenes until the middle of treatment. At the end of the process, there was a significant increase in the number of positive scenes compared to negative scenes (B2 > A2), a significant decrease in the number of negative scenes between the first and second phase of therapy (A1 < A2), and a higher proportion of positive scenes (B2 > B1).

The themes that were most representative of trauma and differed to the most extent between the first and second phase were threat/conflict, wounds/injuries, neglect and defenses (decrease in frequency); and the themes most representative of transformation and psychological improvement were centralization and integration (increase in frequency).

**TABLE 9.7** Test to check for differences between the average frequency of negative themes (A1 and A2) and positive themes (B1 and B2)

|   | Variables | Experimental Group | |
|---|---|---|---|
|   |   | Average | P-value[1] |
| A | Threat/conflict – A1 | 6.4 | **0.005** |
|   | Threat/conflict – A2 | 4.5 | |
|   | Hurt/injured – A1 | 3,0 | **0.028** |
|   | Hurt/injured – A2 | 1.7 | |
|   | Neglect – A1 | 2,4 | **0.021** |
|   | Neglect – A2 | 1,1 | |
|   | Defense/split – A1 | 3.2 | **0.026** |
|   | Defense/split – A2 | 1.8 | |
| B | Centralization – B1 | 3.9 | **0.049** |
|   | Centralization – B2 | 5.2 | |
|   | Integration – B1 | 2.5 | **0.022** |
|   | Integration – B2 | 3.8 | |
|   | Nourishment – B1 | 4.4 | 0.088 |
|   | Nourishment – B2 | 3.1 | |
|   | Protection/care – B1 | 6.1 | 0.098 |
|   | Protection/care – B2 | 4.8 | |

[1]  T-test for paired samples.

Table 9.7 lists the themes most representative of suffering and conflict and that contained significant differences in the first and second phase (threat/conflict, wounds/injuries, neglect and defenses [decrease in frequency]), as well as the themes most representative of transformation and psychological improvement (centralization and integration [increase in frequency]).

Interestingly, there was no change in the frequency of scenes with themes of nurture and protection with a high frequency of these themes throughout the process, possibly expressing the helplessness and lack of resources these children had, who were both physically and emotionally hungry.

Both the statistical analysis and the results of the sandplay process showed an improvement in the symptoms of the participants and a transformation of their behavior toward more adaptive patterns. Thus, ST appeared to result in the transduction and transformation of symptoms, leading to healthier ego development.

## Discussion

This study confirms the efficacy of ST in the treatment of children who are victims of trauma, as well as maintenance of this effect at 6 month follow-up.

Via the children's elaboration of the scenes and the stories they constructed, they developed what Knox (2011) describes as a sense of self-agency: a more mature ego and greater control over impulsiveness. Similar to observations by Kalff (2003), we observed that ST enabled the children to form a greater self-awareness, initially expressing their suffering in terms of chaotic and destructive themes and subsequently revealing a greater degree of organization, harmony, and psychic integration. The act of playing in a free and protected space, in the presence of a qualified therapist, enabled the expression of deep unconscious contents related to abandonment, abuse, and trauma.

The ability to express and symbolize traumatic events led to a reframing, corroborating what Van der Kolk (2005) highlighted as the importance for traumatized children to acquire skills to deal with uncomfortable physiological sensations and to be able to initially process these experiences non-verbally. ST allowed for the development of this process by providing a protected space where children could "look" at their trauma without reliving and repeating it.

## Acknowledgment

This research was supported by a grant from CAPES (Ministry of Education of Brazil).

## References

Adams, K. (2007). Reconnecting to the source: Recovering from sexual molestation. *Journal of Sandplay Therapy, 16*(2), 55–73.

Assumpção, F.B., Jr., Kuczinski, E., Sprovieri, M.H., & Aranha, E.M.G. (2000). Escala de Avaliação de Qualidade de Vida. AUQEI-Autoquestionnaire qualité de vie enfant imagé. Validade e confiabilidade de uma escala para qualidade de vida em crianças de 4 a 12 anos. *Arq. de Neuro-Psiquiatr, 58*(1), 119–127.

Balfour, R.N. (2008). Evolution of Sandplay images in healing: A case of childhood sexual abuse of a 36-year-old woman. *Journal of Sandplay Therapy, 17*(2), 33–49.

Freedle, L.R., Altschul, D.B., & Freedle, A. (2015). The role of Sandplay therapy in the treatment of adolescents and young adults with co-occurring substance use disorders and trauma. *Journal of Sandplay Therapy, 24*(2), 127–145.

Friedman, H., & Mitchell, R. (2003). *Olhando os cenários de Sandplay através de diferentes prismas.* Tradução de Marla Regina Gheller Souza dos Anjos. São Paulo: Sociedade Brasileira de Psicologia Analítica.

Grubbs, G. A. (1995). A comparative analysis of the sandplay process of sexually abused and nonclinical children [Special Issue]. *Arts in Psychotherapy, 22*, 429–446.

Herrmann, S.B. (2008). Treatment of an abandonment Trauma. *Journal of Sandplay Therapy, 17*(2), 51–73.

Herrmann, S.B. (2011). Transformation of violence: The case of Jacob. *Journal of Sandplay Therapy, 20*(1), 117–132.

Hong, G. (2011). *Sandplay therapy: Research and practice.* London-New York: Routledge.

Howe, D. (2005). *Child abuse and neglect: Attachment, development and intervention.* Basingstoke: Palgrave MacMillan.

Kalff, D.M. (2003). *Sandplay: A psychotherapeutic approach to the psyche.* Cloverdale, CA: Temenos Press.

Knox, J. (2011). *Self-agency in psychotherapy: Attachment, autonomy and intimacy.* London and New York: Routledge.

Macdonald, G., Higgins, J.P.T., & Ramchandani, P. (2006). Cognitive-behavioural interventions for children who have been sexually abused. *Cochrane Database of Systematic Reviews 2006*, Issue 4, Art. No.: CD001930. https://doi.org/10.1002/14651858.CD001930.pub2

Matta, R.M. (2006). *A utilização da terapia do Sandplay no tratamento de crianças com transtorno obsessivo-compulsivo*. Master Dissertation. Programa de Estudos PósGraduados em Psicologia Clínica da PUC-SP, São Paulo.

Mitchell, R., & Friedman, H. (1994). *Sandplay: Past, present & future*. London: Routledge.

Pattis, E. (2011). *Sandplay therapy in vulnerable communities, a Jungian approach*. London: Routledge.

Ramos, D.G. (2006). *The psyche of the body*. London: Routledge.

Ramos, D.G., & Matta, R.M. (2008). Sandplay: A method for data analysis. *Journal of Sandplay Therapy*, 17(2), 93–115.

Rivière, Y. (2008). Xena: Healing the abused feminine. *Journal of Sandplay Therapy*, 17(1), 63–79.

Rocha, M.M., Pereira, R.F., Arantes, M.C., & Silvares, E.F.M. (2010). Guia para profissionais da saúde mental sobre o Sistema Achenbach de Avaliação Empiricamente Baseada (ASEBA). Translation from T.M. Achenbach & L.A. Rescorla. São Paulo. In *Mental health practitioners' guide for the Achenbach of System of Empirically Bases Assessment (ASEBA)* (7th ed.). Burlington: University of Vermont, Research Center for Children, Youth & Families (Tiragem de circulação interna).

Schore, A.N. (2003). *Affect regulation & the repair of the self*. New York: W.W. Norton & Company.

Spinazzola, J., Habib, M., Knoverek, A., Arvidson, J., Nisenbaum, J., Wentworth, R., & Kisiell, C. (2013). The heart of the matter: Complex trauma in child welfare. *Child Welfare 360°: Trauma-Informed Child Welfare Practice*. https://cascw.umn.edu/wp-content/uploads/2013/12/CW360-Ambit_Winter2013.pdf, accessed June 2014.

Van der Kolk, B. (2005). Child abuse & victimization. *Psychiatric Annals*. Editorial Introduction: Child Abuse & Victimization, 374–378.

Van Ijzendoorn, M.A., & Juffer, F. (2006). The Emanuel Miller Memorial Lecture: Adoption as intervention. Meta-analytic evidence for massive catch-up and plasticity in physical, socioemotional and cognitive development. *Journal of Child Psychology and Psychiatry*, 47, 1228–1245.

Wechsler, D. (2011). *WISC-III: Escala de Inteligência Wechsler para Crianças: Manual*. Adaptação e padronização de uma amostra brasileira: Vera Lúcia Marques de Figueiredo. São Paulo: Casa do Psicólogo.

Weinrib, E. (1993). *Imagens do Self: O processo terapêutico na caixa de areia*. São Paulo: Summus.

# 10

## PICTURES OF TRANSFORMATION AND THE SYMBOLIC ATTITUDE

### A research perspective on picture interpretation and the therapeutic *mundus imaginalis*

*Manfred Krapp*

Today, Analytical Psychology is faced with the challenge of grounding its theoretical concepts in accordance with current research standards. In this chapter I present my efforts to ground the Jungian pictorial-hermeneutic method and the therapeutic mundus imaginalis. I will present two studies of picture interpretation, one of which also includes an interdisciplinary discourse with qualitative researchers.

### Analytical Psychology and the hermeneutic tradition

"My views are grounded in experience" (Jung, CW 18, para. 1731).[1] "Grounded" is a generous English translation and masks the problem of Jung's empirical attitude, how he developed a theory from his experiences (see also Introduction). "Grounding," however, represents exactly the methodical proceeding of the "Grounded Theory" (see Corbin & Strauss, 1990; Strauss, 1998), a well-known qualitative method.

Postmodern scholars have subsumed Jung's methodical approach under the hermeneutic tradition.

> Jung often interpreted the unconscious as if it were a hermeneutical inquiry of a text, and it can be argued that he was moving in the direction of "depth hermeneutics" with his psychological studies of dreams, mental disturbances, religion, myths and such phenomena as Gnosticism and alchemy.
>
> *(Pietikäinen, 1999, p. 30)*

Despite Jung having emphasized that he was an empirical scientist, "his understanding of phenomenology has more to do with a qualitative and descriptive approach to 'psychic experiences'" (Pietikäinen, 1999, p. 31).

J.J. Clarke (1994, p. 47) compares Jung's method of understanding with the hermeneutic circle of the philosopher Gadamer (2004). ≈) too sees parallels between

Jung and the hermeneutics which are "the close connection between the subject and object in the act of interpretation and the fundamental role of understanding as the imaginative but publicly verifiable method of translating the subjective experiences of the other into objective knowledge" (p. 30). But he attributes an outstanding quality to Jungian hermeneutics. "Myth, dreams, folklore and the delusions of the mentally ill are predominantly pictorial representations for Jung, [. . .] he is undoubtedly the great advocate of the relevancy of 'fantasy' thinking in the twentieth century" (Pietikäinen, 1999, p. 86).

In contrast to direct, rational thinking, indirect, associative fantasy thinking is based on images.[2] Thus the Jewish scholar Brumlik contrasts Jung's pictorial-hermeneutic discourse with Freud's hermeneutic focus on language. The archetypes can be seen as the structural dominants of the collective unconscious:

> these forms of symbolic order, which are represented predominantly in pictorial signs and culturally represented in icons can be deciphered by depth hermeneutics, which applies – like Freudian psychoanalysis – the idea of the human unconscious, but in contrast to Freud's psychoanalysis, does not use a linguistic model of textual understanding, but an iconographic model of imaginal understanding.
>
> *(Brumlik, 2004, p. 133, my translation)*

## The role of images in the therapeutic process

Concepts of cognitive psychology such as "emotional meaning structures" or "image-like prototypes of emotional structures" (see Moser, 1992, p. 183) emphasize the supremacy of images over language within the therapeutic process.

> Meaning does not come into the therapeutic relationship first through language. [. . .] The image the analyst develops of the analysand on the basis of their affective relationship, and which contains parts of him or herself, representing the essence, biography, and sociocultural context of both, [. . .] is certainly not, or not exclusively, a linguistic work of verbal constructions arising from the analyst's interpretations. It is an emotional and image-like world, a cognitive-affective system, the elements of which are stored in both an affective as well as an image-like code.
>
> *(Moser, 1992, p. 34)*

Process research emphasizes the theoretical models at the back of the therapist's mind. Analytical Psychology focuses on the psychic image as a "concentrated expression of the psychic situation in its totality" (Jung, CW VI, para. 760) and the analyst's symbolic attitude, which create the therapeutic mundus imaginalis, "the interactive field which is structured by images" (Schwartz-Salant, 1989, p. 101; see also Samuels, 1985, p. 264). In this interactive field, the patient's and the analyst's inner images correspond to each other and the analyst becomes a container for the imagery of the patient. The following two studies demonstrate how patients intro-ject the analyst's symbolic attitude, his or her way of integrating the images which emerge from the common unconscious between both, the mundus imaginalis.

## Pictorial symbolism of transformation processes in art therapy groups

The first study is an investigation of art therapy in groups with psychotic patients which I applied in the entry ward of a psychiatric hospital.[3] Over a period of almost three years I collected approximately 500 paintings and sculptures which were cre-ated in groups which I treated myself in collaboration with a female art therapist, or in groups which I supervised. I documented the paintings with the comments and associations of patients and therapists, and in the case of the groups I treated myself, with my own countertransference feelings. More than 40 case studies were conducted representing the clinical process of recovering psychotic patients as it was manifested in their paintings.

The theoretical model for my interpretation was the structural analysis of *The Great Mother* (Neumann, 1972). Neumann's book was inspired by a collection of pictures and statues at the Eranos Archive for Symbolic Research, which "deter-mined the whole content and rhythm of my thinking" (Neumann, 1972, p. vii). Thus Paglia (2005) enthusiastically calls it "a visual feast." More than 200 plates of pictures and 74 text figures illustrate the mother archetype in its different ritual and artistic representations. *The Great Mother* illustrates the paramount significance of pictorial representations for forming and grounding a theory within Analytical Psychology. Another example is the first version of *Symbols of Transformation* (Jung, 1952) with 300 illustrations.[4]

Neumann distinguishes two characteristics of the feminine. "As an elementary character we designate the aspect of the Feminine as being the Great Round, the Great Container, tending to hold fast onto everything that springs from it and to surround it like an eternal substance" (Neumann, 1972, p. 25). This is the "participation mystique between mother and child [which] is the original situ-ation of the container and contained" (Neumann, 1972, p. 29). The increasing independence of the ego leads to the transformative character, which, "in contrast to the conservative tendency of the elementary character, drives towards motion, change, and [. . .] transformation" (Neumann, 1972, p. 29). This corresponds to the detachment of the anima figure from the mother archetype. "The anima is the vehicle par excellence of the transformative character" (Neumann, 1972, p. 33). Neumann (1972, p. 82) gives the innumerable manifestations of the mother archetype a coherent shape by means of a structural diagram (see Scheme III in Neumann, 1972, p. 82 and its explanation on pp. 64–83).

I investigated the study paintings from the following viewpoint: in acute psycho-sis, the negative elementary character dominates (e.g., the devouring tendencies), often in combination with the negative transformative character. In Scheme III, Neumann assigns madness to the negative pole of axis A (transformative character) and sickness in general to the negative pole of axis M (elementary character). In the improvement phase of psychosis, the shift in the constellation of the mother archetype to the positive elementary and transformative character was evident. In this process of ego-recovery, the art therapy group functions as a vessel, the center of the mother archetype's symbolism.

These two paintings (Figure 10.1) emerged within one group session and demonstrate already this transformation processes. The theme was Grimm's fairy tale "The Gallant Tailor." Many psychotic patients have difficulties coping with the devouring tendencies of the group. Fairy tales can neutralize these by structuring threatening images and building up a means of identification with the group. Both pictures of Wolfgang, as I call this 25-year-old schizophrenic patient, show the tailor in his workshop, which had become too small after he had slain seven at one blow. Wolfgang projected his family situation onto the fairy tale by painting the tailor's mother, who does not occur in the story at all, behind him. But his biographical conflicts were focused on an ambivalent dependence on his possessive mother, caused by the early death of his father. A remarkable feature of both paintings is the tendency toward the left, which, following the "guidelines" of Jungian picture interpretation (see Abt, 2005; Jacobi, 1981; Riedel, 1988), represents the dominance of the unconscious. Both figures of the first painting have a demonic appearance and evidently represent the negative elementary character in the sense of it holding fast, fixating, bewitching, and devouring (see the negative pole of axis M in Neumann's Scheme III).

**FIGURE 10.1** Two pictures from the session: "The Gallant Tailor"

In the second painting, a remarkable transformation has taken place. Gaining a more realistic view of the fairy tale's story as well as his situation in the group, Wolfgang is about to detach himself from the negative mother archetype by removing the mighty throne of the first painting, "the sacral symbol of the Great Mother" (Neumann, 1972, p. 99), in the background. The mother is replaced with a black hatched area, erased by means of a strong sweep of his chalk resembling a confused mass. This *massa confusa* refers to the prime matter and the nigredo (blackening); both are the matrix of an alchemical transformation processes. Thus, the prime matter in Wolfgang's picture suggests a development toward the positive elementary and transformative character. In both pictures the vertical format represents an opening up to the top and to the paternal, spiritual realm that counterbalances the conflict-burdened horizontal line between mother and son. This also reflects the strong transference Wolfgang built up onto me which became evident in Figure 10.2.

In contrast to analytic group therapy, the art therapy group represents a particular creative group norm. My personal presence for the entire duration of the group setting is unusual for these patients, who are not accustomed to seeing a psychiatrist for such a long time. Being exposed in a totally passive way to the intensity of psychotic emotionality was sometimes a real challenge for me. In the previous group sessions I had experienced a split in my countertransference, which oscillated between fearful feelings and a positive identification with the patient's impressive

**FIGURE 10.2**   Picture from the session: second movement of Mozart's piano concert in C-major (Köchel index 467)

creativity. The second movement of Mozart's piano concert in C-major (Köchel index 467) reconciled the conflict between my threatening emotions and a positive identification and became a uniting symbol for me, which I presented to the group. Art therapy with psychotic patients often challenges the therapist to create transforming images.

In Wolfgang's painting one can see a large "bellied" piano in the lower left-hand corner. "The belly [...] represents the elementary character of the vessel" (Neumann, 1972, p. 44). The vessel is the "essence of the Feminine. The basic symbolic equation woman = body = vessel corresponds to what is perhaps mankind's [...] most elementary experience of the Feminine" (Neumann, 1972, p. 39). The bellied piano expresses a primordial image of the group, and compensates for the tendency toward the left together with the pianist, the devouring character of the unconscious respective the group of his previous paintings. A movement toward the upper right hand corner, toward the bright staves and the musicians is recognizable. This full spectrum of different colors — the alchemical *cauda pavonis* (peacock's tail) which announces the dawn (aurora) of a new day — symbolizes Wolfgang's emotional transformation. Now, he has developed an identification with the therapist and his "instrument," meaning he is listening to Mozart's music within the group.

Wolfgang's next picture (Figure 10.3) originates from 5 weeks later. The theme was the patient's expectations with regard to the art therapy group. On the left-hand side, he depicts his activity in occupational therapy, and on the right how art therapy furthered him to get in touch with other people. The bench between the

**FIGURE 10.3**   Picture from the session: the expectations with regard to the art therapy group

two trees reflects the containing vessel character of the group, which is emphasized by the bellied drawing. There is a distinctive similarity between the piano
in the previous painting and the bench, which symbolizes the introjection of the
symbolic attitude. It epitomizes an encounter between male and female, "me" and
"you" within the group. This coniunctio also is represented by an active male element, craft activity, on the left, and a containing and transforming female element,
the group as a contact medium, on the right. Surprisingly enough, the object of
Wolfgang's craft activity are pots and baskets, which are vessel symbols. The pot,
in particular, is "the belly symbol par excellence" (Neumann, 1972 p. 132). The
rose in Wolfgang's hand and the trees is assigned to the transformative character of
the vessel symbolism (Neumann, 1972, p. 44) and effectively highlights Wolfgang's
amazing transformation.

The painting (Figure 10.4) of a young woman reflects her experiences in the
art therapy group at the end of her 3 months of treatment. She is a seriously ill
borderline patient with prolonged psychotic episodes combined with strong auto-
destructive impulses and actions. In the upper left-hand corner, the square frame
reflects her inner situation at the beginning of the treatment. It contains a broken
round figure with a sun on the right above, and a moon on the left below, as she
explained. Below this square frame, there is a hole into which she fell during her
psychotic states. She herself is the blue point in the center, embedded in earth. The
circle on the right below illustrates her therapeutic process, making its way upwards

**FIGURE 10.4**   Picture from the session: my experiences in the art therapy group

toward the light that is the sun. In the top right-hand corner, darkness still reigns. The ground consists of earth surrounded by water; the green color as nature has an important meaning for her, as she told the group.

The painting illustrates the containing vessel character of the group, which is first the ground, consisting of earth surrounded by water, and green nature. "The natural elements that are essentially connected with vessel symbolism include both earth and water. This containing water is the primordial womb of life [. . .]. But the maternal water not only contains; it also nourishes and transforms" (Neumann, 1972, p. 47). The use of blue and brown, the colors of water and earth, to depict the Great Round accentuates its containing character.

The broken and split ego could be placed on the ground and joined together by diving into the Great Round, which is the group as well as the patient's unconscious. It is no coincidence that its center has the same blue color as the restored ego in the middle of the picture. The Great Round is not merely a circle, however, but rather resembles a wheel with the hub in the center and 10 spokes. That is a complete mandala structure – similar, for instance, to the Tibetan wheel of life – and represents the spiritual transformative character. It becomes the basic condition for her development upwards toward the sun, symbolizing the recovery of her ego. The wheel is assigned to the alchemical operation of "circulatio" or "rotatio," which leads, according to Jung, to a state of "being contained in the opposites" (Jung CW XIV, para. 296, quoted according to Edinger, 1985, p. 143). A kind of rotation also happens within the group when the patients reflect together on her paintings and communicate about them.

## The use of the interpretation support system ATLAS.ti

Now I would like to discuss how qualitative methods can illustrate imaginal processes. By means of the interpretation support system ATLAS.ti (Muhr, 1997), I created a semantic network of this painting which contains the patient's comments and my interpretation. ATLAS.ti (see www.atlasti.com) is a complex QDA (qualitative data analysis) program and offers an effective tool for the analysis of textual, graphical, and audio data. Qualitative strategies are very common in process research, in particular for investigating the therapeutic relationship. They make the bases of interpretations transparent at all stages, from theory-driven data collection to the development and application of categories to the evaluation and interpretation of the results with reference to the starting point of the investigation. This circular procedure (see Flick, 1998) is analogous to the alchemical operation of "circulatio" and "circumambulatio." Qualitative methods are directed at the complexity and totality of the subject under investigation, including both its inner perspective and the subjectivity of the investigator. This is an analogy to the alchemical attitude of investigating nature, the "imaginatio vera et non phantastica" (Jung CW, XII, para. 218).

ATLAS.ti differentiates between textual and conceptual level work. The textual work segments the text, graphic, or audio primary documents into specific passages to which comments, codes, and memos are assigned. On the conceptual level,

"ATLAS.ti's unique networking features allow you to visually 'connect' selected passages, memos and codes, into diagrams which graphically outline complex relations" (Muhr, 1997, p. 7).

> "In contrast to linear, sequential representations (e.g., text) network representations of knowledge resemble more closely the way human memory and thought is structured. Some cognitive 'load' in handling complex relationships is reduced with the aid of spatial representation techniques. ATLAS. ti uses networks to help explore conceptual structures and to make them transparent. The networks add a heuristic 'right brain' approach to qualitative analysis."
>
> *(Muhr, 1997, p. 61)*

A Jungian research strategy requires this right brain methodological approach to do justice to the subtlety of inner images. In analytic psychology, Edinger refers to a network or cluster thinking

> which is neither linear nor meandering and associational. [. . .] It is thinking that is orientated around a center, and moves radially to and from that center, circumambulating it. It goes back and forth returning to the central image again and again, building up a rich associative cluster of interconnecting images.
>
> *(Edinger, 1995, p. 20)*

Thus semantic networks created by ATLAS.ti could be a tool for operationalizing the Jungian hermeneutic approach to images.

I have created a semantic network in order to ground my interpretation of the last painting in the data. My theoretical background focuses on the mother archetype and alchemical imagery. The network consists of codes and code families, like alchemical operations, which are linked to quotations referring to different areas or motives of the painting, the patient's comments, and my interpretation. The codes have a standardized or a specific defined relation to each other. For example the relation "isa" ("is a") is standardized by ATLAS.ti and relates the "circulatio" and "containing" in the painting. A comment can be activated by clicking on "isa" and explains my reasons for this relational reference to Jung, CW XIV, par.296 (see above): Circulatio "means being contained in the opposites." My own creation is the relation between "Great Round" and Ego. I assigned the symbol ">>," which means "is basis of." My theoretical argumentation for this relation which, again, can be activated by a mouse-click on ">>," refers to Neumann's idea of the ego–self axis, that the "Great Round" as a symbol of the mother archetype is the basis of ego formation. In this way, ATLAS.ti provides the facility of operationalizing imaginal processes, as they are manifested in pictures as well as in language.

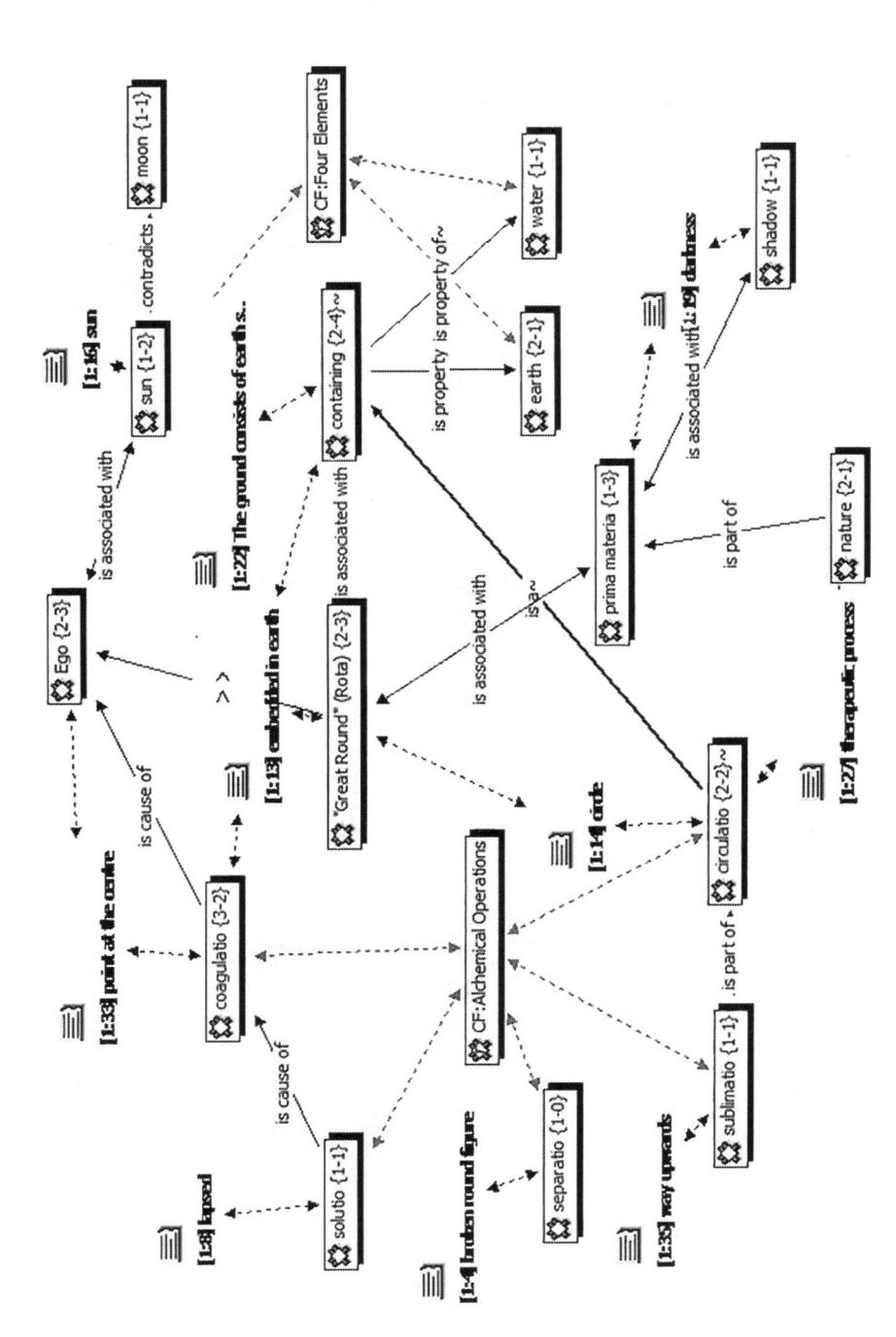

FIGURE 10.5   Semantic network referring to Figure 10.4

## A pilot study: "Analytical Psychology and Pictorial-Hermeneutic, Qualitative Methods"

### *Methodology*

I would now like to present a pilot study which focuses on the imaginal world of a 43-year-old borderline patient. During our first meeting I was very impressed by her lucid account of her inner images. I therefore encouraged her to paint them. Eight watercolors emerged, which became the prime matter of the analytical therapy because of the intensive communication about them. Later on, she also wrote down her comments about the paintings. A mundus imaginalis was formed by the patient's imagination and my symbolic attitude, which led to some 20 paintings and about 150 pages of comments and her imaginative participation concerning her therapeutic process. I called the pilot study "Analytical Psychology and Pictorial-Hermeneutic, Qualitative Methods." The study focused on the interaction and communication about (painted) "Images from the Unconscious" could contribute to therapeutic efficacy which could potentially be specific for Analytical Psychology. Its data consists of the first eight paintings, the patient's comments on them encompassing about 10 pages, and a small section of her documentation, demonstrating how she has introjected the analyst's symbolic attitude. In order to evaluate the data, I also interviewed the patient 3 years after the conclusion of her therapy. The paintings and comments were analyzed by a philosopher and linguist proceeding from Panofsky's iconological-iconographical method, by an art scientist employing semiotics, and by an art therapist and qualitative researcher applying the ethnographic method. My own interpretation focused on alchemical imagery creating a code system by means of ATLAS.ti. Another qualitative researcher who is specialized in QDA supervised the project. Due to the limited financial resources, the evaluation of all the data and interpretations by ATLAS.ti is incomplete.

A main focus of psychotherapy research is based on the fact that "theoretical models are not a super-structure, but they are connected to the interpretative process from the start" (Moser, 1992, p. 39). For the therapeutic process, alchemical imagery is a common Jungian model, regarded as an analogy for transformation.

> If we are not to submit psychic phenomena to the Procrustean bed of a preconceived theory, we must seek the categories for understanding the psyche within the psyche itself. An old alchemical dictum says, "Dissolve the matter in its own water." This is what we do when we try to understand the process of psychotherapy in terms of alchemy.
>
> *(Edinger, 1985, p. 1)*

Qualitative methods exactly reflect this hermeneutic attitude.

A theoretical model already consisting of images like Jungian amplification is easier to transfer into inner images as the basis for therapeutic communication. Edinger has "broken down" alchemical imagery by ordering it around the seven main alchemical operations. These are the calcinatio, solutio, coagulatio, sublimatio, mortificatio, separatio, and coniunctio.

> Each of these operations is found to be the center of an elaborated symbol system. [. . .] They provide basic categories by which to understand the life of the psyche and they illustrate almost the full range of experiences that constitute individuation. [. . .] Each will be accompanied by a chart indicating the major symbolic connections that cluster around the core image.
>
> *(Edinger, 1985, p. 15)*

Edinger's charts or networks "emphasize the structural nature of each symbol system" (p. 15) and could be operationalized by means of ATLAS.ti in order to reflect the therapeutic process.

A pictorial-hermeneutic iconographic method for therapeutic pictures is mainly based on the analyst's symbolic attitude, which is both a theoretical model and an emotional therapeutic attitude. Empathy and identification with the patient's images and paintings create an interactive field (see Stein, 1995) including the subjective experience of both.[5] A Jungian analyst should be able to easily "translate" his theoretical models like individuation, symbolic attitude, or amplification into his inner images and refer them to the patient's images. This kind of therapeutic communication leads to a reciprocal emotional resonance, an interchange of inner images, the mundus imaginalis, which could be a specific Jungian factor of therapeutic efficacy in both individual and group analysis.

## The corresponding inner images of patient and analyst (mundus imaginalis)

Gina, as I call my patient, became conscious of her inner images during psychotherapy in a hospital when she was intensely confronted with being abused by her father. But she did not talk about her images to her therapist. I encouraged Gina to do so during our first meeting nine months later, and she portrayed a dramatic scenario of world-creation threatened by dissolution.

| **The patient's description of her images.** | **The analyst's amplifications.**[6] |
| --- | --- |
| *First image (left side of Figure 10.6):* <br> There is, far-reaching into the horizon, an all enclosing greyish–black background – ; before that a muddy brown area of ground with only a few clumps of grass – ; a shapeless tiny brownish-black mass is emerging slowly from the ground or directly out of the mould – ; probably my "Ego." | In the Orphic cosmogony, the cosmic egg emerges from the darkness, which gives birth to the God of Eros. Eros, however, creates the world from this darkness. <br> In Egyptian creation mythology the god Ptah forms the cosmic egg from the potter's wheel. |

**FIGURE 10.6**    Gina's painting of her first two inner images

I feel that the ground (earth) is very soft and deep and smells like a swamp, and "I want to grow."

*Second image (right side of Figure 10.6):*

Now a movement is starting, the brown muddy ground has a few more clumps of grass – ; the shapeless mass is consolidating a little – ; now a lilac covering is emerging – ; "Ego"

I felt: The covering is transparent, probably consisting of bullet-proof glass, and is slowly forming around my "Ego."

Alchemical symbolism: nigredo, solve et coagula, Die and Become, putrefactio.

Growth

Prime matter (massa informa), coagulatio

vas hermeticum

vas hermeticum

Gina gave the following image (Figure 10.7) the number 2a because it complements the dynamic of the first two images with its non-figurative symbolism. It is a memory of being abused by her father during a Sunday walk. Gina spoke of a "desperate search for the little girl in me, which I had lost at some time in a dark tunnel. I really wanted to find this little girl again, in order to create an opportunity to rebuild a complete person" (Gina's documentary). Her subsequent process fantasy of rebuilding a complete person corresponds to the preceding inner images and its symbolism of the cosmic egg in obscurity, because the abuse occurred in the obscurity of the tunnel. Now she stretches out her hand to the lost child, saving

**FIGURE 10.7**   Gina's painting of her inner image 2a

herself. The black area of Figure 10.7 is framed by a wall which structures and con-solidates (coagulation) the brown, moldy ground as the basis of ego formation. The introjection of the analyst's symbolic attitude is emerging.

*Third image (see Figure 10.8):*
The shapeless black-brown mass has grown, it is
   as big as "I myself" am − ; the lilac (transparent)
   covering encloses the mass up to my shoulder − ;
   now on the right side of the picture there is a tall
   dark pine tree, in the background there is first
   a blue sky, in the foreground there is a meadow
   growing in soft, brown, moist ground.
I feel that the mass is standing in the mud and fear
   it could sink, I don't feel the ground under my
   feet − ; I want to have roots.

The analyst's amplifications:
Prime matter, growth
vas hermeticum
separatio
Nature
Metaphoric idiom: To sink
   into the ground out of
   shame

Gina's paintings and comments represent the mundus imaginalis, the mutual interchange and introjection of images between analyst and patient. A prerequisite is the analyst's interest in the images of the patient, his symbolic attitude, and the capacity to introduce his own imaginations and amplifications into the therapeutic process. "The act of soul-making is imaging" (Hillman, 1983, p. 36). Communi-cation about the paintings furthers the analyst's identification with the patient's

**FIGURE 10.8** Gina's painting of her third inner image

creativity and makes difficult countertransference more tolerable. This was necessary for me, when Gina described in the following a dissociation, probably as a
consequence of the intensified therapeutic communication of the abuse.

In the crane that was in the clinic grounds, she imagined the possibility of a "liber-
ating jump" (Gina's documentary). But in order to prevent herself from committing
suicide, she developed an "inner possibility," as she put it, seeing herself as a sporty,
daring figure on top of the crane, which was roughly 20 meters in height, and at the
same time as a gentle, naked figure with raised arms on a green meadow, looking up
to the figure above. In this state of dissociation, Gina was released from hospital. Over
the next few months, her imagination became motionless and rigid. With the bitter
realization that her husband had a lover, her inner images were overtaking her. She
came to fear that the exuberant figure could kill the naked figure on the ground and
went to a hospital for crisis intervention. Here this inner drama came to a conclusion: "The exuberant figure has slipped into the huge wound of the naked figure and
unites with it in its body. [. . .] Now I feel one single 'I' in me" (Gina's documentary).

Pictures 7 to 9 of the alchemical "rosarium philosophorum" (see CW XVI,
paras. 475–524) were my amplification to Gina's state of dissociation. Picture 7
is titled "The Ascent of the Soul" and illustrates the separation of the soul from
the body, a dissociation and dissolution of ego-consciousness (see CW XVI, para.
476). This requires an attitude of the analyst, "which itself has to be pictorial
and symbolic and has to emerge from the experience of unconscious contents"
(CW XVI, para. 478). Picture 8 ("Purification") and 9 ("The Return of the

Soul") represent an emerging transformation process. Supported by this Jungian background knowledge, I was more able to endure Gina's dramatic portrayal of her psychotic state. Knowing that there was a "return" of her dissociated soul was consoling for me. I only learned at the end of our first session of this "solutio" the happy ending of Gina's picture story, in which her images culminated in the union of the two figures – the alchemical coniunctio.

## Conclusions

Relating Gina's paintings and comments to Edinger's (1985, p. 46) network of the solutio reveals that the purifying effect of the solutio, the fall of Gideon's dew (see also Picture 8 of the "rosarium philosophorum"), is not represented. The solutio becomes menacing and dissolving due to the danger of sinking into the swamp. Here we have a remarkable difference between the emergence of meaning on the textual and pictorial level. The danger of sinking into the swamp is already manifested in Figure 10.6, but is verbalized only as a comment to Figure 10.8. Here, however, pictorially the ground is already more "coagulated." The alchemical "solve et coagula" (dissolving and coagulating) has different expressions on the textual and pictorial level. Those differences were one important question of the pilot study.

Prof. Flader's interpretation proceeded from Panofsky's iconological-iconographical method, which evidently bears a similarity to Analytical Psychology, as the "synoptical table" (Panofsky, 1957, pp. 40–41) demonstrates.

**TABLE 10.1** "Synoptical Table" (Panofsky 1957, p. 40/41)

| Object of Interpretation | Act of Interpretation | Equipment of Interpretation | Corrective Principle of Interpretation (History of Tradition) |
| --- | --- | --- | --- |
| I. Primary or natural subject matter – (A) factual, (B) expressional – constituting the world of artistic motifs | Pre-iconographical description (and pseudoformal analysis) | Practical experience (familiarity with objects and events) | History of style (insight into the manner in which, under varying historical conditions, objects and events were expressed by forms |
| II. Secondary or conventional subject matter, constituting the world of images, stories and allegories | Iconographical analysis | Knowledge of literary sources (familiarity with specific themes and concepts) | History of types (insight into the manner in which, under varying historical conditions, specific themes and concepts were expressed by objects and events) |

(*Continued*)

**TABLE 10.1** (Continued)

| Object of Interpretation | Act of Interpretation | Equipment of Interpretation | Corrective Principle of Interpretation (History of Tradition) |
|---|---|---|---|
| III. Intrinsic meaning or content, constituting the world of "symbolical" values | Iconological interpretation | Synthetic intuition (familiarity with the essential tendencies of the human mind), conditioned by personal psychology and *Weltanschauung* | History of cultural symptoms or "symbols" in general (insight into the manner in which, under varying historical conditions, essential tendencies of the human mind were expressed by specific themes and concepts) |

The interpretation of therapeutic images requires some modifications of the corrective principle. In Figure 10.2, where on the pre-iconographical level the piano, the pianist, the musicians, and the music notes form the "world of artistic motifs," the corrective principle is, as yet, of no significance. On the second, iconographical level, these motifs compose the scenario of a concert, the shared listening of music. Now the corrective principles are the clinical context, that is to say the group theme, the behavior of the patients in the creative process, and the associations and comments on their pictures. These are completed by the therapist's knowledge about the clinical course and biography of the patient as well as his therapeutic experience as a whole. Wolfgang's psychosis had led to social isolation, which he overcame in his picture insofar as the musicians "speak" to him. Mozart's music becomes a unifying symbol by overcoming ambiguous emotions.

Here we have reached the iconological interpretation, which is mainly symbolic and leads to the essence of an artwork. A prerequisite is a synthetic intuition. Now the most important corrective principle is the symbolic, amplificating attitude of the therapist. If, in Panofsky's table, "human mind" also comprises the soul, than the iconologic-iconographic method is very similar to the Jungian approach to the collective unconscious by means of amplification. Here Panofsky also refers to the "philosophy of symbolic forms" (Cassirer, 1977–1985), that the human being as "animal symbolicum" gives meaning to the word through its symbolic activity.[7] In Gina's paintings, e.g., the emerging of a shapeless, tiny brownish-black mass symbolizes the cosmic egg and the creation of a new ego. Clinical knowledge again is part of the corrective principle on this level.

The interpretation of the art therapist and qualitative researcher Dr. B. Ball is enhanced by her clinical experience, especially with abused children. Thus she created a much different approach to Gina's imagery and the therapeutic mundus imaginalis. She applied participant observation, an ethnographic method, reflecting her subjective experience of paintings and comments and opening a dialogue with them. In contrast to this subjective, spontaneous, and intuitive attitude, she developed formal categories for the picture interpretation, which function like codes in the "Grounded Theory." She, too, interpreted the first, non-figurative pictures as a cosmogony, the structuring of the ground in contrast to the danger of falling out of the lilac covering, and came by means of the formal criteria to a similar result as the Jungian approach. A synergy between art therapy and qualitative methods could provide a solid scientific basis for a Jungian pictorial hermeneutic method.

In conclusion, Gina's introjection of my therapeutic, symbolic attitude became evident months later. After the separation from her husband, she was able to withstand auto-destructive suicidal impulses. Instead the feeling came up: "I could know myself in a new way." After the next analytic session she wrote:

> Inwards I have to die "a little bit" in order to create some space for the new. That is the way within the nature and that is happening probably in my soul to. I found it difficult to accept this kind of dying. For more than a half year I have been putting up resistance.

Now the symbol of "Die and Become," which is the matrix of the alchemical transformative operations, unfolds its therapeutic effect. The seed of being emotionally involved in her images and creating a container for her has borne fruit.

Applying the interpretation support system ATLAS.ti, a complex QDA (qualitative data analysis) program, therapeutic microprocesses from only one session illustrate the interchange between the patient's and the therapist's imaginal worlds and its implementation in the therapeutic communication.

## Notes

1 *"Meine durch Erfahrung gewonnenen Anschauungen." Gewinnen* literally means to win, gain, or obtain something.
2 Jung introduces the "two kinds of thinking" in CW V, ch. 2.
3 This study was my dissertation (supervised by Prof. G. Benedetti) and diplom-thesis at the C.G. Jung Institute Zurich (supervised by Prof. V. Kast).
4 In CW 5 the number of illustrations was reduced to 123 because of economic reasons.
5 The qualitative method of ethnography represents this attitude.
6 I summarized my own inner images as they correspond to those of the patient to a greater extent in Krapp (2006).
7 Cassirer's relationship to Analytical Psychology is the topic of Pietikäinen (1999) and Brumlik (2004, p. 144).

## References

Abt, T. (2005). *Introduction to picture interpretation.* Zürich: Living Human Heritage.
Brumlik, M. (2004). *C. G. Jung zur Einführung* (C.G. Jung on introduction). Hamburg: Junius.
Cassirer, E. (1977–1985). *Philosophie der symbolischen Formen* (Philosophy of symbolic forms). Darmstadt: Wissenschaftliche Buchgesellschaft.

Clarke, J.J. (1994). *Jung and eastern thought: A dialogue with the orient*. London: Routledge.

Corbin, J., & Strauss, A. (1990). Grounded theory research: Procedures, canons and evaluative criterias. *Qualitative Sociology, 13*, 3–21.

Edinger, E. (1985). *Anatomy of the psyche*. Chicago: Open Court.

Edinger, E. (1995). *The Mysterium lectures*. Toronto: Inner City Books.

Flick, U. (1998). *An introduction to qualitative research*. London: Sage.

Gadamer, H-G. (2004). *Truth and method* (2nd ed.). New York: Crossroad.

Hillman, J. (1983). *Archetypal psychology: A brief account*. Woodstock: Spring.

Jacobi, J. (1981). *Vom Bilderreich der Seele* (The psyche's realm of images). Olten: Walter.

Jung, C.G. (1952). *Symbole der Wandlung* (Symbols of Transformation). Zürich: Rascher.

Krapp, M. (2006). Bild, metapher, symbol (Image, metaphor, symbol). In L. Cowan (Ed.), *Edges of experience: Memory and emergence. Proceedings of the 16th international congress for analytical psychology*. Einsiedeln: Daimon.

Krapp, M. (2010). *Ich – DU – Wir* (I – You – We: Pictorial symbolism of therapeutic transformation in groups). Stuttgart: opus magnum.

Moser, U. (1992). Two butterflies on my head, or, why have a theory in psychoanalysis? In M. Leuzinger-Bohleber (Ed.), *Two butterflies on my head*. Berlin: Springer.

Muhr, T. (1997). Atlas.ti – A prototype for the support of text interpretation. *Qualitative Sociology, 14*(4), 349–371.

Muhr, T. (1997). *ATLAS/ti: The knowledge workbench*. Berlin: Scientific software development.

Neumann, E. (1972). *The great mother* (Paperback ed.). Princeton, NY: Princeton University Press.

Neumann, E. (1992). *Die Psyche als Ort der Gestaltung* (Psyche as location of formation). Frankfurt am Main: Fischer.

Paglia, C. (2005). *Erich Neumann: Theorist of the Great Mother*. Retrieved from www.bu.edu/arion/Volume13/13.3/Camille/Paglia.htm

Panofsky, E. (1957). *Meaning in the visual art*. New York: Doubleday.

Pietikäinen, S. (1999). *C. G. Jung and the psychology of symbolic forms*. Saarijärvi: Gummerus Oy.

Riedel, I. (1988). *Bilder in therapie, kunst und religion* (Pictures in therapy, art and religion). Stuttgart: Kreuz.

Samuels, A. (1985). *Jung and the post-Jungians*. London: Routledge.

Schwartz-Salant, N. (1989). *The borderline personality: Vision and healing*. Wilmette: Chiron Publications.

Stein, M. (Ed.) (1995). *The interactive field in analysis*. Wilmette: Chiron Publications.

Strauss, A. (1998). *Grundlagen qualitativer Sozialforschung* (Qualitative analysis for social scientists). (2nd ed.). München: Fink.

# 11
# RESEARCH ON THE EFFECTIVENESS OF JUNGIAN PSYCHOTHERAPY
## State of the art

*Christian Roesler*

Jungian psychotherapy has long been blamed for not giving any empirical proof of its effectiveness. Since the 1990s, several research projects and empirical studies on Jungian psychotherapy, its outcome, and process have been conducted, mainly in Germany and Switzerland. The studies are diligently designed and the results are well applicable to the conditions of outpatient practice. This chapter will give a critical overview of the studies and results. All the studies show significant improvement not only on the level of symptoms and interpersonal problems, but also on the level of personality structure and in everyday life. These improvements also remain stable after completion of therapy over a period of up to six years. Several studies show further improvements after the end of therapy. Health insurance data show that after Jungian therapy, patients visits to doctors and hospitals are reduced to a level even below the average of the total population. Results over several studies show that Jungian treatment moves patients from a level of severe symptoms to a level even below the cutoff where one can speak of psychological health. These significant changes are reached by Jungian therapy with an average of 90 sessions, which makes Jungian psychotherapy an effective and cost-effective method. Process studies support Jungian theories on psychodynamics and elements of change in the therapeutic process.

In the early 1990s, the first meta-analyses of empirical studies investigating the effectiveness of psychotherapy were published. Following this, several researchers claimed that there were no studies investigating the effectiveness of Jungian psychotherapy and therefore it should be excluded from the field of psychotherapy (Grawe, Donati, & Bernauer, 1994). This moved several Jungian training institutes, namely Zurich, Berlin, and San Francisco, to design the first empirical studies in the field of Jungian psychotherapy. Even though Jung started his career as a researcher at the psychiatric hospital of the University of Zurich and achieved an international reputation around 1905 because of his empirical research with the association experiment, after 1912 and his break with Freud Jung never took up empirical research again. This might be the reason why in the Jungian community a more skeptical attitude toward empirical research developed over the years. Only recently have systematic attempts to investigate Jungian concepts empirically been undertaken. On the other hand, reviews show that many of Jung's concepts are empirically well founded today (Roesler, 2010). In the field of psychotherapy research, the skepticism about empirical methods in the community of Jungian practitioners has created some difficulties in conducting effectiveness studies (see below). Practitioners worried that research would interfere with the therapeutic relationship; also there was the question of how to capture the details of the psychotherapeutic process methodically.

The studies reported below have found solutions to these questions: different measures have been designed to catch different aspects of the psychotherapeutic process characteristic for analytical psychotherapy. Operationalized Psychodynamic Diagnostics (OPD) have been developed to systemize diagnostic steps in psychoanalysis, and this was adapted for Jungian psychotherapy (Junghan, 2002). The "Heidelberger Umstrukturierungsskala" (Heidelberg scale for changes in personality structure) and measures for analytic focus on and therapeutic alliance and transference are just a few examples of tools that were developed to systematically investigate different aspects of the psychotherapeutic process.

Another problem that was dealt with is the question of manualization of treatment. Even though this is not well known even to Jungian practitioners, there are several handbooks for the application of Jungian psychotherapy (Stein, 1984; Kast, 1990; Eschenbach, 1979–1983; Dieckmann, 1991). Besides these general handbooks there are specialized treatment recommendations for therapeutic work with clients' paintings (Riedel, 2005), the use of dreams and dream interpretation (Adam, 2000), the handling of the transference–countertransference relationship (Jacoby, 1998; Dieckmann, 1980), and active imagination (Kast, 1988). There are also treatment recommendations for specific disorders: narcissistic personality disorder and depression (Asper, 1987; Jacoby, 1985), borderline personality disorder (Schwartz-Salant, 1991), and other personality disorders (Doherty und West, 2007).

From the beginning, there were difficulties in recruiting enough practicing analysts to participate in the studies, which is still a problem today, as can be shown in the latest example, the PAP-study in Switzerland. One of the main arguments against participating in empirical studies was the assumption that the research process would interrupt or at least influence the analytic process and the therapeutic relationship in an unfavorable way. Also it was argued that empirical instruments would never be able to catch the complexity of the analytic process. From my point of view, these critical positions are based on false ideas about the research process, its capacities, and its limitations. Of course, any research design to investigate psychotherapy has its limitations and can only analyze certain aspects of the complex interactions taking place in the process of psychotherapy. But empirical research methods offer the possibility of insight into the psychotherapeutic work and its effects from a more objective position. We have to consider that our perspective as practicing psychotherapists on our own processes is, and has to be, mainly subjective and is subject to interpretation and also to the possibility of error. On the other hand, empirical research can never claim to tell the whole truth about psychotherapy. I think that both viewpoints have value and should be combined as to get a richer picture of the subtle process of psychotherapy.

## Levels of evidence

In empirical research there is a differentiation between different levels of studies, which is described in the *Handbook of Psychotherapy and Behavior Change* (Lambert, 2004). The highest level or gold standard is the randomized controlled trial (RCT), with an experimental and a control group and participants who are randomly divided into these groups. Only RCTs can give proof of the efficacy of a psychotherapy method, which means that the effects in the patients are a result of the method alone (and no other extratherapeutical factors). In general, only RCTs are accepted as a proof for the efficacy of the psychotherapy method. In recent years, however, there has been a discussion about the validity of RCTs, since their internal validity is high in the described sentence but the external validity, its applicability to everyday practice, is low (Westen & Morrison, 2001). Several researchers have argued for naturalistic studies which are conducted in everyday practice and therefore much better applicable to reality conditions. Several of the Jungian studies have applied this design. Generally speaking, prospective data are more valid then retrospective, even though the two Jungian studies described below that have applied a retrospective design have been very carefully designed.

## Overview of Jungian empirical studies

### Prospective, naturalistic outcome studies

- Praxisstudie Analytische Langzeittherapie (PAL) Schweiz (Practice Study Analytical Long-Term Psychotherapy Switzerland; Mattanza, Jakobsen, & Hurt, 2006; Rudolph et al., 2004)
- San Francisco Psychotherapy Research Project (Rubin & Powers, 2005)
- PAP-S practice study outpatient psychotherapy Switzerland (Tschuschke et al., 2010).

### Catamnestic/retrospective studies

- Berlin Jungian Study (Keller et al., 1997)
- Konstanz Study – a German *Consumer Reports* study (Breyer, Heinzel, & Klein, 1997).

## Small sample and case studies

On Jungian sandplay therapy, psychosomatic disorders, etc. (Kleeberg, Schreiber, & Schwinger, 2003; Tavares, 2002; Ramos and da Matta in this volume).

## Qualitative and process studies

On complex theory (Heisig, 2001), picture interpretation method (Krapp, 1997).

## Praxisstudie Analytische Langzeittherapie (PAL) Schweiz (Zurich) (Mattanza et al., 2006)

A group of researchers of the Jung Institute Zurich participated in a larger German study on analytical long-term psychotherapy (Rudolf, 2004) conducted by the University of Heidelberg. The design was a naturalistic prospective outcome study, which means that therapists and patients were monitored from the beginning of therapy in the usual everyday practice context (no control group). Twenty-six therapists with 37 cases were chosen as representative for Jungian psychotherapy in Switzerland and their patients. Fifty-seven percent of these patients suffered from depressive disorders, and with 47% identified as having a personality disorder the sample population had a considerably high burden of disease. The mean duration of treatment was 35 months with a mean of 90 sessions, which is equivalent to a low-frequency treatment. This was a realistic representative sample for Jungian therapy in Switzerland.

There were three different perspectives applied: researchers, therapists, and the patients themselves. On each level a set of objective and self-evaluation research instruments was used.

## Researchers

Operationalized Psychodynamic Diagnostics (OPD), Jungian adaptation (Junghan, 2002)
Psychodynamic focuses (two interviews)
Changes in personality structure: Heidelberger Umstrukturierungsskala
Therapeutic alliance and transference (SGRT, TAB)
Interpersonal problems (IIP)
Changes in life conduct (research interview).

## Therapists

Physical and psychological symptoms, severity score (BSS), status and process ratings, ICD-diagnosis.

## Patients

Psychological and interpersonal symptoms (SCL-90-R, PSKB-Se-R, IIP), personality (TPF), health insurance data.

## Results

### Researchers

- Positive restructuring of patients' personality, effect size: 0.94.
- Positive changes in everyday life, very high effect size: 1.48.

### Therapists

- Global rating of results positive or very positive for 75% of patients.
- Cost-effectiveness good, very good or maximum for 55% of patients.

### Patients

- Global Severity Index reduced highly significant, very high effect size: 1.31, normal level at end of therapy
- Reduction of interpersonal problems (IIP), medium effect size
- Rating of results over 90% positive, very positive or maximum
- Cost-effectiveness 80% good, very good or maximum, 20% satisfying.

### Follow-up

All results remained stable after 1 year and 3 years. An interesting point is that there are findings for further positive effects between the end of therapy and follow-up, which would mean that some effects of the therapy show only after the end of therapy. This is an effect that psychoanalysis has always maintained. The use of health care services was already low during the course of therapy and remained on a low level until the follow-up.

This study could give proof of very positive effects for Jungian psychotherapy in a prospective design that remained stable over three years after the end of therapy. Jungian therapy leads not only to a significant reduction of symptoms and of interpersonal and other problems but also to a restructuring of the personality with the effect that the patients can deal with upcoming problems much better after the end of therapy. Patient satisfaction with the results was extremely high, even though most of the patients had to pay for their therapy by themselves.

### San Francisco psychotherapy research project (Rubin & Powers, 2005)

Originally this study conducted by the San Francisco Jung Institute was designed as a prospective outcome study with four points of measurement (start of therapy, end of therapy, 1-year and 5-year follow-up). In many aspects the design of the San Francisco psychotherapy research project is similar to that of the Zurich study. The instruments applied in the research were: SCL-90-R; IIP, GAF (Global Assessment of Functioning, axis V of the DSM); an additional instrument designed by the institute asking for demographic data, therapy motivation and subjective experience with the therapy; the therapists had an instrument also designed by the institute called "Portrait of My Practice" (POMP). The participants of the study were patients of the outpatient clinic of the San Francisco Jung Institute. The clinic had 100 patients; 57 participated in the study. The participating therapists were 23 professional analyst members of the institute, 17 candidates in training, and seven psychology interns.

Because of the low participation of analysts from the institute, the project had to be terminated early. Due to these problems the original design had to be collapsed into a one-group pretest–posttest design. This included 39 of the original 57 patients and only part of these completed follow-up. So the internal validity of the study could not be secured and the statistical results have to be interpreted given that background. Only data from the start of therapy and the end of therapy could be compared. Regardless of these limitations, the study points in the direction of effectiveness of Jungian therapy. There were significant reductions in SCL-90-R and IIP.

## Berlin catamnestic study (Keller et al., 1997, 2002)

In the early 1990s, the Empirical Psychotherapy Research Group in Analytical Psychology Berlin conducted a nationwide catamnestic, retrospective study. Former patients of Jungian psychotherapies were asked to participate and were tested via questionnaires and interview. All members of the German Society for Analytical Psychology (DGAP) were asked to participate; 78% responded and 24.6% participated. The reasons for refusal to participate were documented and no bias was found. The participating therapists documented all cases terminated in 1987–1988 and gave a global evaluation about the success of therapy. In Germany, psychotherapy is financed quite generously by universal health insurance (up to 300 hours of analysis). At the beginning of therapy, the therapist has to apply for financing. These applications contain numerous data about the health state and symptoms of the patient, personality, social context, psychodynamics, and diagnosis. This information is stored by the health insurance agency for decades and the Berlin study made use of these data. Additionally other health insurance data about the patients could be used, e.g., utilization of health care services, days in hospital, and so forth. The distribution of symptoms and their severity in the sample were the following: 46% affective disorders, 24% other neurotic and psychosomatic disorders, and 17% personality disorders.

Catamnestic studies are affected strongly by bias through selection effects, but these were tested in the study: of 353 documented cases, 111 participated in the study; a bias was found concerning the number of therapy dropouts, which was higher in the sample than in the population; apart from that the sample was representative for the population. The mean duration of treatment was 162 sessions with a frequency of one to two sessions per week.

*Measures*: Patients were sent a follow-up questionnaire which included measures of life satisfaction, well-being, social functioning, personality traits, interpersonal problems, health care utilization, and some psychometric tests (SCL-90-R, VEV, Gießen-Test). The severity of symptoms before treatment was assessed using the Schepank method of impairment severity index (BSS; Schepank, 1994). The psychopathological status and diagnosis at initiation of therapy were reconstructed from patient records (applications to health insurances).

*Results*: Of 60.4% of patients reporting their well-being as very poor (severe set of diagnoses) prior to therapy, 86.6% rated their global well-being at follow-up as very good, good, or moderate (well-adjusted close to normal reference group on all scales of psychopathology). Six years after the termination of treatment, 70%–94% reported good to very good improvements in: psychological distress, general well-being, life satisfaction, job performance, partner and family relations, and social functioning. The global health state of 88% could be described as "normal health" compared to a calibration sample (Gerdes & Jäckel, 1992). Patients were better off than any of the clinical groups with which they shared diagnoses prior to therapy.

*SCL-90-R*: Jungian therapy could move the sample of severely disturbed patients even below the cutoff where one can speak of psychological health after the end of therapy. All of these results were statistically highly significant.

*Gießen-Test*: This personality test is standardized with a normal sample and the results found in this study show that the subjects fell within the normal range on all scales.

There was also a significant reduction in health care utilization: the mean number of 16 days lost due to sickness in the 5 years before psychotherapy was reduced to a mean of 8 days in the 5 years after the end of therapy; the mean number of 8 days of hospitalization in the year before psychotherapy was reduced to a mean of 1 day after the end of therapy; there was a reduction of visits to primary care services below the level of two representative studies of private practice patients (Hoffmeister, 1988; Schach et al., 1989) and a reduction in intake of psychotropic

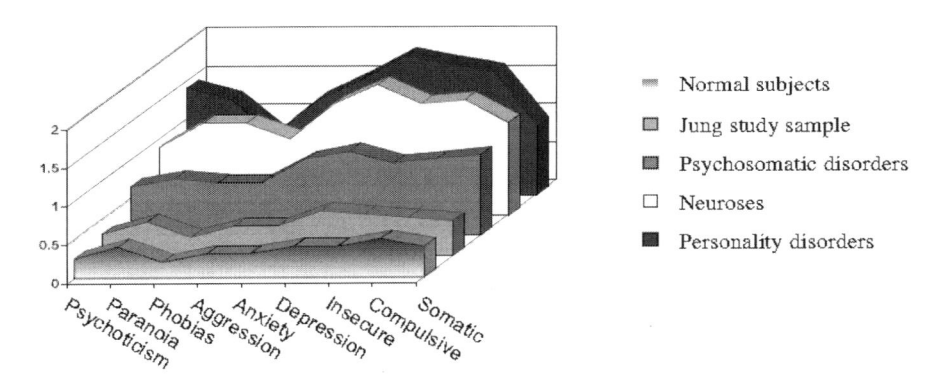

**FIGURE 11.1**   Mean SCL-90-R scales on follow-up compared to standardization sample

drugs. All these reductions were statistically significant. In sum, Jungian psycho-therapy reduced the health insurance claims of the patients even below the level of the average German member of the health insurance system. Other interesting findings are the relationship between improvement and treatment length, and again there are indicators for further improvements after termination of therapy. The results of the Jungian sample in the Questionnaire of Change in Experience and Behavior (VEV) showed significant improvements in various areas of life ($p < 0.01$) compared to the calibrated random sample. They were also compared to an equiva-lent 1-year follow-up sample of inpatient cognitive behavioral treatment ($N = 142$; Zielke, 1993), and practically no differences were found.

Summarizing the results, it can be said that there was not only a high patient satisfaction with the Jungian treatment, but there was also a reduction in symptoms which moved the patients into the area of normal health. The effects of psycho-therapy were long-lasting and touched all areas of the lives of the patients so that even the use of health care services was so drastically reduced that Jungian therapy was also cost-effective in the long run. These results have to be interpreted in term of the background of limitations of the design, even though the study made great efforts to control for biases and secure a representative sample.

### The Konstanz Study – a German replication of Seligman's Consumer Reports *study (Breyer et al., 1997)*

This study conductwed in Konstanz/Germany is a replication of the famous Con-sumer Reports study done by Seligman applied to therapies from several psycho-dynamic schools and in its design comparable to the aforementioned Berlin study. Ninety psychotherapists distributed 979 questionnaires to former patients of whom 66% participated in the study. There were no systematic biases found in the sample. About a fifth of the participating therapists had a Jungian background, and it could be shown that there are no systematic differences between this subgroup and the overall sample, so that the study is representative for psychoanalytic practice in Ger-many in general and for Jungian psychotherapy.

The results are very much comparable to those of the aforementioned Berlin study; in all dimensions the study found significant benefits in health and well-being. There were again significant changes between end of therapy and follow-up. As in the Berlin study, health insurance data were used and a highly significant reduction in health utilization parameters was found. All of these results remained stable in a 6-year follow-up. A special aspect of this study is a cost-benefit com-putation: there were significant savings accrued as a result of individual and group psychotherapy in the first 2 years after therapy. The amount of savings was parallel to the severity of the health status of the patient at the beginning of therapy, that is more severely distressed patients had higher gains in improvement and conse-quently in the reduction of health care utilization.

As this study is a retrospective study, the results have to be interpreted in light of the background of risk of biases, but these were controlled for as far as possible.

**TABLE 11.1** Retrospective reports of subjective well-being from start of treatment to follow-up

| | Start of treatment | Change by termination | Change by follow-up | Change from termination to follow-up |
|---|---|---|---|---|
| Total well-being | 4.33 | −2.06★ | −2.17★★ | −0.11★★ |
| Somatic well-being | 3.21 | −1.01★★ | −1.08★★ | −0.07★ |
| Psychological well-being | 4.44 | −2.16★★ | −2.26★★ | −0.10★ |
| Quality of relationships | 3.66 | −1.19★★ | −1.52★★ | −0.33★★ |

Scale: 1 = very good;  5 = very bad.
★★ p < 0.001 on related t-test (one-tailed).
★ p < 0.05 on related t-test (one-tailed).

**TABLE 11.2** Changes in health utilization parameters (mean values and percents relative to the year previous to therapy, at therapy termination and follow-up)

| Indicator | Start of therapy | At termination (% reduction) | At follow-up (% reduction) | % change from termination to follow-up |
|---|---|---|---|---|
| Number of visits to family doctor | 6.28 | 3.76★★ (40%) | 3.03★ (52%) | 19%★★ |
| Number of visits to medical specialist | 3.97 | 2.65★★ (33%) | −1.59★★ | 10%★ |
| Days of sickness absence | 14.48 | 8.46★★ (42%) | −8.62★★ | 31%★★ |
| Days of hospitalization | 3.39 | 1.17★★ (66%) | −2.22★★ | 0% |

★★ p < 0.001 on related t-test (one-tailed).
★ p < 0.05 on related t-test (one-tailed).

**TABLE 11.3** Savings accrued as a result of individual and group psychotherapy in the first 2 years after therapy

| Savings | Expected reduction in health care events (individual therapy) | Cost of events (individual therapy) (DM) | Expected reduction in number of health care events (group therapy) | Cost of events (group therapy) (DM) |
|---|---|---|---|---|
| Family doctor visits | 7.3 | 130.90 | 7.5 | 134.70 |
| Specialty doctor visits | 3.0 | 101.30 | 7.1 | 235.40 |
| Days sickness | 19.5 | 6,906.10 | 26.0 | 9,198.00 |
| Days in hospital | 3.0 | 1,339.50 | 10.74 | 759.90 |
| Total savings | | 8,477.80 | | 14,330.00 |
| Costs of treatment | | 33,235.00 | | 4,305.00 |
| Savings/costs ratio | | 0.255:1 | | 3.32:1 |

## Praxisstudie ambulante Psychotherapie Schweiz (PAP-S) (Tschuschke et al., 2010)

The main goal of the Naturalistic Psychotherapy Study on Outpatient Treatment in Switzerland, conducted by the Swiss Charta for Psychotherapy, was to compare different types of psychotherapy with regard to specific and nonspecific common therapeutic factors. The design is comparable to that of the Zurich Jungian study but investigated eight different schools of psychotherapy, mainly from the psychodynamic and the experiential field. In Switzerland these different psychotherapeutic schools are organized in the Charta for Psychotherapy, and one aim of this study was to determine the effectiveness of these methods so they could become accredited officially in the new legal system regulating psychotherapy in Switzerland. The choice of measures applied followed the recommendations given by the Society for Psychotherapy Research and includes outcome as well as process variables. The study ran 7 years (2006–2012) including therapies and follow-up.

### Measures

- *Patients*: self-rating of therapy outcome (OQ 45), symptoms (BSI), depression (BDI), Sense of Coherence (SOC-9), congruence (K-INK), therapy motivation (FMP).
- *Researchers*: Standardized Clinical Interview for DSM (SKID), Global Assessment of Functioning Individual (GAF) and Relationships (GARF), Operationalized Psychodynamic Diagnostics (OPD).

The participating psychotherapists included the following groups: process-oriented psychotherapy, gestalt therapy, bioenergetic therapy, transaction analysis, art and expression-oriented therapy, existential analysis and logotherapy, integrative body psychotherapy, and psychoanalysis. The psychoanalysis group contained Jungian Analytical Psychology as well as Freudian psychoanalysis, so there was no differentiation, but since the Jungian approach is the largest school in Switzerland regarding professional membership and training institutions, it can be assumed that the results of this group are representative for Jungian psychotherapy. Since the study emphasized a naturalistic approach, it was designed to have no impact on everyday practice. Recruitment of clients ran from March 2007 to June 2011 and there were no restrictions on client inclusion regarding diagnosis, age, and so forth.

The overall sample includes 379 clients. In Tschuschke et al. (2014) there is a detailed analysis of a subgroup of 81 clients, of which 46 were women and 35 were men with an average age of 39.6 years. In terms of their life situation and education the sample was representative for the client population in psychotherapy in Switzerland. The following diagnoses were included in the sample: substance related disorders 4.8%; mood disorders 23.8%; anxiety, posttraumatic stress disorders, and somatoform disorders 34.0%; eating and sexual disorders 5.4%; personality disorders 10.2%; other diagnoses: 2.7%.

The general results indicated that all the participating schools of psychotherapy were found to be effective. Outcomes were operationalized using the strategy of multiple outcome criteria on the basis of the Global Severity Index of the BSI, the Outcome Questionnaire, and the Global Assessment of Functioning Scale. These three tests were employed within the first probationary sessions before the start of treatment, immediately after the last therapy session, and at follow-up 1 year after the end of therapy. Scores were tested only on the pre–post basis since follow-up data were not available for all the cases. Changes in all three tests pre to post were highly significant. Effect sizes were BSI 0.69, GAF 1.12, and OQ 0.61. On average all clients benefited from the therapies. The authors of the study emphasized the point that generalizations from these results are hampered by several limitations. The most important point here is that the cooperating approaches provided to few cases and too few therapists to allow generalization.

Nevertheless the study produced some interesting findings. One part of the study consisted of describing the interventions applied by the different schools in detail. In the study, therapies were videotaped and external raters evaluated which of the described interventions were practically applied. In each school the majority of interventions applied was not school-specific but either general or stemming from a different school. Only about 15% of the interventions came from the specific background of the therapist. This of course automatically raises the question of whether there is even a specificity in the practical therapeutic work of Jungian therapists and what that would be.

## Conclusion

Since, at this time, there are no level I studies (RCTs) of Jungian therapy, there is no proof of efficacy for Jungian psychotherapy. But the effectiveness of Jungian psychotherapy is now, on the base of the aforementioned studies, empirically proven. The same can be said for its cost-effectiveness. As most of the studies are naturalistic designs, it can be assumed that they give a realistic picture of Jungian therapy in everyday practice. All of the studies report positive effects in a wide variety of disorders with good or very good effect sizes on symptom reduction, well-being, interpersonal problems, change of personality structure, reduction of health care utilization, and changes in everyday life conduct. All of these effects are stable in follow-up up to seven years after therapy. There are even further positive changes between termination and follow-up. With an average of only 90 sessions Jungian therapy is a very time- and cost-effective form of psychodynamic psychotherapy. All the studies realized a high methodological standard with objective measures, different research perspectives (patient, therapist, researcher), control of biases. The most convincing results concerning the effectiveness of Jungian psychotherapy from a review of all studies is that their results all point in the same direction. Nevertheless the efficacy of Jungian psychotherapy is still to be proven in a randomized controlled trial design. We also have to note that in all studies 10%–20% of patients do not profit from Jungian therapy. This should be subject to further research aiming at finding markers for personalities expected to profit from Jungian psychotherapy.

Another serious problem that comes to light in the overview of these studies is the fact that Jungian analysts tend to be very reluctant to participate in empirical studies to an extent that leads almost to the breakdown of studies. From my point of view, this should be a point of discussion in the Jungian community. Insofar as Jungian analysis is a part of psychotherapy as a treatment of psychological problems, it should also apply appropriate measures of quality management (see also Keller in this volume). Even if psychotherapists have the best intentions, the treatment can be ineffective or even harmful to patients. At least it can be said now that the point that was often made by critics of empirical research in the Jungian community that empirical methods would interfere with the special situation of the analytical relationship has been disproved by the above studies. In no study was there any hint of negative interference in the psychotherapeutic process. Some studies made great efforts to adapt or even develop research measures which catch aspects special to the Jungian background, as for example changes in personality or the adaptation of psychodynamic diagnostics (Junghan, 2002). On the other hand, we as Jungians can now offer empirical results about the effectiveness of our psychotherapy method and are no longer subject to the critique that our method is not effective or empirically proven.

## Prospects: current ongoing studies in Germany

Researchers from the Societies of Analytical Psychology in the German-speaking countries (Austria, Germany, Switzerland) have formed a research platform (www.infap3.eu) which is currently planning to conduct several studies in the field of Jungian psychotherapy. The training institutes in Germany agreed that future training candidates will have to apply a couple of empirical measures (symptoms, life satisfaction, operationalized psychodynamic diagnostics) to their training cases in order to form a database and to make ongoing quality management possible (see also Keller in this volume). In the long run, this aims at creating a more open attitude to empirical research in the coming generations of Jungian analysts. On the other hand, this process aims at stabilizing the currently comfortable position Jungian therapy has in the German health care system for the future by delivering empirical results about the effectiveness of the methods and applying standard quality management processes.

## References

Adam, K.U. (2000). *Therapeutisches Arbeiten mit Träumen: Theorie und Praxis der Traumarbeit.* Berlin: Springer.

Asper, K. (1987). *Verlassenheit und Selbstentfremdung: neue Zugänge zum therapeutischen Verständnis.* Olten: Walter.

Breyer, F., Heinzel, R., & Klein, Th. (1997). Kosten und Nutzen ambulanter Psychoanalyse in Deutschland (Cost and benefit of outpatient analytical psychotherapy in Germany). *Gesundheitsökonomie und Qualitätsmanagement, 2*, 59–73.

Dieckmann, H. (Ed.) (1980). *Übertragung und Gegenübertragung in der analytischen Psychologie.* (Transference and countertransference in analytical psychology). Hildesheim: Gerstenberg.

Dieckmann, H. (1991). *Komplexe: Diagnostik und Therapie in der analytischen Psychologie* (Complexes. Diagnostics and therapy in analytical psychology). Berlin: Springer.

Doherty, N.J., & West, J.J. (2007). *The matrix and meaning of character: An archetypal and developmental approach.* London: Routledge.

Eschenbach, U. (Ed.) (1979–1983). *Die Behandlung in der Analytischen Psychologie* (Treatment in Analytical Psychology). Stuttgart: Bonz.

Gerdes, N., & Jäckel, W.H. (1992). Indikatoren des Reha-Status (IRES) (Indicators of rehabilitation status). *Rehabilitation, 31,* 73–79.

Grawe, K., Donati, R., & Bernauer, F. (1994). *Psychotherapie im wandel (Psychotherapy in change).* Göttingen: Hogrefe.

Heisig, D. (2001). *Wandlungsprozesse durch die therapeutische Beziehung* (Transformation processes in the therapeutic relationship). *Analytische Psychologie, 32,* 230–251.

Hoffmeister, J., Hoeltz, J., Schön, D., Schröder, E., & Güther, B. (1988). Nationaler Untersuchungs-Survey und regionale Untersuchungs-Surveys der DHP (Deutsche Herz-Kreislauf-Präventionsstudie) (National survey on the German coronary heart disease prevention study). *DHP Forum, 3,* 18–37.

Jacoby, M. (1985). *Individuation und Narzissmus (Individuation and narcissism).* München: Pfeiffer.

Jacoby, M. (1998). *Grundformen seelischer Austauschprozesse* (Basic forms of psychological exchange). Düsseldorf: Walter.

Junghan, M. (2002). Die Anwendung der Strukturachse der OPD in der Analytischen Psychologie (The application of operationalized psychodynamic diagnostics in Analytical Psychology). In G. Rudolf, T. Grande, & P. Henningsen (Eds.), *Die Struktur der Persönlichkeit (The structure of personality)* (pp. 90–114). Stuttgart: Schattauer.

Kast, V. (1988): *Imagination als Raum der Freiheit (Imagination as a space of freedom).* Olten: Walter.

Kast, V. (1990): *Die Dynamik der Symbole: Grundlagen der Jungschen Psychotherapie* (The dynamic of symbols: Foundations of Jungian psychotherapy). Olten: Walter.

Keller, W., Westhoff, G., Dilg, R., Rohner, R., Studt, H.H., & The Study Group on Empirical Psychotherapy Research in Analytical Psychology. (2002). Efficacy and cost effectiveness aspects of outpatient (Jungian) psychoanalysis and psychotherapy – a catamnestic study. In M. Leuzinger-Bohleber & M. Target (Eds.), *Longer-term psychoanalytic treatment: Perspectives for therapists and researchers.* London: Whurr.

Keller, W., Dilg, R., Westhoff, G., Rohner, R., Studt, H.H., & The Empirical Psychotherapy Research Group in Analytical Psychology Berlin. (1997). On the efficacy of outpatient Jungian psychoanalyses and psychotherapies. In M.A. Mattoon (Ed.), *Proceedings of the 13th international congress for analytical psychology Zürich 1995.* Einsiedeln: Daimon-Verlag.

Kleeberg, A., Schreiber, S., & Schwinger, T. (2003). Symbole als Ausdruck der therapeutischen Beziehung. Eine empirische Untersuchung zur Schattensymbolik in einer jungianischen Psychotherapie. *Analytische Psychologie, 34,* 266–297.

Krapp, M. (1997). Pictorial-hermeneutic, qualitative methods (pp. 581–586). In M.A. Mattoon (Ed.), *Open questions in analytical psychology.* Einsiedeln: Daimon.

Lambert, M.J. (Ed.). (2004). *Bergin and Garfield's handbook of psychotherapy and behavior change* (5th ed.). New York: Wiley.

Mattanza, G., Jakobsen, T., & Hurt, J. (2006). Jung'sche Psychotherapie ist effizient (Jungian psychotherapy is efficient). In G. Mattanza, I. Meier, & M. Schegel (Eds.), *Seele und Forschung (Soul and research)* (pp. 38–82.). Basel: Karger.

Riedel, I. (2005). *Bilder: In Psychotherapie, kunst und religion* (Pictures: In psychotherapy, art and religion). Stuttgart: Kreuz.

Roesler, C. (2010). *Analytische Psychologie heute: Der aktuelle Forschungsstand zur Psychologie C. G. Jungs* (Analytical Psychology today. The state-of-the-art in research on the psychology of Jung). Basel: Karger.

Rubin, S.I., & Powers, N. (2005). *Analyzing the San Francisco psychotherapy research project.* Unpublished report, San Francisco. Retrieved from www.sirseth.net/doc/SFresearch.pdf

Rudolf, G., Dilg, R., Grande, T., Jakobsen, T., Keller, W., Krawietz, B., Langer, M., Stehle, S., & Oberbracht, C. (2004). Effektivität und Effizienz psychoanalytischer Langzeittherapie: die Praxisstudie analytische Langzeittherapie (Efficacy and efficiency of psychoanalytic long-term therapy: the practice study analytical long-term therapy). In A. Gerlach, A. Schlösser, & A. Springer (Eds.), *Psychoanalyse des Glaubens (Psychoanalysis of belief)* (pp. 515–528). Gießen: Psychosozial.

Schach, E., Schwartz, F.W., & Kerek-Bodden, H.E. (1989). *Die EVaS-Studie: Eine Erhebung über die ambulante medizinische Versorgung in der BRD* (An investigation on outpatient medical treatment in West Germany). Köln: Zentralinstitut für die kassenärztliche Versorgung.

Schepank, H. (1994). *Der Beeinträchtigungsschwere-Score (BSS) für psychogene Erkrankungen* (The severity of symptoms score for psychological diseases). Weinheim: Beltz.

Schwartz-Salant, N. (1991). *Die Borderline-Persönlichkeit (The Borderline personality).* Olten: Walter.

Stein, M. (Ed.). (1984). *Jungian analysis.* Boulder, CO: Shambhala.

Tavares, M.L. (2002). *The patient's psyche in cancer terminal phase.* Doctoral dissertation, Pontifica Universidade Catolica de Sao Paulo.

Tschuschke, V., Crameri, A., Koehler, M., Berglar, J., Muthi, K., Staczan, P., von Wyl, A., Schulthess, P., & Koemeda-Lutz, M. (2014). The role of therapists' treatment adherence, professional experience, therapeutic alliance, and clients' severity of psychological problems: Prediction of treatment outcome in eight different psychotherapy approaches. Preliminary results of a naturalistic study. *Psychotherapy Research,* Retrieved from http://doi.org/10.1080/10503307.2014.896055

Tschuschke, V., Crameri, A., Koemeda, M., Schulthess, P., von Wyl, A., & Weber, R. (2010). Fundamental reflections on psychotherapy research and initial results of the naturalistic Psychotherapy Study on Outpatient Treatment in Switzerland (PAP-S). *International Journal for Psychotherapy, 14,* 247–256.

Westen, D., & Morrison, K. (2001). A multidimensional meta-analysis of treatments for depression, panic, and generalized anxiety disorder: an empirical examination of the status of empiricially supported therapies. *Journal of Consulting and Clinical Psychology, 69,* 875–899.

Zielke, M. (1993). *Wirksamkeit stationärer Verhaltenstherapie (Efficacy of inpatient behavior therapy).* Weinheim: Beltz.

# 12

# QUALITY MANAGEMENT AND EMPIRICAL RESEARCH ACTIVITIES IN JUNGIAN PSYCHOTHERAPY IN GERMANY

*Wolfram Keller*

Analytical Psychology was grounded in a strong empirical research base. C.G. Jung began his career as both a clinician and a research scientist. His experimental approach and discovery of the meaning of his early association experiment was the precursor to tools such as the Myers–Briggs instrument that are still used today. His self-exploration that led to the development of the *Red Book* was grounded in scientific observation and documentation. He was a clinician–researcher in his time but did not specifically pursue empirical evaluation of Jungian psychology and psychoanalysis, focusing instead on the development of the theoretical underpinnings and tools to conduct Jungian analysis.

In large measure, this interest in developing the conceptual basis for Jungian analysis rather than the empirical evaluation of its effectiveness has continued. Until recently, the main focus of scientific interest in Analytical Psychology has been on more theoretical aspects and concepts in a social and cultural context or in clinical topics and case studies. The tradition of being both analyst and scientist simultaneously has continued. This so-called *Junctim* attitude, introduced from Freud, means the ability to focus on conducting research and providing therapy as dual aspects of professional life. Until now, most of the emphasis of this dual perspective has not included an interest in empirical studies (Kaiser, 1993).

However, interest in empirical studies has been growing within the Jungian community in Germany. Psychotherapy research such as empirical research on effectiveness of treatment can offer a third independent perspective on the evaluation of Jungian therapy. This approach to psychotherapy research might contribute to new findings in terms of efficacy of treatment and therapeutic development. This chapter will summarize major empirical studies on the effectiveness of Jungian psychotherapy and analysis in Germany, examine their conclusions, and offer directions for future research.

## The beginnings of Jungian empirical research in Germany

Interest in the development of empirical research in psychotherapy in Germany began with a longitudinal study. In 1962, Dührssen conducted a prospective empirical study that showed a long-lasting, substantial reduction in the burden of symptoms and in health care costs on the basis of sick-leave days and inpatient clinic visits 5 years after patients' termination of analytical psychotherapy and psychoanalysis. A partial result of this study was that analytical psychotherapy became eligible for coverage by insurance companies. At the same time, behavioral psychotherapy methods gained more and more popularity demonstrating empirical evidence and effectivity, especially in short-term psychotherapy. In the late 1980s, a new law was enacted in Germany that would provide psychological psychotherapists increased access to the health care system. It was evident in this context and criticized by empirical scientists and researchers that no empirical studies existed on Jungian psychotherapy. A great many Jungians focused solely on the individual needs and treatment of their patients and did not conduct research.

Increasing pressure from health care administrations for data supporting Jungian therapy effectiveness motivated some in the Jungian community to take part in empirical analysis of the quality of their treatment. In the early 1990s, a group of interested and engaged Jungian psychoanalysts in Berlin with connections to university took on the challenge. Working under pressure, they organized an elaborate and empirical retrograde psychotherapy study using health care provider data as well as a retrospective assessment of diagnoses and impairment of disease on the basis of psychoanalyst's written applications for cost coverage.

## Available health care system data in Germany

The entire working population in Germany has health insurance that covers the cost for both illness and temporary pay loss due to illness. Each examining physician provides a sick note or hospital admission for a patient. Each health insurance provider documents the number of sick days, hospital days, and corresponding diagnoses. Every patient in Germany is entitled to any treatment required and has a free choice of therapists. The physician or psychotherapist decides on the necessity for treatment. The prerequisite for provider coverage of psychotherapy according to psychotherapy guidelines is a written detailed report (containing a description of symptoms, history of complaints, diagnosis, biography, psychodynamics, treatment plan, and assessment of prognosis).

Data on sickness behavior can be drawn from comparing the frequency of sick and hospital days before and following therapy. The pre–post comparison of sick or hospital days is regarded as a direct outcome measure of psychotherapy (Dührssen, 1962; Richter, 1994).

These reports preceding the therapy notes served as the basis for our retrospective classification according to ICD-10 and the assessment of the severity of disease before the start of treatment and the duration of indicating symptoms.

In a naturalistic follow-up study, the patients could only be contacted by their former therapists. The therapists have to get in contact with and obtain consent from their patients to take part on the study. Obviously, this causes an unsurprisingly complex selection process of patients.

## The Berlin Jungian study: on the effectiveness and efficacy of outpatient (Jungian) psychoanalysis and psychotherapy – a catamnestic study (Keller et al., 1998, 2001)

In 1993, the members of the Deutsche Gesellschaft für Analytische Psychologie (DGAP, all working with adult clients) were asked to participate in a retrospective catamnestic, naturalistic multi-level study to investigate the effectiveness of long-term psychotherapy and psychoanalysis. Seventy-eight percent of those contacted responded to our inquiry, and 24.6% participated in the study and contacted their former patients. A central component of the study was a follow-up examination of former patients via a questionnaire 6 years after termination of psychotherapy or analysis, and the recording of treatment-seeking data from health insurance companies 5 years before and after treatment. The objectives were (1) to investigate the effectiveness of long-term analyses (more than 100 sessions) and examining the stability of treatment results by a follow-up study 6 years after therapy; (2) evaluate health care utilization data; and (3) analyze Jungian psychotherapy and analysis in terms of its cost-effectiveness for the cost carrier and the health-care administration.

In 1993–1994, 111 individuals who finished their psychoanalysis or psychotherapy in 1987 or 1988 were identified and included in the study. The selection of the participating therapists was controlled by a separate survey of the members of the DGAP consisting of personal characteristics and data on their patients. The selection of the included patients was controlled against a total of 353 therapist-documented therapies completed between 1987 and 1988.

More than three-fourths of the patients examined underwent psychoanalysis. Of the study participants, 70%–94% reported good to very good improvement of their physical and psychological state and social functioning 5 to 6 years after therapy. We could find a marked reduction of health insurance claims – disability days, hospital days, number of visits to a doctor, and drug intake; thus one can conclude a reduction of health care costs.

Three psychometric tests were administered 5 to 6 years after the end of psychotherapy evaluating the health status in terms of symptomatic strain using the Symptom Checklist-90-R (SCL-90-R), personality traits Gießen Test, and Change in Experience and Behavior (VEV).

The Symptom Checklist 90-R (SCL-90-R) is a widely applied self-assessment instrument for a broad range of mental disorders that assesses the subjective symptom burden in patients with mental disorders. This test has a high acceptance and extensive worldwide application as an outcome instrument in psychotherapy research. The version we used consists of 90 items and nine subscales: somatization, obsessive-compulsive, interpersonal sensitivity, depression, anxiety, hostility, phobic anxiety, paranoid ideation, psychoticism, and the Global Severity Index (GSI) as an expression of the total strain. This test refers to experience within the last 7 days, and it allows a comparison with a normal population or different clinical reference groups.

The Gießen Test (GT; Beckmann & Richter, 1972) is widely used in Germany in psychotherapy research. It refers to personality traits and comprises 40 7-point bipolar items (three positive, three negative, and one indifferent) and six subscales: social resonance, dominance, control, basic mood, and social potency.

The VEV (Zielke & Kopf-Mehnert, 1978) questionnaire aims at the change in experience and behavior in psychotherapy and serves as control for success. In 42 7-stepped bipolar items concerning relief, calmness, optimism, strain, insecurity, and pessimism, patients can sign three steps positive or negative tendencies and one indifferent position.

Compared to reference samples of healthy subjects or other clinical groups, our study sample did not show any contrasting difference.

*Study conclusion and summary*: The effectiveness of Jungian psychoanalysis and psychotherapy was determined on the basis of a number of different perspectives and success criteria in a selected and not necessarily representative sample. Three-quarters (76%) of the patients examined had Jungian psychoanalysis so that empirical proof of the effectiveness of long-term analyses could be examined after an average of 6 years. Even after 5 years, the improvement in the patients' state of health and attitude toward the disease resulted in a measurable reduction of health insurance claims (work days lost due to sickness, hospitalization days, doctor's visits, and psychotropic drug intake) in a significant number of the patients treated. This suggests that psychoanalysis is associated with a reduction of health care use and related costs. Cost-effectiveness increasingly plays an important role as outcome criteria for health care purchasers and providers. This retrospective study demonstrated that psychoanalysis also has long-lasting effects on the patients' psychological well-being. Limitations of design and methods aside, the data here provide some convincing arguments for the effectiveness of psychoanalysis. This is encouraging, as the design could be readily replicated on other patient populations. The study offers substantial evidence that the self-assessed health status of patients improved significantly associated with psychoanalytic therapy.

## Which patients had additional psychotherapy after finishing the Jungian psychoanalysis in the catamnestic period? (Westhoff et al., 1996)

This examination is part of the above catamnestic Jung study. Thirty-eight percent ($N = 42$) of the investigated study population from 111 former patients underwent another psychotherapy after finishing the Jungian analysis within the period 5 to 6 years after the end of the Jungian psychotherapy.

In our large catamnestic questionnaire, we had a lot of scales and data allowing a comparison of these patients with an additional psychotherapy with the sample that had only a Jungian psychotherapy. So we could try answering the question of why 42 patients sought additional psychotherapy.

What is difference about these patients compared with patients who did not have an additional psychotherapy?

Which socio-demographic, personality patterns, and somatic characteristics distinguish these patients, and how can we understand their patient–therapist relationship and their health care utilization in comparison to patients without additional psychotherapy?

For 63% of the study sample of 111 patients the Jungian psychotherapy was the first psychotherapy, but 37% had previous psychotherapy with an average duration of 19 months. This is quite the same percentage of patients who have had an additional psychotherapy after the Jungian psychotherapy (38%).

## Socio-demographic comparison

Except for a higher educational attainment, the group of patients with additional psychotherapy (+ patients) show no difference from the sample which had only the Jungian psychotherapy (0 patients). As to education, 40.5% versus 25.4% of the group + patients had an academic degree.

## Biographic background

Likewise, with regard to life-influencing events – we used an Inventory of Stressful Life events (ILE; Siegrist, 1983)[1] in the catamnestic questionnaire – again we could not find any difference between the group with only Jungian psychotherapy and the group with additional psychotherapy.

Both groups had, on average, the same number of siblings and experienced the relationship to their parents in the childhood on a 7-point scale from very good to very bad as moderate to rather bad.

The burden of disease before Jungian psychotherapy in both groups was equal with regard to the duration of the disease and impairment by symptoms assessed from the research rating group on a physical, psychological, and social relationship level in terms of an impairment severity score (BSS, Schepank, 1995),[2] but single individual symptoms showed a difference between both groups: + patients had more problems with contact, anancasm, phobic symptoms, and eating problems. This group of + patients initiated their psychotherapies more by themselves (71% vs. 57%). Three-quarters of the + patients complained of the same symptoms in the catamnesis period as in average 10 years before their Jungian psychotherapy and these symptoms have been the reason for seeking an additional psychotherapy. Half of the 42 + patients decided on individual psychotherapy, seven preferred group therapy, and nine had more than one additional psychotherapy.

## Effectiveness of psychotherapy from the point of view of the patients

Of the entire sample, 45.6% ($n$ =111) would decide in future for another school of psychotherapy. This was due in majority for male patients (67%). The effectiveness of the additional psychotherapy was assessed by the + patients as 28% analogous to the Jungian psychotherapy, 21% experienced their second psychotherapy as worse than their Jungian psychotherapy, and 51% felt it was better. This assessment of the + patients had no association to their mental state. As expected, those who had a better experience in the next psychotherapy would not recommend a Jungian psychotherapy.

The additional psychotherapies had in average a duration of 35 months, had mostly a higher frequency and a mean of 144 sessions over different settings.

Whether these patients (+ patients) did not confirm finishing their (Jungian) psychotherapy too early, nor they would have preferred a higher amount of sessions. But (+ patients) in 38.1% versus 20.9% they estimate the Jungian psychotherapy as not deep enough and failing intensity and they were doubtful about the goal of the psychotherapy. And 26.1% versus 11.8% of the + patients confirmed that their psychotherapy did not provide them a better life.

In different scales of an inventory for rehabilitation (IRES, Gerdes & Jäckel, 1992)[3,] + patients show clear differences compared to 0 patients, they had a lower life satisfaction. In general, 40.5% versus 17% are discontented with their own life, with their family life, and with their occupation – even though they had a better education.

## Health care utilization

Neither in the frequency of recurrent physical diseases in the medical history nor the kind and number of different physical symptoms assessed by a validated list showed any difference between the groups. + Patients did not search more frequently for medical visits because of physical symptoms. They had on average the same number of sick leave days. But they had significantly more frequent visits to psychologists and psychiatrists, alternative practitioners and support groups. + Patients answered the question with respect to the change of symptomatic impairment compared before and after the Jungian psychotherapy like the group of 0 patients. But the findings of the symptomatic complain list SCL-90-R revealed a higher self-rated level of symptomatic strain in all different subscales of this test. Impressive are the high ratings in the subscales somatization, insecurity with social contact, anxiousness. The + patients are doubtful about themselves, have a tendency to more self-blaming, and show a tendency toward being involved in discussions and struggle more frequently with others.

We conclude that the higher degree of psychological strain associated with the kind of disease behaviors identified may account for the patient dissatisfaction rather than an insufficient psychotherapy.

Twenty-six of the + patients living with a partner indicated in the self-rating Inventory of Interpersonal Problems (IIP; Horowitz et al., 2000; Horowitz et al., 1988)[4] having problems with trusting others, opening themselves to others, and having more problems showing their feelings to others. They have a greater need to distance themselves from others compared to 0 patients.

In psychotherapy research the quality of the patient-therapist relationship is one of the best predictors for the outcome. In our study we used a 5-point scale (Strupp, 1969) describing the quality of the therapeutic relationship. We found that 21% versus 6% + patients felt that their therapist did not understand them, they doubt that their therapist paid enough attention to them, and they supposed that their therapist believed the therapy with them is not worth the trouble. They experience the speaking of the therapist as formal; they missed feelings of warmness and security.

In summary, both groups had a benefit from the Jungian psychotherapy but + patients experience a higher mental strain. We suppose from a point of view of nowadays that + patients might have developed a dysfunctional, repetitive relationship pattern and disease behavior with their social partners which too might have been constellated in the patient–therapist relationship. As a consequence of this pattern, a unresolved involvement with the therapist probably followed. It could be that both therapist and patient in such cases have not been aware of this involvement. In those cases, usually patients experience their therapists as disappointing and as one of the important persons in his childhood or biography.

We conclude the reason for the patient's seeking an additional psychotherapy is not primarily the kind of psychotherapy or the doses of psychotherapy, but different qualities of the patient–therapist relationship as an expression of an unfavorable relationship experience as a repetitive dysfunctional pattern in their past life.

## Survey of the German Jungian society (DGAP), (Westhoff et al., 1994)

This survey was performed to collect information for use in the selection of therapists from within DGAP membership to participate in the study summarized in the previous section.

In 1993, all members of the German Society for Analytic Psychology (DGAP) were asked to provide information about the membership, structure of this society, school orientation, preferred advanced training, setting characteristics, therapist assessment of success of treatment with individual patients, and professional satisfaction.

Patient and procedural characteristics from a completed case were described, as were the characteristics of outpatient Jungian psychotherapy and analysis. A summary of the findings from this survey include the following: psychotherapy patients still enter therapy about 7 years after the onset of symptoms; they are on average 35 years old at the beginning of treatment; and require a mean of 228 therapy sessions of mostly 2 hours' duration. A total of 1,054 cases were reported in the survey. These were all patients who finished their psychotherapy within the 12-month period prior to the survey. Therapists' global assessment of patient improvement was recorded in six categories: 20.6% were evaluated by their therapists as showing "very good" improvement, 40.5% as "good," and 26.5% as "moderate" improvement. However, 12% of the patients could not improve and were assessed as unchanged, and another 1.1% finished therapy from the point of view of their therapists as "worsened" or "distinctly worsened." In summary, 13.1% of the patients did not improve during treatment.

From the sample of "exemplary cases" we found male therapists proportionally treat male patients more frequently (28%) than female therapists (9%). In contrast, female therapists treat more female patients (90.3%) than male therapists (72%). The number of treatment sessions of male therapists with male patients was 198 – 8 sessions on average – in contrast with female patients who had on average 247 sessions.

It is possible that skepticism among psychotherapists in private practice regarding empiricism and their rejection of quantitative methods led to a general refusal to participate in the survey. In fact, a considerable rate of "hard" exclusion criteria must be taken into consideration in psychotherapy studies. Significant exclusion of subjects occurred due to the fact that current members did not belong to the society in the years relevant to the study (1987–1988) or that older therapists refused additional participation, especially if it clearly extended over the retirement age as in a planned prospective study. Willingness to participate in empirical studies is thus highly dependent on age – an effect that plays a relatively major role in retirement age limits in private practice.

## Current research activities

Empirical research as continued since the start of the initial Berlin Jungian Study. In the Berlin-Heidelberg study (PAL study; Rudolf et al., 2004), both Freudian and Jungian analysts participated in a naturalistic prospective outcome study. Jungian analysts from the the Swiss Society of psychoanalysis (SGAP) took over the study-design from the Berlin–Heidelberg study and conducted a separate study by exclusively Jungian analysts under auspices of the Heidelberg-Berlin team (Mattanza, 2006). The objective of this research was to investigate the effects of long-lasting psychodynamic psychotherapy and psychoanalysis on symptomatic burden and change of structural personality characteristics.

One central instrument used in the PAL-study is the Operationalized Psychodynamic Diagnostic system (OPD Task Force, 2001, 2008)[5] that allows definition of central foci of the patient in terms of dysfunctional, repetitive relationship patterns, unconscious conflicts, and structural characteristics at the onset of psychotherapy and in the development during the course of psychotherapy. Furthermore, the Heidelberg Structural Change Scale (HSCS) measures structural change on the basis of an operationalized and validated scale (Rudolf et al., 2000).[6]

The Berlin-Heidelberg study was among others funded by the International Association for Analytical Psychology (IAAP). A high percentage of the Jungian analysts participated in the Heidelberg-Berlin study. Three publications cited here address the central findings of the long-lasting study and 3-year cooperative catamnestic study (PAL study, Berlin-Heidelberg).

## Differential effects of two forms of psychoanalytic therapy: results of the Heidelberg-Berlin study (Grande et al., 2006)

This study was funded and promoted by the German umbrella society of psychoanalysts (DGPT).

This is a prospective naturalistic quasi-experimental study. Two psychodynamic therapy approaches that make up about 65% of all forms of psychotherapy currently financed by the health insurance system in Germany were compared. Psychodynamic therapy (PD) is a focal therapy approach involving supportive elements, whereas psychoanalytic therapy (PA) encourages regressive processes, works with transference, and aims at more extensive changes to the personality (structural changes). PAs take longer and involve more sessions per week. By international standards, both approaches are regarded as long-term forms of therapy. This study investigates two groups of diagnostically heterogeneous patients, one PA and the other PD, matched with regard to several important parameters. The success of this matching was tested and comparability checked and substantiated on a wide range of features and scales. Treatment effects measured at the end of therapy and at 1-year follow-up were analyzed with reference to the Global Severity Index (GSI) of the Symptom Checklist-90-R (SCL-90-R; Derogatis, 1980) and the Inventory of Interpersonal Problems (IIP; Horowitz et al., 1988; Horowitz et al., 2000). Both the GSI of the SCL-90-R and the total IIP score showed highly significant main effects in the whole group at the end of therapy and at follow-up. A significant interaction effect between the two groups indicating higher efficiency for PA was found for the IIP total score with regard to the pre–post changes, with a corresponding trend in the pre-therapy follow-up changes. Evidence shows that a supplementary investigation of the specific effects of psychodynamic therapies (structural changes) is required for an accurate appreciation of their potential.

## Structural change in the Heidelberg-Berlin study as a predictor of long-term follow-up outcome (Grande et al., 2009)

Based on data from psychoanalytic long-term psychotherapies, the predictive value of three measures of pre–post change for retrospective patient assessments of outcome at 1-year and 3-year follow-up was investigated. Pre–post changes were measured using the Global Severity Index (GSI; Derogatis, 1980), the Inventory of Interpersonal Problems (IIP; Horowitz, 1988; Horowitz et al., 2000) total score, and the Heidelberg Structural Change Scale (HSCS; Rudolf et al., 2000). In line with psychoanalytic theory, it was assumed that structural changes cause especially persistent modifications and would, therefore, be most suitable to predict the follow-up criterion. This expectation was confirmed: pre–post changes in GSI and IIP were only weakly associated with assessments at 1-year follow-up and not at all with assessments at 3-year follow-up. In contrast, correlations between changes in HSCS and outcome assessments were highly significant at both occasions.

## Structural change as an outcome paradigm in psychodynamic psychotherapy: results of the PAL study (long-term psychoanalytic psychotherapy study) (Rudolf et al., 2012)

The objective of psychodynamic psychotherapies has proved to lead to relevant and stable symptomatic improvement. An unresolved question, however, is what amount of psychodynamic change can be expected beyond symptom relief. For theoretical and methodological reasons rooted in the psychodynamic approach, this question was difficult to answer until now. In the German PAL study (long-term psychoanalytic psychotherapy), 32 patients in psychoanalytic therapy and 27 patients in psychodynamic psychotherapy were studied from the perspective of therapists, patients and researchers through 3 years post-treatment. In this paper we studied dysfunctional relations, unconscious conflicts, and structural aspects as diagnosed by the OPD method. Structural change was rated using the HSCS. A comparison of the two forms of therapy shows more structural change in long-term psychoanalytic psychotherapy compared to the shorter psychodynamic psychotherapy. A comparison of patients with a high level and a low level of structural change revealed that the highly changed patients showed greater symptom relief and greater satisfaction with therapy, and that their therapists perceived a better overall result of treatment. For psychodynamic psychotherapies, structural change seems to be a relevant paradigm of outcome in addition to symptom relief. In longer and more frequent psychoanalytic therapies, more structural change occurs compared to shorter psychodynamic psychotherapies. Beside the amount and length of treatment, the different therapy targets – working through versus supportive treatment – seem to be important.

## Comparison of the structural axis of OPD with structural concepts within Analytical Psychology (Junghan, 2002)

This study (Junghan, 2001) came in the context of the Berlin-Heidelberg-Zurich study (PAL study).

The Operationalized Psychodynamic Diagnostic (OPD, 2001) is a systematic manual used in psychotherapy and psychoanalysis as well, meanwhile widespread in Germany.

Based on conceptual work by C. G. Jung, J. Jacobi, E. Neumann, and M. Fordham in this paper, it is demonstrated that the OPD structure axis (axis IV) can well be described using the terminology of Analytical Psychology. General terms in psychoanalysis like ego or self are analyzed and compared with Jungian conceptions.

Concordant analogue aspects were processed. As a consequence it states that the structure axis of the OPD is suited to be used in Analytical Psychology to achieve more precision and an operationalization of the clinical diagnostic process. This could be of some relevance to clinical practice and is of basic importance to any attempt of process or outcome research in Analytical Psychology.

## Symbols as an expression of a therapeutic relationship: an empirical investigation of the shadow in a Jungian psychotherapy (Kleeberg et al., 2003)

Kleeberg investigated the development of shadow symbols in several psychotherapy processes and showed that unconscious symbols pictured important aspects of the therapeutic relationship, investigated in a single case study based on the complex theory.

## Transformation processes through the therapeutic relationship (Heisig, 2001)

This study investigates in a single case study of how patients' therapeutic relationship changed their inner and outer relationship patterns. The central focus of this study is the processes of constellation and transformation of complex patterns. The investigation shows that the ego-complex developed and got more differentiated from pathological complex-patterns at the end of psychotherapy, and strengthening of the ego complex could be demonstrated. Theses transformation processes were described during 2 years of expert interviews and dream analysis and in a follow-up study. Heisig could develop several qualitative methodological approaches to analyze the therapeutic relationship, "present moments," and the change of symbols in the dreams.

## Current quality insurance, quality management and empirical research activities in Jungian psychotherapy in Germany

There are different reasons for introducing quality management into the health care system in Germany. One of the most important reasons for this is the health administration's need to assess quality for both medical care by the German health system and also psychotherapy and psychoanalysis which is generally is covered by insurance companies, if indication is proved. At the same time, there is also a growing interest in the Jungian community to show evidence of the effectiveness and scientific background of Jungian theoretical positions.

In 2012 a group of Jungian psychoanalysts with research experience founded an international network for research and development in analytical psychotherapy organized in the DGAP and including members of DGAP, SGAP, ÖGAP (Infap3: International Network for Research and Development in Analytical Psychotherapy,

Dreiländergruppe, www.infap3.eu). As a first step, this research network decided to introduce a standardized and consistent basic documentation system in three German Jungian training centers (Stuttgart, Munich, Berlin) in order to systematically collect data on patients searching for psychotherapy in these training centers before and after treatment conducted with either psychodynamic psychotherapy or psychoanalysis.

This documentation system comprises validated patient-related questionnaires handed out before and after treatment concerning basic information on socio-demographic status, symptomatic strain, structural impairment, and quality of life. At the current time of introduction we established from the perspective of the psychoanalysts only the ICD-10 diagnosis used in Germany, recorded from the psychotherapist's written sheets for covering cost expenditure.

This first step of introducing a standardized documentation system serves as a basic instrument of quality insurance and management revealing evidence of the effectiveness from the experience and perspective of the patient's view.

In a second step, our research network intend to unite the data from all three centers together in one data file in order to increase the number of included patients to get a more extended data basis.

The objective of this documentation system is to provide a basic tool for additional research projects and instruments which could be added to the basic questionnaires. At the same time, those empirical funded results could meet expected regulatory issues and laws from government and insurance companies.

Data collection started in Munich and Stuttgart in 2015. Berlin introduced data collection 3 years ago. Now the post-treatment data recruitment has to be organized.

For 3 years Infap3 has organized a "research day" once a year in one of the Jungian training centers to promote research activities in the Jungian community. Training candidates were invited to present their qualification works like bachelor's, master's thesis, or dissertations. Additionally, findings of our documentation system are presented. Experienced researchers give advice for future study designs. Furthermore, a growing network of interested colleges in research has been established.

This process aims at stabilizing the current position of psychoanalysis and psychotherapy including Jungian therapy in the German health care system for the future, by delivering empirical results on the effectiveness of the methods and applying standard quality management processes.

## Summary and future prospects

In the past some encouraging approaches to empirical research have been conducted in Germany to demonstrate the effectiveness of Jungian psychotherapies. The intended purpose of this approach was to provide information about the efficacy of Jungian psychoanalysis to the German health care system and to evaluate the long-term results of treatment with Jungian analysis and psychotherapy against other psychotherapeutic approaches. In particular, when compared with behavioral psychotherapy, an approach that has gained favor in recent years within the German health care system, Jungian therapy approaches have been shown to be effective in numerous empirical studies – mainly short-term psychotherapies and only short-term follow-ups. The need to provide accurate outcomes data is still present and vitally important. Until now there have been no empirical studies that could meet actual empirical methodological standards.

At this time, few research approaches and empirical studies with regard to specific Jungian concepts except for some single case studies. But there is a growing interest in training candidates using empirical approaches for their master-thesis or dissertation. There are a lot of research activities around Christian Roesler's (in this volume) conceptual qualitative approaches to Jungian concepts.

The task force of some Jungian psychoanalysts and researchers in the network of Infap3 has initiated, and promotes the exchange of ideas and discussion about research in the Jungian community. Their goal is to encourage access to scientific knowledge for young analysts and training candidates. The Infap3 will discuss a future study design that meets the RCT criteria (randomized controlled trial). To provide prerequisites for future research in three German Jungian training centers, a basic inventory of instruments for quality insurance was established. This will serve a basic tool for future research. These research activities are promoted by definitive engagement of the managing board of the IAAP. I hope the growing interest of the predominantly younger analysts in an empirical grounded approach for psychotherapy research will result in new studies and new perception and knowledge about Jungian psychotherapy effectiveness and conceptual basis and continued validation of Jungian psychodynamic therapy in the health care system.

## Notes

1 Inventory of Stressful Life Events (ILE). We used a self-rating version. It measures the physical and psychological consequences of critical life events such as separation, loss of job, or death of a close person. It is a standardized questionnaire consisting of 34 items covering quality, quantity, and time patterns of defined life events.
2 BSS–Beeinträchtigungs Schwere Score (Impairment Severity Score; Schepank, 1995) is an expert rating assessment independent from the theoretical background. This assessment comprises three dimensions: physical, psychological, and psychosocial (interpersonal) impairment by mental disease. Rating steps from 0 to 4 with reference to the three dimensions can be summarized to a total score between 0 and a maximum of 12. For benchmarking, a comparison with reference samples of different clinical groups is possible.
3 IRES: Indicator for the Status of Rehabilitation is an assessment questionnaire to evaluate the need and efficiency of the status of rehabilitation. This standardized measurement assesses the physical and psychosocial status and quality of life satisfaction of patients who intend to finish or who have finished rehabilitation. It also can be used in the field of psychotherapy outcome and follow-ups. This questionnaire is validated and allows a comparison with a healthy reference sample.
4 IIP (Inventory of Interpersonal Problems; Horowitz, 2000). is a standard instrument in both psychotherapy research and quality control of psychotherapy that has a wide acceptability across theoretical orientations. This self-report assessment measures maladaptive relationship behavior, distress arising from interpersonal sources. It describes the types of interpersonal problems that patients experience and the level of distress associated with

them before, during, and after psychotherapy. The 64 items make up a circumplex of problems which is composed of eight subscales: domineering, vindictive, cold, socially inhibited, nonassertive, overly accommodating, self-sacrificing, and intrusive. Participants respond to each item using a 5-point scale from 0 (not at all) to 4 (extremely).

5 Operationalized Psychodynamic Diagnosis (OPD) is a multiaxial diagnostic and classification system based on psychodynamic principles. It is based on five axes: I = experience of illness and prerequisites for treatment, II = interpersonal relations, III = conflict, IV = structure, and V = mental and psychosomatic disorders (in line with Chapter V (F) of the ICD-10). After an initial interview lasting 1–2 hours, the clinician (or researcher) can evaluate the patient's psychodynamics according to these axes and enter them in the checklists and evaluation forms provided.

6 HSCS (Rudolf et al., 2000): The Heidelberg Structural Change Scale is an assessment for measuring the stages of re-structuring of the patient's personality in the course of analytic therapies. It is an expert rating scale on basis of a psychodynamic background. One prerequisite of this scale is the definition of a central focus (dysfunctional relationship pattern, unconscious conflict, or structural problem) in terms of the OPD. Seven stages are defined from the focus on unconscious handling and behavior of the patient to a focus on conscious coping with the unconscious, and finally in the seventh stage to a structurally changed experience and behavior with respect to inner focus. This instrument relies in its formal structure on the APES Scale of Stiles (Stiles et al., 1990; Stiles et al., 1992). The stages of development are orientated on a specific model of the psychoanalytic process. This measure is not only an instrument of research, but also of practice for planning and evaluating of psychodynamic treatments and quality assurance.

## References

Beckmann, D., & Richter, H.E. (1972). *Der Gießen-Test (GT)*. Bern: Huber.

Derogatis, L.R. (1980). *SCL-90R*. Weinheim: Beltz Testgesellschaft.

Dührssen, A. (1962). Katamnestische Ergebnisse bei 1004 Patienten nach analytischer Psychotherapie. *Zeitschrift für Psycho-somatische Medizin, 9*, 94–113.

Gerdes, N., & Jäckel, W.H. (1992). "Indikatoren des Reha-Status (IRES)" – Ein Patientenfragebogen zur Beurteilung von Rehabilitationsbedürftigkeit – und Erfolg. *Rehabilitation, 31*, 73–79.

Grande, T., Dilg, R., Jakobsen, Th., Keller, W., Krawietz, B., Langer, M., Oberbracht, C., . . . Rudolf, G. (2006). Differential effects of two forms of psychoanalytic therapy: Results of the Heidelberg-Berlin study. *Society for Psychotherapy Research*. https://doi.org/10.1080/10503300600608082

Grande, T., Dilg, R., Jakobsen, Th., Keller, W., Krawietz, B., Langer, M., Oberbracht, C., . . . Rudolf, G. (2009, May). Structural change as a predictor of long-term follow-up outcome. *Psychotherapy Research, 19*(3), 344–357.

Heisig D. (2001). Wandlungsprozesse durch die therapeutische Beziehung. *Analytical Psychology, 32*, 230–251 (in German).

Horowitz, L.M., Alden, L.E., & Wiggins, J.S. (2000). *IIP – Inventory of interpersonal problems manual*. San Antonio, TX: The Psychological Corporation.

Horowitz, L.M., Rosenberg, S.E., Baer, B.A., Ureño, G., & Villaseñor, V.S. (1988, December). *Journal of Consulting and Clinical Psychology, 56*(6), 885–892. https://doi.org/10.1037/0022-006X.56.6.885

Junghan, M. (2002). Die Anwendung der Strukturachse der OPD in der Analytischen Psychologie (The application of operationalized psychodynamic diagnostics in Analytical Psychology). In G. Rudolf, T. Grande, & P. Henningsen (Eds.), Die Struktur der Persönlichkeit (The structure of personality) (pp. 90–114). Stuttgart: Schattauer

Kaiser, E. (1993). Quantitative Psychotherapieforschung: Modernes paradigma oder Potemkinsches Dorf? *Forum der Psychoanalyse, 9,* 348–366.

Keller, W., Westhoff, G., Dilg, R., & Rohner, H.H. (2001). Berlin department of psychosomatics and psychotherapy, University Medical Center Benjamin Franklin, Free University of Berlin, Studt and the study group on empirical psychotherapy research in analytical psychology. Wirksamkeit und Inanspruchnahme bei Langzeitanalysen: Ergebnisse einer empirischen Follow-up-Studie zur Effektivität der (jungianischen) Psychoanalyse und Psychotherapie. *Analytical Psychology, 32,* 202–229.

Keller, W., Westhoff, G., Dilg, R., Rohner, R., Studt, H.H., & The study group on empirical psychotherapy research in analytical psychology Berlin. *Department of psychosomatics and psychotherapy,* University Medical Center Benjamin Franklin, Free University of Berlin. The Berlin Jungian study: On the effectiveness and efficacy of outpatient (Jungian) psychoanalysis and psychotherapy – a catamnestic study. In P. Fonagy (Ed.), An open door review of outcome studies in psychoanalysis. https://doi.org/10.13140/2.1.3458.0160 (pp. 180–199). In book: Publisher: International Psychoanalytic Association.

Kleeberg, A., Schreiber, S., & Schwinger, T. (2003). Symbole als Ausdruck der therapeutischen Beziehung. Eine empirische Untersuchung zur Schattensymbolik in einer jungianischen Psychotherapie. *Analytical Psychology, 34,* 266–297 (in German).

Mattanza, G., Jacobsen, T., & Hurt, J. (2006). Jung'sche psychotherapie ist effizient. In Mattanza, G., Meier, I., & Schlegel, M. (Hrsg.), *Seele und Forschung: Ein Brückenschlag in der psychotherapie* (pp. 38–82). Basel: Karger.

OPD Task Force. (Ed.) (2001). *Operationalized psychodynamic diagnostics: Foundations and manual.* Seattle: Hogrefe & Huber.

OPD Task Force. (Ed.) (2008). *Operationalized psychodynamic diagnosis (OPD-2): Manual of diagnosis and treatment planning.* Cambridge: Hogrefe & Huber.

Richter, R., Hartmann, A., Meyer, A.E., & Rüger, U. (1994). Die Kränkesten gehen in eine psychoanalytische Behandlung. Kritische Anmerkung zu einem Artikel in Report Psychologie. *Zeitschrift für Psychosomatische Medizin und Psychoanalyse, 40,* 41–51.

Rudolf, G., Grande, T., Dilg, R., Jakobsen, T.H., Keller, W., Krawietz, B., Langer, M., . . . Oberbracht, C. (2004). Effektivität und Effizienz psychoanalytischer Langzeittherapie: Die Praxisstudie analytische Langzeittherapie. In A. Gerlach, A. Schlösser, & A. Springer (Hgs.), *Psychoanalyse des glaubens* (pp. 515–528). Gießen: Psychosozial-Verlag.

Rudolf, G., Grande, T., & Oberbracht, C. (2000). Die Heidelberger Umstrukturierungsskala: Ein Modell der Veränderung in psychoanalytischen Therapien und seine Operationalisierung in einer Schätzskala [The Heidelberg Structural Change Scale. A model for change in psychoanalytic therapies and its operationalization in an assessment scale]. *Psychotherapeut, 45,* 237–246.

Rudolf, G., Jakobsen, Th., Keller, W., Krawietz, B., Langer, M., Oberbracht, C., Stehle, S., Stennes, S., & Grande, T. (2012). Umstrukturierung als Ergebnisparadigma der psychodynamischen Psychotherapie: Ergebnisse aus der Praxisstudie Analytische Langzeittherapie (Structural change as an outcome paradigm in psychodynamic psychotherapy – results of the PAL-Study (long-term psychoanalytic psychotherapy study). *Zeitschrift für Psychosomatische Medizin und Psychotherapie, 58,* 55–66.

Schepank, H. (1995). *Der Beeinträchtigungs-Schwere-Score (BSS): Ein Instrument zur Bestimmung der Schwere einer psychogenen Erkrankung. Handanweisung.* Göttingen: Beltz Test GmbH.

Siegrist, J., & Dittmann, K. (1983). *Inventar Lebensverändernder Ereignisse* (ILE). ZUMA-Handbuch sozialwissenschaftlicher Skalen, Bd 3. Mannheim: Zentrum für Umfragen, Methoden und Analysen e.V.

Stiles, W.B., Elliott, R., Lewelyn, S.P., Firth-Cozens, J.A., Margison, F.R., Shapiro, D.N., & Hardy, G. (1990). Assimilation of problematic experiences by clients in psychotherapy. *Psychotherapy*, 27, 411–420.

Stiles, W.B., Meshot, C.M., Anderson, T.M., & Sloan, W.W., Jr. (1992). Assimilation of problematic experiences: The case of John Jones. *Psychotheraphy Research*, 2, 81–101.

Strupp, H.H., Fox, R.E., & Lessler, K. (1969). *Patients view their psychotherapy*. Baltimore: Johns Hopkins University Press.

Westhoff, G., Dilg, R., Keller, W., Köller, K., die Arbeitsgruppe Analytische Psychologie, Berlin, Abteilung für Psychosomatik und Psychotherapie des Universitätsklinikums Benjamin Franklin der Freien Universität Berlin. (1994). *Rahmenbedingungen ambulanter jungianischer Psychoanalysen und Psychotherapien in den neunziger Jahren und Haltung niedergelassener Psychotherapeuten gegenüber empirischer Psychotherapieforschung – Ergebnisse einer Fachverbandsbefragung im Rahmen einer Psychotherapie-Wirksamkeitsstudie*. Unpublished paper.

Westhoff, G., Dilg, R., Keller, W., Rohner, R., & Studt, H.H. (1996). *Welche Patienten unterziehen sich aus welchen Gründen mehrfach einer ambulanten Psychotherapie?* (Which reasons patients motivate to undergo an additional outpatient psychotherapy?) Unpublished paper.

Zielke, M., & Kopf-Mehnert, C. (1978). *VEV: Veränderungsfragebogen des Erlebens und verhaltens manual*. Weinheim: Beltz Test Gesellschaft.

# 13

# RESEARCH ON TRAINING

## Findings from the evaluation of the IAAP's International Router training program

*John Merchant*

The International Association for Analytical Psychology's (IAAP) International Router training program began in 1996 in response to those professionals who wanted to train as Jungian analysts but who were in countries where no Training Societies existed and who were precluded from traveling to established institutes because of issues like costs, political difficulties, and language barriers. Since that time the program has grown into five world regions and currently deals with over 200 trainees. While the program continues to fulfill its IAAP aim of leading to new Societies, it was understandably necessary to evaluate its strengths and weaknesses which the IAAP initiated through its Research and Evaluation Working Group (currently comprising Nataliya Alexandrova, Graham Fuller, John Merchant [Chair], Denise Ramos, Christian Roesler, Yasuhiro Tanaka, and Jan Wiener).

### Previous research within Analytical Psychology

Within Analytical Psychology, issues to do with training have been addressed mainly in terms of symposia, conferences, and professional commentary as in conference papers and publications. Consequently, systematic research on training has been sparse.

In 1960, the Society of Analytical Psychology, London, held a symposium on training with discussions being subsequently published in the *Journal of Analytical Psychology* (Plaut, Newton, & Fordham, 1961; Hillman, Plaut, & Fordham, 1962; Plaut, 1962). A following symposium in 1980 focused on professional supervision (Plaut et al., 1982).

In 2006, the *Journal of Analytical Psychology* devoted its conference to "Jungian Analytic Training for the 21st Century – New Contexts and New Directions," at which Horne (2007) stressed the need to attend to the intellectual context in which a training is embedded. Egger-Biniores (2007) saw training primarily as a process of immersion and personal transformation as distinct from just learning. Kelly (2007) noted that despite their being different trainings around the world, there were common core values among trained analysts, a central one being a capacity to work with the symbolic in a meaningful way, and he suggested that from this can follow a dynamic and living relationship with the unconscious as real, objective, and as other. Beginning with a definition of analytic talent, Wiener (2007) presented a Jungian framework for assessing trainees' progress which emphasizes the significance of both character and competence and the developing relationship between them.

More recently, those involved in the IAAP Router training program have discussed their experiences either as trainers or trainees (Bortuleva, 2014; Connolly, 2006, 2011; Crowther & Wiener, 2002, 2015; Crowther et al., 2011; Gordon, Perry, & Wright, 2012; Kalinowska, 2012; Korinteli, 2003; Korinteli, Lavrova, & Rebeko, 2012; Mathers, Palmer Barnes, & Noack, 2006; Pourtova, 2013; Rudakova, 2002, 2003; Tsivinsky, 2014; Zalessky & Zalesskaya, 2012). These contributions highlight a number of issues including the flexibility and limits of such a model of cross-cultural training; mutual adaptation to other cultures without losing tradition and identity; cultural complexes and trauma; moving on from doctrinaire Soviet attitudes in education to embrace "not knowing"; the learning from mistakes and from joint experience without guilt or shame; the pros and cons of shuttle analysis; curriculum issues; group dynamics; and post-training issues and the need to protect reflective space amid the constraints of time and geography. These range of issues provided much initial material for the Working Group to consider in relation to its evaluation.

## Previous research within the broader psychoanalytic school

As with Analytical Psychology, issues to do with training within the broader psychoanalytic school have often been addressed through professional commentary as in conference papers and publications, although certain groups have undertaken surveys and interviews. The literature reveals a number of important issues.

Drawing on an ongoing project undertaken by European International Psychoanalytical Association (IPA) institutes, Tuckett (2005) saw the need for transparent assessment criteria and proposed a subsequent model. This transparency issue was also addressed by Doll-Hentschker (2006).

In relation to curriculum issues, Jordan and Emde (2006) conducted a survey of the 30 American Psychoanalytic Association (APA) institutes and found that while most saw the evaluation of what candidates learn from the curriculum as important, few did any such evaluation. This finding raised the whole issue of the specification of teaching goals and the evaluation of learning within psychoanalytic training.

Shuttle analysis also emerged as an issue. Szonyi and Stajner-Popovic (2008) and later Diatkine (2010) both overviewed its pros and cons as experienced within the Psychoanalytic Institute for Eastern Europe (PIEE), highlighting that the repeated separation experiences inherent in shuttle analysis often give a new meaning to past trauma.

Following a comprehensive study of its own training institutions by the Transparency Commission of the German Psychoanalytic Association (DPV), Brodbeck (2008) put forward suggestions to help make unconscious structures and related unconscious acting out in the training, especially under the influence of idealizations, more transparent, thereby alleviating the build-up of anxieties that hamper an optimal learning and development process. Brodbeck also proposed that it would be useful to apply the psychoanalytic method to group processes as well as organizational structures.

Important evaluative work has also been done by the Working Party on Education (WPE) of the European Psychoanalytical Federation (EPF) and Junkers, Tuckett, and Zachrisson (2008) have summarized the findings from this ongoing project to do with training, which particularly looked at what constitutes competent psychoanalytic work and what criteria are used to evaluate it. Subsequently, on how best to facilitate training, Francois-Poncet (2009) put forward a model designed to deal with the inevitable conflicts between transmission by means of analysis (which was seen to be difficult to regulate through institutional standards) and training by means of apprenticeship (which can be evaluated by objective and public criteria). One final recommendation was that the observation and analysis of transference be taken beyond the framework of treatment to that of supervision.

Following the founding of the Han Groen Prakken Psychoanalytic Institute for Eastern Europe by the IPA and the European Psychoanalytical Federation (EPF) in 2002, Fonda (2011) extensively overviewed the development of psychoanalysis and of analytic training in Eastern Europe through this institute after the fall of the Iron Curtain. The issues that required thought and attention had to do with shuttle analysis; the formation of groups; the involvement of international staff with their similarities and differences; the need for systematic teaching; determining criteria for selection of candidates; and the diversity of candidates in terms of languages, cultures, and histories.

More recently, Kahl-Popp (2014) delineated the affinities between learning in psychoanalysis, psychoanalytic treatment, and learning in supervision and went on to show how a patient- and supervisee-centered psychoanalytic concept of evaluation can be used for research purposes to investigate the impact of supervision on the learning of psychoanalytic-psychotherapeutic competence.

In addition to Kernberg's (2000, 2006, 2016) extensive overviews of psychoanalytic trainings, other topics addressed in the literature have included the role, functions, and dynamics of report reading (Hanna, 1998); issues of power and regression in the supervisory relationship (Frawley-O'Dea & Sarnat, 2001); the evaluative components and learning objectives of supervision (Frijling-Schreuder, Isaac-Edersheim & Van der Leeuw, 1981; Levy, 2001; Watkins, 2016; Weiss & Fleming, 1975); transference and countertransference dynamics in training (Lauro, 1994; Martin, Mayerson, Olsen, & Wiberg, 1978); candidate selection, progression, and evaluation (Cabaniss, Schein, Rosen, & Roose, 2003; Greenacre, 1961; Kappelle, 1996; Mander, 2004; Rothstein,

2016); organizational issues (Garza-Guerrero, 2004); and the training analysis itself (Caligor, 1985; Kernberg, 2014; Lifschutz, 1976; Meyer, 2003; Shapiro, 1976; Stone, 1974; Torras de Bea, 1992; Wallerstein, 2010).

The issues and suggestions raised in the aforementioned literature proved useful to the IAAP Working Group in orienting their evaluation.

## Initial considerations and the subsequent research method

A number of members of the IAAP Working Group had opportunity of meeting with past and current Routers at the 2013 IAAP Copenhagen Congress. One major issue that emerged had to do with the use of Skype, its suitability to the analytic process as well as the IAAP's rules in terms of its frequency of use, confidentiality issues, and individuals' ease (or not) in using Skype. Evaluation of the use of Skype in the Router program and a review of any research on the efficacy of Skype in analysis, psychotherapy, and supervision was clearly indicated, which ultimately led to Merchant's (2016) paper "The Use of Skype in Analysis and Training: A Research and Literature Review" in the *Journal of Analytical Psychology*.

Other main points which emerged from the meetings at the 2013 IAAP Copenhagen Congress meetings had to do with cultural trauma and how it influenced the Router experience; language and translation issues; group dynamics in the Developing Groups; clarification as to the Liaison Person's responsibilities; Router feedback mechanisms; ways to strengthen the Router community; delivery of the theoretical component of the training; shuttle analysis (its benefits and difficulties) and the impact of interpreters. These comments gave the Working Group useful information as to the issues which needed to be addressed in the evaluation.

One major difficulty the Working Group faced in terms of its data collection was feasibility. The Current Routers (hereinafter CRs), Router Graduates (hereinafter RGs), the Regional Organizers (hereinafter ROs) and Liaison Persons for particular local groups (hereinafter LPs) were spread across five regions, making the use of focus groups difficult although individual face-to-face interviewing did become possible. Second, there were language and translation issues to consider. The other major issue had to do with validity. Triangulation is the generally agreed method to enhance validity in the kind of qualitative research this evaluation required (Bryman, 2012), so data was gathered using a three-pronged approach:

1   Anonymous surveys through Survey Monkey were sent to CRs, RGs, and analysts (who have had involvement in the program).
2   Face-to-face interviews of CR, RG, and analyst volunteers occurred. From a practical point of view, these interviews had to rely on volunteers who were able to meet at available conferences. As a consequence, the CR, RG, and analyst interviewees came from Europe and Asia only, although feedback from the other regions is contained in the surveys.
3   A review of any published literature relevant to the Router program.

If consistent themes emerged across these three areas, it would be reasonable to conclude they had validity.

## The surveys

### Surveys to the CRs and RGs

A number of preliminary meetings with CRs and RGs as well as the Working Group's reflections highlighted the kinds of issues needing inclusion in the surveys. Questions were divided into three sections to do with the *structure*, the *process*, and the *content* of the program. The RG survey contained an additional question about the Final Examination.

Respondents first specified the region from which they came, but not all went on to answer every question.

The structure questions targeted the initial screening interview; the yearly Self-Evaluation Forms; the yearly Supervisor's Consultation Evaluation; the Intermediate Examination; the Final Examination (for RGs only); the RO; the LP; and any suggested improvements.

The process questions asked about shuttle analysis; the use of interpreters; Skype and analysis (including the IAAP's rules); cultural differences and analysis; the overall experience of analysis; Skype and supervision; cultural differences and supervision; group and individual supervision; the overall experience of supervision and the use of Skype in the Router's own practice.

The content questions asked about the required readings, the overall curriculum, and any suggested improvements.

There was a concluding question where respondents could make any final comments.

### Results of the survey to CRs and RGs

Out of 190 CR contacts, 104 accessed the survey but the numbers who responded to the questions ranged from 71 to 47, giving an average response rate of 64/190 (34%). Of the 63 RG names on the Secretary's list, 45 accessed the survey, but those who responded to the questions ranged from 25 to 16, so that the average response rate was 21/63 (33%).

The CR respondents came from the following regions: Asia and the Chinese region, 14 (13.46%); Latin and Central America, 19 (18.27%); Central Europe, 38 (36.54%); Eastern Europe, 23 (22.12%); other, 10 (9.62%), giving a total of 104. The majority of respondents therefore came from Europe – 61/104 (58.65%) – and although the total number here is 104, not all answered every question, so the average response rate was 64/190 (34%).

The RG respondents came from the following regions – Asia and the Chinese region, 3 (6.67%); Latin and Central America, 11 (24.44%); Central Europe, 18 (40%); Eastern Europe, 11 (24.44%); other, 2 (4.44%) giving a total of 45. Again, the majority of RG respondents came from Europe – 29/45 (64%) – but not all answered every question, so the average response rate was 21/63 (33%).

The following summary is made by truncating the individual responses of the CRs and RGs. General comments have been included later in the themes section.

## The initial screening interview

The screening interviews were understandably anxiety provoking but provided a personal reflective space where the sensitivity and support of the interviewers and any feedback was appreciated. Comments indicated the following:

- Assessment criteria and interviewers' procedures may need specifying;
- Timely (and perhaps written) feedback needs to be considered;
- Further attention could be given to the presence of dual relationships.

## The yearly Self-Evaluation Forms

The comments here indicated Routers gained knowledge of their strengths and · weaknesses and they found this useful to compare with their Supervisors' Reports. One concern seems to be a perceived "surveillance aspect" raising questions like these: Who reads the form and why? Is its purpose assessment? What is done with the information? Finally, many respondents commented that they received no feedback and there were no guidelines for the form's completion.

## The yearly Supervisor's Consultation Evaluation

The comments here indicated Routers again gained knowledge of their strengths and weaknesses but timely implementation and a lack of feedback were mentioned as problems as well as the question, who wrote what?

## The Intermediate Examination

The goodwill of the examiners was appreciated and the immediate feedback was very valued as it gave direction for the Final Examination. The combining of theory with practice was also valued. A lack of feedback issue was again raised by some as was the desire for more up-front guidelines about the examination. Difficulties doing the examination during an IAAP Congress were also raised.

## The Final Examination (only RGs answered this question)

Again the goodwill of the examiners was appreciated and the immediate feedback was very valued as was having continuity with previous examiners. The issue of written feedback was again raised. Other comments mentioned guidelines by which to do the examination; how to write for this kind of assessment; the timing of examinations and the issue of the qualification – can it be a diploma?

### The Regional Organizer (RO)

The majority of CRs are finding the RO to be useful (or very useful) [59/67 (88.06%)]. The majority of RGs [16/22 (73%)] feel the same but the overall percentage is lower, and 3/22 (14%) found the RO "not useful." This probably reflects historical issues so more reliance should be placed on the feedback for the CRs. Aspects of the previous Router situation in Poland highlight the issue of the RO and group supervisor always being separate individuals.

### The Liaison Person (LP)

The majority of CRs are finding the LP to be useful [52/61 (85.25%)], but this has not been the experience for many RGs where only 14/25 (56%) found the LP useful. Conversely, about one third of RGs [8/25 (32%)] had an issue with their LP. This is a high rate and indicates further analysis of the data is required to see if this was a regional issue or one to do with role clarification and/or impractical expectations of Routers at the time or an historical issue no longer relevant. As with the RO, more reliance should be placed on the feedback from the CRs as being indicative of the current state of affairs.

### Shuttle analysis

Individual comments mentioned the in-built lack of continuity so that intervening Skype sessions were found to be helpful. It can also be financially costly if it is the Router who has to move.

### The use of interpreters

Interestingly, no problems were raised by the CRs on this issue. Some RGs mentioned the additional cost it entailed but that the translation pause facilitated reflection. Others did find the presence of a third person discommoding and commented that the interpreters need to be professional and as "invisible" as possible.

### The Skype issue

Overall, the repeated issues raised were the continuity in analysis that Skype can provide; the access it gave to a diversity of analysts; the value of in-person start-points before transitioning to Skype; the preparation it requires and its limitations compared to its cost-effectiveness.

### The IAAP's recent increase in the number of allowed Skype sessions

Noticeably, 34/64 (53%) of the CRs think the number of allowed hours is just right, while 19/64 would want it increased. Four suggested that half the number of hours should be allowed by Skype. There is a possibility there could be regional differences being expressed here. Of the RGs, the vast majority [16/22 (73%)] also agree with the current allocation, while the remainder (apart from one) maintain it is too high. This latter result is in contrast to that from the CRs and raises the question for future research: why this difference? Perhaps the use of Skype was less available when most of the RGs were training, or there was more of an emphasis on shuttle analysis for them. Furthermore, as the Router program extended into more distant regions, the use of Skype by the CRs became more necessary alongside the possibility that the CRs come from a younger, more cyber-friendly generation. It is also possible that the CRs prefer to access a more diverse pool of analysts via Skype and that the analysts themselves are becoming more used to and willing to use Skype.

## Cultural differences

Overall, 36/47 (77%) of CRs rate the impact of cultural differences on their analysis as low to insignificant, while less than a quarter 11/47 (23%) rate it as having some significance. There may be specific regional issues indicated here. Nonetheless, it is noticeable that cultural differences are not a major issue for the vast majority of CRs. Responses by the RGs are not that dissimilar to those from the CRs, where 12/16 (75%) rate the impact of cultural differences on their analysis as low to insignificant. However, it needs to be noted that 4/16 (25%) of the RGs said the impact was high but these numbers do not come from an extensive enough sample. A better-sized sample is that from the CRs (47), so more emphasis should be placed on those responses. Again, we may be dealing here with specific regional issues or those from a past state of affairs. Further regional input on this issue is indicated but again it is noticeable that cultural differences were not a major issue for the majority of RGs.

## The experience of analysis

Of the CRs, 68/71 (96%) are having either a positive or very positive experience of analysis and of the RGs, 20/21 (95%) gave similar responses. These responses high-light the very personal nature of analytic training and these results are encouraging.

## Supervision by Skype

For the CRs, 48/71 (68%) are doing their supervision by Skype and of those 30/51 (59%) do more than half their supervision via Skype. Of the RGs, 9/22 (41%) have not used Skype in supervision at all. Of those who did, 14/18 (78%) used it less than 50% of the time. This result is in marked difference to that from the CRs. It has to be noted that the CR data represents a better sample size (71 and 51 compared to 22 and 18) but the question remains – why this difference? Both regional and generational differences are likely to be implicated here, and some of the same reasons may apply for the difference seen in the issue of the recent increase in the number of allowed Skype sessions (see above).

Individual comments to do with the positive aspects of doing supervision by Skype included the frequency, access, and continuity it enabled; how it was both time and cost-effective and the way it gave access to a diversity of supervisors. Negative aspects mentioned Skype as not enabling a deep enough experience and that things can be hindered (as in presenting drawings), there can be connection failures, and the IAAP's requirements were too stringent.

### Cultural differences and supervision

Over one third of the CRs [27/69 (39%)] rate cultural differences as having an impact on their supervision, but when these cultural differences are rated, 34/43 (79%) said they were of "low" to "no significance." While present, cultural differences do not appear to be a major issue for most of the CRs. This is interesting compared to the responses to do with cultural differences impacting analysis where the significance is rated lower [11/47 (23%)]. Similarly, however, these 47 respondents rate the impact of cultural differences on their analysis as being low or insignificant. We may be dealing here with specific regional issues.

For the RGs, 10/20 (50%) rated cultural differences as having an impact on their supervision. The drop from 50% among the RGs to 39% for CRs is noticeable, and the CRs did have a more reliable number of respondents – 69 compared to 10. This probably reflects a greater awareness of these issues among the trainers and the way the Router program has been extended into other regions. It indicates a positive shift on this issue in the current context. Furthermore, 12/15 (80%) of the RGs said the influence of cultural differences on their supervision was "low" or of "no significance." This is virtually the same result as for the CRs, so while cultural differences are present they do not appear to have been a major issue for these RGs during their training.

### Group and individual supervision

Comments indicated that both are useful but different. While group supervision was seen to provide a diversity of insights, the group process needed containing/holding. Some also commented on certain confidentiality/ethical issues arising in group supervision like presenting session recordings and the introduction of new members to the group. Large group sizes can also be an issue. Individual supervision was seen by most respondents to be more effective, more in-depth and where more attention could be given to transference/countertransference issues.

### The experience of supervision

The vast majority of CRs [68/71 (96%)] are having a positive experience in supervision, and this is similar to the RGs responses [21/22 (96%)]. No RGs selected the "negative" or "very negative" alternatives to this question.

## The use of Skype in their own practices

More than half of the CRs [40/70 (57%)] use Skype in their own practice but of these, the vast majority [36/43 (84%)] only use Skype up to a quarter of the time. Of the RGs, the majority use Skype in their practices [16/22 (73%)] but of these, the vast majority use it only "0 to 24% of the time" [17/18 (94%)]. The latter result is similar to the results for the CRs. Individual comments do not reveal a major use of Skype as a predominant part of CR and RG practices. The main use seems to be to maintain continuity when patients go out of town.

## The required readings

The vast majority of CRs [52/64 (81%)] have sufficient access to the required readings (but about one-fifth do not) and similarly, the vast majority of CRs [59/61 (97%)] find the readings helpful. For the RGs, the majority also had sufficient access to the required readings [15/21 (71%)], but the percentage is less for them compared to the CRs, so that over one-quarter of the RGs did not have sufficient access [6/21 (29%)]. The vast majority of RGs [18/19 (95%)] found the readings helpful. More than likely, any differences here between the CRs and RGs probably reflect regional issues (which require further investigation) as well as positive changes and developments in the Router training.

## The curriculum

The vast majority of CRs [61/63 (96.83%)] find the curriculum helpful, and this is encouraging. The majority of RGs also found the curriculum helpful [17/20 (85%)]. There were, however, three "no" responses, which is likely to reflect a situation from the historic past or from a particular region.

## The analyst's survey

The analyst's survey contained questions to do with their involvement across what region(s) and over what year(s); what they see as having worked well and not well for themselves and the Routers; what strengths and weaknesses they see in the program; any suggestions for improvement; and any comments on the Skype issue.

Of the analysts surveyed, 48 (out of 94) from the Secretary's list accessed the survey, but those who responded to the questions ranged from 34 to 26, so that the overall average response rate was 29/94 (31%). Significantly, 18 analysts indicated their willingness to do a follow-up interview, which speaks to the interest and commitment to the program despite the practical logistics of getting such interviews arranged (as yet).

Following are the themes/issues which emerged:

1 Cultural issues and their impact on analysis, supervision, and group processes;
2 The Router isolation factor, in that most Routers have either few or no local trainees;

3    Shuttle analysis including the "abandonment" experience many Routers have when their analyst departs;
4    Assessment standards: is the Router training rigorous enough?
5    Group processes to do with a range of impacting issues like cultural differences to do with leadership and deference, ethics, democratic processes, and grievance procedures;
6    Administrative procedures and structures both in the delivery of the program by the trainers and in the Developing Groups;
7    The program's strength being its flexibility and adaptability;
8    The need for a basic curriculum with available readings to provide theoretical grounding and understanding to the Routers;
9    The issue of funding and costs both in relation to the analyst volunteers and the Routers.

## The interview

Interviews with the CRs and RGs followed the method of appreciative inquiry, which emphasizes "what worked?" before exploring "what did not work?" and eliciting suggestions for improvement (Bushe, 2012; Bushe & Kessler, 2013). In terms of ethics, the interviews followed the protocols of the National Statement on Ethical Conduct in Human Research, 2007 (updated March 2014). Specifically, interviewees had to give informed consent; they had indicated to them a person disconnected from the Working Group or the IAAP Executive Committee whom they could contact if they were in any way distressed by the interview, and they also had a person specified to them to contact if they wanted to make a complaint.

Overall, a total of 26 interviews were conducted with 12 analysts; 7 RGs (two from Central Europe, three from Eastern Europe, and two from Asia) and 7 CRs (one from Central Europe and six from Asia).

The positive aspects of the program consistently mentioned by the CRs and RGs were the value of the personal analysis in terms of personal change, self-knowledge, initiation, and aspects of personal (emotional) connection with the trainers and others, that is, the analytic community. For the analysts, the positives had to do with the program reaching its objectives, that is, new Societies forming; the program's flexibility; the commitment and enthusiasm of the trainers; and the supervision courses which emerged.

A summary of the other themes from the interviews follow and they are ranked according to the number of interviewees who commented thereon and who are listed by their interview number after the sub-heading. Current Routers are designated as "CR"; Router graduates as "RG"; Central Europe as "CE"; Eastern Europe as "EE"; Asia as "As"; and analyst as "A."

### The European Router interviews

The majority of the interviewees from Europe were RGs from Eastern Europe, and since this is where the program started, we have valuable feedback as it gives insight into how things may have been which can be compared to the current situation. The main themes (ranked) that emerged were:

1a  Administration issues [RG1(CE); RG2(EE); RG3(EE); RG5(CE)]
1b  Assessment and selection issues [RG1(CE); RG2(EE); RG4(EE); RG5(CE)]
1c  Curriculum and faculty issues [CR1(CE); RG2(EE); RG3(EE); RG4(EE)]
1d  Financial cost issues [CR1(CE); RG1(CE); RG2(EE); RG5(CE)]
1e  The Router and Router Graduate community [CR1(CE); RG3(EE); RG3(EE); RG5(CE)]
2a  Cultural differences/complexes [RG1(CE); RG2(EE); RG5(CE)]
2b  Group processes [RG1(CE); RG2(EE); RG5(CE)]
2c  Language issues [RG1(CE); RG3(EE); RG4(EE)]
3a  Ethics issues [CR1(CE); RG1(CE)]
3b  Post-graduation issues [RG2(EE); RG5(CE)]
4a  Potential program expansion issues [CR1(CE)]
4b  Shuttle analysis and Skype [RG3(EE)]
4c  The personal analysis [RG3(EE)].

### The Asian Router interviews

The main themes (ranked) that emerged were:

1a  Diversity and continuity of the analysts [CR2(As); RG9(As); CR4(As); CR6(As); CR7(As)]
1b  The Router community and group meetings [CR2(As); CR3(As); CR4(As); CR5(As); CR7(As)]
1c  Curriculum issues [CR3(As); RG8(As); RG9(As); CR6(As); CR7(As)]
2a  Supervision [CR2(As); RG8(As); CR5(As); CR6(As)]
2b  Ethics issues [CR2(As); RG8(As); RG9(As); CR7(As)]
3a  Skype issues [CR2(As); RG8(As); CR7(As)]
3b  Language issues [CR2(As); CR4(As); CR6(As)]
4a  Sandplay [CR3(As); CR6(As)]
4b  Administration issues [CR2(As); CR7(As)]
4c  Financial cost issues [CR4(As); CR7(As)].

### The analyst interviews

The main themes (ranked) that emerged were:

1a  Assessment, examinations, and rigor issues [A1(EE); A3(CE); A4(EE); A5(EE); A6(As); A8 (EE/As); A10(As); A11(As); A12(As)]
1b  Cultural issues, cultural complexes, and trauma [A1(EE); A4(EE); A5(EE); A6(As); A7(As); A8(EE/As); A10(As); A11(As); A12(As)]

2   The issue of Skype usage [A1(EE); A2(EE); A3(CE); A8(EE/As); A9(As); A10(As); A11(As); A12(As)]
3   Shuttle analysis and abandonment issues [A1(EE); A2(EE); A3(CE); A9(As); A10(As); A11(As); A12(As)]
4a  Administration issues [A1(EE); A3(EE); A4(EE); A5(EE); A10(As); A11(As)]
4b  Curriculum issues [A1(EE); A3(CE); A6(As); A9(As); A10(As); A11(As)]
4c  Group processes [A1(EE); A3(CE); A7(As); A8(EE/As); A10(As); A11(As)]
5   Router selection [A1(EE); A4(EE); A5(EE); A6(As)]
6   Funding issues [A1(EE); A4(EE); A5(EE)]
7a  Recognition of the Router training [A3(CE)]
7b  The "incest" issue and dual relationships [A3(CE)].

## The literature

Since the beginning of the Router training program in Russia in the 1990s, quite a number of papers have appeared in the *Journal of Analytical Psychology* addressing various issues. Rudakova (2002) specifically mentioned the curriculum, personal development, clinical techniques, the interpreter experience, and emerging collegiality, while others explored specific cultural issues that could intersect with clinical work: Korinteli (2003); Kalinowska (2012); Pourtova (2013); Bortuleva (2014); Rudakova (2003); and Tsivinsky (2014).

In 2002, Crowther and Wiener overviewed their experience in Russia and described the interactive field between participants, the cultural unconscious, and the way the different learning styles between East and West impacted on transference/countertransference dynamics. Subsequently, in 2011 they published "Fifteen Minute Stories About Training" in collaboration with some RGs from Eastern Europe where the themes identified were mutual adaptation, the embracing of "not knowing", learning from mistakes, and the need to protect reflective space. Crowther and Wiener specifically mentioned the positives and negatives of shuttle analysis, the positive involvement of translators, specific cultural differences that needed addressing, post-training issues, and collegiality. Common themes for the RGs were cultural differences and complexes. Volodina highlighted cultural trauma and her own transcendence of it, while Alexandrova presented particular details about cultural complexes and how she worked with them. Other issues mentioned were maintaining the frame, regular curriculum delivery, the centrality of the personal over the intellectual in analytic work, isolation and the finishing-up process (Tserashchuk), personal and cultural shadow projections, interpreters, the analyst's (developmental) style, "not knowing," and collegiality (Tsivinsky).

Additionally, Connolly (2006, 2011) has considered the different cultural responses to the frame as well as cultural trauma in Russian patients, while Mathers, Palmer Barnes, and Noack (2006) addressed language and translation issues, cultural trauma, and specific archetypal patterns that emerged in their work in Poland.

More recently, Crowther and Wiener (2015) have edited contributions from 18 involved in the Router program either as supervisors, analysts, trainers, or RGs and listed the themes which emerged:

1 The analysts found their involvement in the Router program to be "moving, challenging, meaningful and life-changing," and this with a sense of "vocation";
2 The personal emotional engagement that occurred between participants;
3 Despite cultural differences, both parties can learn and be mutually transformed – "the bi-directionality of influence," as Cambray put it in his chapter;
4 Cultural differences can also lead to shadow projections;
5 Language issues can have negative consequences (as in the blurring of meaning) but also positive outcomes (as in decelerating the process, which allows for greater reflection).

Crowther and Wiener (2015) also noted two different perspectives among their contributors. Shuttle analysis can facilitate an analysis, but on the other hand, the in-built "abandoning" breaks can activate pre-existing trauma in Routers. This raised an additional question: will the use of shuttle analysis have a negative impact on the eventual ethos and infrastructure of new Training Societies if they continue to use it in their own region?

The second different perspective had to do with the analysts being the "outsiders" which can lead, on the one hand, to "colonization" perceptions, and on the other hand to an enabling of deeper confidentiality since the "outsiders" are not connected either to the Routers' personal circle or cultural norms.

Interestingly, given the issue of Skype in the surveys, it was only mentioned eight times in the book: once in passing by Abramovich and by Jasiński and Kalinowska; twice by Cavalli who uses it in overseas supervision with no problem; and by Beebe, who mentions it four times in a positive way in relation to analysis and supervision within a shuttle context.

## Overall themes (with suggestions)

As indicated previously, the surveys to CRs and RGs contained directed questions, but the surveys also contained an "Any other comments" section so that entries mentioned there were summarized. These were then compared with the themes emerging from the interviews and any alignment with the published literature could then be assessed so as to complete the triangulation. Overall then, there were 10 data strands (excluding the published literature and apart from the CR and RG surveys' directed questions summarized above):

1 CR survey "Any other comments" on structure
2 RG survey "Any other comments" on structure
3 CR survey "Any other comments" on content
4 RG survey "Any other comments" on content

5  CR survey final "Any other comments"
6  RG survey final "Any other comments"
7  Analysts' survey themes
8  Analysts' interview themes
9  Asia Region CR and RG interview themes
10  Europe Region CR and RG interview themes.

## The emerging issues (ranked according to the number of data strands mentioning the issue)

1  *The curriculum and its delivery*: All ten data strands commented upon it (with six placing it first – #1, #2, #4, #6, #9, #10). As noted from the CR and RG surveys above, curriculum issues do not seem to be a major difficulty, but overall there is a desire for a core curriculum to be established (specifying learning and teaching aims, staged modules, and pivotal/primary and recommended texts) as the basis for focused and continuous tutorials/seminars (with suggestions to include online and e-learning resources and groups, films/DVD, Skype group discussions, and a distance library) in contrast to individual lectures so as to provide sound theoretical understanding enabling Routers to develop their "own theory" as a basis to their clinical work. In terms of triangulation, various aspects of the issue appear in the published literature (see above).

2  *The Router community and cohort*: Nine data strands commented upon it (NOT #4 and two placed it first – #9, #10). The isolation factor for Routers can be intensified by shuttle analysis, and so a very real need for collegial support is indicated. Suggestions included using internet resources to foment a Router community, e.g., an internet forum/chat room; the starting of a Router newsletter; establishing a mentor and/or "buddy" system for Routers; establishing regular regional and interregional group meetings; and expanding the supervision courses. In terms of triangulation, the issue also appears in the published literature in terms of Router graduates wanting to maintain an ongoing dependence on their former trainers, the need for a safe and holding structure, and collegiality (Crowther & Wiener, 2015; Rudakova, 2002).

3  *Administrative issues*: Eight data strands commented upon it (NOT #3 or #4 but three placed it first – #2, #5, #10). Administrative procedures and structures that promote smooth organizational running and program delivery were mentioned so that requirements, expectations, and communication should be as clear as possible. There seems to have been improvement in this area over the past years. Other suggestions were:

   - The specification of clear role descriptions for the ROs and LPs;
   - An ongoing refining of the documentation as the program continues to expand;
   - Consider centralizing the program delivery;
   - Expand the range of analysts involved in the program;

- Clarify the procedures for when requirements are changed and how these are to effect CRs;
- Re-consider the graduates' credential and the wait time between the Final Examination and the next Congress;
- Find ways to minimize all the costs to Routers and to the analysts involved in the program;
- Standardization of the fees.

In terms of triangulation, the issue also appears but minimally in the published literature as in the need for democratic group processes/procedures including ethics (Crowther & Wiener, 2015). Understandably, the particular focus of the literature has not been on administration issues.

4   *Group issues*: Seven strands commented upon them (NOT #3 or #5 or #9). Group processes can have either a positive or negative impact on the Router program including Developing Group functioning as well as on new Societies once they form. Specific consultative processes with the IAAP were requested by some, as well as an acknowledgment that appropriate structures/procedures (including a manual) for Developing Groups and Societies covering ethics codes, committees, democratic protocols, training manuals, and grievance procedures would be advantageous. Training in group processes was also mentioned. In terms of triangulation, the issue also appears in the published literature (Crowther et al., 2011; Crowther & Wiener, 2015).

5   *Assessment issues (including standards)*: Six strands commented upon it (NOT #3 or #4 or #6 or #9 but two placed it first – notably #8, the Analyst interviews, and #10). The human component in what is being examined needs to be acknowledged. Comments indicated that some Routers become more focused on the assessment aspects of the training and lose sight of the personal journey that analysis is. The questions raised about assessment were as follows: Does shuttle analysis lead to an adequate training? Does the curriculum cover all Jungian schools? Are some Routers being graduated too quickly? The latter raises the issue of having to short-cut training requirements so as to get something started – which may not be a problem in the initial stages. Also mentioned was the need for clear documentation in terms of criteria, guidelines, and procedures for each assessment component including feedback provisions. In terms of triangulation, the issue does not really appear in the published literature, again indicating the focus of the literature has not been on assessment standards.

6   *Financial costs*: Six strands commented upon it (NOT #2 or #3 or #4 or #6, but #10 placed it first). Two of these data strands were the analysts (#7, #8), and their concerns can be split between IAAP funding of the Router program (as in the British FAJP), awareness of the direct costs to Routers as well as the time and expense the analysts' commitments require. Money issues can also lead to status/discrimination issues among Routers. In terms of triangulation, the issue does not really appear in the published literature.

7    *The diversity of analysts*: Five strands commented upon it (#1, #2, #4, #5, #9, with #9 placing it first). There was an expressed need for more analysts and supervisors to be available, and with continuity especially for in-person sessions, as this provided a wider range of experienced input and enhanced the experience of an analytic community while also overcoming any perceived "jobs for the boys" phenomenon. There was a view that a lack of diversity can lead to boundary issues and potential dual relationships in the Developing Groups which can interfere with transference resolution (out of which a reliance on the internet can emerge). In terms of triangulation, this issue does not appear directly in the published literature.

8a   *Language, translation and interpreter issues*: Five strands commented upon them (#1, #2, #5, #9, #10). The reliance on English is an understandable burden for some Routers, and while the use of translators can be initially challenging, it can become workable with time and can facilitate a slowing down of the process enabling greater reflection. In terms of triangulation, the issue also appears in the published literature (see above).

8b   *Post-training issues*: Five strands commented upon them (#2, #5, #6, #8, #10). The sense of separation and loss once the training is completed seems an issue for some RGs. There is an issue of aftercare here, for once Routers graduate, they can feel further abandonment and experience "sibling replacement" so that it becomes difficult for these graduates to focus on developing themselves locally. There was an expressed need for help in establishing new Societies (and this without rushing). In terms of triangulation, the issue also appears in the published literature (see above).

8c   *The use of Skype*: Five strands commented upon it (#5, #7, #8, #9, #10). Not only do Routers find difficulty in accruing their required number of in-person hours, but the intensification of attachment/abandonment problems in the shuttle analysis context does raise the whole issue of the use of Skype as a bridging tool in analysis and whether the number of IAAP allowable hours needs to be reviewed. Overall comments across all groups indicated there was a preference to start with in-person sessions but that a genuine analytic process can unfold using Skype. This view was supported by Merchant's (2016) paper. By the completion of the evaluation, Skype usage did not seem to be such a major area of concern as it had been in the preliminary meetings with CRs and RGs, indicating that changes have occurred on this issue over time. Participants seem to be getting used to it and to working with it. In terms of triangulation, the issue also appears but minimally in the published literature and noticeably, it is not spoken of negatively (Crowther & Wiener, 2015).

9a   *Cultural issues*: Four strands commented upon them (#6, #7, #8, #10, with #8 placing it first). Views were expressed that the differences in cultural background could underpin mutual projections and foment misunderstandings apart from actual cultural trauma. These impacted in a lack of trust of others (who could report on one); on projections onto office bearers; on leadership styles; and on a lack of familiarity with democratic procedures and the way ethics committees could be experienced. One suggestion was that trauma be included as a curriculum topic. Nonetheless, a consensus seemed to be that cultural issues could be worked with and through over time and despite initial reservations, the presence of interpreters was helpful. A number of very specific cultural issues were mentioned in the Asia context: the place of the individual in relation to the community; an apparent precedence given to rote learning with a deference to authority; and the place of sandplay. In terms of triangulation, the issue also appears in the published literature (see above).

9b *Ethics*: Four strands commented upon it (#6, #8, #9, #10). The issue of dual relationships in the Developing Groups was raised as was the expressed need for courses on ethics, the need for guidelines around confidentiality when presenting case material, that there are no grievance procedures for Routers, and that the presence of translators raises ethical concerns. It would appear that Developing Groups and post-Router groups may need more help in developing their ethics codes and procedures. In terms of triangulation, the issue also appears but minimally in the published literature as in the need for ethics procedures in the Router groups (Crowther & Wiener, 2015).

10 *Shuttle analysis (its benefits and difficulties)*: Three strands commented upon it (#7, #8, #10), and see 8c, where further incorporation of the internet as a bridging tool needs consideration. The other main issue mentioned had to do with the unsuitability of some trainees to shuttle analysis as in those with borderline personality organization, schizoid dynamics, and those prone to suicidal ideation. In terms of triangulation, the issue also appears in the published literature (see above).

11 *Supervision*: Two strands commented upon it (#6, #9). A number of Asian interviewees in particular requested more opportunities for supervision (especially individual supervision) as well as more courses on supervision. Comments from other regions requested facilitation of Routers in moving to work with local supervisors. In terms of triangulation, the issue also appears in the published literature (Crowther et al., 2011; Crowther & Wiener, 2015).

12 *The remaining issues* were commented upon by one group only: dynamics of the training (#6); idealization of the trainers (#6); the training credential (#6); selection processes (#8); the place of sandplay (#9); potential expansion of the program (#10); and the experience of analysis (#10).

## Conclusions

At the 2016 IAAP Kyoto Congress, when the preliminary results of this evaluation were presented, George Hogenson asked the appropriate question: "so where are we at now?" This evaluation goes somewhat to addressing that question as it would be reasonable to conclude from the outcomes that the "visionary" and establishment phase of the Router program is likely to be over and a phase of consolidation is required, its priorities being the curriculum, refining of administrative procedures, fomenting of ongoing CR and RG communities, and the honing of procedures for the smooth running of regional Developing Groups. Nonetheless, it needs to be kept in mind that the IAAP aims of the program are progressively being achieved as evidenced at the 2016 Kyoto Congress where approval was given to 77 new Independent Members, four new Societies and where three Societies were elevated to Training Society status. None of these outcomes would have occurred without the Router training program, and this is in addition to the overwhelmingly positive comments made by the CRs and RGs in this evaluation about their analysts, the opportunity the Router program provides for them to be trained, and the appreciation they have of the commitment and dedication of all those involved as trainers and supervisors.

## Acknowledgment

John Merchant wishes to acknowledge his appreciation of a research grant from the IAAP's Academic Sub-committee that enabled aspects of this evaluation to proceed.

## References

Bortuleva, E. (2014). Rivers of milk and honey – an exploration of nurturing the self in a Russian context. *Journal of Analytical Psychology*, *59*, 531–547.

Brodbeck, H. (2008). Anxiety in psychoanalytic training from the candidate's point-of-view. *Psychoanalytic Inquiry*, *28*, 329–343.

Bryman, A. (2012). *Social research methods*. Oxford: Oxford University Press.

Bushe, G.R. (2012). Appreciative inquiry: Theory and critique. In D. Boje, B. Burnes, & J. Hassard (Eds.), *The Routledge companion to organizational change* (pp. 87–103). Oxford: Routledge.

Bushe, G.R., & Kessler, E. (Eds.) (2013). The appreciative inquiry model. In *The encyclopedia of management theory*. London: Sage.

Cabaniss, D.L., Schein, J.W., Rosen, P., & Roose, S.P. (2003). Candidate progression in psychoanalytic institutes: A multicenter study. *International Journal of Psychoanalysis*, *84*, 77–94.

Caligor, L. (1985). On training analysis: Or Sometimes analysis in the service of training. *Contemporary Psychoanalysis*, *21*, 120–129.

Connolly, A. (2006). Through the iron curtain: Analytical space in post-Soviet Russia. *Journal of Analytical Psychology*, *51*, 173–189.

Connolly, A. (2011). Healing the wounds of our fathers: Intergenerational trauma, memory, symbolization and narrative. *Journal of Analytical Psychology*, *56*, 607–626.

Crowther, C., & Wiener, J. (2002). Finding the space between East and West: The emotional impact of teaching in St Petersburg. *Journal of Analytical Psychology*, *47*, 285–300.

Crowther, C., & Wiener, J. (2015). *From tradition to innovation: Jungian analysts working in different cultural settings*. Los Angeles: Spring Journal.

Crowther, C., Wiener, J., Tserashchuk, A., Tsivinsky, V., Volodina, E., & Alexandrova, N. (2011). Fifteen minute stories about training. *Journal of Analytical Psychology*, *56*, 627–652.

Diatkine, G. (2010). Shuttle analysis in the Han-Prakken Psychoanalytic Institute for Eastern Europe (PIEE). *The International Journal of Psychoanalysis*, *91*, 1250–1253.

Doll-Hentschker, S. (2006). On my becoming a psychoanalyst. *Psychoanalytic Inquiry*, *26*, 751–766.

Egger-Biniores, D. (2007). The alchemy of training. *Journal of Analytical Psychology, 52*, 143–155.

Fonda, P. (2011). A virtual training institute in Eastern Europe. *International Journal of Psychoanalysis, 92*, 695–713.

Francois-Poncet, C-M. (2009). The French model of psychoanalytic training: Ethical conflicts. *The International Journal of Psychoanalysis, 90*, 1419–1433.

Frawley-O'Dea, M., & Sarnat, J. (2001). *The supervisory relationship: A contemporary psychodynamic approach.* New York: Guilford Press.

Frijling-Schreuder, E., Isaac-Edersheim, E., & Van der Leeuw, P. (1981). The supervisor's evaluation of the candidate. *International Review of Psycho-Analysis, 8*, 393–400.

Garza-Guerrero, C. (2004). Reorganisational and educational demands of psychoanalytic training today: Our long and marasmic night of one century. *International Journal of Psychoanalysis, 85*, 3–13.

Gordon, E., Perry, C., & Wright, S. (2012). Analysis in the Borderlands – experiences in St. Petersburg. *Paper presented at the Second European Conference on Analytical Psychology*, St. Petersburg, Russia.

Greenacre, P. (1961). A critical digest of the literature on selection of candidates for psychoanalytic training. *The Psychoanalytic Quarterly, 30*, 28–55.

Hanna, E. (1998). Some thoughts on the role of independent report reading in psychoanalytic training. *Canadian Journal of Psychoanalysis/Revue Canadienne de Psychanalyse, 6*, 113–132.

Hillman, J., Plaut, A., & Fordham, M. (1962). Symposium on training: Part 2. *Journal of Analytical Psychology, 7*, 3–28.

Horne, M. (2007). There is no "truth" outside a context: Implications for the teaching of analytical psychology in the 21st century. *Journal of Analytical Psychology, 52*, 127–142.

Jordan, L., & Emde, R. (2006). How do we evaluate learning from the curriculum? Thirty phone interviews with institutes of the American Psychoanalytic Association. *Journal of the American Psychoanalytic Association, 54*, 231–249.

Junkers, G., Tuckett, D., & Zachrisson, A. (2008). To be or not to be a psychoanalyst—How do we know a candidate is ready to qualify? Difficulties and controversies in evaluating psychoanalytic competence. *Psychoanalytic Inquiry, 28*, 288–308.

Kahl-Popp, J. (2014). Evaluation of learning in psychoanalytic clinical practice and supervision. *Psychoanalytic Inquiry, 34*, 538–553.

Kalinowska, M. (2012). Monuments of memory: Defensive mechanisms of the collective psyche and their manifestation in the memorialization process. *Journal of Analytical Psychology, 57*, 425–444.

Kappelle, W. (1996). How useful is selection? *International Journal of Psychoanalysis, 77*, 1213–1232.

Kelly, T. (2007). The making of an analyst: from "ideal" to "good enough." *Journal of Analytical Psychology, 52*, 157–169.

Kernberg, O. (2000). A concerned critique of psychoanalytic education. *The International Journal of Psychoanalysis, 81*, 97–120.

Kernberg, O. (2006). Review of Impossible training: A relational view of psychoanalytic education. *Journal of the American Psychoanalytic Association, 54*, 281–286.

Kernberg, O. (2014). The twilight of the training analysis system. *Psychoanalytic Review, 101*, 151–174.

Kernberg, O. (2016). *Psychoanalytic education at the crossroads: Reformation, change and the future of psychoanalytic training.* New York: Routledge.

Korinteli, R. (2003). On the psycho-social conditions of psychotherapy in post-Soviet Georgia. *Journal of Analytical Psychology, 48*, 371–380.

Korinteli, R., Lavrova, O., & Rebeko, T. (2012). Border crossings: Boundaries and frame in Router analysis. *Paper presented at the Second European Conference on Analytical Psychology,* St. Petersburg, Russia.

Lauro, L. (1994). Psycho-analytic education: Unique and not so unique aspects. *Psychoanalytic Psychotherapy in South Africa, 2,* 56–62.

Levy, I. (2001). Superego issues in supervision. In S. Gill (Ed.), *The supervisory alliance: Facilitating the psychotherapist's learning experience* (pp. 91–106). Lanham, MD: Jason Aronson.

Lifschutz, J. (1976). A critique of reporting and assessment in the training analysis. *Journal of the American Psychoanalytic Association, 24,* 43–59.

Mander, G. (2004). The selection of candidates for training in psychotherapy and counselling. *Psychodynamic Practice: Individuals, Groups and Organisations, 10,* 161–172.

Martin, G., Mayerson, P., Olsen, H., & Wiberg, J. (1978). Candidates' evaluation of psychoanalytic supervision. *Journal of the American Psychoanalytic Association, 26,* 407–424.

Mathers, D., Palmer Barnes, F., & Noack, A. (2006). "Held in mind" or "Hell in mind": Group therapy in Poland. *Journal of Analytical Psychology, 51,* 191–207.

Merchant, J. (2016). The use of Skype in analysis and training: A research and literature review. *Journal of Analytical Psychology, 61,* 309–328.

Meyer, L. (2003). Subservient analysis. *International Journal of Psychoanalysis, 84,* 1241–1262.

*National statement on ethical conduct in human research 2007 (Updated March 2014).* The National Health and Medical Research Council, the Australian Research Council and the Australian Vice-Chancellors' Committee. Commonwealth of Australia, Canberra.

Plaut, A. (1962). Symposium on training Continued. *Journal of Analytical Psychology, 7,* 149–152.

Plaut, A., Dreifuss, G., Fordham, M., Henderson, J., Humbert, E., Jacoby, M., Ulanov, A., & Wilke, H-J. (1982). How do I assess progress in supervision? *Journal of Analytical Psychology, 27,* 105–107.

Plaut, A., Newton, K., & Fordham, M. (1961). Symposium on training. *Journal of Analytical Psychology, 6,* 95–115. Pourtova, E. (2013). Nostalgia and lost identity. *Journal of Analytical Psychology, 58,* 34–51.

Rothstein, A. (2016). Fostering the educational value of candidate evaluation. *The International Journal of Psychoanalysis.* https://doi.org/10.1111/1745–8315.12613

Rudakova, T. (2002). Diversity of learning psychoanalysis and analytical psychology. *Journal of Analytical Psychology, 47,* 301–306.

Rudakova, T. (2003). Comment on Rezo Korinteli's "On the psycho-social conditions of psychotherapy in post-Soviet Georgia." *Journal of Analytical Psychology, 48,* 381–382.

Shapiro, D. (1976). The analyst's own analysis. *Journal of the American Psychoanalytic Association, 24,* 5–42.

Stone, L. (1974). The assessment of students' progress. *The Annual of Psychoanalysis, 2,* 308–322.

Szonyi, G., & Stajner-Popovic, T. (2008). Shuttle analysis, shuttle supervision, and shuttle life–Some facts, experiences, and questions. *Psychoanalytic Inquiry, 28,* 309–328.

Torras de Bea. (1992). Towards a "good enough" training analysis. *International Review of Psycho-Analysis, 19,* 159–167.

Tsivinsky, V. (2014). The spatial metaphor of Utopia in Russian culture and in analysis. *Journal of Analytical Psychology, 59,* 47–59.

Tuckett, D. (2005). Does anything go? Towards a framework for the more transparent assessment of psychoanalytic competence. *The International Journal of Psychoanalysis, 86,* 31–49.

Wallerstein, R.S. (2010). The training analysis: Psychoanalysis' perennial problem. *Psychoanalytic Review, 97,* 903–936.

Watkins, C. (2016). Psychoanalytic supervision in the new millennium: On pressing needs and impressing possibilities. *International Forum of Psychoanalysis, 25,* 50–67.

Weiss, S., & Fleming, J. (1975). Evaluation of progress in supervision. *The Psychoanalytic Quarterly, 44*, 191–205.

Wiener, J. (2007). Evaluating progress in training: Character or competence? *The Journal of Analytical Psychology, 52*, 171–183.

Zalessky, D., & Zalesskaya, O. (2012). The social, personal and group dynamic issues arising from the Developing Group in Kiev, Ukraine. *Paper presented at the Second European Conference on Analytical Psychology*, St. Petersburg, Russia.

# PART V
# Synchronicity

# 14

# SYNCHRONICITY AND THE EXPERIENCE OF PSYCHOPHYSICAL CORRELATIONS

*Harald Atmanspacher*

## Dual-aspect monism according to Pauli and Jung

### The overall picture

The Pauli–Jung version of *dual-aspect monism* merges an ontic monism, reflected by a psychophysically neutral background reality, with an epistemic dualism of the mental and the physical as perspectival aspects of the underlying ontic reality (Atmanspacher, 2012). Jung coined the notion of the *unus mundus*, the one world, for this domain. In dual-aspect monism, the aspects are not *a priori* given, but depend on epistemic issues and contexts. Distinctions of aspects are generated by "epistemic splits" of the distinction-free, unseparated underlying realm, and in principle there can be as many aspects as there are contexts. In somewhat more abstract terms, distinctions can be conceived as symmetry breakings.[1]

According to the Pauli–Jung conjecture,[2] mind and matter appear as *complementary* aspects: they are mutually incompatible but both together necessary to describe mind–matter systems exhaustively. A straightforward reason for this is the fundamentally non-Boolean nature of the underlying reality. As is well known in mathematics, representations of non-Boolean systems are generally incompatible, and complementarity can be formally characterized as a maximal form of incompatibility.

There are important respects in which this framework differs from *neutral monism* à la Mach, James, or Russell. In neutral monism, the mental and the physical are *reducible* to the underlying domain, whereas they are *irreducible* in dual-aspect monism. The reason for this difference is that neutral monism conceives the underlying domain to consist of psychophysically neutral elements whose combinations determine whether the compound products appear mental or physical. In dual-aspect monism, the underlying domain does ultimately not consist of separate elements at all.[3] It is radically holistic, and the mental and physical aspects emerge by a *decomposition of the whole rather than a composition of elements.*[4]

In the Pauli–Jung conjecture, the psychophysically neutral domain is apprehensible only indirectly, by its manifestations in the aspects. Their dual-aspect monism is a metaphysical position including both epistemic and ontic elements. Although large parts of the 20th century witnessed an often pejorative connotation with metaphysics, insights into the nature of reality are in general impossible without metaphysical assumptions and regulative principles. The metaphysical nature of the Pauli–Jung conjecture *implies* a lack of concrete illustrative examples which is not due to missing imagination but represents an important feature of their approach.

This resembles the situation in quantum theory repeatedly expressed by one of its main architects, Niels Bohr (1934, p. 5):

> we are concerned with the recognition of physical laws which lie outside the domain of our ordinary experience and which present difficulties to our accustomed forms of perception.

Accordingly, so-called "intuitively appealing thinking" may mislead us by inhibiting rather than advancing our ways to insight.[5] Along the same lines, Heisenberg (1971, p. 64) remembers a conversation with Bohr at Göttingen in 1922. He asked Bohr:

> If the inner structure of the atoms is inaccessible to an illustrative [*anschauliche*] description, as you say, if we basically have no language to speak about this structure, will we ever be able to understand the atoms? Bohr hesitated for a moment, then he replied: Yes we will. But at the same time we will have to learn what the word "understanding" means.

As we will see below, it may not be entirely accidental that the issue of meaning arises here – pretty astonishing for a typical physics discussion but absolutely pivotal for Jung's concept of synchronistic events and the symbolic expression of their meaning.

### *Synchronicities as psychophysical correlations*

Conceiving the mind–matter distinction in terms of an epistemic split of a psychophysically neutral reality implies psychophysical correlations between mind and matter as a direct and generic consequence. Pauli and Jung discussed psychophysical correlations extensively in their correspondence between June 1949 and February 1951 (Meier, 1992, pp. 40–73), when Jung drafted his article on "synchronicity" for the book that he published jointly with Pauli (Jung & Pauli, 1952). In condensed form, two (or more) seemingly accidental, but not necessarily simultaneous events are called synchronistic if the following three conditions are satisfied.

1   Each pair of synchronistic events includes an internally conceived and an externally perceived component.

2　Any presumption of a direct causal relationship between the events is absurd or even inconceivable.

3　The events correspond with one another by a common meaning, often expressed symbolically.

The first criterion makes clear that synchronistic phenomena are intractable when dealing with mind or matter alone. The second criterion expresses that synchronistic correlations cannot be explained by (efficient) causation in the narrow sense of a conventional cause-and-effect relation as usually looked for in science. And the third criterion suggests the concept of meaning (rather than causation) as a constructive way to characterize psychophysical correlations.

Since synchronistic phenomena are not necessarily "synchronous" (in the sense of "simultaneous"), synchronicity is a somewhat misleading term. For this reason Pauli preferred to speak of "meaningful correspondences" under the influence of an archetypal "acausal ordering." He considered both Jung's synchronicity and the old teleological idea of finality (in the general sense of a process oriented toward a goal) as particular instances of such an acausal ordering. Meaningful coincidences cannot be set up fully intentionally or controlled reproducibly. On the other hand, "blind" chance (referring to stochastically accidental events) might be considered as the limiting case of meaning*less* correspondence.

What Pauli here postulates is a kind of lawful regularity *beyond both deterministic and statistical laws*, based on the notion of *meaning* and, thus, entirely outside the natural sciences of his time and also, more or less, of today. It remains to be explored how this key issue of meaning can be implemented in an expanded worldview not only comprising but rather exceeding both psychology and physics. A comprehensive substantial account of psychophysical phenomena needs to address them beyond the distinction of the psychological and the physical (including the brain).

For a psychologist like Jung, the issue of meaning is of primary significance anyway. For a long time, Jung insisted that the concept of synchronicity should be reserved for cases of distinctly numinous character, when the experience of meaning takes on existential dimensions. With this understanding synchronistic correlations would be extremely rare, thus contradicting their supposedly generic nature. In later years, Jung opened up toward the possibility that synchronicity might be a notion that should be conceived as ubiquitous, as indicated above. Meier (1975) has later amplified this idea in an article about psychosomatics from a Jungian perspective.

## From quantum physics to (depth) psychology

According to Pauli and Jung, the role which measurement plays as a link between epistemic and ontic realities in physics is mirrored by the act in which subjects become consciously aware of "local mental objects," as it were, arising from unconscious contents in psychology.[6] In this sense, they postulated the possibility of transitions between the mental and/or the material mediated by the psychophysically neutral *unus mundus*. This idea is most clearly elaborated in Jung's supplement to his

*On the Nature of the Psyche* (Jung, 1969).[7] Let me first quote from a letter by Pauli which Jung cites in footnote 130 in this supplement (Jung, 1969, para. 439):[8]

> the epistemological situation regarding the concepts of "consciousness" and the "unconscious" seems to offer a close analogy to the situation of "complementarity" in physics, sketched below. On the one hand, the unconscious can only be made accessible in an indirect way by its (ordering) influence on conscious contents, on the other hand every "observation of the unconscious," i.e., every attempt to make unconscious contents conscious, has a *prima facie* uncontrollable reaction back onto these unconscious contents themselves (as is well known, this precludes that the unconscious can be "exhaustively" brought to consciousness). The physicist will *per analogiam* conclude that precisely this uncontrollable backlash of the observing subject onto the unconscious limits the objective character of its reality and, at the same time, provides it with some subjectivity. Although, moreover, the *position* of the "cut" between consciousness and the unconscious is (to a certain degree) up to the free choice of the "psychological experimenter," the *existence* of this "cut" remains an inevitable necessity. Thus, the "observed system" would, from the viewpoint of psychology, not only consist of physical objects, but rather comprise the unconscious as well, whereas the role of the "observing device" would be ascribed to consciousness. The development of "microphysics" has unmistakably led to a remarkable convergence of its description of nature with that of the new psychology: While the former, due to the fundamental situation known as "complementarity," faces the impossibility to eliminate actions of observers by determinable corrections and must therefore in principle relinquish the objective registration of all physical phenomena, the latter could basically complement the merely subjective psychology of consciousness by postulating the existence of an unconscious of largely objective reality.

This excerpt describes Pauli's position concerning objective and subjective aspects of the mental, a distinction that he adopted from Jung quite early. Already in a letter to Kronig of August 3, 1934 (letter 380 in von Meyenn, 1985, pp. 340–341), he talks about the "autonomous activity of the soul" as "something objectively psychical that cannot and should not be explained by material causes." Hence, the "objective reality" at the end of the quote refers to the psychophysically neutral background reality, while the "subjective" relates to its contextual, epistemic manifestation in the psyche.

As a consequence of Pauli–Jung style dual-aspect monism, mind–matter relations, or psychophysical relations, can be understood due to their common origin in the underlying domain of reality. Although there is no direct causal pathway between the mental and the physical, Pauli and Jung conjectured indirect kinds of influence via their underlying domain. These influences are possible because the relation between ontic (psychophysically neutral) and epistemic (mental and material) domains is conceived as *bidirectional* (see the discussion of psychophysical correlations).

If, for instance, unconscious contents become conscious, this very transition changes the unconscious left behind. Analogously, physical measurement entails a transition from an unobserved to an observed state, and this very measurement changes the state of the system left behind. This picture, already outlined in Pauli's letter to Fierz of October 3, 1951 (von Meyenn, 1996, p. 377), represents a genuine interdependence between ontic and epistemic domains. It can entail mind–matter correlations in addition to those *unidirectional* correlations that are due to mere epistemic manifestations of the ontic realm.

The Pauli quote above emphasizes parallels between basic conceptual structures of quantum theory and psychology. One of the key common features in these two scientific areas is arguably the fact that an observation does not only register an outcome, as in classical thinking, but also changes the state of the observed system in a basically uncontrollable manner. This holds for physical quantum systems as well as for mental systems and, as simple as it sounds, it has far-reaching consequences which psychology and cognitive science are just about to realize (cf. Aerts, Durt, Grib, Van Bogaert, & Zapatrin, 1993; Atmanspacher, Römer, & Walach, 2002; Khrennikov, 2010; Busemeyer & Bruza, 2012; Wendt, 2015).

A most evident effect of this backreaction on mental states is the almost ubiquitous appearance of order effects in surveys and questionnaires. This has recently been addressed in detail (Atmanspacher & Römer, 2012; Wang, Solloway, Shiffrin, & Busemeyer, 2014) on the basis of non-commutative structures of mental observables. Since the mathematics of such structures is at the heart of quantum theory as well, this parallel is not a mere analogy – it points to a constitutive joint principle underlying the mental and the physical: "almost too good to be true," as one recent commentator expressed it (Tresan, 2013).

## Relative onticity

As appealing and compact as the sketch outlined in the preceding section may appear, it is not subtle enough. For instance, the boundary between the mental and physical aspects on the one hand and their underlying domain on the other is unsharp: there is always a gray area between conscious and unconscious states, and no physical state is ever exactly disentangled from the rest of the material world.

In fact, one might conceive of a whole spectrum of boundaries, each one indicating the transition to a more comprehensive level of wholeness until (ultimately) the distinction-free unus mundus is approached. A viable idea in this context might be archetypal levels with increasing degrees of generality: the unus mundus at bottom, the mental and physical on top, and intermediate levels in between. Depending on the status of the individuation process of the individual concerned, Jung's *transcendent function* regulates the exchange among these levels.

This entails that a tight distinction of one fundamentally ontic and two derived epistemic domains is too simplistic. However, an idea originally proposed by Quine

(1969), developed by Putnam (1981, 1987) and later utilized by Atmanspacher and Kronz (1999), comes to help here: *ontological relativity* or, in another parlance, *relative onticity*.[9]

The key motif behind this notion is to allow ontological significance for any level, from elementary particles to ice cubes, bricks, and tables – and all the same for elements of the mental. One and the same descriptive framework can be construed as either ontic or epistemic, depending on which other framework it is related to: bricks and tables will be regarded as ontic by an architect, but they will be considered highly epistemic from the perspective of a solid-state physicist. Schizophrenia, depression, or bipolar disorders will be considered as basic ontic features in psychiatry, yet a detailed psychological or philosophy-of-mind analysis will try to find its own ontic terms with which these impairments can be described as epistemic manifestations.

Quine proposed that a "most appropriate" ontology should be preferred for the interpretation of a theory, thus demanding "ontological commitment." This leaves us with the challenge of how "most appropriate" should be defined, and how corresponding descriptive frameworks are to be identified. Here is where the notion of *relevance* becomes significant. For particular degrees of complexity, the "most appropriate" framework is that which provides those features that are relevant for the question to be studied. And the referents of this descriptive framework are those which Quine wants us to be ontologically committed to.

This can be applied to the Pauli–Jung conjecture in an interesting way: an archetype which may be regarded as ontic relative to the perspective of the mind–matter distinction can be seen epistemic relative to the unus mundus. This twist is additionally interesting because it also relativizes Jung's (overly) stern Kantian stance that archetypes *per se* as formal ordering factors in the collective unconscious must be *strictly inaccessible* epistemically, and thus empirically.[10] A relativized notion of ontology allows us to see clearer why and how a more sophisticated blend of epistemic and ontic realms in dual-aspect monism can acquire systematic and explanatory status.

Taken seriously, this framework of thinking entails a farewell to the centuries-old conviction of an absolute fundamental ontology (usually that of basic physics). This move is in strong opposition to many mainstream positions in the philosophy of science until today. But in times in which fundamentalism – in science and elsewhere – appears increasingly tenuous, Quine's philosophical idea of an ontological relativity offers a viable alternative for more adequate and more balanced worldviews. And using the scientifically tailored concept of relative onticity, this is not merely a conceptual idea but can in fact be used for an informed discussion of concrete issues in the sciences.

Coupled with an ontological commitment to context-dependent "most relevant" features in a given situation, the relativization of onticity does not mean dropping ontology altogether in favor of a postmodern salmagundi of floating beliefs. The "tyranny of relativism" (as some have called it) can be avoided by distinguishing more appropriate descriptions from less appropriate ones. The resulting picture is more subtle and more flexible than an overly bold reductive fundamentalism, and yet it is more restrictive and specific than a patchwork of arbitrarily connected opinions.

## More than physics "plus" psychology

### *A semi-fictitious historical excursion*

Imagine a scientist specializing in electricity in the early 19th century. At this point in time, Faraday just started the investigations that ultimately led him to the concept of electric and magnetic fields. Later, Maxwell developed them into a unified theory of electromagnetism, culminating in the set of four basic equations which he published under the title "On Physical Lines of Force."[11]

At the beginning of the 19th century, however, electricity and magnetism were still regarded as basically unrelated phenomena. Now consider our imagined scientist experimenting with electric currents on his laboratory desk. Incidentally, a compass, unwittingly left by a visitor the other day, is sitting on a side table not far from the desk. The scientist starts his experiments and connects the wires on the table with a battery (invented by Volta just a few years back).

He looks around in the room for some additional equipment, and suddenly rivets on the compass. The compass needle trembles, and points into an entirely wrong direction – not north, not south, but something completely different! What happened? An outright spooky apparition it seems, inexplicable by anything he ever learned. Which impudent specter tries to fool him with such a kind of nuisance? Did the compass get inhabited by naughty spirits, moving the needle at their pleasure?

Indeed, the body of knowledge in physics at the time of this fictitious story did not offer any compelling explanation of the distorted behavior of the compass. Of course, this changed half a century later, when it became well known that electric currents generate a magnetic field, and that this field naturally moves the compass needle, such that it deviates from the orientation of the magnetic field of the earth.

Maxwell's electrodynamics succeeded in describing both electric and magnetic phenomena in the same compact framework, specifying the relations by which the two are linked together. Without this framework, magnetic phenomena in the presence of electricity and electric phenomena in the presence of magnetism were regarded as inexplicable magic, miracles, or misconduct – depending on who reported them and for what purpose.

What can this little narrative teach us? It expresses an analogy (not a perfect one, of course) of the contemporary situation concerning the psychophysical problem of how mind and matter are related. Exactly as the moving compass needle (due to electric current), a moving hand (due to mental decision) represents a paradigm example of an anomaly not understood by the science of the time. Needless to say, there are more stunning psychophysical anomalies such as out-of-body experiences, premonitions, and so forth – more about them later.

At present, we do not have a theoretical framework for psychophysical phenomena, just as the early 19th century did not have electrodynamics. The analogy tells us also that it is misleading to try and study psychophysical phenomena as if they were either mental or physical, exactly as electromagnetic phenomena are neither solely electric nor magnetic. It is likely that psychophysical phenomena need to be recast in a way even more radical than Maxwell's breakthrough has been.

### Structural and induced psychophysical correlations

The development of Pauli's and Jung's views about psychophysically neutral archetypes and their role in manifesting psychophysical correlations (e.g., "synchronicities") suggests a distinction between two basically different kinds of mind–matter correlations for which we propose the notions of "structural" and "induced" correlations.

*Structural correlations* refer to the role of archetypes as ordering factors with an exclusively *unidirectional* influence on the material and the mental (Pauli's letter to Fierz of 1948; von Meyenn, 1993, pp. 496–497). They arise due to epistemic splits of the unus mundus, and manifest themselves as correlations between mental and material aspects. These correlations are a straightforward consequence of the basic structure of the Pauli–Jung conjecture, and they are expected to be ubiquitous, persistent, and empirically reproducible.

*Induced correlations* refer to the backreaction that changes of consciousness induce in the unconscious and, indirectly, in the physical world as well.[12] (Likewise, measurements of physical systems induce backreactions which can lead to changes of mental states.) In this way, the picture is extended to a *bidirectional* relation (Pauli's letter to Jung of 1954, Jung, 1969, para. 439). In contrast to structural, persistent correlations, induced correlations depend on all kinds of contexts (e.g., personal situation, environment). They occur occasionally and are evasive and not (easily) reproducible.

What Pauli wrote to Fierz on June 3, 1952 (von Meyenn, 1996, pp. 634–635), yields an almost seamless fit with this distinction:

> synchronistic phenomena . . . elude being captured in natural "laws" since they are not reproducible, i.e., unique, and are blurred by the statistics of large numbers. By contrast, "acausalities" in physics are precisely described by statistical laws (of large numbers) . . . . I would personally prefer to begin with always reproducible acausal dispositions (incl. quantum physics) and try to understand psychophysical correlations as a special case of this general species of correlations.

Pauli's proposal to begin with "always reproducible acausal dispositions" relates perfectly well to the structural mind-matter correlations due to epistemic splits of the unus mundus. What he referred to as special cases of psychophysical correlations can then be mapped to the induced correlations superimposing those structural "general species of correlations."

Pauli speculated that synchronicities exhibit a kind of lawful regularity beyond both deterministic and statistical laws, based on the notion of *meaning* and, thus, outside the natural sciences of his time (and also of today): "a third type of laws of nature consisting of corrections to chance fluctuations due to meaningful or purposeful coincidences of causally unconnected events" (von Meyenn, 1999, p. 336). It remains to be explored how the key issues of meaning and purpose can be implemented in an expanded worldview not only comprising, but also exceeding both psychology and physics (compare Atmanspacher, 2014c). A comprehensive substantial account of psychophysical phenomena needs to address them beyond the distinction of the mental and the physical. This excludes considering them as a simplistic ("additive") composition of these two domains.

While structural correlations define a baseline of ordinary, robust, reproducible psychophysical correlations (such as mind–brain correlations or psychosomatic correlations), induced correlations may be responsible for alterations and deviations (above or below) this baseline. Induced excess correlations, above the baseline, are experienced as unusual "coincidence" phenomena.[13] Numinous synchronistic events in the sense Jung proposed originally clearly belong to this class. Induced missing correlations, below the baseline, are experienced as unusual "dissociation" phenomena. Later in this chapter we will relate these features to the phenomenology of exceptional human experiences.

It is important to keep in mind that in both induced and structural correlations there is no direct causal relation from the mental to the physical or vice versa (i.e., no direct "efficient causation"). The problem of a direct "causal interaction" between categorically distinct regimes is thus avoided. Of course, this does not mean that the correlations themselves are causeless (cf. Atmanspacher, 2014c). The ultimate causes for structural correlations are the epistemic split of the unus mundus and the ordering influence of psychophysically neutral archetypes. The causes for induced correlations are interventions in the conscious mental domain or the local material domain, whose backeffects on archetypal activity must be expected to manifest themselves in the complementary domain, respectively.

## *Formal and experienced meaning*

In the characterization of synchronistic events given above, the common meaning of mental and material events figures prominently. However, meaning is a notoriously difficult notion, used differently in different areas. Formally speaking, meaning is a two-place relation between a sign and what it designates, or a representation and what it represents. Meaning in this formal sense is simply a reference relation, in accordance with the philosophical usage of the term intentionality since Brentano (1874).

What Jung had in mind when he emphasized meaning is different, however. He did aim at meaning as an element of experience, not as a formal relationship.

This can be rephrased in Metzinger's (2003) representational account of the mental, where intentionality – a reference relation between a representation and its referent – is itself encoded as a (meta-)representation. In Metzinger's parlance this (meta-)representation is a "phenomenal model of the intentionality relation" (PMIR).[14]

Mental representations have intentional content and they have phenomenal content. While the intentional content explicates their reference, as mentioned above, their phenomenal content refers to "what it is like to" instantiate a representation – in other words, to experience it. So the phenomenal content of a PMIR refers to "what it is like to" experience a particular meaning. Jung's usage of meaning refers to the phenomenal content of PMIRs: the subjectively experienced meaning of a synchronistic event.

It should be stressed that the meaning of synchronistic events, although being subjectively ascribed (by the experiencing subject), is not completely arbitrary. It depends on a subject's life situation as a whole, likely including conditions that are not consciously available to the subject. According to Jung, synchronistic events arise due to constellated archetypal activity. This activity limits the range of possibly attributable meanings by "objective," metaphysical constraints.

In typical situations of "ordinary" structural psychophysical correlations, the *formal intentionality* due to plain reference is hardly experienced explicitly – subjects are not actually aware of its phenomenal quality. This is different for induced psychophysical correlations: their deviation from the ordinary baseline stimulates that *experienced intentionality* is incurred, referring to the phenomenal content of the appropriate PMIR. In this case, the corresponding meaning is distinctly and phenomenally inflicted upon the experiencing subject.

It is plausible to assume that the extent to which contextually induced correlations deviate from the baseline of persistent structural correlations complies with the degree to which the corresponding PMIR is phenomenally experienced. Small deviations indicate quasi-persistent, almost reproducible correlations, while large deviations signify what Jung insisted on for truly synchronistic events: the "numinous" dimension of the experience.

In his concept of synchronicity, Jung typically emphasized induced psychophysical correlations in the sense of meaningful coincidences, i.e., excess correlations above the ordinary baseline. The more comprehensive approach presented here also includes baseline correlations and missing correlations below the baseline, appearing in dissociation events rather than coincidence events. Jungian synchronicities may be regarded as special cases of induced excess psychophysical correlations with large deviations above the baseline.[15]

## Exceptional human experiences

The rich material of exceptional psychophysiological correlations comprehensively reviewed by Kelly (2007) suggests various concrete types of psychophysical phenomena of the deviating kind. Moreover, a recent statistical analysis of a large body of documented cases of exceptional experiences (Fach, 2011; Belz & Fach, 2012; Atmanspacher & Fach, 2013; Fach, Atmanspacher, Landolt, Wyss, & Rössler, 2013; Fach, 2017) provides significant evidence that the Pauli–Jung conjecture matches with existing empirical material surprisingly well.

Particularly relevant with respect to the discussion of psychophysical correlations are exceptional experiences which refer to the way in which mental and physical states are merged or separated, connected or disconnected, above or below ordinary baseline correlations. In coincidence phenomena, ordinarily disconnected elements of self and world, inside and outside, appear connected; in dissociation phenomena, ordinarily connected elements of self and world appear disconnected.

1   *Coincidence phenomena* refer to experiences of psychophysical excess correlations above the persistent ordinary baseline. Typically, these correlations are experienced as acausal meaningful links between mental and material events, e.g., meaningful coincidences such as Jungian "synchronicities." Spatiotemporal restrictions may appear as inefficacious, as in several kinds of "extrasensory perception."

2   *Dissociation phenomena* refer to experiences of missing psychophysical correlations below the persistent ordinary baseline. For instance, subjects are not in full control of their bodies, or experience autonomous behavior not deliberately set into action. Out-of-body experiences, sleep paralysis, and various forms of automatized behavior are among the most frequent phenomena in this class.

In order to assess whether and how these classes are empirically relevant, they have been compared with empirical data from the counseling department of the Institute for Frontier Areas of Psychology (IGPP) at Freiburg (Germany) since 1996. For details of the documentation system and the statistical analyses, see Bauer et al. (2012). It is important to note that the patterns obtained by statistical factor analyses reflect the subjective views of the clients about their experiences – not their veridicality. The collected data yield an exclusively phenomenological classification scheme, not a system for clinical diagnosis.[16]

It turned out that coincidence and dissociation phenomena represent key patterns in the documented material from IGPP clients.[17] An additional study, together with the Psychiatric University Hospital Zurich, based on subjects from ordinary population (rather than advice-seeking clients) was recently published (Fach et al., 2013). As expected, the average intensity of their reported experiences is rated significantly lower than for IGPP clients. However, the patterns extracted from the ordinary population sample as well as their relative frequencies are in good agreement with the IGPP sample.

Meanwhile, further studies with hundreds of additional subjects have been conducted at IGPP, at the University of Giessen, and at the Psychiatric University Clinic Zurich (Fach et al., 2013; Wyss, 2016; Fach, 2017). Many of the corresponding analyses were based on a questionnaire about the phenomenology of experiences, developed and validated at IGPP (which is now also available in the English language). The results of these recent studies confirm the results of previous work.

The large-scale project on exceptional experiences at the Psychiatric University Clinic Zurich investigates, beyond the phenomenology of the experiences, also their potential psychophysical and psychophysiological correlates, using a whole arsenal of methods up to functional magnetic resonance imaging (fMRI) and positron emission tomography (PET). The comprehensive databases from these studies are still under analysis. However, there are clear indications that an experimental distinction of different classes of experiences is possible already by psychophysical tests (Wyss, 2016).

## *From relational to immanent experiences*

Exceptional experiences are typically difficult to communicate in conventional language. This often leads to paradoxical formulations (Bagger, 2007) or metaphorical descriptions in which (Boolean) categories are used to circumscribe the experience. One way to do this amounts to projections onto physical or mental phenomena, e.g., experiences of joy, bliss, and lucidity are then referred to as experiences of "inner light." Repeating a point made earlier, this should be understood as a genuinely *psychophysical phenomenon* – neither a physical (electromagnetic) field within the body nor a mental image of light.

As discussed before, it is crucial for such experiences to be experiences of meaning. Insofar as explicit (or explicated) meaning is a two-place relation between a representation and what it represents,[18] psychophysical phenomena might thus be conceived as meaningful *relations* between the physical and the psychological. Dual-aspect monism suggests that this relation of meaningfulness arises due to the epistemic split of the mental from the physical: without this split there would be no mental and physical referents which could be related by the meaning.

Alternative to an explicitly relational view, it might also be possible to understand the experience of meaning *implicitly*, not as a relation between distinguishable entities. Such experiences transcend the realm of Boolean categories and could be examples for the refinement indicated by relative onticity. Elements of the psychophysically neutral reality could be apprehensible without a mind–matter distinction, as *immanent experiences* (Kerslake, 2007), thus relaxing Pauli and Jung's neo-Kantian conviction that elements of the unconscious are strictly inaccessible in themselves.

More systematically speaking, archetypal activity could be the carrier of that implicit meaning which can be explicated in terms of meaningful psychophysical phenomena. This adds a further kind of "meaningfulness" to formal and experienced meaning as addressed above. As Aziz (1990) indicated and Main (2004, ch. 2) demonstrated, Jung referred extensively to such a kind of "objective" meaning in his synchronicity essay (Jung, 1952). Dual-aspect monism provides places for all these kinds of meaning, from the purely formal notion of intentionality to the experience of meaning as a relation and further to the metaphysical dimension of meaning in archetypal activity itself.

In this spirit, a key difference between the experience of archetypal activity and psychophysical phenomena would be the difference between implicit and explicated meaning. Perhaps Pauli's understanding of the "reality of the symbol" (in Jung's sense) comes close to the notion of implicit, not yet explicated meaning (letter of Pauli to Fierz of August 12, 1948, von Meyenn, 1993, p. 559):

> When the layman says "reality," he usually thinks that he is talking about something evident and well-known; by contrast it seems to me that it is the most important and exceedingly difficult task of our time to work out a new idea of reality. . . . What I have in mind concerning such a new idea of reality is − in provisional terms − the idea of the reality of the symbol.

## Conclusions

The conceptual framework of dual-aspect monism according to Pauli and Jung stipulates that phenomena based on psychophysical correlations are misconstrued if they are described physically (plus some mental context) or mentally (plus some physical context). It is suggested that genuinely psychophysical phenomena are more properly regarded as relations between the physical and the mental rather than *entities* in the physical or mental realm. This challenging idea elucidates why meaning is so essential for psychophysical phenomena − either as an explicitly relational concept or an implicitly holistic experience.

In a recent commentary, Tresan (2013) expressed the intuition that the theory of complex systems, which has been widely applied to the description of synchronicities and their archetypal origin, still relies "on dependency (neither strictly reductive nor random, but nonetheless still causal, albeit diluted)" (p. 252). By contrast, the more radical vision of the Pauli–Jung conjecture hits the core of psychophysical phenomena: a holism in which *wholes do not consist of parts* to begin with. Elements of the theory of complex dynamical systems, such as networks of attractors (archetypes) and their basins of attraction (complexes) can be useful descriptive tools within epistemic contexts (cf. Cambray, 2009). However, Pauli's and Jung's daring ideas in their full scope may persuade us to believe that the repertoire of complex dynamical systems is not deep enough.

Unlike numerous neuroscientists and philosophers of mind still seem to assume, the Pauli–Jung conjecture implies that brain science alone will be unable to unveil the mysteries of psychophysical phenomena, neither in past "decades of the brain" nor in decades to come. What is needed is a new idea of reality, implying novel and refined metaphysical structures. If we can make progress on this route, it will provide us, and our culture, with a satisfactory and beneficial worldview − a key element of Jungian psychology besides its therapeutic values.

## Acknowledgment

This article is a slightly extended and updated version of *Notes on Psychophysical Phenomena*, published in Atmanspacher and Fuchs (2014).

## Notes

1 Symmetries in this parlance are invariances under transformations. For instance the curvature of a circle is invariant under rotations by any arbitrary angle. A circle thus exhibits complete rotational symmetry. Symmetry breakings are a powerful mathematical tool in large parts of theoretical physics, but we can only speculate which symmetries must be ascribed to the psychophysically neutral unus mundus. See Atmanspacher (2014a) for some of those speculations.

2 This notion is the title of a recently published collection of essays from a conference on dual-aspect monism à la Pauli and Jung, edited by Atmanspacher and Fuchs (2014). See the introduction to this collection for explanatory comments.

3 This is crucial because it avoids the so-called "combination problem" in various accounts of panpsychism and panexperientialism; see Seager (2010) for a detailed discussion and a proposed solution.

4 A review of the most prominent versions of dual-aspect thinking in the 20th century is due to Atmanspacher (2014b).

5 This implies an emphatic plea against misunderstood (misplaced) concreteness and simplification. As cognitive scientists found not long ago, learning processes can be substantially improved if abstract principles are learned first and concrete examples for them thereafter (Kaminski et al., 2008). This result counters a carefully nurtured long-time dogma in education.

6 We use the term "local mental objects" to emphasize the analogy with local material objects, meaning that neither of them are non-local or non-Boolean. More concretely, local mental objects should be understood as distinct mental representations or categories endowed with a Boolean (yes–no) structure: a mental state is either in a category or it is not. Using the formal apparatus of the theory of complex systems, such categories can be defined, e.g., as attractors in an appropriately defined phase space (van Gelder, 1998; Fell, 2004).

7 The German version of this essay was first published as "*Der Geist der Psychologie*" in 1946, and later revised and expanded (essentially by the mentioned supplement) as "*Theoretische Überlegungen zum Wesen des Psychischen*" in 1954.

8 This letter is contained neither in the published Pauli–Jung correspondence (Meier, 1992) nor in Pauli's correspondence edition by von Meyenn. Since Jung presents the quotation with the remark that Pauli "was gracious enough to look over the manuscript of my supplement," the letter is likely of 1954.

9 Similar ideas have been developed independently by van Fraassen (1980) in terms of "relevance relations" and Garfinkel (1981) in terms of "explanatory relativity," though with less, or less explicit, emphasis on issues of ontology.

10 See Kime (2013) for more discussion. The contribution by Kime in this volume also picks up Quine's approach in terms of ontological relativity.

11 "On Physical Lines of Force" is a four-part article that appeared in the *Philosophical Magazine* in 1861 and 1862. The four parts are devoted to "the theory of molecular vortices applied to magnetic phenomena" (I), "to electric currents" (II), "to statical electricity" (III), and "to the action of magnetism on polarized light" (IV).

12 Jungian psychology describes this in more detail: when a subject becomes aware of some problematic unconscious content, the corresponding unconscious complex may be (partially) dissolved. This affects the archetypal core that is constellated in the complex, which in turn is supposed to manifest itself in the physical world.

13 The notion of "salience" has been introduced to address such phenomena in psychiatry (cf. Kapur, 2003; van Os, 2009). But this does not mean that all such phenomena are indicators of psychiatric impairments.

14 Metzinger's overall philosophical position *differs from* dual-aspect monism – it is basically an attempt to naturalize mental processes such that they are conceived as a result of physical brain activity. Nevertheless, his (epistemic) categories of self-model and world model are in one-to-one correspondence with the (epistemic) mental and material aspects of the Pauli–Jung conjecture.

15 Occasionally, Jung also characterized out-of-body experiences as synchronicities (Jung, 1952, paras. 949–955). This expands his understanding of synchronistic events from excess deviations from baseline correlations to deviations in general, including missing correlations – which will be addressed in more detail in the following subsection.

16 Such systems are the *Diagnostic and Statistical Manual of Mental Disorders* (DSM) of the American Psychiatric Association or the *International Classification of Diseases* (ICD) of the World Health Organization. While both the DSM and ICD are continually developed based on more or less heuristic criteria, the classification scheme used by Belz and Fach (2012) can be systematically derived from the basic structure of a dual-aspect picture.

17 The full spectrum of exceptional experiences reported by those clients contains internal and external phenomena in addition to coincidence and dissociation phenomena. See also Atmanspacher and Fach (2013) and Fach (2017).

18 On Metzinger's account, this relation would be (meta-)represented by a PMIR. This is logically consistent as long as PMIRs are neither ascribed as belonging to the physical nor to the mental – possibly a problematic point in Metzinger's approach.

# References

Aerts, D., Durt, T., Grib, A., Van Bogaert, B., & Zapatrin, A. (1993). Quantum structures in macroscopical reality. *International Journal of Theoretical Physics, 32*, 489–498.

Atmanspacher, H. (2012). Dual-aspect monism à la Pauli and Jung. *Journal of Consciousness Studies, 19*(9/10), 96–120.

Atmanspacher, H. (2014a). Levels of unconsciousness and their formal structure. *Journal of Analytical Psychology, 59*, 386–391.

Atmanspacher, H. (2014b). 20th century variants of dual-aspect thinking (with commentaries and replies). *Mind and Matter, 12*, 245–288.

Atmanspacher, H. (2014c). Roles of causation and meaning for interpreting correlations. *Journal of Analytical Psychology, 59*, 429–434.

Atmanspacher, H., & Fach, W. (2013). A structural phenomenological typology of mind-matter correlations. *Journal of Analytical Psychology, 58*, 219–244. Atmanspacher, H., & Fuchs, C.A. (Eds.) (2014). *The Pauli-Jung conjecture and its impact today*. Exeter: Imprint Academic.

Atmanspacher, H., & Kronz, F. (1999). Relative onticity. In H. Atmanspacher, A. Amann, & U. Müller-Herold (Eds.), *On Quanta, mind and matter* (pp. 273–294). Dordrecht: Kluwer.

Atmanspacher, H., & Römer, H. (2012). Order effects in sequential measurements of non-commuting psychological observables. *Journal of Mathematical Psychology, 56*, 274–280.

Atmanspacher, H., Römer, H., & Walach, H. (2002). Weak quantum theory: Complementarity and entanglement in physics and beyond. *Foundations of Physics, 32*, 379–406.

Aziz, R. (1990). *C. G. Jung's psychology of religion and synchronicity*. Albany, NY: University of New York Press.

Bagger, M. (2007). *The uses of paradox*. New York: Columbia University Press.

Bauer, E., Belz, M., Fach, W., Fangmeier, R., Schupp-Ihle, C., & Wiedemer, A. (2012). Counseling at the IGPP: An overview. In W.H. Kramer, E. Bauer, & G.H. Hövelmann (Eds.),

*Perspectives of clinical parapsychology* (pp. 149–167). Bunnik: Stichting Het Johan Borgman Fonds.

Belz, M., & Fach, W. (2012). Theoretical reflections on counseling and therapy for individuals reporting ExE [exceptional experiences]. In W.H. Kramer, E. Bauer, & G.H. Hövelmann (Eds.), *Perspectives of clinical parapsychology* (pp. 168–189). Bunnik: Stichting Het Johan Borgman Fonds.

Bohr, N. (1934). *Atomic theory and the description of nature* (p. 5). Cambridge: Cambridge University Press.

Brentano, F. (1874). *Psychologie vom empirischen Standpunkt.* Leipzig: Duncker & Humblot.

Busemeyer, J.R., & Bruza, P.D. (2012). *Quantum models of cognition and decision.* Cambridge: Cambridge University Press.

Cambray, J. (2009). *Synchronicity: Nature and psyche in an interconnected universe.* College Station: Texas A&M University Press.

Fach, W. (2011). Phenomenological aspects of complementarity and entanglement in exceptional human experiences. *Axiomathes, 21,* 233–247.

Fach, W. (2017). *Das Spektrum des Aussergewöhnlichen* (Ph.D Thesis). University of Bern.

Fach, W., Atmanspacher, H., Landolt, K., Wyss, T., & Rössler, W. (2013). A comparative study of exceptional experiences of clients seeking advice and of subjects in an ordinary population. *Frontiers in Psychology, 4*(65), 1–10.

Fell, J. (2004). Identifying neural correlates of consciousness: The state space approach. *Consciousness and Cognition, 13,* 709–729.

Garfinkel, A. (1981). *Forms of explanation.* New Haven: Yale University Press.

Heisenberg, W. (1971). *Physics and beyond: Encounters and conversations.* New York: Harper and Row. German original: *Der Teil und das Ganze* (p. 64). München 1969: Piper.

Jung, C.G. (1952). Synchronicity: An acausal connecting principle. In *The structure and dynamics of the psyche, collected works Vol. 8,* London: Routledge & Kegan Paul, 1969.

Jung, C.G., & Pauli, W. (1952). *Naturerklärung und Psyche.* Zürich: Rascher. English: *The interpretation of nature and the psyche.* London: Routledge & Kegan Paul, 1955.

Kaminski, J.A., Sloutsky, V.M., & Heckler, A.F. (2008). The advantage of abstract examples in learning math. *Science, 320,* 454–455.

Kapur, S. (2003). Psychosis as a state of aberrant salience: A framework linking biology, phenomenology, and pharmacology in schizophrenia. *American Journal of Psychiatry, 160,* 13–23.

Kelly, E.W. (2007). Psychophysiological influence. In E.F. Kelly & E.W. Kelly et al. (Eds.), *Irreducible mind* (pp. 117–239). Lanham, MD: Rowman & Littlefield.

Kerslake, C. (2007). *Deleuze and the unconscious.* London: Continuum Press.

Khrennikov, A. (2010). *Ubiquitous quantum structure.* Berlin: Springer.

Kime, P. (2013). Regulating the psyche: The essential contribution of Kant. *International Journal of Jungian Studies, 5*(1), 44–63.

Main R. (2004). *The rupture of time: Synchronicity and Jung's critique of modern Western culture.* New York: Brunner-Routledge.

Meier, C.A. (1975). *Psychosomatik in Jungscher Sicht.* In C.A. Meier (Ed.), *Experiment und symbol* (pp. 138–156). Olten: Walter.

Meier, C.A. (Ed.) (1992). *Wolfgang Pauli und C.G. Jung. Ein Briefwechsel 1932–1958.* Berlin: Springer. English: *Atom and archetype: The Pauli/Jung letters 1932–1958.* Princeton, NJ: Princeton University Press, 2001.

Metzinger, T. (2003). *Being no one.* Cambridge, MA: MIT Press.

Putnam, H. (1981). *Reason, truth, and history.* Cambridge: Cambridge University Press.

Putnam, H. (1987). *The many faces of realism.* La Salle: Open Court.

Quine, W.V.O. (1969). Ontological relativity. In *Ontological relativity and other essays* (pp. 26–68). New York: Columbia University Press.

Seager, W. (2010). Panpsychism, aggregation and combinatorial infusion. *Mind and Matter, 8*, 167–184.

Tresan, D. (2013). A commentary on "A structural phenomenological typology of mind-matter correlations" by H. Atmanspacher and W. Fach. *Journal of Analytical Psychology, 58*, 245–253.

van Fraassen, B. (1980). *The scientific image*. Oxford: Clarendon.

van Gelder, T. (1998). The dynamical hypothesis in cognitive science. *Behavioral and Brain Sciences, 21*, 615–661.

van Os, J. (2009). A salience dysregulation syndrome. *British Journal of Psychiatry, 194*, 101–103.

von Meyenn, K. (Ed.) (1985). *Wolfgang Pauli: Wissenschaftlicher Briefwechsel, band III: 1930–1939*. Berlin: Springer.

von Meyenn, K. (Ed.) (1993). *Wolfgang Pauli: Wissenschaftlicher Briefwechsel, band III: 1940–1949*. Berlin: Springer.

von Meyenn, K. (Ed.) (1996). *Wolfgang Pauli: Wissenschaftlicher Briefwechsel, band IV/1: 1950–1952*. Berlin: Springer.

von Meyenn, K. (Ed.) (1999). *Wolfgang Pauli: Wissenschaftlicher Briefwechsel, band IV/2: 1953–1954*. Berlin: Springer.

Wang, Z., Solloway, T., Shiffrin, R.M., & Busemeyer, J.R. (2014). Context effects produced by question orders reveal quantum nature of human judgments. *Proceedings of the National Academy of Sciences of the USA, 111*, 9431–9436.

Wendt, A. (2015). *Quantum mind and social science*. Cambridge: Cambridge University Press.

Wyss, T. (2016). *Behavioral, physiological, and subjective aspects of exceptional experiences* (Ph.D Thesis). ETH Zurich.

# 15

# SYNCHRONISTIC EXPERIENCES IN PSYCHOTHERAPY

## Empirical studies

*Christian Roesler*

As is well known, the main theoretical product of the Pauli–Jung dialogue is the concept of synchronicity. In his publications on synchronicity (*Synchronizität als ein Prinzip akausaler Zusammenhänge* in 1952 *and Über Synchronizität* in 1951), Jung defined it as a coincidence of an inner psychological state or event and an external or objective event. There is no causal connection between the two events and no causal explanation can be given for the connection, but it appears meaningful, at least for the experiencing individual. Jung as well as Pauli struggled over decades to form a theoretical model for explaining synchronicity by making use of analogies from quantum theory; see Atmanspacher (in this volume) and Gieser (2005) for a detailed discussion.

In his publication of 1951, where he introduced the term synchronicity, Jung gave the classical example for a case of synchronicity which is placed in the context of psychotherapy. A female patient of Jung's presented the following dream in a therapy session: she had received a golden scarab as a present. Right at that moment they heard a noise tapping at the window. When Jung stood up and opened the window a beetle flew into the room, which was the closest equivalent of a *Scarabeus* occurring in the middle of Europe, a so-called rose beetle. The patient was deeply moved by this experience. Before that, the therapy had become difficult and made no progress. Through this irrational experience it was possible for the patient to change her inflexible identification with the totally rational orientation of her consciousness and to start a process of psychological transformation. Within the archetypal symbolism of the *Scarabeus* beetle Jung saw a relationship to the mystery of death and rebirth and an analogy to the psychological situation of his patient. She had to give up her one-sided orientation on rationality and ego control and move toward a new balance between consciousness and the unconscious.

So it becomes clear from this example that from the beginning Jung connected the concept of synchronicity strongly with the process of psychotherapy and the individuation process. Individuation here is seen as a spontaneous process developing out of the unconscious psyche moving the individual toward his or her potential wholeness. In this process the unconscious confronts the ego with symbols, as for example dreams, to foster a constructive dialogue between consciousness and the unconscious. In Jungian theory, the situation of analytic therapy and its special interpersonal relationship is seen as a field where this internal dialogue is promoted and, in the course of spontaneous production of symbols from the unconscious, the probability for synchronistic events to appear is heightened. This comes about through the constellation of collective unconscious/archetypal material. Archetypes, which structure the unconscious, are organized in opposites, which links them to the concept of complementarity in quantum theory (Atmanspacher, in this volume; Walach, 2003; Atmanspacher, Römer, & Walach, 2002; v. Lucadou, Römer, & Walach, 2007). In this sense synchronistic events carry a meaning and can be interpreted in the context of psychotherapy like other symbolic material as for example dreams, images, and so forth (Fordham, 1957; Main, 2004; Hopcke, 2009). Several Jungian authors have developed therapeutic methodologies for working with synchronicity in the context of psychotherapy (Bolen, 1979; Keutzer, 1984).

## State of empirical research

Even though there has been extensive publication activity since the time Jung and Pauli formulated the concept (Cambray, 2004; Donati, 2004), there have been very few studies on synchronicity from the background of Analytical Psychology using systematic empirical research methods (Coleman, Beitman, & Celebi, 2009). Also these are mostly single case studies with no systematic methodology and free interpretation in the sense of a general psychoanalytic approach (Williams, 1957; Bender, 1966; Keutzer, 1984; Wharton, 1986; Hopcke, 1990; Kelly, 1993; Guindon & Hanna, 2002). The following studies have applied a systematic scientific methodology: Hanson and Klimo (1998) have conducted a systematic analysis of reports on coincidences with negative consequences. In these, 56% of the subjects interviewed reported synchronistic events. Hill (2011) developed a study of synchronistic events in mourning. He demonstrated that these synchronistic experiences have a healing function for people who are grieving. Meyer (1998) investigated the correlation between the proneness to experience synchronistic events and personality factors. He found a strong correlation for the finding that introverted feeling types have more synchronistic experiences. He could also show that synchronistic experiences appear especially in stressful life situations.

Several studies that were undertaken in Germany have investigated the occurrence of synchronistic experiences and exceptional experiences in a descriptive sense. In a representative panel investigating the frequency of exceptional experiences, it was found that 36.7% had dreams that later became true and 18.7% experienced extrasensory perceptions in correlation with death or crises (Schmied-Knittel & Schetsche, 2003). In another nationwide representative telephone panel in Germany with 1,510 participants, 40.3% stated that they had the experience of meaningful coincidences which they could not explain by chance at least once (Deflorin, 2003). Temme (2003) found 36.7% of interviewees in a representative study saying they had at least once dreamed something that later became true. She could also show that the content of the reported dreams circled around a limited number of topics, especially death and existential crises as well as great changes in the life of the subjects, as for example meeting a future spouse. The most common forms of synchronistic experience are dreams and visions (47.9%), premonitions (26.7%), and dreams and visions with a more symbolic nature (15.1%) (Sannwald, 1959). Precognitive dreams are often experienced as especially clear, emotionally intensive, and easy to remember (Schredl, 1999). In a database containing 1,465 cases of exceptional experiences developed by the counseling department of the Institute for Frontier Areas of Psychology (IGPP) in Freiburg, Germany, 6% of these were "meaningful coincidences" (Atmanspacher et al., 2013).

These studies show that the descriptive side of the phenomenon is fairly well documented, but the small number of systematic empirical studies investigating the connection between inner and external events shows the need for more systematic studies that connect reports of Synchronistic Experiences (SE) with context data.

A key problem in studies of synchronicity is that chance expectations can never be exactly computed (or even excluded). The reason is that the base rate for the occurrence of single events is fundamentally inaccessible (Diaconis & Mosteller, 1989). Similarly, causal connections between synchronistic events can hardly be excluded with certainty; they could just be too complex to be identified or hidden as common causes for the two events observed (Primas, 1996). As a consequence, the difficulties of investigating synchronicities in an experimentally well-defined study design are extreme indeed.

## An empirical study on synchronicity in the field of psychotherapy

This situation has led the author to design a study on synchronicity using empirical research methods and placing it in the field of psychotherapy. Psychotherapy as a research field has several advantages:

- Psychotherapy is a highly standardized and reduced situation (referring to the setting: persons involved, time frame, space, topic, etc.).
- Patient information (patient's pathology and psychodynamics, biography, transference, course of therapy, etc.) is available.
- This information is available prior to the synchronistic event.
- Dreams are documented right after their occurrence (this is the case at least in Jungian psychotherapies, where clients are usually asked at the beginning to document their dreams regularly).
- The relationship is usually stable over several years.
- A follow-up of development after the synchronistic event is possible.

This means that analytical psychotherapy is the ideal field for empirical research on synchronicity. It allows for systematic documentation of the events and includes the possibility of interpretation of the events in context, which means connecting it with the biography and the psychodynamics of the patient as well as with his life situation and the current situation in therapy. So the problem of retrospective reinterpretation or manipulation of the original data can be reduced. Also a follow-up on the impact of the event on further development is possible.

## Design of the study

The general idea of the study is to create conditions under which it will be possible to collect data about synchronistic events in the field of psychotherapy in a systematic way, and at the same time to collect patient data in the way described above so it will be possible to form interpretations about the connections between individual psychological conditions and the occurrence of such events. To make systematic data collection possible, it is necessary to form a documentation scheme. In this first step we built a sample of cases accessible in the public literature or in collections of cases. Cases and case reports were taken from the following publications:

- Ryback, D., & Sweitzer, L. (1990). *Wahrträume: ihre transformierende und übersinnliche Kraft.* München: Droemer Knaur, 23 case reports.
- Tart, C.T. (1990). *TASTE (The Archives of Scientists' Transcendent Experiences).* Retrieved from www.isse-taste.org, 9 case reports.
- Demoll, R., Oliass, G., & Schumacher, J. (1960). Berichte über spontane Erlebnisse. *Zeitschrift für Parapsychologie und Grenzgebiete der Psychologie 3*(2/3), (185–191), 2 case reports.
- Bauer, E., & Schetsche, M. (Hrsg.) (2003). *Alltägliche Wunder: Erfahrungen mit dem Übersinnlichen – wissenschaftliche Befunde.* Würzburg: Ergon, 6 case reports.

This collection of 40 case reports circling around synchronistic experience was analyzed via Qualitative Content Analysis (Mayring, 2010), an interpretive method aiming at finding categories inherent in the empirical material. This analysis produced the following system of categories (Table 15.1).

The results of this qualitative analysis show some first systematic structures inherent in the empirical material. It becomes obvious that synchronistic experiences occur under special conditions, especially in life situations that are characterized by rapid change, crises, or even illness and death. Also it becomes clear that the synchronistic experience is always organized around a so-called focus person who is connected with the change situation. This can be either the reporting person or a representative. In many cases the experience leads to changes in the world or the self-concept of the person or is part of a dynamic which changes psychological or interpersonal conditions.

To illustrate the application of the category system, the following case example will be analyzed and put into the scheme.

**TABLE 15.1** Categories for synchronistic experiences

| | | |
|---|---|---|
| **Context** | Change | 1. General |
| | | 2. Crisis |
| | | 3. Growth |
| | Stability | 1. General |
| | | 2. Conflict |
| | Specific | 1. Couple relationship |
| | | 2. Family |
| | | 3. Other social relationship |
| | | 4. Work |
| | | 5. Other |
| | Psychological | 1. Hope |
| | | 2. Fear |
| | | 3. Personal affective relation |
| **Event I: The inner state** | Topic | Negative affect |
| | Content | Positive affect |
| | Symbolism | |
| | Type of experience | 1. Dream |
| | | 2. Hallucination |
| | | 3. Vision |
| | | 4. Premonition (emotion, spontaneous behavior, physiological reaction, physical effect, information) |
| | | 5. Inner voice |
| | | 6. Illusion |
| | | 7. Statement |
| | Focus person(s) | 1. Self |
| | | 2. Other: familiar, unfamiliar, anonymous |
| **Event II: The coinciding event** | Topic | Negative affect |
| | Content | Positive affect |
| | Symbolism | |
| | Manifestation | 1. Psychological state |
| | | 2. External event |
| | Focus person(s) | 1. Self |
| | | 2. Other: familiar, unfamiliar, anonymous |
| **Coincidence** | Subjective explanation | 1. God/higher being |
| | | 2. Magic causality |
| | | 3. Transcendental reality |
| | | 4. Unexplainable/anomaly |
| | Consequences | 1. Topic/focus |
| | | 2. Subjective changes (world concept, self-concept, emotions, social relations) |
| | | 3. Persistence (temporary vs. ongoing) |
| | | 4. Dynamic (beginning of, end of, part of development) |

(*Continued*)

**TABLE 15.1** (Continued)

| | | |
|---|---|---|
| **Context** | Change | 1. General |
| | | 2. Crisis |
| | | 3. Growth |
| | Stability | 1. General |
| | | 2. Conflict |
| | Specific | 1. Couple relationship |
| | | 2. Family |
| | | 3. Other social relationship |
| | | 4. Work |
| | | 5. Other |
| | Psychological | 1. Hope |
| | | 2. Fear |
| | | 3. Personal affective relation |
| **Relations** | Time | 1. Synchronic |
| | | 2. Asynchronic |
| | Space | 1. Coinciding |
| | | 2. Distant |
| | Focus person(s) | 1. Participant |
| | | 2. Observer (with[out] focus person) |
| | | 3. Representative (active/passive) |
| **Type of coincidence** | | 1. Realistic |
| | | 2. Symbolic |
| | Subtype | 1. Precognition |
| | | 2. Telepathy |
| | | 3. Clear sight |

## Case example from Tart (1990)

My best friend, Mike, was in a car accident and for approx. a month was in a coma. One night I dreamed that he came to my parent's house. The dream was extremely vivid. We sat and talked for what seemed about an hour, about all kinds of subjects. Mike told me about the wreck, that his girlfriend had not died instantly (like the papers had reported) but that she was okay now, and that he was fine and would see me again one day. The odd thing about the dream was that it was completely real, but not surreal like most of my "vivid" dreams. It really felt like reality. When Mike got up to leave, he mentioned that he wouldn't see me again for a long time, but that I wasn't to be upset, because he was fine. As he walked out the door, he looked back and said that his mom was about to call, and to let her know everything would be okay. I awoke with a start from the dream, and sat up in my bed. About one minute later, at around five in the morning, the phone rang. I had a room downstairs that had been a family room, and it had a phone. I got to the phone before the third ring and answered it. It was Mike's mother. She simply said Mike had died earlier that morning. I was still quite groggy from my sudden awakening, and all I could think of to say was, "I know. He told me." She started crying and hung up the phone. The thing that struck me about this incident was that at the time, it did not seem odd at all. It was simply a fact that Mike and I had talked prior to his leaving. It did not surprise me that Mike had died, because we had talked about that in our conversation, and Mike had told me that his mom would call, so the call did not even seem notable. I did notice a sudden change in my attitude after this event. Prior to Mike's death, I had been consumed by fear of death, often crying myself to sleep worrying about dying, even though I was brought up in a church environment that taught that death was not to be feared. After this incident, I lost my fear of death, but more than that, I gained a love of life, the absence of which had stifled my childhood. I never considered this a case of transcendental experience, in part because it was so normal and natural. However, had I not had this experience, I don't believe I would have had the courage to follow my creative scientific thoughts that lead to my leading an R&D team.

If we take the information from the case reports and put it into the category system the following description results (Table 15.2).

**TABLE 15.2** Application of the category system to a case from Tart (1990)

| Context | Stability | Crisis: car accident |
|---|---|---|
| | Specific | Other social relationship: close friend |
| | Psychological | Fear of death |
| **Event I** **The inner state** | Topic | (Positive affect) |
| | Content | Assurance about well-being of friend, goodbye, departing in hope |
| | Symbolism | Information about telephone call by mother |
| | Type of experience | Dream |
| | Focus person(s) | 1. Self |
| | | 2. Other: familiar |
| **Event II** **The coinciding event** | Topic | Telephone call by mother |
| | Content | Information about Mike's death |
| | Symbolism | |
| | Manifestation | External event |
| | Focus person(s) | 1. Self |
| | | 2. Other: familiar |
| **Coincidence** | Subjective explanation | None (transcendental?) |
| | Consequences | 1. Topic/focus: lost fear of death, gained love of life, courage to follow his creative scientific thoughts 2. Subjective changes in self-concept, emotions 3. Persistence ongoing 4. Dynamic: beginning of development |

*(Continued)*

**TABLE 15.2** (Continued)

| Relations | Time | Asynchronic |
|---|---|---|
| | Space | Distant |
| | Focus person(s) | Participant |
| | | Observer (with focus person) |
| **Type of coincidence** | Subtype | Realistic |
| | | Precognition |

The aim of this first step of the study was not primarily to gain insight into the conditions and consequences of synchronicity. The resulting system of categories makes it possible to design a documentation scheme which can be used for further data collection.

For this aim, especially in the field of psychotherapy, the documentation scheme has to be extended to include data from the context of psychotherapy (see Table 15.3).

## *Psychotherapeutic context*

The second part of the documentation scheme is designed for the psychotherapist to provide the necessary context data from psychotherapy and diagnosis. In psychodynamic psychotherapy in general and especially in Jungian psychotherapy, the necessary information should be available or is already documented before the occurrence of a synchronistic event. It is necessary to collect detailed data about the therapist as well as the patient because from the Jungian perspective, the synchronistic event is a phenomenon taking place in an interpersonal unconscious sphere which is influenced by unconscious conditions from both partners of the relationship.

The documentation scheme has been circulated in the German Jung Society (DGAP) inviting participation. In Germany, psychotherapy is integrated into the legal system of health care and psychotherapists have to provide extensive information about diagnosis, biography, and psychodynamics as well as the personality of the patient, a plan of the therapy, and prognosis to apply for financing of the therapy. So in general, the necessary information for the second part of the documentation scheme is available. In this way it was possible to create a collection of cases with extensive data to which a number of cases from single case studies (provided by R. Hopcke and B.D. Beitman) were added resulting in a corpus of 56 cases. This corpus of cases was analyzed interpretively as well as statistically in the attempt to gain more insight into the structure and conditions of the occurrence of synchronistic events in the field of psychotherapy and their potential meaning. First results make clear that synchronicity is a frequent phenomenon in psychotherapy and that it is often very clear that these events carry a meaning which can be interpreted and made useful for the progression of the psychotherapeutic process. The overall aim of this study is to form a more empirically grounded theory of synchronicity in the context of psychotherapy.

**TABLE 15.3** Extension of the category system including dimensions of psychotherapy

| | | |
|---|---|---|
| **Patient** | Psychopathology | e.g., depression, trauma |
| | Biographical background | |
| | Psychodynamics | 1. Complexes |
| | | 2. Conflict(s) |
| | | 3. Defense mechanisms |
| | | 4. Interpersonal relationships |
| | Personality | 1. Typology: e.g., introverted – extraverted |
| | | 2. Psychodynamic: e.g., anancastic, hysteric |
| | Earlier synchronistic/ paranormal experience | |
| | External life situation | e.g., divorce, crisis |
| **Therapist** | Personality | 1. Typology: e.g., introverted – extraverted |
| | | 2. Psychodynamic: e.g., anancastic, hysteric |
| | Earlier synchronistic/ paranormal experience | |
| | External life situation | e.g., divorce, crisis |
| **Psychotherapy** | Transference– countertransference | |
| | Development | 1. Therapeutic goals |
| | | 2. Course of therapy |
| | | 3. Current issues/ situation |
| | Consequences | 1. For life of patient |
| | | 2. For psychotherapy |
| | | 3. For therapeutic relationship |

Hypotheses about meaning of synchronistic event and interconnections with psychodynamics and course of therapy/development of patient (individuation)

## References

Atmanspacher, H., & Fach, W. (2013). A structural-phenomenological typology of mind-matter correlations. *Journal of Analytical Psychology, 58*, 219–244.

Atmanspacher, H., Römer, H., & Walach, H. (2002). Weak quantum theory: Complementarity and entanglement in physics and beyond. *Foundations of Physics, 32*, 379–406.

Aziz, R. (1990). *C. G. Jung's psychology of religion and synchronicity.* Albany, NY: State University of New York Press.

Bauer, E., & Schetsche, M. (Hrsg.) (2003). *Alltägliche Wunder: Erfahrungen mit dem Übersinnlichen – wissenschaftliche Befunde.* Würzburg: Ergon.

Bender, H. (1966). The Gotenhafen case of correspondence between dreams and future events. *International Journal of Neuropsychiatry, 2*, 114–197.

Bolen, J.S. (1979). *The Tao of psychology: Synchronicity and the self.* New York: Harper & Row.

Cambray, J. (2004). Synchronicity as emergence. In J. Cambray & L. Carter (Eds.), *Analytical psychology: Contemporary perspectives in Jungian analysis.* Hove and New York: Brunner and Routledge.

Coleman, S.L., Beitman, B.D., & Celebi, E. (2009). Weird coincidences commonly occur. *Psychiatric Annals, 39*(5), 265–270.

Deflorin, R. (2003). Wenn Dinge sich verblüffend fügen: Außeralltägliche Wirklichkeitserfahrungen im Spannungsfeld zwischen Zufall, Unwahrscheinlichkeit und Notwendigkeit. In E. Bauer & M. Schetsche (Hgs.), *Alltägliche Wunder.* Würzburg: Ergon.

Demoll, R., Oliass, G., & Schumacher, J. (1960). Berichte über spontane Erlebnisse. *Zeitschrift für Parapsychologie und Grenzgebiete der Psychologie, 3*(2/3), 185–191.

Diaconis, P., & Mosteller, F. (1989). Methods for studying coincidences. *Journal of the American Statistical Association, 84*, 408, 853–861.

Donati, M. (2004). Beyond synchronicity: The worldview of Carl Gustav Jung and Wolfgang Pauli. *Journal of Analytical Psychology, 49*, 707–728.

Fordham, M. (1957). Reflections on the archetypes and synchronicity. In M. Fordham (Hrsg.), *New developments in analytical psychology.* London: Routledge & Kegan Paul.

Gieser, S. (2005). *The innermost kernel: Depth psychology and quantum physics – Wolfgang Pauli's dialogue with C.G. Jung.* New York: Springer.

Guindon, M.H., & Hanna, F.J. (2002). Coincidence, happenstance, serendipity, fate or the hand of god: Case studies in synchronicity. *The Career Development Quarterly, 50*, 195–208.

Hanson, D., & Klimo, J. (1998). Toward a phenomenology of synchronicity. In R. Valle (Hrsg.), *Phenomenological inquiry in psychology: Existential and transpersonal dimensions.* New York: Plenum Press.

Hill, J. (2011). *Synchronicity and grief: The phenomenology of meaningful coincidence as it arises during bereavement* (Dissertation). Palo Alto, CA: Institute of Transpersonal Psychology.

Hopcke, R. (1990). The barker: A synchronistic event in analysis. *Journal of Analytical Psychology, 35*, 459–473.

Hopcke, R. (2009). Synchronicity and psychotherapy: Jung's concept and its use in clinical work. *Psychiatric Annals, 39*(5), 287–296.

Jung, C.G. (1951). Über synchronizität. In C.G. Jung (Ed.) (1967), *Die Dynamik des Unbewussten* (2. Aufl., Gesammelte Werke, Bd. 8, pp. 579–591). Zürich: Rascher.

Jung, C.G. (1952). Synchronizität als ein Prinzip akausaler Zusammenhänge. In C.G. Jung (Ed.) (1967), *Die Dynamik des Unbewussten* (2. Aufl., Gesammelte Werke, Bd. 8, pp. 475–577). Zürich: Rascher.

Kelly, S. (1993). A trip through lower town: Reflections on a case of double synchronicity. *Journal of Analytical Psychology, 38*, 191–198.

Keutzer, C. (1984). Synchronicity in psychotherapy. *Journal of Analytical Psychology, 29*, 373–381.

Main, R. (2004). *The rupture of time: Synchronicity and Jung's critique of modern Western culture.* Hove: Brunner and Routledge.

Mayring, P. (2010). *Qualitative Inhaltsanalyse: Grundlagen und techniken.* Weinheim: Beltz.

Meyer, M.B. (1998). *Role of cognitive variables in the reporting of experienced meaningful coincidences or "synchronicity."* San Francisco, CA: Saybrook Institute. Diss.

Primas, H. (1996). Synchronizität und Zufall. *Zeitschrift für Parapsychologie und Grenzgebiete der Psychologie, 38*(1), 61–91.

Roesler, C. (2010). *Analytische Psychologie heute: Der aktuelle Forschungsstand zur Psychologie C.. Jungs.* Basel, Freiburg: Karger.

Ryback, D., & Sweitzer, L. (1990). *Wahrträume: ihre transformierende und übersinnliche Kraft.* München: Droemer Knaur.

Sannwald, G. (1959). Statistische Untersuchungen an Spontanphänomenen. *Zeitschrift für Parapsychologie und Grenzgebiete der Psychologie, 3*, 59–71.

Schmied-Knittel, I., & Schetsche, M. (2003). Psi-report Deutschland: Eine repräsentative Bevölkerungsumfrage zu außergewöhnlichen Erfahrungen. In E. Bauer & M. Schetsche

(Hrsg.), *Alltägliche Wunder: Erfahrungen mit dem Übersinnlichen – wissenschaftliche Befunde* (pp. 13–38). Würzburg: Ergon.

Schredl, M. (1999). Präkognitive Träume: Überblick über die Forschung und Zusammenhang zum Traumerleben. *Zeitschrift für Parapsychologie und Grenzgebiete der Psychologie, 41,* 134–158.

Tart, C.T. (1981). Causality and synchronicity: Steps toward clarification. *Journal of the American Society of Psychical Research, 75,* 121–141.

Tart, C.T. (1990). *TASTE: The Archives of Scientists' Transcendent Experiences.* Online-Journal, Retrieved June 2, 2012, from www.issc-taste.org

Temme, T. (2003). "Ich sehe was, was Du nicht siehst": Wahrträume und ihre subjektive Evidenz. In E. Bauer & M. Schetsche (Hrsg.), *Alltägliche Wunder.* Würzburg: Ergon.

von Loucadou, W., Römer, H., & Walach, H. (2007). Synchronistic phenomena as entanglement correlations in generalized quantum theory. *Journal of Consciousness Studies, 14*(4), 50–74.

Walach, H. (2003). Generalisierte Quantentheorie (Weak Quantum Theory): Eine theoretische Basis zum Verständnis transpersonaler Phänomene. In W. Belschner, L. Hofmann, L., & H. Walach (Hrsg.), *Auf dem Weg zu einer Psychologie des Bewusstseins* (pp. 13–46). Oldenburg: BIS.

Wharton, B. (1986). Deintegration and two synchronistic events. *Journal of Analytical Psychology, 31,* 281–285.

Williams, M. (1957). An example of synchronicity. *Journal of Analytical Psychology, 2,* 93–95.

# INDEX

Note: Page numbers in *italics* indicate figures; **bold** indicates tables.

abstract, defined 19
academic psychology 1
Adler, Alfred 30
AE *see* association experiment
affect dictionary 63
age, and dreams under conditions of continuous stress 96–97
Ainsworth, Mary 121
alchemical imagery 164–165, 169
alchemy 105
American Psychoanalytic Association 204
amplification: in SDA 73; of symbols in SDA 77, **79**
analysts for Router program: diversity of 219; interviews of 214–215; surveys of 212–213
Analytical Psychology: movement into academic environment 1; research overview 4–6; scientific reputation of 3
Animus dreams 94, 95
Archetypal Psychology 44
Archetypal Symbol Inventory (ASI) 46, 50
archetypes: cultural context of 122; defined 41–42; empirical studies on 46–47; images and 57; as image schemas 45–46; *kanji* as archetypal image 48–50; modern approaches to 42–44; as organized in opposites 245
arousal phase of referential process model 62
art therapy groups 156–161, *157*, *158*, *159*, *160*
ASI (Archetypal Symbol Inventory) 46, 50

Asian Routers, themes of interviews of 214
association experiment (AE): overview 29–30, 38–39; research with 33–34; standardized diagnostic measures compared to 35–38
ATLAS.ti 161–162, *163*
attachment patterns 122
attachment theory 31, 126
autism spectrum disorder and default mode network 111–112
autonomous complexes 56–57

Beeinträchtigungs Schwere Score (BSS) 199n2
Berlin catamnestic study 178–180, *179*, 189–193
Bleuler, Eugen 29
borderline patient, pictorial–hermeneutic pilot study with 164–169, *166*, *167*, *168*
bottom-up empiricism 20–21
brain networks: altered states, trauma, and 112–114, 117; types of 109–112
BSS (Beeinträchtigungs Schwere Score) 199n2
Bucci, Wilma 58–59, 61–62, 63, 65
Burghölzli psychiatric asylum, Zurich 104

central executive network (CEN) 110, 114, 117
centroversion 97
Change in Experience and Behavior (VEV) questionnaire 190

children: with OCD 138–140, *139*, **141**, 142, **143–144**; traumatized 144–152, **149**, **150**, **151**; *see also* infant observation method

China: Cultural Revolution in 131; cultural skin in 123–124; emergence of self in 127–129; infant observation in 126–127; one child policy in 133–134; social contract in 129

cognition and action, approaches to 42

cognitive behavioral therapy for traumatized children 145

cognitive psychology 17–18, 21, 31–32

coincidence phenomena 237

collective unconscious memory: cross-cultural evidence of 50–52; empirical study of 46–47; mechanism for 47; transmission of 44

complexes: in neuro-imaging studies 34–35; overview 30–31; pathological 32–33; schemas as 2

complexity/complex systems theory 106, 239

conceptual research 23–24

concrete traumatic dreams 90–91, 92, 98

consciousness 56, 57–58

content analysis of dreams **93**, 93–94

continuous stress, dreams under conditions of 92–98, **93**

cross-cultural evidence of collective unconscious memory 50–52

cultural differences in Router training 210, 211, 219–220

cultural skin: Chinese 123–124; overview 121–123; *see also* infant observation method

cure of words 61

default mode network (DMN) 109–112, 117

definitional activity in psychology 23–24

Deutsche Gesellschaft für Analytische Psychologie (DGAP) 189, 193–194, 251

Discourse Attributes Analysis Program (DAAP) 63–64

disfluency dictionary 63

dissociation 32–33

dissociation phenomena 237

dissociative model of psyche 104

DMN (default mode network) 109–112, 117

documentation system, standardized 198

dreams: interpretation of 69–70, 72; psychological function of 70, 91–92; research on 70–72; theories of 70; *see also* structural dream analysis; traumatic dreams

dual-aspect monism 21, 227–231, 238–239

dual code theory of cognition 58

dual perspective 187

dynamic systems approach to cognition and action 42

effectiveness of Jungian psychotherapy: Berlin catamnestic study 178–180, *179*, 189–193; Konstanz study 180, **181**; levels of evidence 175; overview 173, 183–184; Praxisstudie ambulante Psychotherapie Schweiz 182–183; Praxisstudie Analytische Langzeittherapie 176–177, 194–196; research on 5–6, 173–176; research platform for 184, 198; San Francisco psychotherapy research project 177–178

empathy and mirror neurons 106

empirical, Jung use of term 3

empirical research: attitude toward 174, 194; beginnings of, in Germany 188; on dreams 69; interest in 187; Jung and 1, 2, 30, 33, 187; participation of analysts in 184

empiricism, data coding in 21–22

enacted cognition approach 42

episodic memory 108

episodic models in SDA 75, **76**

epistemological foundations and controversies 2–3

epistemology, naturalized 13–15

Erikson, Erik 121

European International Psychoanalytical Association 204

European Psychoanalytical Federation 205

European Routers, themes of interviews of 213–214

exceptional experiences 236–238, 245–246

experienced intentionality 236

extraversion *versus* introversion 1–2

fate of protagonist in SDA 75–76, **76**

fathers in China 133–134

feeling-toned complex 104

feminine, characteristics of 156

fictions, study of 17–20

finalistic aspect 38

folk tales as examples of proxy functions 17–20

Fordham, Michael 124–125, 127

formal intentionality 236

Freiburg Personality Inventory (FPI-R) 36–38

Freud, Sigmund 1, 30, 90

functional analysis in SDA 76–77, **78**

future, imagining events in 108

Galton, Francis 29
gender and traumatic dreams 94–95
German Psychoanalytic Association 205
Germany: approaches to research in
  198–199; beginnings of empirical
  research in 188; health care system
  in 188–189, 197–198, 251; Jungian
  psychotherapy in 6
Giegerich, W., Hegelian program of 24
Gießen Test 190
global efficiency of brain 112
grandparents in China 133
Great Round 156, 161

Han Groen Prakken Psychoanalytic
  Institute for Eastern Europe 205
Hartmann, Ernest 90, 91
health care system in Germany 188–189,
  197–198, 251
health care utilization after psychotherapy
  192–193
Heidelberger Umstrukturierungsskala 174
Heidelberg Structural Change Scale
  (HSCS) 200n6
"Helpless Heroes" 94–95
hermeneutic tradition 154–155
Hogenson, George 42, 43, 220
HSCS (Heidelberg Structural Change
  Scale) 200n6
*Human Inference* (Nisbett and Ross) 21, 22

IAAP *see* International Association for
  Analytical Psychology (IAAP)
*I Ching* 123
IGPP (Institute for Frontier Areas of
  Psychology) 237, 246
IIP (Inventory of Interpersonal Problems)
  199–200n4
ILE (Inventory of Stressful Life Events)
  199n1
images: clinical research based on 61–65;
  multiple code theory of emotional
  information processing and 59–61,
  65; origins and meaning of concept
  of 55–58; in psychotherapy 65–66,
  155–156; as research construct 58–59;
  *see also* art therapy groups; image
  schemas; pictorial-hermeneutic method
image schemas: archetypes as 42, 45–46;
  *kanji* as 48–50
imaginal psychology 18–20
immanent experiences 238–239
Indicator for the Status of Rehabilitation
  (IRES) 199n3
individuation 245

induced correlations 234–235
infant observation method: in China
  126–127; emergence of self and
  127–129; Jungian approach to 122–123;
  one child policy and 133; overview
  121, 124–126; psychic skin concept and
  129–131
infap3 (International Network for
  Research and Development in Analytical
  Psychotherapy) 184, 197–198, 199
innateness of archetypes 43–44
inner world, as simulated interaction with
  environment 45–46
Institute for Frontier Areas of Psychology
  (IGPP) 237, 246
integration in SDA 77, 79, **80–81**
inter-generational transmission of trauma
  131–133
International Association for Analytical
  Psychology (IAAP): Kyoto Congress 220,
  221; Research and Evaluation Working
  Group 203, 206; research funded by 194,
  199; *see also* training
International Network for Research
  and Development in Analytical
  Psychotherapy (infap3) 184,
  197–198, 199
interpretation support system ATLAS.ti
  161–162, *163*
interviews: of analysts 214–215; of Current
  Routers and Router Graduates 206–212
introversion 111
Inventory of Stressful Life Events (ILE)
  199n1
IRES (Indicator for the Status of
  Rehabilitation) 199n3
Italian Weighted Referential Activity
  Dictionary (I-WRAD) 64–65

JAKOB narrative method 72–73
James, William 56
Janét, Pierre 104
*Journal of Analytical Psychology* 203, 215
*Junctim* attitude 187
Jung, Carl Gustav: developmental history
  of 103–104; Freud and 2; psychiatric
  training of 104; on psychology 103;
  psychosis, experience of 104–105;
  as researcher 1, 2, 30, 33, 187;
  transformative experience of 102

Kalff, Dora 137
*kanji*, as archetypal images 48–50
K (Knowledge) link 13
Konstanz study 180, **181**

Liaison Person in Router training 209
local mental objects 229
LSD and brain networks 112

Maloney paradigm 46
manualization of treatment 174
Maskit, Bernhard 63
maternal reverie 126
meaning: dual-aspect monism and 228–229;
    experiences of 238–239; formal and
    experienced 235–236; of psychophysical
    phenomena 239; of synchronistic
    events 245
*Memories, Dreams and Reflections* (Jung) 102
memory studies 107–109
mental images *see* images
Mill, Stuart 29
mirror neurons 106–107
moment of complexity (MoC) 116
mother-infant metaphor 126
multiple code theory of emotional
    information processing 59–65
mundus imaginalis 164, 165–169, *166,
    167, 168*
mythologems and images 56

narrative/symbolizing phase of referential
    process model 62
naturalism and psychological empiricism
    11–12
naturalized epistemology 13–15
natural science, psychology as 3
Neumann, Erich: centroversion principle of
    97; *The Great Mother* 156–157; on infant
    development 122
neuro-imaging studies 34–35
neuronal activation maps, image schemas
    as 45, 50
neurosciences: Jungian and post-Jungian uses
    of 105–107; unconscious and 32
neutral monism 227
non-verbal symbolic code 59

obsessive compulsive disorder (OCD) *see*
    sandplay
*On the Nature of the Psyche* (Jung) 230
ontological relativity 231–233
ontology and research 15–17
Operationalized Psychodynamic
    Diagnostics (OPD) 174, 194, 196–197
out-of-body experiences 241n15

Paivio, Allan 58
PAL (Praxisstudie Analytische
    Langzeittherapie) Schweiz 176–177,
    194–196

PAP-S (Praxisstudie ambulante
    Psychotherapie Schweiz) 174, 182–183
pathological complexes 32–33
patients, effectiveness of psychotherapy
    from point of view of 192
Pauli, Wolfgang 2, 105, 234–235; *see also*
    dual-aspect monism
Pauli-Jung conjecture 227–228, 230, 232,
    237, 239
personality: development of, and association
    experiment 38; dimensions of 1–2;
    partial personalities 32–33
phenomenal model of intentionality
    relation (PMIR) 236
pictorial-hermeneutic method: ATLAS.
    ti interpretation support system
    161–162; interpretations 169–171;
    mundus imaginalis 165–169, *166,
    167, 168*; overview 154–155; research
    methodology 164–165
pictorial symbolism of transformation
    processes 156–161, *157, 158, 159, 160*
PMIR (phenomenal model of
    intentionality relation) 236
Popper, Karl 3, 17
posttraumatic stress disorder (PTSD) 89–90,
    91, 112–113
Praxisstudie ambulante Psychotherapie
    Schweiz (PAP-S) 174, 182–183
Praxisstudie Analytische Langzeittherapie
    (PAL) Schweiz 176–177, 194–196
pregnancy, dreams during 97
Propp, Vladimir 72
proxy functions: folk tales as examples
    of 17–20; forms of 22–23; overview
    15–16
psyche: dissociative model of 104; naturally
    dissociated 56–57; as self-regulating
    system 70, 71
psychic skin 129–131
Psychoanalytic Institute for Eastern Europe
    204–205
psychoanalytic process, study of, and
    referential activity 59–61
psychodynamic therapy compared to
    psychoanalytic therapy 195
psychology: academic 1; building from
    ground up 20–23; cognitive 17–18, 21,
    31–32; defined 19; definitional activity in
    23–24; form of 12; imaginal 18–20; Jung
    and 102–103; as natural science 3; *see also*
    Analytical Psychology
psychophysical correlations: exceptional
    experiences 236–238; formal and
    experienced meaning 235–236; problem
    of explanation for 233–234; relational

and immanent experiences 238–239; structural and induced 234–235; synchronicities as 228–229
psychotherapy: additional course of 190–193; course of, and results of SDA 83–84; financing of, in Germany 178; mundus imaginalis 165–169, *166, 167, 168*; role of images in 155–156; synchronicity in 244–247, 249–251; use of dreams in 71–72; *see also* effectiveness of Jungian psychotherapy
psychotic patients, art therapy groups for 156–161, *157, 158, 159, 160*
PTSD (posttraumatic stress disorder) 89–90, 91, 112–113

qualitative analysis 137–138
qualitative research, triangulation in 206
quality management in health care system in Germany 197–198
quantum physics 229–231
Quine, W.V. 13–16, 21, 22, 231–232

randomized controlled trials (RCTs) 175
rapid eye movement (REM) sleep 105
*Red Book* (Jung) 104, 187
referential activity (RA): building on measurement of 63–64; clinical research on 61–63; Italian research on 64–65; overview 59–61
referential process model 62
reflection dictionary (REF) 63–64
Regional Organizer in Router training 209
relational experiences 238–239
relative onticity 231–233
REM (rapid eye movement) sleep 105
reorganizing phase of referential process model 62
repetitive structure identification in SDA 77
research: conceptual 23–24; ontology and 15–17; philosophical and epistemological questions in 11–12; qualitative analysis 137–138; *see also* empirical research
Rosen and Smith paradigm 46–47, 48
Router training *see* training

salience 241n13
salience network (SN) 110, 113–114
sandplay: category frequency assessment 140, **141**, 142; data analysis 138; efficacy of 151–152; evaluation questions 142; evolution of categories **143–144**; expressions, capturing 138; overview 137; research methodology 138–140, 146; results of research 148–149, **149**; scene classification 139–140, 149–151,

**150, 151**; survey of miniatures in scenes 138–139, *139*; with traumatized children 144–146; treatment procedure 147–148
San Francisco psychotherapy research project 177–178
SCL-90-R (Symptom Checklist-90-R) 36–38, 189
SDA *see* structural dream analysis
Sderot 89, 98
self: defined 57; emergence of, in China 127–129
Sensory Integration 145
serial reaction time tests 34
shuttle analysis 204–205, 209, 216, 220
skin disorders in infants in China 130–131
Skype: in practices 212; in Router program 206, 209–211, 216, 219
social containment, culture as providing form of 121
Sperry, Roger 105–106
spindle neurons 107
structural analysis/functional analysis 72
structural change, evidence of 195–196
structural correlations 234–235
structural dream analysis (SDA): amplification of symbols 77, **79**; case description 82–83; course of therapy and 83–84; episodic models 75, **76**; exemplary dream series 73–75; fate of protagonist 75–76, **76**; functional analysis 76–77, **78**; identification of repetitive structural elements 77; integration of previous steps 77, 79, **80–81**; overview 72–73; segmentation 75; summarizing interpretation 79, 82
structure, as essential feature of theory 16
structure axis of OPD 196–197
subsymbolic code 59
summarization in SDA 79, 82
supervision of training: issues in 211–212, 220; by Skype 210–211
suppression 35
Switzerland, Jungian psychotherapy in 6
symbolic code 59
symbolic traumatic dreams 90–91, 94, 96, 97, 98
symbolization process 61, 126
symbols: amplification of, in SDA 77, **79**; as expression of therapeutic relationships 197; formation of 60; *see also* pictorial symbolism of transformation processes; symbolic traumatic dreams
*Symbols of Transformation* (Jung) 55, 156
sympathetic mirroring 11–12
Symptom Checklist-90-R (SCL-90-R) 36–38, 189

synchronicity: archetypes and 44; case example 249–250; categories for experiences of **248–249, 250–251**; dual-aspect monism 227–231; hypotheses about **252**; *I Ching* and 123; in psychotherapy 244–247, 249–251; relative onticity 231–233; in treatment of trauma 114–116; *see also* psychophysical correlations
synoptical table 169–170

*Tao Teh Ching* (Lao-tzu) 123
theory: attachment 31, 126; complexity 106, 239; of dreams 70, 91; dual code theory of cognition 58; structure as essential feature of 16; testability of 17; *see also* multiple code theory of emotional information processing
therapist, role of, with sandplay 137
training: emerging issues 217–220; initial considerations and research methodology 206–207; interviews of analysts 214–215; interviews of Current Routers and Router Graduates 213–214; literature on 215–216; previous research on 203–206; recommendations for 220–221; surveys of analysts 212–213; surveys of Current Routers and Router Graduates 206–212, 216–217
transcendent function 57, 231
transformation: pictorial symbolism of 156–161, *157, 158, 159, 160*; through therapeutic relationship 197
transmission: of culture 121, 129; of trauma 131–133
trauma: brain networks and 112–114, 117; in children 144–145; inter-generational

transmission of 131–133; Jung orientation to studies of 104; massive, collective 105; synchronistic phenomena in treatment of 114–116; *see also* sandplay
traumatic dreams: characteristics of 90–92; under continuous threat and in times of war 92–94, **93**; "Dream Dome" 96–98; history of research on 89–90; of Israelis and Palestinians 98–99, **99**; of men 94–95; PTSD and 89–90; working with 100
traumatic memories 109
treatment handbooks and recommendations 174
Tresan, David 106
triangulation in qualitative research 206

unconscious: association experiment and 29–30; cognitive psychology and 31–32; dreams and 70, 71; Jung, Freud, and interpretation of 55; neurosciences and 32; sandplay and 137; *see also* collective unconscious memory
*unus mundus* 227

verbal symbolic code 59
VEV (Change in Experience and Behavior) questionnaire 190
vitality forms 128
von Economo neurons 107

war trauma 90
Weighted Referential Activity Dictionary (WRAD) 63–64
Wilmer, Harry A. 91
Word Association Test 46
Wundt, Wilhelm 29